MW00534272

Who shall ascend the mountain of the Lord?

NEW STUDIES IN BIBLICAL THEOLOGY 37

Series editor: D. A. Carson

Who shall ascend the mountain of the Lord?

A BIBLICAL THEOLOGY OF
THE BOOK OF LEVITICUS

L. Michael Morales

APOLLOS

INTERVARSITY PRESS
DOWNERS GROVE, ILLINOIS 60515

APOLLOS
(an imprint of Inter-Varsity Press, England)
Norton Street
Nottingham NG7 3HR, England
ivpbooks.com
ivp@ivpbooks.com

InterVarsity Press, USA
P.O. Box 1400
Downers Grove, IL 60515-1426, USA
ivpress.com
email@ivpress.com

InterVarsity Press®, USA, is the book-publishing division of InterVarsity Christian Fellowship/ USA® and a member movement of the International Fellowship of Evangelical Students. Website: intervarsity.org.

Inter-Varsity Press, England, is closely linked with the Universities and Colleges Christian Fellowship, a student movement connecting Christian Unions throughout Great Britain, and a member movement of the International Fellowship of Evangelical Students. Website: uccf.org.uk.

Unless otherwise indicated, all Scripture quotations are the author's own translation.

First published 2015

Set in Monotype Times New Roman
Typeset in Great Britain by CRB Associates, Potterhanworth, Lincolnshire
Printed in the United States of America ∞

USA ISBN 978-0-8308-2638-4 (print)
USA ISBN 978-0-8308-9986-9 (digital)
UK ISBN 978-1-78359-368-2

As a member of the Green Press Initiative, InterVarsity Press is committed to protecting the environment and to the responsible use of natural resources. To learn more, visit greenpressinitiative.org.

British Library Cataloguing in Publication Data

A catalogue record for this book is available from the British Library.

Library of Congress Cataloging-in-Publication Data

Names: Morales, L. Michael.
Title: Who shall ascend the mountain of the Lord? : a biblical theology of the Book of Leviticus / L. Michael Morales.
Description: [Nottingham, England] : Apollos ; Downers Grove, Illinois : InterVarsity Press, 2015. | Series: New studies in biblical theology ; 37 | Includes bibliographical references and index.
Identifiers: LCCN 2015037779 | ISBN 9780830826384 (pbk. : alk. paper)
Subjects: LCSH: Bible. Leviticus—Criticism, interpretation, etc.
Classification: LCC BS1255.52 .M67 2015 | DDC 222/.1306—dc23

LC record available at http://lccn.loc.gov/2015037779

| P | 20 | 19 | 18 | 17 | 16 | 15 | 14 | 13 | 12 | 11 | 10 | 9 | 8 | 7 | 6 | 5 |
| Y | 31 | 30 | 29 | 28 | 27 | 26 | 25 | 24 | 23 | 22 | 21 | 20 | | | | | |

Contents

Series preface

New Studies in Biblical Theology is a series of monographs that address key issues in the discipline of biblical theology. Contributions to the series focus on one or more of three areas: (1) the nature and status of biblical theology, including its relations with other disciplines (e.g. historical theology, exegesis, systematic theology, historical criticism, narrative theology); (2) the articulation and exposition of the structure of thought of a particular biblical writer or corpus; and (3) the delineation of a biblical theme across all or part of the biblical corpora.

Above all, these monographs are creative attempts to help thinking Christians understand their Bibles better. The series aims simultaneously to instruct and to edify, to interact with the current literature and to point the way ahead. In God's universe, mind and heart should not be divorced: in this series we will try not to separate what God has joined together. While the notes interact with the best of scholarly literature, the text is uncluttered with untransliterated Greek and Hebrew, and tries to avoid too much technical jargon. The volumes are written within the framework of confessional evangelicalism, but there is always an attempt at thoughtful engagement with the sweep of the relevant literature.

Hebrews 7:11–28 reminds us that the priestly system of the old covenant is so important that should a change take place in the priesthood, there must be a change in the entire law-covenant structure. That strongly underscores the importance of the sacrificial system and its priesthood to the law covenant. One might suppose that such a reflection would drive us to study Leviticus. Most of us, however, find the prospect of teaching or preaching from Leviticus a wee bit discomfiting. We can cite choice bits ('Love your neighbour as yourself'), but we have no feel for the book, little grasp of its structure and movement, no sense of its place in the Pentateuch and in the canon. This book by Dr Michael Morales, carefully read, will for ever banish such limitations. It promises to give us not only a theology of Leviticus, but also a richer theology of the Pentateuch and finally of the whole Bible. I predict this volume will spawn some excellent sermon series on Leviticus!

D. A. Carson
Trinity Evangelical Divinity School

Author's preface

As the central book of the Pentateuch, Leviticus contains the heart of its theology and has much to unfold regarding the nature of God and the plight of humanity. The church's understanding of Leviticus is foundational for grasping the story of the Bible in its depth and beauty, and for discernment concerning a whole array of pressing issues, such as the substance and nature of the Mosaic covenant, the worship of God, and the person and work of Jesus Christ. My hope and prayer in this endeavour is to provide the church with a theological entry into Leviticus in the context of both the Pentateuch and the New Testament, an entry that will strengthen feeble hands and make firm the weak knees, and lead to a renewed glorying in her heavenly access to the Father through the new and living way. To pursue this aim has meant that many aspects of Leviticus, from defining atonement to competing methodologies in ritual theory, and so on, which are topics of scholarly debate requiring much nuanced discussion and argumentation, have necessarily been avoided.

Much of this work was written while teaching at Reformation Bible College, and I remain grateful for blessed days there – for the leadership of Dr R. C. Sproul, Mr Chris Larson and Dr Steve Nichols; for the friendship of my former colleagues Dave Briones, Aaron Denlinger, Ben Dunson, Keith Mathison and R. C. Sproul Jr.; for Heidi Fraser and the rest of the kind staff; and for the students who made teaching at RBC such an insightful joy. Keith was kind enough to read a draft of the manuscript and to offer helpful feedback. I also express my gratitude to Mr Ryan Fraser who turned my whiteboard line drawings into digital illustrations, both helpful and beautiful – thank you, my friend.

This book's last chapter was written during my transition to the post of professor of biblical studies at Greenville Presbyterian Theological Seminary, and I offer here my warm gratitude to Dr Joseph Pipa Jr., along with the board of directors, the faculty, staff and students for their kind reception. Rev. Peter van Doodewaard and his dear family hosted me for three weeks during this transition, for which I remain grateful. My family and I were then hosted for months by the Ben Daniel family (I write this preface from their basement). May the Lord repay your kindness according to his riches in glory.

Some of this material was taught during courses for which I served as an adjunct at Reformed Theological Seminary in Orlando – my thanks to Drs Ligon Duncan and Scott Swain for those opportunities. Thank you also to Michael Farrell, a most resourceful librarian, who graciously obtained for me so many of the books and articles I needed for this and various other projects.

For their patient and careful editorial labours on this project, I thank Don Carson and Philip Duce; it has been a privilege to have their help and guidance. Much appreciation also goes to Eldo Barkhuizen for his diligence as copy editor of this work.

My gratitude to the Lord continues to abound for the session (including my father), deacons and flock of Grace Presbyterian Church in America (Stuart, Fla.), and now also for Woodruff Road Presbyterian Church in America (Greenville, S.C.).

Finally, I give thanks for my dear wife, Elise, and for my sons Armando, Diego, Alejandro and Andres. This book is dedicated, with much love and affection, to Elise.

> Now unto the GODHEAD all glory be;
> And eternal bliss to Israel, his saints redeemed.
> FATHER, SON and SPIRIT – blessed, hallowed THREE;
> – O happy lot to join that holy COMPANY!

L. Michael Morales
11 April 2015

Abbreviations

AB	Anchor Bible
ABD	*Anchor Bible Dictionary*, ed. D. N. Freedman, 6 vols., New York: Doubleday, 1992
AnBib	Analecta biblica
ANE	ancient Near East(ern)
AOAT	Alter Orient und Altes Testament
AOTC	Apollos Old Testament Commentary
AR	*Adventist Review*
AUSS	*Andrews University Seminary Studies*
BBR	*Bulletin for Biblical Research*
BBRSup	Bulletin for Biblical Research Supplements
BHS	*Biblia Hebraica Stuttgartensia*, ed. K. Elliger and W. Rudolph, Stuttgart: Deutsche Bibelstiftung, 1983
Bib	*Biblica*
BibInt	*Biblical Interpretation*
BIS	Biblical Interpretation Series
BM	*Beth Miqra*
BN	*Biblische Notizen*
BSac	*Bibliotheca sacra*
BT	*Bible Translator*
BTB	*Biblical Theology Bulletin*
BThSt	Biblisch-theologische Studien
CBQ	*Catholic Biblical Quarterly*
CBQMS	Catholic Biblical Quarterly Monograph Series
CC	Concordia Commentary
Chm	*Churchman*
Colloq	*Colloquium*
CTJ	*Calvin Theological Journal*
CTR	*Criswell Theological Review*
DBI	*Dictionary of Biblical Imagery*, ed. L. Ryken, J. C. Wilhoit and T. Longman III, Downers Grove: InterVarsity Press, 1998

DDD	*Dictionary of Deities and Demons in the Bible*, ed. K. van der Toorn, B. Becking and P. W. van der Horst, 2nd ed., Leiden: Brill, 1995
DOTP	*Dictionary of the Old Testament: Pentateuch*, ed. T. D. Alexander and D. W. Baker, Downers Grove: InterVarsity Press; Leicester: Inter-Varsity Press, 2003
ECC	Eerdmans Critical Commentary
EgT	*Eglise et théologie*
ErIsr	*Eretz-Israel*
EvQ	*Evangelical Quarterly*
ExpTim	*Expository Times*
Gen. R.	*Genesis Rabbah*
HBM	Hebrew Bible Monographs
HBS	Herders Biblische Studien
HBT	*Horizons in Biblical Theology*
HSM	Harvard Semitic Monographs
HSS	Harvard Semitic Studies
HTR	*Harvard Theological Review*
IDBSup	*Interpreter's Dictionary of the Bible: Supplementary Volume*, ed. K. Crim, Nashville: Abingdon, 1976
IEJ	*Israel Exploration Journal*
Int	*Interpretation*
IRT	Issues in Religion and Theology
JAAR	*Journal of the American Academy of Religion*
JANES	*Journal of the Ancient Near East Society*
JAOS	*Journal of the American Oriental Society*
JATS	*Journal of the Adventist Theological Society*
JBL	*Journal of Biblical Literature*
JETS	*Journal of the Evangelical Theological Society*
JHS	*Journal of Hebrew Scriptures*
JNES	*Journal of Near Eastern Studies*
JPSTC	Jewish Publication Society Torah Commentary
JR	*Journal of Religion*
JRC	*Journal of Religion and Culture*
JSHJ	*Journal for the Study of the Historical Jesus*
JSJ	*Journal for the Study of Judaism in the Persian, Hellenistic, and Roman Periods*
JSNTSup	Journal for the Study of the New Testament, Supplement Series
JSOT	*Journal for the Study of the Old Testament*

JSOTSup	Journal for the Study of the Old Testament, Supplement Series
JSQ	Jewish Studies Quarterly
Jub.	Jubilees
LB	Linguistica biblica
Lev. R.	Leviticus Rabbah
LNTS	Library of New Testament Studies
LTJ	Lutheran Theological Journal
LXX	Septuagint
m. Šebu.	Mishna Šebu'ot
MT	Masoretic Text
m. Yom.	Mishna Yoma
NAC	New American Commentary
NCBC	New Century Bible Commentary
NIB	New Interpreter's Bible
NICOT	New International Commentary on the Old Testament
NIDOTTE	New International Dictionary of Old Testament Theology and Exegesis, ed. W. A. VanGemeren, 5 vols., Carlisle: Paternoster; Grand Rapids: Zondervan, 1997
NTS	New Testament Studies
NU	Novum Testamentum Graece, 27th ed., ed. E. Nestle, K. Aland et al., Stuttgart: Deutsche Bibelstiftung, 1993; The Greek New Testament, 4th rev. ed., ed. B. Aland, K. Aland et al., Stuttgart: Deutsche Bibelgesellschaft/United Bible Societies, 1993
OBO	Orbis biblicus et orientalis
OtSt	Oudtestamentische Studiën
pl.	plural
ProEccl	Pro ecclesia
Proof	Prooftexts: A Journal of Jewish Literary History
RB	Revue biblique
RestQ	Restoration Quarterly
SBJT	Southern Baptist Journal of Theology
SBLSP	Society of Biblical Literature Seminar Papers
SBS	Stuttgarter Bibelstudien
SEAJT	South East Asia Journal of Theology
SJOT	Scandinavian Journal of the Old Testament
SNTSMS	Society for New Testament Studies Monograph Series

SR/SR	*Studies in Religion/Sciences Religieuses*
STDJ	Studies on the Texts of the Desert of Judah
Targ. Neof	*Targum Neofiti*
TBN	Themes in Biblical Narrative
TDOT	*Theological Dictionary of the Old Testament*, ed. G. J. Botterweck, H. Ringgren and H.-J. Fabry, 15 vols., Grand Rapids: Eerdmans, 1974–2006
ThW	Theologische Wissenschaft
TJT	*Toronto Journal of Theology*
TOTC	Tyndale Old Testament Commentaries
tr.	translation, translated, translated by
TynB	*Tyndale Bulletin*
VE	*Verbum et Ecclesia*
VT	*Vetus Testamentum*
VTSup	Supplements to Vetus Testamentum
WBC	Word Biblical Commentary
WTJ	*Westminster Theological Journal*
WW	*Word and World*
WUNT	Wissenschaftliche Untersuchungen zum Neuen Testament
ZAW	*Zeitschrift für die alttestamentliche Wissenschaft*

The glory of God's house: the lampstand and the table of the Presence

What is the Sabbath? . . . The Sabbath is an ascent to the summit.

(Abraham Joshua Heschel)

The instructions for making the lampstand of the tabernacle's holy place describe it as a stylized almond tree, hammered out of pure gold and having a central shaft with three branches on either side – all made 'according to the pattern' that was shown to Moses on the mountain of God (Exod. 25:31–40). YHWH gives Aaron, the high priest of Israel, the particular duty of tending the lampstand in the following manner:

> And YHWH spoke to Moses saying: 'Speak to Aaron, and say to him, "When you set up the lamps, the seven lamps shall give light in front of the lampstand."' And Aaron did so; he set up the lamps to face toward the front of the lampstand, as YHWH commanded Moses. Now this workmanship of the lampstand was hammered gold; from its base to its flowers it was hammered work. According to the pattern which YHWH had shown Moses, so he made the lampstand. (Num. 8:1–4)[1]

In his commentary on this passage Gordon J. Wenham notes that the text is insistent on one point in particular, namely on Aaron's duty to direct the menorah's seven lamps forward, ensuring they give light in front of the lampstand. Why such emphasis upon this curious duty of ensuring the lamps beam their light in front of the lampstand? He explains that the meaning of this action becomes apparent when the design of the holy place is taken into account:

---

[1] All translations are my own, unless otherwise stated.

15

If the light beamed forwards it would have fallen on the table of shewbread, where twelve loaves of bread, symbolizing the twelve tribes of Israel, were heaped up (Lev. 24:5–9). Light and fire represent the life-giving presence and blessing of God (e.g. Exod. 13:21–22). Thus Aaron had to arrange the lamps so that their light always illuminated the shewbread. *This arrangement portrayed visually God's intention that his people should live continually in his presence and enjoy the blessing mediated by his priests.*[2]

Wenham further remarks that this priestly duty symbolizes what the Levitical blessing in Numbers 6:23–27 affirms verbally:[3]

> YHWH bless you and keep you;
> YHWH make his face shine upon you
> and be gracious to you;
> YHWH lift up his face upon you
> and give you peace.

So shall they put my name upon the sons of Israel, and I myself will bless them.

This blessing, which in the Hebrew utilizes a threefold use of the divine name plus twelve remaining words, is itself not free of symbolic import. Here two brief observations are in order. First, the divine blessing, in both Numbers 6 and 8, is portrayed as God's shining his light upon his people, which is further explained as putting 'his name' upon them (6:27) – a significant gloss to which we will return later on in this book. Secondly, the significance of the lampstand should be understood together with that of the bread of the Presence, forming one symbolic picture, just as the light of God's countenance in the Levitical blessing of Numbers 6 is cast upon his people. Indeed, the forward-facing arrangement of the lamps is an integral part of the instructions for manufacturing the lampstand (Exod. 25:37), intimately woven into its meaning, not to mention that these instructions follow immediately upon the directions to 'set the bread of the Presence before me always' (v. 30). Aaron's instructions require, then, the reader's awareness of the bread's position before the lampstand in the holy place: according to Exodus 26:35 (cf. 40:24), the golden

---

2 Wenham 2008: 106–107; my emphasis.
3 Ibid. 107.

table with the twelve loaves of bread was placed on the north side of the holy place, and the golden, seven-branched lampstand was set directly across from it on the south side (the tabernacle itself facing eastward).

In summary, the light of the lampstand represents the life-giving Presence of God, his blessed glory, while the twelve loaves represent the twelve tribes of Israel. Aaron's role of regularly arranging the lamps so that they shone upon the loaves summarizes the role and function of the priesthood to mediate God's blessings to his people. One might say, in short, that these references in Numbers summarize the role of the cultus for Israel's relationship with God, as it relates to the goal of the covenant.[4] Numbers 6:23–27 and 8:1–4 present the blessing of God upon the people of God, mediated by the priesthood of God.

The arrangement of the holy place of the tabernacle, therefore, portrayed the ideal of Israel basking in the light of the divine Presence in the house of God, abiding in the fires of his glory. As we will come to understand in the following chapters, this cultic symbolism depicted the Sabbath day in particular, as Israel entered the renewing Presence of YHWH *through the Levitical way* he had opened for them – a foretaste of life at the consummation of history. Indeed, this glimpse into the glory of the house of God may be appreciated more fully when we recall that the panelled walls of the holy place were overlaid with gold, a feature that, together with the golden lampstand and golden table, would have caused the light of the seven lamps to be reflected in a wondrous manner. And so this symbolic picture of Israel abiding in the blessed Sabbath-day Presence of YHWH is one that portrays life in the house of God, a prospect foretasted in Israel's Sabbath day worship.

Life with God in the house of God – this was the original goal of the creation of the cosmos (which, as we will see, may be thought of as a house), and which then became the goal of redemption, the new creation. The prophets offer glimpses of this reality in their descriptions of God's final redemption of his people, when, after he has purged and made them utterly holy, he dwells with them on his holy mountain:

Then YHWH will create over the whole place of
Zion's mountain, and over her assemblies,

---

[4] As Kapelrud (1965: 56) expresses it, 'That ladder [of Jacob's dream, connecting heaven and earth] symbolizes the role of the cult in old Israel.'

> a cloud by day and smoke, and the shining
>   of a flaming fire by night –
> for over all the glory there will be a canopy.
>
> (Isa. 4:5)

> 'For I will be to her [Jerusalem]' – utterance of YHWH –
>   'a wall of fire surrounding her,
> and I will be the glory in her midst.'
>
> (Zech. 2:5)

In the closing pages of John's Apocalypse we are given a final glimpse of holy Jerusalem 'having the glory of God', a fire with such radiance from YHWH God that there will be neither night nor need of the sun (Rev. 21:10–11, 23; 22:5) as God's people dwell in the light of his glory. This consummation of the messianic kingdom of God is presented to us by John as the historical fulfilment of the divine intention, as expressed in the covenant formula

> And I heard a loud voice from heaven saying, 'Look! The tabernacle of God is with humanity and he will dwell with them, and they shall be his people and God himself will be with them and be their God.' (Rev. 21:3)

As the innermost aim of the covenant, dwelling with God in the house of God, for fullness of life in abundant joy and fellowship, is the great promise held out before God's people, and the ardent desire expressed in Israel's liturgy:

> I will dwell in the house of YHWH for ever.
>
> (Ps. 23:6)

Those whom YHWH brings into his house receive divine hospitality. Much like a magnanimous ANE host, God spreads a table for his guests, anointing their heads with oil and pouring wine liberally into their cups (Ps. 23:5). Indeed, YHWH's house is described as the source of all life and abundance:

> They are abundantly satisfied with the
>   fatness of your house,
> And you give them drink from the
>   river of your pleasures ['dn].

> For with you is the spring of life;
> In your light we see light.
>
> (Ps. 36:8–9)

Note the allusion to Eden's river of life, with the word 'pleasures' being merely the plural form of 'Eden'. Dwelling in the house of God is, more deeply, a hope inflamed with the longing to behold YHWH himself – for he is the fountain of life:

> You will make known to me the path of life;
> There is fullness of joy in your Presence;
> And pleasures at your right hand for evermore.
>
> (Ps. 16:9–11)

> O YHWH, I love the habitation of your house
> And the place where your glory dwells.
>
> (Ps. 26:8)

The same yearning, to dwell with YHWH in a life suffused by the beatific vision, is expressed as the 'one thing' the psalmist asks for in Psalm 27:4:

> One thing I have asked of YHWH – that will I seek:
> That I may dwell in the house of YHWH
>   all the days of my life,
> To behold the beauty of YHWH,
> And to contemplate in his temple.

But just here the question comes how can this be possible? How is it that God's own abode may become the end of his people's journey? How can becoming a member of the household of God be a real hope for creatures made from dust? Considering that only the high priest had been allowed entrance into the holy of holies within the tabernacle and later temple, how is it songs could be sung about dwelling in YHWH's house 'for ever' and 'all the days of my life'? In many ways, this is the fundamental question of Israel's cult – and indeed of life itself:

> O YHWH, who may abide in your tabernacle?
> Who may dwell on your holy mountain?
>
> (Ps. 15:1)

19

> Who may ascend the mountain of YHWH?
> Or who may stand in his holy place?
>
> (Ps. 24:3)

This question of ascending God's mountain to his house was probably recited by pilgrims upon approaching the temple on Mount Zion during the annual pilgrimage festivals, and is referred to as a gate (or entrance) liturgy. As we will see in the chapters ahead, the gate liturgy runs as an undercurrent throughout the narratives of the Pentateuch, and is found at the heart of its central book, Leviticus. Such a point comes as no surprise when we consider that the Pentateuch itself is a thoroughly Levitical work, a priestly torah, whose traditional author, Moses, was a thoroughgoing Levite (Exod. 2:1–2; 6:14–27). Its dominating concern, as well as that of the rest of the Bible, is the way in which humanity may come to dwell in the house of God. Under the Mosaic covenant, that way opened by YHWH was through the tabernacle and later temple, its priesthood and rituals – that is, through the Levitical cult. The advent of Christ would open a new and living way into the house of God; indeed, that was the goal of his taking our humanity upon himself, of his suffering, of his resurrection and ascension.

This biblical theology of Leviticus, then, is a book about the theme of dwelling with God in the house of God, and how that reality is finally made possible. Israel's deepest hope, to dwell in YHWH's house upon his holy mountain, was not merely a liturgical question but a historical quest. A gravely confounding quest, to be sure, for who may 'dwell with the devouring fire?' (Isa. 33:14). And yet Israel's destiny, nevertheless, is to become just such a wonder, akin to the burning bush, to be 'burning with fire, but not consumed', alight with the glory of the Presence of God (Exod. 3:2–3). In Exodus 15, having just seen the deliverance of YHWH through the sea, Moses leads Israel in song, perhaps the most ancient in Scripture. The theological heart and structural centre of the song, verse 11, is the adoration of God:

> Who is like you, O YHWH, among the gods?
> Who is like you, glorious in holiness,
>> fearful in praises,
>> doing wonders?

Again, we are confronted with 'the deepest and innermost nature of the God of the Old Testament',[5] his absolute holiness. From the heavens, the angels declare, 'Holy, holy, holy is YHWH of hosts' (Isa. 6:3); that is, YHWH is like 'no other'. This heavenly indicative is matched by an earthly interrogative. From the earth, Israel, having experienced his salvation, cries up, 'Who is like you, O YHWH?' The question itself is the highest acclamation of praise. And yet, even in the depths of such a fearful marvel, the song moves on with undaunted hope to a nearly unimaginable promise – namely, that God's people have been delivered precisely for the purpose of abiding with this One to whom none can be compared:

> You in your loving-kindness will lead forth the people
> you have redeemed;
> You will guide them by your strength to your holy
> habitation . . .
> You will bring them in and plant them in the mountain
> of your inheritance,
> In the place, O YHWH, you have made for your
> own dwelling,
> The sanctuary, O Lord, which your hands have
> established.
> (Exod. 15:13, 17)

The emphatic threefold 'you will' of these verses is the source of Israel's life and hope for dwelling in God's house. YHWH, out of an eternal love, purposes to make a way – and, is anything too difficult for God? The following pages endeavour to unfold the wonder of that way. Anchored thus to YHWH's own will, his people's longing will not be in vain.

The Heidelberg Catechism, question and answer six, teaches that humanity was created to truly know and love God and to live with him in eternal happiness, all to his praise and glory. Similarly, the Westminster Confession of Faith Shorter Catechism, question and answer one, states that humanity's chief end is to glorify God and enjoy him for ever. These historic confessions capture precisely the biblical theology of the Bible. Entering the house of God to dwell with God, beholding, glorifying and enjoying him eternally, I suggest, is *the* story of the Bible, the plot that makes sense of the various acts, persons and places of its pages, the deepest context for its doctrines.

---

[5] Sellin 1936: 19.

21

For this ultimate end the Son of God shed his blood and poured out the Spirit from on high, even to bring us into his Father's house, in him, as sons and daughters of God.

> How lovely is your dwelling, O YHWH of hosts!
> My soul longs, even faints, for the courts of YHWH,
> My heart and flesh cry out with joy to the living God!
> . . . How happy are those who dwell in your house,
>   ever singing your praise!
>
> (Ps. 84:1–4)

Chapter One

Leviticus within the Pentateuch: a theological structure

Introduction

The primary theme and theology of Leviticus (and of the Pentateuch as a whole) is *YHWH's opening a way for humanity to dwell in the divine Presence*. This theme will be found to encompass the narrative storyline of the Pentateuch, as well as the prominent role of the tabernacle cultus within it. Indeed, the theme of dwelling in the divine Presence, like a kernel sprouting up from the soil of the Pentateuch's heart, wends its way through biblical history and branches out literarily into various cluster-bearing vines, vines never severed from their root.

Increasingly, scholars have come to appreciate the significance of literary structure for determining the meaning of a work: that the form conveys meaning. In this chapter, therefore, we will consider the structure of the Pentateuch in its final form, examining how that structure contributes to the stated theological theme of Leviticus.

The structure of the Pentateuch

We will now explore the Pentateuch's overarching structure. I will argue that by examining the highest macrostructural level of the Pentateuch one is able to sound out the deepest level – the bedrock – of its meaning. In doing so we will find that the final shape of the Pentateuch sets up the priestly cultus quite literally as a light upon a hill.

The centre of the Pentateuch: Leviticus

Perhaps the most obvious structural feature of the Pentateuch is that it *is* a 'Pentateuch', a 'five-volume' or 'five-scrolled' book. Many scholars have noted that this five-book structure, with Leviticus at the centre, is not likely to have been coincidental.[1] The notion that it simply took five scrolls to fit the entire Torah, an idea justly dubbed 'flimsy' by Auld,[2] does not adequately account for the cut-off points of each book nor for the symmetry of the collection taken together: Exodus and Numbers are nearly the same length (16,713 and 16,413 words respectively) while Leviticus, the central book, is by far the shortest (11,950 words – half the length of Genesis).[3] Moreover, chronological markers set off all five books of the Pentateuch as separate units.[4] Likewise, that the psalter was deliberately divided into five books manifests a relevant awareness that the Pentateuch's fivefold structure is theologically significant.[5]

Once the fivefold nature of the Pentateuch is in view, the centrality of Leviticus becomes readily apparent. Thematically, there is also good reason to believe the Pentateuch is structured concentrically. Genesis and Deuteronomy both end with a patriarch (Jacob, Moses) blessing the twelve tribes before dying outside the land,[6] and Exodus and Numbers have many parallel events, framing Leviticus as the central book. A. C. Leder summarizes:

In the concentric structure of the Pentateuch parallels between Exodus and Numbers suggest that they constitute a frame for Leviticus. Parallels between Genesis and Deuteronomy not only frame Exodus, Leviticus and Numbers thematically, they also provide the beginning and conclusion to the linear sequence of the entire pentateuchal narrative. Thus, Genesis through Deuteronomy exhibits an ABCB'A' organizational format in which Deuteronomy returns to and complements the themes of Genesis, and Numbers returns to and complements the themes of Exodus. This leaves Leviticus occupying the narrative centre of the Pentateuch, as illustrated in the chart below.[7]

[1] See e.g. Klingbeil 2007: 155–157; Radday 1972; Shea 1986; Christensen 1996: 539. Sailhamer (1992: 1–2) downplays the Pentateuch's fivefold structure, a point that may be connected to his marginalization of the cultus.
[2] Auld 1996: 40.
[3] Blenkinsopp 1992: 42–47; Ska 2006: 16–19.
[4] M. Smith 1999: 201; Knierim 1995: 353; Auld 1996; 2003; Bibb 2008: 18–26.
[5] Interestingly, Book Three of the Psalms is 'dominated by songs of the Levites Asaph, Korah and Ethan' (Auld 1996: 41), in addition to the further similarity of its being the central and shortest of the five books.
[6] Note also the shared vocabulary, exclusive to the beginning of Genesis (1:2) and end of Deuteronomy (32:10–11).
[7] Leder 2010: 34–35.

A GENESIS	Separation from the nations/Blessing/ Seeing the land/ Descendants and the land		
B EXODUS		Israel's desert journeys/ Apostasy and plagues/ Pharaoh and magicians/ First-born/Levites	
C LEVITICUS			Sacrifices/ Cleanliness/ Holiness
B' NUMBERS		Israel's desert journeys/ Apostasy and plagues/ Balak and Balaam/ First-born/Levites	
A' DEUTERONOMY	Separation from the nations/Blessing/ Seeing the land/ Descendants and the land		

Moshe Kline (2006) proposes a similar schematic structure of the Pentateuch:

Genesis	Prologue
Exodus	Leaving Egypt
	Building the **tabernacle**
Leviticus	The **tabernacle** service
Numbers	Dedicating the **tabernacle**
	Preparing to enter Canaan
Deuteronomy	Epilogue

The symmetry is more than broadly thematic however. Wenham notes, for example, that while Genesis appears to serve as an introductory prologue and Deuteronomy as a reflective epilogue, Exodus, Leviticus and Numbers hang closely together by three extended journey-stop cycles:[8]

---

[8] Wenham 2008: 18. On pp. 19–20 Wenham charts the journey-and-stops parallels.

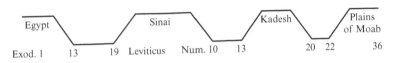

More narrowly, the ring structure of Exodus 15:22 – Numbers 21:18 proposed by A. Schart highlights both the similarities between Exodus and Numbers and the significance of Sinai within the Pentateuch:[9]

A Exod. 15:22–25 transformation of water from bitter to sweet
  B   17:1–7   water from the rock
    C   17:8–16   Amalekite–Israelite war
      D 18   leadership relief for Moses
        E   18:27   the Midianite Hobab, Moses' father-in-law
          F   19:1–2   arrival at Sinai

          SINAI

          F' Num. 10:11–23 departure from Sinai
        E'   10:29–32   the Midianite Hobab, Moses' father-in-law
      D' 11   leadership relief for Moses
    C' 14:39–45   Amalekite–Israelite war
  B' 20:1–13   water from the rock
A' 21:16–18   the spring

The centrality of Sinai, the locus for the archetypal advent of YHWH, demonstrates the theological emphasis of theophany and divine Presence within the Pentateuch.[10] Narrowing further within this central Sinai section (Exod. 19 to Num. 10), which is itself set off by itinerary notices, there are significant signals as to the literary integrity of the book of Leviticus.[11] With reference to the tabernacle, the book is framed by a date notice:

G Exod. 40:17 1st day of 1st month of 2nd year – 'the tabernacle was raised up'

    SINAI   Book of Leviticus

G' Num. 1:1   1st day of 2nd month of 2nd year – 'the tabernacle of meeting'

That the tabernacle structure coincides with the book of Leviticus supports Mary Douglas's reading of Leviticus as something of a

---

[9] Schart 1990: 52. J. Milgrom (1990: xvii–xviii) also argues for a general chiastic arrangement. See also the chiasm of Exod. 19:3 to Num. 10:10 proposed by D. A. Dorsey (1999: 80–81).
[10] See Polak 1996; Lawlor 2011: 30–31.
[11] Cf. Ruwe 2003: 58–59.

literary tour of the tabernacle.[12] C. R. Smith also points out how the second half of Exodus deals primarily with setting up the tabernacle, while the first half of Numbers is concerned with taking it down, Leviticus itself comprising God's speeches from the tabernacle.[13] He notes, along with Knierim,[14] that Leviticus 1:1 ('YHWH summoned Moses, and spoke to him *from the tent of meeting*') signals the highest level in the macrostructure of the Sinai pericope, and is bookended by Numbers 1:1 ('YHWH spoke to Moses in the wilderness of Sinai, *in the tent of meeting*'), betraying a deliberate effort to seclude Leviticus as a distinct section. Rendtorff likewise points out the intentional nature of its composition,[15] being 'the only book in the Pentateuch that takes place completely and exclusively at Sinai – and which at the same time takes place at and in the tent of meeting, the sanctum'.[16] With relative confidence, then, we may affirm Damrosch's statement that Leviticus is the very heart of the Pentateuch's narrative.[17]

The centre of Leviticus: day of Atonement

Setting our focus now within the confines of Leviticus, atonement is one of the major themes of this central book, and several scholars have posited the Day of Atonement in Leviticus 16 as the book's literary centre. This conclusion appears well founded as it can be reached from a variety of approaches. Outlining Leviticus according to its alternating genres of law and narrative, C. R. Smith proposes a sevenfold division: law, narrative, law, narrative, law, narrative, law, with the central section being the narrative description of the Day of Atonement in Leviticus 16.[18] Zenger comes to a concentrically arranged sevenfold structure,[19] with chapters 16–17 at the centre: 1–7,

---

[12] Douglas 1999a. See also G. Rendsburg's (2008) additional support. While affirming Leviticus as dominated literarily by the tabernacle, I do not embrace Douglas's structural outline (see brief critique below).

[13] C. R. Smith 1996: 18–19. Lawlor (2011: 39–42) posits Exod. 33:7–11 not only as the turning point in the Sinai pericope (which he defines as Exod. 18 to Num. 10) but also as referring to the content of Leviticus and Num. 1 – 6 (revelation in which the tent of meeting is central).

[14] Knierim 1985: 405.

[15] Rendtorff 2003: 253.

[16] My translation of 'Damit wird zugleich bewusst gemacht, dass Leviticus als einziges der fünf Bücher des Pentateuch ganz und ausschliesslich am Sinai spielt – und das heisst zugleich: am und im Zelt der Begegnung, dem Heiligtum.'

[17] Damrosch 1987: 76. Knierim's (1985: 405) conclusion is much the same, that the 'Sinai-pericope aims at the book of Leviticus. This book is the centre of the Pentateuch.'

[18] C. R. Smith 1996: 22. He (24) also suggests the two goats of the Day of Atonement highlight the concerns of the set of laws on either side of it: cleanness and holiness.

[19] Zenger 1999.

sacrifice regulations; 8–10, priestly duties; 11–15, daily purity; 16–17, atonement and reconciliation; 18–20, daily holiness; 21–22, priestly duties; 23–26, sacrifice and festival regulations – and here Ruwe critiques well his failure to isolate chapter 16.[20] Although Ruwe himself posits Leviticus 1 – 8 and 9 – 26 as the highest structural division of Leviticus, his subdivisions (e.g. positing a concentric structure for chs. 11–15, a coherent independent complex for chs. 17–27 and delineating ch. 16 as its own section due to the chronological notice of v. 1, and the exclusive address to Aaron in v. 2) mark the central character of the Day of Atonement.[21] And in his published doctoral dissertation Warning analyses the structure of Leviticus according to its thirty-seven divine speeches, arriving at Leviticus 16 as the literary centre, with eighteen divine speeches on either side.[22] Finally, based on formal devices, such as repetitions and interconnections, and marking Leviticus 1:1, 16:1–2aα and 25:1 as macrostructural divine-speech introductions, Luciani also proposes a concentric structure, with Leviticus 16 at the centre.[23] Rendtorff's conclusion appears judicious, therefore, that on both a formal and thematic level there are sound reasons to speak of the central position of chapter 16 within the book of Leviticus.[24] Thus construed, the Day of Atonement becomes the literary and thematic centre of the Pentateuch. Bibb comes to a similar conclusion:

> The chapter itself [16] is a microcosm of the book's ritual world, a subtle integration of narrative past and timeless, disembodied ritual. In any case, it is clearly the central pivot point of the book and any literary analysis must account for its importance in the structure and the message of Leviticus.[25]

Based on an article by Shea (1986), R. M. Davidson's diagram of the Pentateuch, which I have altered slightly, highlights the structural position and role of Leviticus 16:[26]

[20] Ruwe 2003: 69, n. 35. The second half of Ruwe's article, furthermore, argues cogently for maintaining chs. 17–26 as a unit – ensuring the distinctness and complete-ness of ch. 16. On this point, see also Otto 1994: 242–243.
[21] Ruwe 2003: esp. 68–69.
[22] Warning 1999.
[23] Luciani 2005. He marks the following parallels: chs. 1–7 and 25–27 (A–A'); 8–10 and 23–24 (B–B'); 11–12 and 22:17–33 (C–C'); 13–15 and 17:1 – 22:16 (D–D'); with ch. 16 at the centre.
[24] Rendtorff 2003.
[25] Bibb 2008: 33.
[26] Davidson 1988: 20.

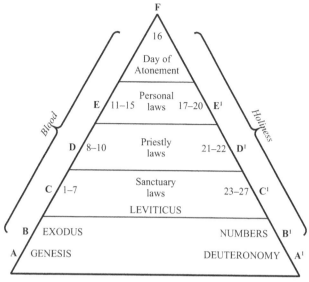

Diagram of Leviticus

Therefore, while precise markers and thematic labels will undoubtedly vary among scholars who propose a sevenfold structure (at some level), the following outline offers a suitable overview to Leviticus:

Lev 1 – 7 Sacrifices
   8 – 10 Institution of priesthood/inauguration of cultus   *Approaching God*
      11 – 15 Clean/unclean in daily life   ATONEMENT
         16 Day of Atonement   —   JUDGMENT/CLEANSING
      17 – 20 Holy/profane in daily life   *Communion with God*
   21 – 22 Legislation for the priesthood
23 – 27 Festivals / sacred time   HOLINESS

As is evident from the stepped arrangement, and in agreement with Zenger (1999) and Luciani (2005) among others, I posit a concentric structure, leading up to the Day of Atonement as the 'capstone of the sacrificial rituals' and flowing out of that ceremony into 'the subject of holy living'.[27] From, perhaps, the most basic vantage point, one may consider Leviticus in two halves, with chapter 16 serving as the fulcrum, summing up the sacrificial cult and functioning as a segue to the call for holiness. The first half deals primarily with the approach to God through blood, while the second half is taken up

---

[27] Shea 1986: 131–132.

with life in God's Presence through increasing holiness, the overall goal being fellowship and union with God.[28] Once more, the *aim* of Levitical legislation must be kept in view. Whether the laws pertain to sacrifice, to distinguishing between clean and unclean, or to ethical and moral behaviour, the aim of the laws is fellowship and union with the living God. For this reason, though Leviticus is often characterized thematically by holiness,[29] it is preferable to discern holiness not as an end in itself but rather as a means to an end, which is the real theme, the abundant life of joy with God in the house of God. This point may be illustrated according to the primary subject matter characterizing each half of Leviticus, blood and holiness, respectively. Leviticus 17:11 sets the whole sacrificial legislation of chapters 1–16 within this framework when it explains *life* as the significance of (cultic or sacrificial) blood:

> For the life ['soul', *nepeš*] of the flesh, it is in the blood, and I myself have given it to you upon the altar to make atonement upon your lives ['souls', *napšōtêkem*], for it is the blood that, by means of the life ['soul', *bannepeš*], makes atonement.

While the idea of death is certainly present in the ritual immolation of animals, yet the pervasive emphasis throughout the first half of Leviticus upon the blood of animals is to be understood rather as an emphasis upon life. This is especially the case as that life is brought into the divine Presence in the holy of holies in Leviticus 16. The overlap between blood and the holiest place occurs, furthermore, precisely upon the holiest ritual act on the Day of Atonement, at the transition point to the second half of Leviticus, with its emphasis upon

---

[28] This broad approach to Leviticus also enables one to grasp the twofold nature of reconciliation with God: approaching God through the means he has ordained, namely *atonement* (in the first half of Leviticus); and then deepening fellowship and communion with God by the increase of *holiness* (in the second half of Leviticus). Stated differently, the two halves of Leviticus may also be contemplated under the theological categories of justification and sanctification, respectively (see e.g. ibid. 149–151), although this is somewhat overly simplistic – the sacrifices are ever as much about sanctification. It was precisely the cultic foundation for these theological categories that enabled the apostles of the new covenant to understand the accomplished work of Jesus Christ. The apostle Paul, therefore, wrote that we have 'now been justified by his blood', being 'reconciled to God through the death of his Son' and that, having been reconciled, we shall all the more 'be saved by his life' (Rom. 5:8–10; cf. 3:21–26).

[29] Turnbull (1926: 17; emphasis original; cf. 13–14) expresses this well: 'Leviticus was given to direct Israel how she might live as a *holy* nation; that being holy, she might come into God's Presence [chs. 1–16]; that being holy, she might live in communion with God [chs. 17–27].'

holiness – an emphasis that begins with the sanctity of blood in ch. 17, though the root for holiness (*qdš*) is not used. The set-apartness of blood for sacred use, because of its significance as life, leads to the subject of holy living (chs. 17–27). Then, just as with the blood's signifying life in the first half of Leviticus, so, too, with holiness in the second half. Holiness, properly conceived, pertains to fullness of life, a perspective that will be grasped more clearly when we consider in the next chapter the correspondence between the holy of holies and the garden of Eden. Suffice it to say here that the holy of holies derives its status from being the locale of God's Presence on earth, and, so, from God's nature as absolute life, the fountain of life – the God of the living. Understood in this manner, *the tabernacle's grades of holiness are seen rather as grades of life*, with *the holy of holies representing fullness of life*. Not only does this point help to explain various require-ments for the high priest, as well as to unfold the logic behind aspects of ceremonial uncleanness, but for our present purpose it also enables us to understand holiness legislation as an invitation to life with God: 'You shall be holy because I YHWH your God am holy' (Lev. 19:2; cf. Lev. 11:44–45; 20:7; cf. 1 Peter 1:16). The realm outside the gates of Eden is polluted with death; approaching God and communing with him must of necessity entail being set apart from sin and un-cleanness (realm of death) to God himself, who is utterly holy (realm of life).

How the Day of Atonement relates to the theme of YHWH's opening a way for humanity to dwell in the divine Presence is readily recognized when the significance of atonement is understood, namely *that it makes possible life in the divine Presence*.[30] Atonement is recon-ciliation, at-one-ment. This is in keeping with Nihan's basic theme for Leviticus as 'Israel's gradual initiation (by Yahweh himself) into the requirements of the divine Presence, an initiation taking place in three successive stages' of growing intimacy.[31] In bringing the divine Presence near, the book of Leviticus itself sharpens the focus of what may be called the central theological dilemma (and drama) of human-ity's relationship with God, namely the danger posed by intimacy with a 'consuming fire' – a threat relieved *somewhat* by cultic legislation.[32]

---

[30] Cf. Crüsemann 1996: 313.

[31] Nihan 2007: 108–110. For a similar reading of the Pentateuch in relation to the divine presence, see Blum 1990; Ruwe 2003.

[32] Cf. e.g. Bibb 2008: 46, 68, 75, 86. Throughout his monograph Bibb notes the tension and ambiguity underlying cultic legislation. The cultus does not amount to 'magic' – it can neither control nor contain the deity.

At the heart of the Pentateuch, then, one finds humanity's deepest penetration into the divine Presence – this by way of the cultic means opened by YHWH. As we will see, however, the book of Leviticus holds out the prospect of deeper communion with God, through the Day of Atonement, but also beyond it. That is, the Day of Atonement represents the deepest *cultic* penetration into God's Presence, while chapters 17–27 of Leviticus will draw out the prospect of life with God enabled through the tabernacle cultus, as Israel grows steadily sanctified through its mediation.

Returning to the book's outline, while academic dispute over the structure of Leviticus will probably continue, it is significant that a number of scholars, perhaps the widest consensus,[33] accept Leviticus 16 as the literary and theological centre. A few who have posited Leviticus 19 as the centre of Leviticus nonetheless suggest that atonement appears thematically central to the book. Mary Douglas infers that atonement is the central theme of Leviticus,[34] as does Moshe Kline, who believes the reader of Leviticus is placed in a position analogous to the high priest on the Day of Atonement, following the path of holiness through the courtyard, holy place and holy of holies to the centre of the book.[35]

Nihan has given a satisfactory critique of Douglas's proposed structure,[36] and I merely add that positioning the reader analogously to the high priest on the Day of Atonement is a more reasonable premise when the Day of Atonement itself is found to be the literary and thematic focus of the book.

Finally, turning our attention to the shape of Leviticus 16 itself, a number of scholars have posited a chiastic arrangement for this chapter.[37] My own objective does not require being dogmatic on the form of Leviticus 16, as we are considering the thematic importance of the chapter (and Day of Atonement) as a whole. However, such a structure, if valid, serves to isolate Leviticus 16 as a textual unit, fits the central function of the chapter and further focuses attention

---

[33] See e.g. Averbeck 1997a: 910; Davidson 2000a; Hartley 1992: 217; Luciani 2005; Radday 1972; Rendtorff 2003; Rooke 2007: 342; Shea 1986; C. R. Smith 1996; Zenger 1999: 71; Jürgens 2001: 126–86 (Zenger and Jürgens both posit chs. 16–17 as the centre).

[34] Douglas 1999a: 231–234.

[35] Moshe Kline 2006: 11.

[36] Nihan (2007: 84) notes e.g. the significant incongruity whereby the high priest's only entrance into the holy of holies in Lev. 16 is assigned in Douglas's schema to the outer court, representing the structural parallel to Lev. 2.

[37] Luciani 2005: 386; Hartley 1992: 232; Rodriguez 1996.

upon the purpose of the ritual (vv. 16–17) – a salient point, given my suggested theme. Rodriguez argues for the following concentric outline,[38] to which I have made slight alterations and have added the concentrically arranged Pentateuch:

```
FRAME: 'And YHWH said to Moses . . .' (16:1)
              A. Aaron should not go into holy of holies any time he wishes
                 (16:2)
                 B. Aaron's sacrificial victims, special vestment (16:3–4)
                    C. Sacrificial victims provided by people (16:5)
                       D. Aaron's bull, goat for sin-offering, goat for Azazel
                          (16:6–10)
A. Genesis             E. Aaron sacrifices bull (16:11–14)
  B. Exodus              F. Goat sacrificed as sin-offering (16:15)
     X. Leviticus – ch. 16 →       X. Atonement (16:16–20a)
  B.' Numbers             F.' Goat sent to wilderness (16:20b–22)
A.' Deuteronomy         E.' Aaron's closing activities (16:23–25)
                       D.' Goat for Azazel, Aaron's bull, goat for sin-offering
                          (16:26–28)
                    C.' People rest and humble themselves (16:29–31)
                 B.' Anointed priest officiates wearing special garments
                    (16:32–33)
              A.' Anointed priest makes atonement once a year (16:34)
FRAME: 'As YHWH commanded Moses . . .' (16:34)
```

Notably, Luciani's chiastic outline of the same chapter contains significant overlap,[39] tending to confirm the general structure's focus on the accomplished purgation of the tabernacle and camp of Israelites – 'so shall he make atonement . . .' (v. 16):

```
16:1–2a  Narrative Speech Frame
I. 16:2aβ–10
        A. YHWH's address to Moses (2aβ–b)
           B. Animals, clothes and bath to begin the ritual and penetrate into the
              holy of holies (3–5)
           C. Presentation of the sacrificial animals and drawing of lots (6–10)
II. 16:11–20
                       X. Entrance, in 2 phases, into holy of holies with the blood
                          of the hatta't bull, with frankincense and with the
                          blood of the hatta't goat (11–15)
                          Y. The purpose of the ritual: Purge the holy of holies
                             and the holy place of the impurities of the
                             assembly of Israel (16–17)
                       X.' Exit to the sacrificial altar and completion of cleansing
                          the sanctuary (18–20)
```

---

[38] Rodriguez 1996: 283.
[39] Luciani 2005: 386.

III. 16:21–34a
>> C.' Load the sins of Israel onto scapegoat and drive it into the desert (21–22)
>> B.' Procedures for ritual exit: disrobe, bath of the high priest and his assistants, burnt offerings, a provision of the remains of sacrificial materials (23–28)
> A.' YHWH addresses the Community (29–34)

16:34b Narrative Speech Frame

At issue, once more, is the significance, thematic and theological, of this Day of Atonement chapter as a whole. Nihan, for example, who sees a threefold structure to the book of Leviticus (chs. 1–10, 11–16 and 17–26 [+27]), each section concluding with a reference to the divine Presence (chs. 9–10, 16, 26), notes the centrality of chapter 16, 'undoubtedly the most important ritual in the whole book', for the following reasons: (1) it is the annual occasion whereby both the sanctuary and the community are purified from all impurities, (2) it is the only ceremony whereby Aaron is given entrance into God's Presence in the holy of holies, (3) formal devices, utterly unique and unparalleled so far in Leviticus, set off the chapter.[40]

In basic agreement with Nihan's proposal, I will approach the drama of Leviticus by a threefold movement, even as I highlight the significance of its central chapter.

While, certainly, not every detail of the Pentateuchal structures reviewed thus far is equally convincing,[41] yet the structural centrality of the Sinai pericope (Schart's outline), the framing of Leviticus (with Exodus and Numbers mirroring each other) and the theological centrality of the Day of Atonement within Leviticus are firm and widely held positions. Accepting the role of the Day of Atonement as the structural keystone and theological centre of Leviticus,[42] it will, however, require the rest of this present study to affirm that *YHWH's opening a way for humanity to dwell in the divine Presence* – particularly through atonement – is a theme that stretches throughout the horizon of the Pentateuch, its rays finding their source at its highest arc, the Day of Atonement in Leviticus 16.

---

[40] Nihan 2007: 96–97. See also Ruwe (2003: 63–64), who speaks of a 'theology of encounter'.

[41] See C. Nihan's (2007: 76–95) review and critique of the main proposals.

[42] Hartley 1992: xxxv.

A sacred journey to YHWH's abode

Finally, I supplement here my conclusions by an alternative angle of approach, which also enables me to map out the place of Leviticus within the Pentateuch. M. Smith persuasively demonstrates a symmetrical shaping of Exodus and Numbers by studying their geographical and temporal markers, long considered by commentators a staple of the priestly organization of Pentateuchal material.[43] The itinerary notices in Exodus and Numbers balance one another with six notices charting the Israelites' journey from Egypt to Rephidim, the station before Sinai (Exod. 12:37a; 13:20; 14:1–2; 15:22a; 16:1; 17:1) and six notices following the Israelites from Sinai to the plains of Moab in Numbers (Exod. 19:2; Num. 10:12; 20:1, 22; 21:10–11; 22:1), manifesting a correspondence between the journey to and from Sinai:[44]

Exodus	1:1 – 15:21	in Egypt
	15:22 – 18:26	in the wilderness
	chs. 19–40	at Mount Sinai
Numbers	1:1 – 10:10	at Mount Sinai
	10:11 – 21:35	in the wilderness
	chs. 22–36	in Transjordan

The chronological markers are no less significant, marking special events according to Israel's liturgical calendar. In the book of Exodus, for example, the chronological markers (12:2, 41; 19:1, 16; 40:17) 'suggest a year arranged primarily according to the first two of three main pilgrimage feasts: Passover begins the series with the exodus from Egypt, the Israelites arrive at Sinai on the feast of Weeks, and the tabernacle (*miškān*) is completed around the New Year'.[45] The same is true for the book of Numbers, so that Passover is celebrated not only to begin the journey to Sinai (Exod. 12 – 13) but to begin the journey from Sinai (Num. 9 – 10). Sacred time, Smith observes, is arranged chiastically around Leviticus: while Genesis 1 to Exodus 12 and Numbers 10 to Deuteronomy 34 are reckoned by years, Exodus

---

[43] M. Smith 1999. See also Ruwe 2003: 58–67.

[44] M. Smith 1999: 186–187. 'In general, the priestly arrangement of Exodus and Numbers presents the geographical progression in the book of Numbers in part as an inversion of the progression in Exodus' (ibid. 187).

[45] Ibid. 193.

12 to Numbers 10 is counted by months, evoking the liturgical year through the feasts of Passover, Weeks and Booths.[46]

Thus illustrating a deliberate concern with sacred space and time, Smith also notes throughout how the book of Leviticus itself contains neither itinerary notices nor chronological markers, that the book is, in a sense, timeless and spaceless and thus marked out as a separate book. Indeed, he stresses the central position of Leviticus in the Pentateuch, with the tabernacle being the centre of Israel's holy and liturgical life.[47] However, because it lacks chronological markers, Leviticus is left out of Smith's examination.[48] Still, Smith's structuring categories of space and time are equally operative within the bounds of Leviticus, though of a different nature. The tabernacle plan structures the book in such a way that emphasis is placed upon both sacred space and time as they converge in ch. 16 – the most sacred time, within the most sacred space. Smith's argument that the Exodus to Numbers material has been shaped and structured according to the categories of sacred space and liturgical time, and this so as to stress the centrality of the book of Leviticus, I suggest, leads inevitably to the threshold of the veil – that is, to the Day of Atonement, the highest holy day of Israel's calendar, the day of humanity's nearest approach into the Presence of YHWH.

As we pan back once more beyond the Sinai narrative to the literary structure of the Pentateuch, particularly with the central Exodus, Leviticus and Numbers material in view, the following 'geographic' pattern is evident, providing a double frame around the tabernacle:

wilderness journey – Mt Sinai – tabernacle – Mt Sinai – wilderness journey

This sequence, then, is not merely linear, but has the tabernacle as the culminating centre. In ancient literature the literary centre is often thematically central, form following function – especially so within a chiastic structure. Yehudah Radday, for example, stated that the centre of a chiastic structure is

> a key to meaning. Not paying sufficient attention to it may result in failure to grasp the true theme . . . Biblical authors and/or editors

---

[46] Ibid. 206–207.

[47] Ibid. 204. He also quotes (202) favourably J. W. Watts (1995): 'The close relationship between P's narratives and lists suggests that the priestly writers and editors worked with the larger context in mind and intentionally structured the whole to highlight Levitical legislation as the central lists in the Pentateuch's rhetoric.'

[48] Although he (1999: 206–207) does note, interestingly, that Lev. 16:1, in refering back to the deaths of Aaron's sons in Lev. 10, does assume some lapse of time.

placed the main idea, the thesis, or the turning point of each literary unit, at its center . . . If true, the significance of this salient feature cannot be overestimated.[49]

Thus reading an ancient work may be likened justly to traversing a mountain, with the two halves – the ascent and descent – mirroring each other, and the central summit constituting the literary height. Applying this insight to both the shape and content of the Pentateuch renders a reading along the lines of a journey to the abode of YHWH atop his holy mountain:[50]

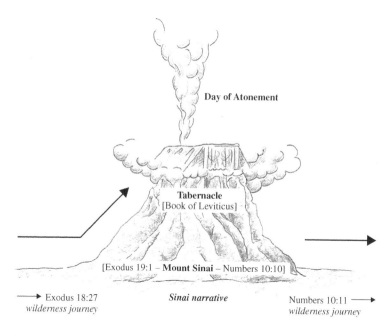

Day of Atonement

Tabernacle
[Book of Leviticus]

[Exodus 19:1 – **Mount Sinai** – Numbers 10:10]

Exodus 18:27
wilderness journey

Sinai narrative

Numbers 10:11
wilderness journey

Like the psalmist's journey to the abode of God in Psalm 23 (a pertinent analogy to which we will return later in this work) the Pentateuch is shaped as a journey led by YHWH to himself at Mount Sinai – and particularly to his abode, the tabernacle. As Blenkinsopp noted, the Pentateuch's narratives 'lead up to the moment when God has

[49] Radday 1981: 51. Cf. also Dorsey 1999: 31; Waltke and Yu 2007: 120. V. M. Wilson (1997: 49; emphasis original) refers to the centre of a chiasm as its '*theological* heart'.
[50] The sketches on pp. 37, 50 and 101 are my own. For somewhat similar approaches, highlighting the centrality of the divine Presence, albeit for the hexateuch, see Newing 1981; 1985; Milgrom 1990: xviii.

ordained to be indefectibly present to his people through its legitimate cult'.[51] Keeping in mind that when reading 'linearly' one must be ever mindful that both halves of a work inform and are informed by the centre, focusing attention upon the centre and deriving meaning from it will help us to read the Pentateuch, as it were, with 'cultic glasses'.

Conclusion

Like moving inwardly along the rings of a target, this chapter has surveyed the structure of the Pentateuch concentrically, moving from its fivefold arrangement to the inner books of Exodus, Leviticus and Numbers, then to the Sinai narrative (Exod 19 to Num 10), then to the central book of Leviticus, and, finally, to the innermost ring itself, the Day of Atonement in Leviticus 16 – the narrowest aim of the Pentateuch's formation. The shape of the Pentateuch, I posit, follows (and forms) its unifying theme: *YHWH's opening a way for humanity to dwell in the divine Presence*. The essence of that *way* and the heart of the Pentateuch's theology is the Day of Atonement.

---

[51] Blenkinsopp 1976: 282. Although Blenkinsopp himself limits this remark to the purported priestly strand in relation to the covenants (Gen. 9:16; 17:7, 13), it nevertheless remains true within a final-form reading of the Pentateuch.

Chapter Two

Longing for Eden: Genesis, the narrative context of Leviticus

Toward understanding the theology of Leviticus, we turn now to consider the narrative arc of Genesis 1 to Exodus 40, particularly as it develops the theme of dwelling with God. This chapter will trace the growing alienation from God's house – that is, from the divine Presence – in the book of Genesis, and the next chapter will follow the drama of YHWH's opening a way for humanity to dwell with him in the book of Exodus as he establishes his house in the midst of Israel. Under the first major heading ('Created to dwell in God's house') we will examine the various parallels between the cosmos and the tabernacle, along with the role of the seventh day, endeavouring to establish that the goal of creation – and therefore the plot of the Bible – is for humanity to dwell with God. Under the second major heading ('Deepening exile from the presence of God') we will begin looking at the story between the bookends of Eden and the tabernacle cultus, tracing the deepening alienation between God and humanity in the book of Genesis as the fundamental plotline leading up to Leviticus. My aim, once more, is to trace the development of the Pentateuch's main theme: *YHWH's opening a way for humanity to dwell in the divine Presence*, particularly as this theme unfolds in the book of Leviticus.

Created to dwell in God's house: the Pentateuch's prologue

Aside from acknowledging the utility of beginning 'with the beginning', few interpreters sufficiently weigh the function of the Genesis 1:1 – 2:3 creation account as a prologue within the overall narrative drama of the Pentateuch.[1] Indeed, the fundamental plotline of the Pentateuch (and redemptive history) is often missed precisely from the failure to discern the ultimate goal of creation, namely *for humanity to dwell with God*. As I will go on to argue, everything else derived from the creation account – every 'mandate', 'commission', and so on – must be subsumed under this chief end of humanity. Creation, in other words, manifests God's purpose, the same purpose and promise found at the heart of the covenant with his people (namely that he will be their God and they will be his people, and he will dwell among them). Because one cannot understand the tabernacle cultus apart from grasping the nature of creation, along with humanity's deepest purpose within it, we will examine how the creation account portrays the cosmos as God's house, and the Sabbath day's communion with God as the goal for humanity.[2]

God's house: parallels between the cosmos and the tabernacle

In the ANE the analogy between cosmos and temple was common-place.[3] The cosmos was understood as a large temple and the temple as a small cosmos. Approaching the biblical account of creation, there are various indications that such a parallel between cosmos and temple (or tabernacle) is in view. For example, the Spirit or 'Wind of God' (*rûaḥ 'ĕlōhîm*) as a phrase appears in Genesis 1:2 for the construction of the cosmos and in Exodus 31:3 and 35:31 for the construction of the tabernacle. Moreover, the Spirit's endowment of Bezalel, the chief artisan of the tabernacle, is described in terms of wisdom,

---

[1] Utilizing the *tôlĕdôt* formula of headings (built off *yld*, 'to give birth') often trans-lated as 'These are the generations of', the book of Genesis may be structured along three major units, by which we will proceed: the opening prologue (Gen. 1:1 – 2:3), which stands outside the scheme of headings and serves as an introduction to the whole book; the primeval age (Gen. 2:4 – 11:26, containing five *tôlĕdôt*); and the patriarchal history (Gen. 11:27 – 50:26, also containing five *tôlĕdôt*, with one duplicated in 36:9) (Wenham 2003: 18–19).

[2] Much of what follows has been dealt with more extensively in a previous work (Morales 2012b).

[3] Levenson 1984; Lundquist 1984. The literature on this point is extensive; I recently edited the volume *Cult and Cosmos*, which republishes some of the pivotal essays on the topic (Morales 2014). For our purpose, John H. Walton (2001a: 151) offers a helpful summary of some of the data: 'The connection of cosmos and temple can be seen in Mesopotamian cosmological texts such as Enuma Elish, in Mesopotamian temple-building texts (esp. the Sumerian account of Gudea's temple project), in Ugaritic mythology concerning Baal's seeking a house for himself, and in Egyptian temple texts. These often portray the temple as related to the cosmic mountain or the first primeval hillock to emerge from the waters of chaos. The temple is portrayed as being in the center of the cosmos, with waters flowing forth from its midst.'

understanding and knowledge (Exod. 31:3), the same attributes by which God is said to have fashioned the cosmos:[4]

> YHWH by wisdom founded the earth
> He established the heavens by understanding;
> By his knowledge the deeps were broken up . . .
>
> (Prov. 3:19–20)

Other creation terminology shared with the tabernacle includes the word *mā'ôr* (light, lamp) in Genesis 1:14–15, which always in the Pentateuch designates the lamps of the tabernacle.[5] Vogels makes the same observation, adding, 'The sun and moon are like sacred lamps in the sanctuary of the universe. A better translation would be: "Let there be lamps . . .", or "luminaries." This word confirms the liturgical character of the narrative.'[6]

Elsewhere in the Hebrew Bible, creation is likened to a tabernacle pitched by God (Ps. 104; Job 9:8; Isa. 40:22) or to a house God has established, with pillars, windows and doors (Job 26:11; Gen. 7:11; Ps. 78:23), the cosmos being thought of as a three-decked house of heavens, earth and sea.[7] As the main character of Genesis 1, God is indeed portrayed as something of a workman who builds his house, inspects, pronounces upon his work and then takes his Sabbath rest,[8] the house itself, inasmuch as it is the house of God, being a temple.

More broadly, the seven-day structure of the creation account appears to be mirrored by the tabernacle instructions in Exodus 25 – 31, structured along seven speeches of God. Kearney goes further, positing that each of the seven speeches alludes to the corresponding day of creation.[9] While some of his correspondences are not entirely convincing, the parallel between the overall shape of the two accounts is supported historically, and the correspondence between the seventh day and the seventh speech is beyond question, both pertaining to Sabbath rest:

[4] Berman 1995: 15–16; Middleton 2005: 87.
[5] Wenham 1987: 22.
[6] Vogels 1997: 175. See also Rudolph 2003. Fletcher-Louis (2004: 90) suggests that the menorah's being tended 'evening' and 'morning' was a cultic action reflecting creation's first day so that the high priest's role in the cult-as-microcosm mimics the Creator's in the cult-as-macrocosm.
[7] Stadelmann 1970; Jacobs 1975; Gage 2001: 54.
[8] Gordon 2007; M. Smith 2010: 13.
[9] Kearney 1977.

And YHWH spoke to Moses, saying, 'Now you speak to the sons of Israel, saying "Surely my Sabbaths you will keep, for it is a sign between me and you throughout your generations, in order for you to know that I am YHWH who sanctifies you . . . It is a sign between me and the sons of Israel for ever; because in six days YHWH made the heavens and the earth, and on the seventh day he rested and was refreshed."' (Exod. 31:12–17)

Already we see that in a profound sense both the cosmos and the tabernacle tilt toward the same Sabbath end; both are constructed for the same purpose. Moreover, the completion of the tabernacle construction at the end of Exodus is described in terms that echo the completion of creation, using similar words and phrases:[10]

Exodus 39 – 40	Genesis 1 – 2
And Moses saw all the work and, behold, they had done it (39:43)	And God saw all that he had made, and, behold it was very good (1:31)
Thus was completed all the work of the Tabernacle of the tent of meeting (39:32)	The heavens and the earth were completed and all their array (2:1)
When Moses had finished the work (40:33)	God finished the work which he had been doing (2:2)
Moses blessed them (39:43)	And God blessed (2:3)
to sanctify it and all its furnishings (40:9)	and sanctified it (2:3)

The various intertextual parallels between the creation and tabernacle accounts affirm that there is an analogical relationship between creation and tabernacle: again, the cosmos is a large temple; the temple is a small cosmos. Two further points follow logically: first, the tabernacle cultus (personnel, furnishings and rituals) must be understood in the light of that analogical relationship, as related fundamentally to creation (so that the high priest, for example, may be understood as an Adam figure); and secondly, the end or purpose of the tabernacle cultus correlates with the end or purpose of the cosmos. We turn now to establish that humanity's dwelling in the divine Presence *is* the purpose of creation (and, thus, also of the tabernacle cultus).

---

[10] Weinfeld 1981: 503. Weinfeld (506) also notes that Moses' going up the mountain, which comes mainly in order to receive the instructions concerning the construction of the tabernacle (Exod. 25:9, 40; 26:30; 27:8; Num. 8:4), was bound up with six days' waiting (Exod. 24:16), similar to the six days required in order to bring the work of creation to completion.

The Sabbath day: humanity's chief end

'"Last in creation, first in intention," the Sabbath is "the end of the creation of heaven and earth."'[11] This statement by Abraham Heschel, that the Sabbath is the *telos* or goal of creation, accurately captures the emphasis of Genesis 1:1 – 2:3 on the Sabbath, leading other scholars to refer to the creation account as a 'cosmic liturgy of the seventh day',[12] and even as the 'creation of the Sabbath'.[13] Indeed, beginning with a seven-word sentence, developed through seven paragraphs, and climaxing on the consecration of the Sabbath where the seventh day is given threefold emphasis, the role of the Sabbath is dominant, leaving its impress on the account in strong ways, as in the literary structure, and in more subtle ways, as in the number of times key words appear, being some derivative of seven.[14] The most common outline of the creation account, using two triads of days to overcome formlessness and void respectively, highlights the uniqueness of the seventh day as the only day that is not paired:

Formless → habitat	*Void → inhabitants*
Day 1 light	**Day 4** luminaries
Day 2 sky and water	**Day 5** fish and fowl
Day 3 land, vegetation	**Day 6** animals, humans
Day 7 The Sabbath	

The seventh day is literarily set apart in another way as well, separated from the other six days by the summary statement in Genesis 2:1. This is a case of form following substance, since Genesis 2:2–3 narrates God's setting apart – that is, 'he sanctified' (*wayĕqaddēš*) – the seventh day. Probably, then, the seventh day should be understood as paired with the first six days taken together, an inclusio serving to explain their goal.

Alternatively, one may also justly outline the creation narrative from the perspective of time, highlighting the first, central and last days as an approach to the divine Presence. Each of the six days concludes with a reference to time ('there was evening, there was morning, day . . .'),

[11] Heschel 2003: 2. Heschel quotes Rabbi Solomo Alkabez, *Lechah Dodi* and 'The Evening Service for the Sabbath', respectively.
[12] Vervenne 2001: 45.
[13] Guillaume 2009: 33–52.
[14] Wenham 1987: 6.

propelling the account steadily toward the goal of the seventh day.[15] Day one establishes 'evening and morning' (the period of a day) through the creation and separation of light; day four establishes, as we will see, the calendric cycle for the annual cultic feasts; and day seven climaxes the whole account with the weekly Sabbath.

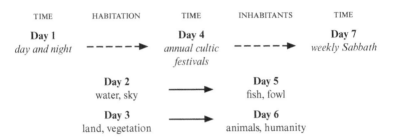

Corresponding to the light of the first day and anticipating the religious festivals of the seventh, the fourth day (Gen. 1:14–18) stands as the structural and thematic centre of the creation account,[16] and was composed as a beautiful palistrophe, outlined here according to function (using the lamed of purpose: 'to', 'for') by Wenham:[17]

A   to divide the day from the night (14a)
    B   for signs, for 'cultic festivals', for days and years (14b)
       C   to give light on the earth (15)
          D   to rule the day (16a) *God made the*
          D' to rule the night (16b*) two lamps*
       C' to give light on the earth (17)
    B' to rule the day and the night (18a)
A' to divide the light from the darkness (18b)

We have already noted how the word *māʾôr* in these verses is the same word used for the tabernacle lamp. Another significant term is *môʿădîm* (pl. of *môʿēd*), rendered as 'cultic festivals' above. Often mistranslated as 'seasons', *môʿēd* refers most often (135 out of 160 times in the Pentateuch) to the 'tent of *meeting*', with the majority of the other cases referring either to the 'fixed time' of a cultic festival or as a synonym for the cultic festival itself – never referring to the seasons of the year (winter, spring, etc.).[18] Thus the chief function of the

---

[15] Westermann 1964: 10–11.
[16] Beauchamp 1969: 67–68.
[17] Wenham 1987: 21–23.
[18] Vogels 1997: 164–165; cf. Rudolph 2003: 40.

'lamps' (sun, moon and stars) is for fixing the annual days of cultic celebration – the heavenly lamps serve as a call to worship for humanity. The B and B' sections of the outline above correlate this cultic function with what it means 'to rule' (*mĕšōl*) the day and night, this ruling then forming the heart of the structure itself (v. 16). Though different words will be used for humanity's call to 'subdue and have dominion over' (*kibšuhā ûrĕdû*) creation, the purpose of that ruling is the same: to gather all of creation into the worship of God. Here we also note that while humanity is called to rule over the earth and its creatures, the lamps rule within the firmament – there is a limit and boundary to humanity's rule, the *rāqîa'* (dome) of Genesis 1:6–8 serving as a 'barrier'.[19] Furthermore, in ruling over time (day and night, cultic festivals), to which humanity is subject as well, these lamps shape, order and guide human life.[20]

Turning to the seventh day, we find a threefold climactic emphasis lacking in the other days of creation:

> Gen 2:2a: And God completed on *the seventh day* his work which he had done.
> Gen 2:2b: And he rested on *the seventh day* from all his work which he had done.
> Gen 2:3: Then God blessed *the seventh day* and sanctified it because on it he rested from all his work which God had created and done.

The seventh day is not only the first day to be blessed, and the only day mentioned three times, but it is also the first object ever to be set apart as holy by God. Moreover, the seventh day is the *only* object of sanctification in the entire book of Genesis; 'he sanctified/made it holy' is the book's only verbal use of the root *qdš*.[21] As the first, mid and final days each relate to time, the account's movement builds toward this sanctification: the reality of one day established by the creation of 'evening and morning', the ability to appoint times for annual cultic festivals established by the heavenly 'lamps', day seven's consecration of *the* cultic day, the weekly Sabbath.[22]

[19] This point will be of interest when we discuss the 'bow' as a sign of the covenant in Gen. 9:12–17.

[20] Vogels (1997: 177) e.g. notes that humanity is not given authority over time, with the moon generally determining the appointed times for liturgical festivals.

[21] Nominal forms of this root include only the place name 'Kadesh' in Gen. 14:7, 16:14, 20:1 and the title (presumably) 'cult prostitute' in Gen. 38:21–22.

[22] Sarna (1989: 14) affirms that the 'ascending order of Creation, and the "six-plus-one" literary pattern that determines the presentation of the narrative, dictates that the seventh day be the momentous climax'. Greenstein (2001: 4) writes, 'The narrative is structured by the recurrent formula, "There was sunset, there was daybreak, one day," "second day", "third day", etc., into seven sections, seven days. . . . The significance of time is made explicit in the narrative with the creation of the luminaries . . .

As we consider now the goal for humanity, it would make sense to do so in the light of this emphasis upon the seventh day. Nevertheless, the dominant role of the Sabbath is rarely factored into discussions about the purpose of creation, many turning rather to the sixth day's creation of humanity as the 'climax' of the account. Typically, arguments for the sixth day's significance relate to the many words used for the sixth day in comparison to the other days.[23] Yet, without minimizing the significance of the sixth day, such reasoning may be faulty on at least two counts. First, one may challenge whether or not it really is the case that the sixth day is more emphatic than the seventh day. Such a view fails to appreciate the Sabbath imprint on the creation account, as I have already established (beginning with a seven-word sentence and structured by seven days, etc.). Secondly, word-allotment alone is insufficient in any case for determining the significance of the sixth day, apart from analysing the *function* of what is being recounted. Indeed, as I will argue, humanity's special place as elaborated on the sixth day is relevant only in the light of the seventh day. The extensive description of humanity's creation on the sixth day is primarily for the sake of understanding the prospect of communion with God on the seventh, actually serving to underscore its significance. As the 'crown' of creation, humanity is made in the 'image' (*ṣelem*) and 'likeness' (*dĕmût*) of God the Creator (Gen. 1:26–27).[24] No doubt this status entitles man (*hā'ādām*), male and female, to rule and subdue the rest of creation, but the primary blessing of being created in God's image is in order to have fellowship with the Creator in a way the other creatures cannot. The 'rule and subdue' command, along with

(*cont.*)
"to be signs of sacred occasions (*mô'ădîm*), days, and years" (v. 14). Days need to be counted for the sake of sacred time. The climax of the creation narrative is not, as some have said, the creation of humanity, but rather the establishment, setting apart, and blessing of the day that has been anticipated by the division of the story into days, the day that retrospectively gives significance to the counting of days, the day that will always be different, God's day, the seventh day, the Sabbath.' See also Gorman 1993: 52–53.

[23] Dempster's fine work may be cited as an example. He (2004: 56–57) refers to the creation of humanity as the 'goal to which everything . . . is directed', and states the 'goal of creation is anthropological', supporting his case by 'the number of words allotted to each day of creation'.

[24] Judging by the Aramaic use of the terms 'image' and 'likeness' in the bilingual inscription of a statue (of a ruler in suppliant's pose) dating to the mid-ninth century BC discovered at Tell Fakhariyeh, 'image' seems to be used as the ruler functions to represent the god's rule over the region/to others (downward), while 'likeness' is used as that aspect which allows the ruler to relate to the god in prayer (upward) (cf. Garr 2000). While this distinction may be intended in Gen. 1, I will proceed by using 'image of God' more comprehensively, as summarizing both aspects.

the 'be fruitful, multiply and fill the earth' blessing, should be directed to this chief end and highest goal – *hāʾādām* is to gather all creation into the life-giving Presence and praise of God.[25] The seventh-day blessing comes, in other words, as a fruition of the radical words 'And God said *to them*' (Gen. 1:28). The *image of God* describes 'the unique-ness of human existence by virtue of which the individual can enter a relationship with God. The human being is regarded as God's counterpart on earth, the "You" who is addressed by God, and the "I" who is responsible to God.'[26] Until this wonder sets in deeply, that the Potter has crafted a vessel with whom he can interact and engage relationally, understanding the image of God will be limited to the goings on of the first six days. Humanity, nevertheless, is not the culmination of creation, but rather humanity in Sabbath day communion with God. This engagement with the divine is what – and what alone – can fulfil the purpose and potential for the image of God, not merely as keeper of the lower creation, but as lover of the fathom-less Uncreated; in this way and for this purpose the image of God itself becomes the wonder of creation. In short, humanity was created for the heavenward gaze, the human soul for a life of prayer. Wester-mann expresses the point well:

> This [the image of God], then, shows us the goal of creation. God made man after his image so that the stream of life might flow in the encounter between God and man, in that which transpires between God and man, through which, even though we cannot fully understand it, God works toward the goal of all creation. . . . This description of man means . . . that man can maintain his humanity only in the presence of God. Man separated from God has not only lost God, but also the purpose of his humanity. . . . man is *not* the goal of God's creation. From the very beginning the seven-day framework has been progressing toward the seventh day. The goal is really the solemn rest of that day. In the blessing and

---

[25] B. M. Palmer (1980: 56) expresses the thought well: 'Stamped with the divine image as being made "a living soul," man's high prerogative is to catch upon the mirror of his own nature the glory of the Creator, and to reflect it back upon him in intelligent and holy worship. His headship over nature is to this end: that, in the interpretation of her secrets, he may disclose the "eternal power and Godhead" hidden in them from the creation of the world; and, as the organ of her hitherto silent praise, may pour it forth in psalms of joy before his throne. Man is ordained a priest to render vocal the worship of all the creatures; which is first made instinct with the life and heart his intelligence and love shall supply. It is a high and solemn function, binding on all who possess the powers of thought and feeling which distinguish men from brutes.'

[26] Och 1995: 228.

hallowing of the seventh day, we may detect the still veiled goal, the day of worship on which the responding congregation audibly utters the praise of the Creator which at creation was still implicit in God's own contemplation of his work.[27]

Humanity's spiritual elevation, made in the image of God, was designed for the spiritual exaltation of the Sabbath. The Sabbath thus becomes *the* day for humanity to enjoy its privileged status of being created in God's image. As later Sabbath legislation would indicate (Exod. 20:8–11), the *image of God* is for the sake of the *imitation of God* (i.e. keeping the Sabbath day holy), and the imitation of God is for the sake of Sabbath *union with God*. As Blocher explains:

> What is the basis of the subordination of work to this 'chief end' of mankind, 'to glorify God and to enjoy him forever' (The Shorter Catechism)? It is nothing other than his creation in the image of God. But what is also meant by the presentation of the divine work at the beginning as a workman's week, as an archetype of the human week, except that mankind is to live according to the image of his Creator? So we see linking together the meaning of the Sabbath and the theme of the image of God, which are in a manner interdependent. . . .[28]

The abundant life, then, is found in engagement with the divine, in the Sabbath day encounter with God.

Returning to the creation and tabernacle parallels, we begin to anticipate something of the wonder opened at the end of Exodus 40: when the cloud of YHWH's glory fills the tabernacle, a new cosmos has broken into the old. These parallels, moreover, find their deepest relation within the context of the Sabbath, so that humanity's purpose established at creation may be realized now only through Israel's tabernacle cultus. 'My Sabbaths you shall guard and my sanctuary you

---

[27] Westermann 1964: 21–22; emphasis original.

[28] Blocher 1984: 57–58. See also Och 1995: 240, and Middleton (2005: 89–90), whose words are worth quoting in full: 'But the *imago Dei* also includes a priestly or cultic dimension. In the cosmic sanctuary of God's world, humans have pride of place and supreme responsibility, not just as royal stewards and cultural shapers of the environment, but (taking seriously the temple imagery) as priests of creation, actively mediating divine blessing to the nonhuman world and – in a postfall situation – interceding on behalf of a groaning creation until that day when heaven and earth are redemptively transformed to fulfill God's purposes for justice and shalom. The human vocation as *imago Dei* in God's world thus corresponds in important respects to Israel's vocation as a "royal priesthood" among the nations (Exod. 19:6).'

shall revere: I am YHWH' (Lev. 19:30). How the tabernacle cultus came to be necessary for humanity's re-engagement with God is part of the Pentateuch's story, to which we now turn.

Deepening exile from the presence of God: the Pentateuch's plot

Broadly, Genesis moves from the life-giving Presence of God in Eden (Gen. 2 – 3) to the death and burial of Joseph in Egypt (Gen. 50:26) – that is, from the heights of Eden upon the mountain of God down to Sheol, the grave.[29] This movement reflects an archetypal pattern related to what we may call 'cultic cosmology'.[30] In short, sacred space was poetically conceived as a world-mountain surrounded by the primeval waters. At the cloud-covered summit of the mountain is the temple, the dwelling of God, and at the base are the chaos waters, underneath which lies Sheol, the place of the dead. Representing God's life-giving Presence, the waters of life flow from the summit of the mountain. Movement away from God is therefore understood as a descent away from life (creation) toward death (chaos); and, conversely, movement toward God is expressed as an ascent from death to life.[31] Thanksgiving and lament psalms often conform to this pattern of describing an individual's deliverance through the archetypal geography of being rescued from the waters of Sheol and being brought to the heights of the divine Presence at the temple mount. Psalm 18 serves well as an example of this movement:[32]

[29] In the Hebrew Bible, Egypt often symbolizes Sheol. N. Wyatt (2001: 40) e.g. notes, 'Egypt serves as a symbolic location in many biblical passages, as a cipher for exile, a "land of the dead." Consequently, one always "goes down (*yārad*) to Egypt," as though entering the underworld. The supreme sacrifice, the burnt offering, or holocaust, is in Hebrew *'ōlâ*, "a going up".'

[30] For the relationship of this cosmology to modern scientific cosmology, with regard to the issue of the Bible's inerrancy, see chs. 6–7 of Beale 2008 (161–218).

[31] Similarly, Batto (1983: 33–34) writes, 'God's holy mountain, where his temple is located, is the center of the cosmos, or orderly creation. The farther away from the center of the cosmos one goes, the more one moves into the realm of chaos or non-creation. The spatial image is equally vertical and horizontal. Vertically, the heavens are the source of existence and creation; the underworld and the abyss are the place of death and nonexistence. Horizontally, the land around the mountain of one's god is known and understood and therefore thought of as most "created"; the sea which lay beyond the limits of the land was unsolid, non-formed – in other words, "uncreated."'

[32] The 'broad place' underscores the sense of safety, and particularly as a refuge from the waters should be understood as a high place. Note also the characteristic righteousness and blamelessness ('clean hands') of the one delivered, defined further as keeping the 'ways of YHWH'. See also Pss 30; 40; 71; 86; and Jon. 2. Cf. G. A. Anderson 1991: 25–32; Gunkel 1988: 199–221.

The sorrows of Sheol surrounded me;
    the snares of death confronted me.
In my distress I called upon YHWH,
    and cried out to my God;
He heard my voice from his temple,
    and my cry came before him, to his ears . . .
                              (Vv. 4–6)

He sent from above, he took me;
    he drew me out of many waters . . . (v. 16)
He also brought me out into a broad place;
    he delivered me because he delighted in me.
YHWH rewarded me according to my righteousness [*ṣidqî*];
   According to the cleanness of my hands
    he has recompensed me.
  For I have kept the ways of YHWH,
    and have not wickedly departed from my God.
                           (Vv. 19–21)

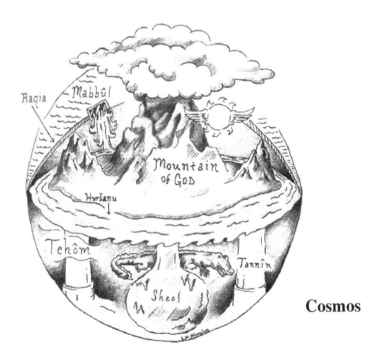

Cosmos

Similarly, the psalm in Jonah 2 states

> Out of the belly of Sheol I cried . . .
> for you cast me into the deep.
> (Vv. 2–3)

Though driven (*grš*) from God's sight, Jonah declared his confidence that he would yet 'look again to your holy temple' (v. 4). Grateful for the deliverance out of the overwhelming waters, the suppliant then ascends the mountain of God to fulfil his vow through a sacrificial offering at the temple (v. 9). Hence the movement from death to life, from exile to entry into God's Presence, involves a pattern of deliverance: through the waters to the mountain of God for worship (i.e. for life in the Presence of God). Noah and his household, as another example, will be delivered through the waters of the deluge to the Ararat mount whereupon he will offer sacrifices and receive divine blessing. Later, Israel will be delivered through the waters of the sea and brought to Sinai, entering into covenant with YHWH. The pattern of exile or expulsion entails the reverse movement: from the temple of God to the waters of destruction.

The pattern of exile from God's Presence is repeated within the internal structure of Genesis, as the primeval age in Genesis 2 – 11 moves from Eden's summit (temple/life) to the deluge waters (exile/death), and from Ararat's summit (temple/life) to the scattering from the tower of Babylon (exile/death), and then the patriarchal history in Genesis 12 – 50 moves from Canaan (temple/life) to Egypt (exile/death). The book of Exodus, as already noted, narrates the pattern of redemption as God's people are delivered through the waters of death and brought to Sinai,[33] upon whose summit the fiery glory of God descends.

The primeval age, from Eden to Babylonian exile: Genesis 2 – 11

Eden, mountain of God in the beginning

While Genesis 1 portrays creation as a tabernacle, Genesis 2 – 3 portrays the garden of Eden as something of an archetypal holy of holies – the place of most intimate communion and fellowship with YHWH God. The book of *Jubilees*, composed around 200 BC, offers

---

[33] See Batto 1983, who parallels the mythological language of the 'song of the sea' (Exod. 15:1–18) with that of Ps. 18 and Jon. 2, and translates *yam-sûp* as 'sea of end/extinction'.

a clear example of interpreting Eden in this way: 'And he [Noah] knew that Eden was the holy of holies and the dwelling of YHWH' (8:19). There are, moreover, various features of the Eden narrative itself that would lead us to the same understanding as well. Gordon J. Wenham noted many parallels between the garden and the later tabernacle (and temple) of Israel.[34] The description of YHWH's 'walking to and fro' (*hithallēk*) in Eden (Gen. 3:8), for example, is also used to describe the divine Presence in the later tent sanctuaries (Lev. 26:12; Deut. 23:15; 2 Sam. 7:6–7). Eden's eastward orientation corresponds to the eastward entrance of the tabernacle. The lushness of Eden as a well-watered garden filled with fruit-bearing trees, and especially with the tree of life in its midst, also finds correspondence with the fullness of life associated with the tabernacle, including the menorah as a stylized tree of life.[35] Many of the symbolic features of the tabernacle would become more pronounced in Solomon's temple, and probably conveyed to pilgrims that the Israelite sanctuary 'recreated or incorporated the garden of Eden, Yahweh's terrestrial residence'.[36] All of these parallels find their explanation within the temple ideology that was common throughout the ANE, whereby a temple was understood to be the architectural embodiment of the 'cosmic mountain';[37] for our purposes, the tabernacle represents the holy mountain of God. The garden of Eden, then, would have been understood as resting upon the summit of the mountain of God. The prophet Ezekiel (28:13–14) makes this precise connection:

> You were in Eden, the garden of God . . .
> You were on the holy mountain of God . . .

Furthermore, Genesis 2:6, 10–14 describes a spring-fed river that runs through the garden and then flows *down* from Eden, branching out into four riverheads to water the rest of the earth, suggesting a high locale that corresponds well with a mountain summit. The temple being an embodiment of this mountain of God, wherein the source of abundant waters is located, explains similar descriptions of a river flowing out of the temple's holy of holies (see Ezek. 47; cf. Ps. 46:5), the holy of holies corresponding to the mountain summit. In sum, then, 'Eden is thought to be a cosmic mountain upon which Adam

---

[34] Wenham 1986.
[35] Meyers 1976.
[36] Bloch-Smith 2002: 88.
[37] Lundquist 1983.

serves as priest.'[38] Or, to reverse the point, the later high priest of Israel serving in the tabernacle must be understood fundamentally as an Adam-figure serving on the (architectural) mountain of God.

While various other parallels between Eden and the tabernacle will be mentioned in relation to the expulsion, the sanctuary symbolism pervading the Eden narrative considered so far is already suggestive of Adam's priestly role within it. Here we note one more significant point, confirming such a view of the primal man: the verbs used to describe Adam's work in 2:15, translated most accurately as 'to worship and obey' (*lĕ'obdāh ûlĕšāmrāh*),[39] are used together elsewhere in the Pentateuch only to describe the duties of the Levites pertaining to the tabernacle (Num. 3:7–8; 8:26; 18:5–6). Adam is hereby depicted as the original high priest abiding in Eden, the original holy of holies. The association between Adam and priest is strengthened by the parallel of Adam's post-transgression vestments and the investiture of the Levitical priests, both needing their nakedness covered (Gen. 3:21; Exod. 20:26; 28:42) and the utilization of the same verb 'to clothe' (*lābaš* in hiphil) and the same noun for 'tunics' (*kuttōnet*):

Gen. 3:21: YHWH God made for Adam and for his wife tunics [*kotnôt*] of skins and clothed [*wayyalbišēm*] them.

Lev. 8:13: And Moses brought Aaron's sons and clothed [*wayyalbišēm*] them with tunics [*kuttŏnōt*].

There has been, in fact, a continuous tradition of interpretation with respect to Adam as priest and sacrificer, from the late post-exilic through the rabbinic periods, Adam sometimes portrayed specifically as primal high priest.[40] I would suggest, further, that the early chapters of Genesis were not composed merely to rehearse origins, but to inform the worship of ancient Israel, explaining the rituals of the tabernacle cultus. Genesis 1 – 3 conforms to the general priestly categories of sacred space (the cosmos as a tabernacle, Eden as the holy of holies), sacred time (the Sabbath) and sacred status (Adam's priestly role),[41] all of which will inform our understanding of the tabernacle cultus.

---

[38] G. A. Anderson 1989: 147.
[39] For the translation 'worship and obey', see Cassuto 1961: 122–123; Morales 2012b: 99–100.
[40] Marcus 2003: 374.
[41] Gorman 1990: 44–45.

Exiled from Eden

Within the garden YHWH had set both a tree of life and a tree of the knowledge of good and evil. Taken together, with their fruits procuring life and death respectively, the trees may be seen to function like the Torah, imploring Adam to choose life: 'Behold, today I have set before you life and good, and death and evil . . . life and death, blessing and cursing; therefore choose life, that both you and your seed may live' (Deut. 30:15, 19).[42] Resisting the second tree, the fruit of which offered wisdom independent of God, *was* Adam's wisdom, allowing him to perfect the fear of YHWH through the submission of his will.[43] The first point of note is simply the dichotomy itself, of life versus death, which is at the heart of the Pentateuch's cultic theology, expressed particularly in the book of Leviticus. Secondly, much like the role of heathen women in the tragic apostasy of Israel, as exemplified by Solomon (1 Kgs 11:4; cf. Exod. 34:14–16), so too for Adam the choice between the two trees becomes recast as the choice between YHWH God and the woman, with whom he is 'one flesh' – this, through the cunning orchestration of the serpent, is *the* test for Adam. Aware that Adam fell, a question imposes itself upon us: What alternative act might Adam have taken when faced with the woman's transgression? For now this question, like a seed, must lie buried and be given time to mature as this work progresses. (We will return to Genesis 2 – 3 and to this question in an excursus when we reflect on the Day of Atonement in chapter 5.)

Upon their transgression, Adam and his wife hid from the Presence (*pānîm*, 'face') of YHWH God (3:8), and then, after experiencing both God's judgment and grace, were driven out from his Presence in Eden: 'So he drove out Adam and he stationed [*wayyaškēn*] the cherubim at the east of the garden of Eden, and a flame of the swirling sword to guard the way [*derek*] to the tree of life' (Gen. 3:24). This primal exile is emphasized by the narrative in several ways. First, there is a repetition of YHWH's expulsion of Adam (vv. 23–24), along with an intensification of its description from 'sent out' to 'drove out'. Then, having driven him out, YHWH God bars Eden's entrance in a twofold manner, stationing the cherubim (fierce, quasi-divine guardians) and the flaming, whirling sword. Finally, the nature of the

---

[42] Emmrich 2001.

[43] The rich reception history of the sapiential theme in Gen. 3 is explored by Lanfer (2012), who unfortunately does not integrate enough the biblical opposition between YHWH's wisdom and the (false) wisdom of human autonomy at play in this narrative. Cf. Wenham 1987: 63.

exile as death is manifest by the divine purpose, narrated climactically with barred life (*haḥayyîm*) as the final word in the sentence: 'to guard the way to the tree of life'. The movement of the Eden narrative, from intimacy (Gen. 2) to alienation (Gen. 3), focuses upon humanity's displacement as a major motif.[44] Outside Eden, Adam is now an exile and a wanderer.[45] Having lost the Presence of God, humanity has also lost its purpose. The children of Adam now sojourn outside the door of God's dwelling, outside the light of his countenance. This expulsion from the divine Presence is *the* central tragic event that drives the history of redemption, determining and shaping the ensuing biblical narrative. Indeed, all of the drama of Scripture is found in relation to this singular point of focus: *YHWH's opening up the way for humanity to dwell in his Presence once more.*

Adam had been the righteous one able to ascend the mountain of YHWH, able to abide in the divine Presence. We have already noted the priestly portrayal of Adam. In a later reflex of this tradition (Ezek. 28:11–19) the expelled primal human is described in ways suggestive of 'an excommunicated priest'.[46] Having been expelled – caused to descend – by God himself, who now dares ascend? This fundamental question is, in fact, at the heart of the Israelite system of worship, the gate liturgy:

> YHWH, who may sojourn in your tabernacle?
> Who shall dwell on your holy mountain?
> > (Ps. 15:1)

> Who shall ascend the mountain of YHWH?
> Who shall stand in his holy place?
> > (Ps. 24:3)

The answer provided by Psalm 15, presumably recited by the priests guarding the temple precincts on Zion's mount, is (v. 2) whoever's walk is 'blameless' (*tāmîm*), whoever works 'righteousness' (*ṣedeq*), whoever speaks 'truth' (*'ĕmet*) in his heart, such a one may ascend the mount of YHWH's abode.[47] Already, then, we begin to see how intimately Israel's cultus is linked to the early accounts of Genesis – how

---

[44] Hauser 1982; Bartholomew 2007.
[45] Cf. Gros Louis 1974: 58.
[46] Callender 2000: 89. 'I cast you as a profane thing from the mountain of God . . . you profaned your sanctuaries' (Ezek. 28:16, 18).
[47] See Morales 2012b: 32–44; Keel 1997: 114, 126.

this Eden narrative may serve to explain the nature and drama of worship as approaching the house of YHWH upon the mountain of God. Adam's expulsion generates the gate liturgy.

Further east of Eden

Reading the narratives of Genesis 2 – 3 as pertaining merely to origins, unrelated to the rest of the biblical story, is a regrettably common approach. From the perspective of the Pentateuch's overall composition, however, the theological role and paradigmatic function of Eden is deeply significant.[48] As stated previously, the expulsion from Eden becomes the central tragic event propelling the entire drama of the Pentateuch (and of the rest of the Bible). Indeed, throughout the history narrated in Genesis, this dilemma is only intensified.

After Adam and Eve have been expelled from the garden of Eden, it appears they did not stray from the bounds of Eden itself – Eden being broader than the garden within it. Though the lines are subtle and sparse, a definite landscape surfaces through the sketch: no longer able to abide in the divine Presence within the garden (holy of holies), humanity now meets with God at the gate of Eden's garden, which has become the cultic site for sacrifice and worship.[49] We have already considered various features that mark out the garden as an archetypal holy of holies; perhaps the most obvious one, however, was not addressed – namely the cherubim posted at the eastward entrance. 'The cherubim reappear in only one other context in the entire Pentateuch, and that is in the Holy of Holies in the Sanctuary.'[50] Cherubim and other like creatures were the traditional guardians of sacred space in the ANE. The veil of the tabernacle's holy of holies was embroidered with cherubim (Exod. 26:1, 31), and cherubim were also fashioned upon the atonement lid of the ark (Exod. 25:18–22). Later, the inner sanctuary of Solomon's temple too would be guarded by large cherubim statues (1 Kgs 6:23–28). As explained in Leviticus, the tabernacle's eastward door served as *the* place where Israelites would come to present their offerings before the Presence of YHWH:

> 'Speak to the sons of Israel and say to them: "When *'ādām* [any man] brings near an offering to YHWH . . . he shall offer it at the door/entrance [*petaḥ*] of the tent of meeting that it may be accepted before YHWH."' (Lev. 1:3; cf. Exod. 40:29; Lev. 4:7)

[48] Bolger 1993.
[49] See Davidson 2000b: 112.
[50] Berman 1995: 21.

Conceivably, then, it was to the original sanctuary door, the gate of Eden guarded by cherubim, that Cain and Abel would have brought their offerings. Indeed, an alternative translation of Genesis 4:7, once common, makes this door the probable referent in YHWH's address to Cain, reading 'a sin offering lies at the door/entrance [*petaḥ*]' (rather than 'sin crouches at the door', as in the door of Cain's heart or tent).[51] In Hebrew both 'sin' and 'sin offering' are rendered by the same word (*ḥaṭṭā'ṭ*), the meaning of which must be determined by context, and the participle rendered 'crouching' or 'lurking' (*rōbēṣ*) by some translations is, in fact, more commonly used in the Hebrew Bible with reference to an animal lying down tranquilly. Psalm 23, for example, expresses the psalmist's reflection upon YHWH as shepherd with this same word: 'he makes me lie down [*rbṣ*] in green pastures'. It could be, then, that YHWH had revealed to Cain the means by which he might be restored to divine fellowship, precisely the same means he would later reveal to Israel through Moses in the book of Leviticus: a sin offering at the sanctuary doorway. While there is much to unfold within this narrative of Genesis 4, here we merely note its emphasis on worship and that, after the murder of Abel, the story resolves with Cain's deepened exile *in relation to the divine Presence within Eden*: 'Cain went out from the Presence of YHWH' to dwell 'east of Eden' (Gen. 4:16). This should certainly be considered a second expulsion, for, aside from various other parallels with Genesis 3, Cain is also 'driven out' (*gēraštā*), and plainly understands the departure from the countenance of God as certain death, contesting, 'I shall be hidden from your face . . . anyone who finds me will kill me' (Gen. 4:14).[52] While vouchsafed divine protection, Cain and his posterity have become wanderers further removed from the life of God that flows from life with God.

The waters of chaos

Humanity's alienation from God deepens further still when the sons of God take to themselves the daughters of men, bearing mighty heroes of 'name' (*'anšê haššēm*), and YHWH resolves to wipe out 'man' (*hā'ādām*) from the face of the 'ground' (*hā'ădāmâ*) (Gen. 6:1–7)

---

[51] Translated 'sin offering' by Adam Clarke (1762–1832), Adoniram Judson (1788–1850), Young's Literal Translation (1862), Jamieson, Fausset, and Brown (1877); Matthew Henry (1662–1714) recognized the validity of both translations. For a defence of this translation, along with a suggestion as to why it fell out of use although it makes better sense of the syntax and context, see Morales 2012a. Cf. also Azevedo 1999.

[52] On the parallels between the expulsion of Adam and Cain, see Westermann 1984: 285–286, 303; Hauser 1980; Edenburg 2011.

by a deluge of waters – a third divine expulsion. However one understands the phrase 'sons of God', whether as referring to the line of
Seth,[53] or, by the traditional interpretation, as indicating angelic
beings,[54] what is clear is that a boundary separating human from
divine was in some sense crossed, and this transgression is weighted
with colossal proportions as defining and ushering in 'the end'. To
the point, the result of this transgression was that knowledge of the
way of YHWH had been abandoned, almost utterly lost – 'all flesh
had corrupted [*nišḥātâ*] his [YHWH's] way upon the earth' (Gen.
6:12).[55] The only previous use of this word 'way' (*derek*) was when
YHWH had installed the cherubim and flaming sword to guard '*the
way* to the tree of life' (Gen. 3:24) – the way of YHWH is also
the way to YHWH. Later, God would know Abraham 'in order that
he may command his children and his household after him, that they
guard/keep the way of YHWH' (Gen. 18:19). Later still, Moses, interceding for Israel on the cloud-covered summit of Sinai, would plead
with God, 'Please now, if I have found grace in your eyes, please show
me your way that I may know you . . .' (Exod. 33:13).

Ararat, mountain of God at the new beginning
Now it is of particular interest to us that the one man whose household
is delivered from the waters of death happens to be described with
the very attributes that would qualify him to ascend into the Presence

[53] Gen. 5 had begun by recalling that Adam was created in the 'likeness of God',
God's firstborn human as it were, while Seth, we read, was born in Adam's likeness
and after his (Adam's) image. By contrast, having forfeited his right of the firstborn to
Abel (who was replaced by Seth), Cain's line begins with himself (Gen. 4:17–22), and
is marked separately from that of Seth, whose line 'began to call upon the name of
YHWH' (Gen. 4:26) and traced its origin to Adam as son of God. Thus we read in
Luke's genealogy of Christ, 'Enosh, the son of Seth, the son of Adam, the son of God'
(3:38). It is possible then that the 'sons of God' are to be defined as Seth's line and the
primary nature of their sin was that of intermarriage with the line of Cain – this aside
from the form of that transgression, be it by tyrannical kings, cult prostitution, etc.

[54] See VanGemeren 1981.

[55] Unfortunately, various English versions erroneously translate the masculine
singular pronominal suffix ('his way') as plural ('their way'), obscuring the theology.
Aside from the grammatical concerns, the parallel occasion in Exod. 32 bolsters the
correct translation as 'his way'. Upon the golden calf idolatry, YHWH declares to
Moses that Israel has acted 'corruptly' (*šiḥēt*), by turning aside quickly from 'the way
which I commanded them' (vv. 7–8). The parallels with the deluge continue in v. 10 as
YHWH says he will destroy the Israelites and begin anew with Moses as he once
destroyed humanity, beginning anew with Noah. See also, among many references to
the way of YHWH, Gen. 18:19; Judg. 2:22. For a parallel on intermarriage, see Judg.
3:5–6. In sum, 'God delivers those who "walk with" him and who do not "corrupt his
way"' (Sailhamer 1992: 124).

of YHWH. Noah, we are told, was a 'righteous' (*ṣaddîq*) man, 'blameless' (*tāmîm*) in his generations (Gen. 6:9). These qualifications become the answer to the gate liturgy question in Psalm 15:

> YHWH, who may abide in your tabernacle?
>   Who may dwell on your holy mountain?
> He who walks blamelessly [*tāmîm*],
>   and works righteousness [*ṣedeq*] . . .
>   (Vv. 1–2)

Relatedly, entrance into the ark is conditional, and the narrative is careful to describe Noah as one qualified to enter, YHWH himself underlining the point explicitly: 'Enter into the ark, you and all your household, *because* [*kî*] I have seen that you are righteous [*ṣaddîq*] before my face / in my Presence in this generation' (Gen. 7:1). It is also probably no coincidence that scholars have noted allusions to Israel's tabernacle in the description of the ark,[56] even suggesting that its dimensions correspond proportionately to that of Solomon's temple.[57] While popular depictions of the ark often portray it as a boat, this vessel, having no sails, rudder, and so on, was not a ship. Perhaps the oddest feature of the ark – and yet the central focus of the narrative – is the doorway (*petaḥ*) on its side. In the flood story recounted in the Gilgamesh epic, the floating vessel appears to be shaped in seven stages like a ziggurat, so that the biblical ark's resemblance to Israel's tabernacle is not so inconceivable.[58] Westermann notes the 'profound meaning' of the parallel between the ark and the tabernacle,[59] the only buildings described in the Pentateuch, each one the climactic point of history before and after the flood respectively. A further correspondence between the ark and the tabernacle is that the plans and measurements for each were revealed by God. The ark, moreover, is presented as a cosmos in miniature, to serve as a substitute refuge while the cosmos itself is being cleansed of its uncleanness. 'Lower, second and third decks you shall make,' YHWH commands, reflecting the three-decked world of ANE cosmography.[60] Even as the world was made (habitat) and then filled (inhabitants), so the three-storey

---

[56] See e.g. Fretheim 1996: 238; Blenkinsopp 1976: 283; Fletcher-Louis 2002: 41; Wenham 1987: 173.
[57] Holloway 1991.
[58] Ibid.
[59] Westermann 1984: 421.
[60] Morales 2012b: 151–154.

ark is made and then filled with living creatures – and Noah, a new Adam, abides with them in peace. The ark comes to 'rest' (*nûah*) on the highest Ararat mount – the same verb describing God's 'resting' Adam within the garden (2:15). As various commentators observe, Ararat is the region of the headwaters of the Tigris and Euphrates, the locale of Eden. 'Thus the ark,' Miller writes, 'representing the sanctuary and resting in the region of Eden, also represents Eden from which the human race goes forth to populate the earth, as the garden of Eden is itself a sanctuary.'[61] From various angles, then, the ark becomes a literary symbol, a reflection of the garden of Eden and a foreshadowing of the tabernacle.

Returning to the word 'rest' (*nûah*), this same root is at the heart of Lamech's hope as he names his son 'Noah' (5:28–29). Noah fulfils his name by offering up ascension offerings (*'ōlōt*) from the summit of the Ararat mount.[62] Only when YHWH smells the 'soothing' (*nûah*) aroma of atonement does his wrath relent, so that he covenants not to destroy the present cosmos by means of a deluge, although the problem of evil within the human heart remains (8:20–21). Thus at the foundation of the new world, at the very root of its history, one finds atonement – the means, that is, by which the world in spite of its rebellion is able to go on existing before a holy God.

This covenant, however, does not imply that life with God after the floodwaters would be the same as it was before humanity's fall into sin. Some scholars even interpret the rainbow as establishing something of a boundary line between heaven and earth, demarcating heaven as God's sphere and abode, and earth as the sphere and abode of humanity. In this light the demarcation of the bow itself – with God retiring, as it were, to the clouds – becomes part of the guarantee of his restrained wrath.[63] This is an interesting suggestion on two counts. First, before the deluge we read about some in Seth's line walking with God: Enoch 'walked with' God (Gen. 5:22); Noah 'walked with' God (Gen. 6:9). But after the deluge, we never read about this experience of God in Genesis – even to Abraham, the friend

[61] Miller 1996: 117.

[62] Built from the Hebrew verb for 'ascend' (*'ālâ*), 'ascension offering' is preferred over the translation 'burnt offering', and captures its theology well.

[63] Nihan 2007: 233; Zenger 1983; Janowski 2008. This theory may be combined plausibly with the suggestion that the rainbow symbolizes the reconstituted *rāqîa'*, 'firmament' (after it had allowed the waters of the heavenly ocean above to rejoin with the waters of the deep below for the deluge), divinely pledged and upheld as a barrier (L. A. Turner 1993). Ezekiel 1:22–23, as Turner points out, describes 'something like a *rāqîa'*/firmament', separating the creatures below from God's throne above.

of God, God says, 'Walk *before* me' (17:1). Thus while humanity is guaranteed existence, nevertheless the alienation from God remains. The second observation relates to the tower of Babylon narrative,[64] and will be addressed in the next section.

Ziggurat of Babylon, city of man as mountain of God

In the tower of Babylon episode, humanity, gathered to the east (*miqqedem*) – presumably east of the Ararat mount/ark – attempts to build a ziggurat 'whose summit is in the heavens' (11:4). Their building project appears to involve an attempted ascent into the sphere and abode of God, for, in Eliade's language, 'the man of traditional societies could only live in a space opening upward, where the break in plane was symbolically assured and hence communication with the *other world*, the transcendental world, was ritually possible'.[65] Given the previous suggestion that the bow may serve as something of a boundary marker,[66] such a breach into the heavens would have been especially defiant and in accord with previous divine–human barrier transgressions throughout the primeval age. In this regard Och is correct in noting a correspondence between the tower episode and the initial act of transgression in Eden, both acts 'guilty of over-stepping the limits of human creaturely existence', God's punishment in both cases serving to underline 'the basic teaching of the primeval period: man must learn his limits; the unbridled drive for power and security is ultimately counterproductive and results in death, destruction, and alienation'.[67] For their hybris, God scattered them across the face of the earth, dividing them by tongues into separate nations. The broad movement from Genesis 1 to 11, then, is a descent from the heights of the mountain of God down to the depths of exile, from Eden to Babylon. Similarly, the history of Israel will parallel that of the Gentiles, ending in exile – Israel being scattered away from the divine Presence. The tower of Babylon narrative also makes explicit what would probably already have been obvious to the

[64] This Hebrew term *bābel* is consistently translated 'Babylon' everywhere else (some 260 times) except here in Gen. 11:9 and 10:10.

[65] Eliade 1987: 43; emphasis original. To be sure, arguments against reading this narrative as a 'storming of heaven' are valid. Too often, however, such arguments unnecessarily dismiss all significance from the phrase 'whose top is in the heavens' (11:4).

[66] On this scenario the bow would function somewhat like the pillar and heap of stones in the covenant between Laban and Jacob, serving as a witness 'that I will not pass beyond this heap to you, and you will not pass beyond this heap and this pillar to me, for harm' (Gen. 31:52).

[67] Och 1995: 231–232; cf. Fishbane 1975: 12–13.

original audience: a 'city' is centred around a ziggurat, an architectural 'mountain of God'. It is no mystery then why, having been expelled further east of Eden (the mountain of God), Cain's first project was to build a city. Through culture and *technē* (craft), he had defiantly attempted to reclaim the benefits of God apart from God himself, naming the city after his son.[68] The innermost motivation for building a city, beyond the desire for preservation, is manifest through the speech of the tower builders (11:4): 'Come, let us build for ourselves [*lānû*] a city, and a tower whose top is in the heavens; let us make for ourselves [*lānû*] a name [*šēm*], lest we be scattered abroad over the face of the whole earth.' 'Let us build for ourselves' is paralleled by 'let us make for ourselves', bringing into focus that deepest impulse for constructing a city: a name. 'Name' (*šēm*) is *the* key word of this little story, not only resulting in YHWH's poetic judgment, whereby the city does receive a name, but also alluded to by frequent alliteration, such as the fivefold use of 'there' (*šām*), along with 'heavens' (*šāmayim*). As Fokkelman puts it, 'what they want to attain, *šēm* = make a name, they make conditional on the *šāmayim*, the abode of God'.[69] Who shall ascend the mountain of YHWH, or who shall stand in his holy place? Their answer to this question, if ever they paused to ask it at all, is: *We will!* Wenham aptly remarks that Isaiah seems to recall this Genesis story when he describes the king of Babylon in the following manner:[70]

> You said in your heart,
> I will ascend to heaven;
> above the stars of God
> I will sit on the mount of assembly in the far north
>   [i.e. the divine council]
> I will ascend above the heights of the clouds
> I will make myself like the Most High.
> But you are brought down to Sheol,
> to the depths of the pit.

(Isa. 14:13–15)

Thus the irony of the name 'Babylon' – for the Babylonians it meant the gate of heaven, literally 'the gate of god' (*bab-ili*), while for YHWH

---

[68] See Ellul's (1973) classic analysis of the city theme.

[69] Fokkelman 2004: 17. Burrows (1935: 52–53) notes a twofold purpose for the tower: to reach up to heaven (bond of heaven and earth) and to prevent being dispersed (bond of the land).

[70] Wenham 1987: 245.

and his people it is a pun on the word for 'confusion'. In retrospect one may affirm similar motivations for Cain's city as that of the ziggurat builders, who wanted (1) to make a 'name' for themselves (*immortality*), (2) to keep from being scattered (*permanence*) and (3) access to the divine through the gate of heaven (*power/control*). Cain, we recall, had built a city and called it after the name of his son (4:17),[71] and the city itself is presented as an endeavour to escape his lot as a fugitive and 'wanderer' (*nôd*) – ironically, he settles in the land of 'wandering' (*nôd*) (4:12, 16). If, moreover, one can take a cue from Babylon, then Cain's city centred upon a ziggurat as well – and 'city' may have been naturally understood as such by the original audience, which would also be in accord thematically with Cain's fear of being driven from God's face. The representation of humanity after the fashion of Cain sounds a troubling chord, and the consequent judgment on the nations serves to reassert Adam's expulsion in a deeper way: all humanity is in exile, wandering outside home – outside the house of God.

Before concluding this section on the primeval age, we should note that humanity's progressively deepened exile from God is expressed by a corresponding intensification in the human experience of sin and depravity. Von Rad captures the point well when he states that

> this story is characterized on the human side by an increase in sin to avalanche proportions. The sins of Adam and Eve, Cain, Lamech, the angel marriages, the Tower of Babel – these are stages along that way which has separated man farther and farther from God. This succession of narratives, therefore, points out a continually widening chasm between man and God. But God reacts to these outbreaks of human sin with severe judgments. The punishment of Adam and Eve was severe; severer still was Cain's. Then followed the Flood, and the final judgment was the Dispersion, the dissolution of mankind's unity. Thus at the end of the primeval history a difficult question is raised: God's future relationship to his rebellious humanity, which is now scattered in fragments.[72]

---

[71] There may be a double emphasis on Cain's desire for immortality inasmuch as children and building projects may be considered ways to leave one's name (see the Epic of Gilgamesh for the latter) – both converging upon Cain's naming the city after his son. We are probably meant to see something of this motivation as well in the sons of God episode of Gen. 6, with v. 4 noting the 'men of renown', literally 'men of name' (*šēm*).

[72] Von Rad 1972: 152.

Especially in the light of ANE parallels where, for example, the deluge was due to the capriciousness of the gods (with minimal human culpability), the biblical account of the primeval age develops a solid theology of sin, assessing human nature with a devastating pessimism.[73] That 'way which has separated man farther and farther from God' must, therefore, be countered by a new way that leads back to God, a way that overcomes sin and enables humanity to draw near to him. The theology of sin thus becomes a backdrop for a theology of sacrifice, as the consuming flames of the altar shine into the all-engulfing darkness of human depravity. Finding fuller expression in the book of Leviticus, the way of YHWH already begins to open as Noah's altar accomplishes what the deluge of waters could not, quelling the wrath of God. Although the root of humanity's heart remains evil, the soothing aroma of the ascent offerings pacifies YHWH's own heart, abating his curse and releasing his blessing (Gen. 8:20 – 9:1; 6:5).

Excursus: cultic theology in the primeval history

Before moving on to the patriarchal history, it is worth reflecting on the threefold descent from God's Presence that ends in the abyss of the deluge, where the earth has become 'uncreated', as it were, covered by the primordial waters once more (Gen. 7:24; cf. 1:2).[74] All three transgressions, of Adam, Cain and the sons of God, not only involve the crossing of forbidden boundaries,[75] but also *result* in the crossing of boundaries, a progressive displacement from God's Presence *of life*: from within the garden of Eden to outside the garden of Eden (eastward), from within Eden to outside Eden (further eastward), and from the land of Nod (east of Eden) to the waters of chaos and destruction – a threefold expulsion from life to death. Now given that the garden of Eden is widely understood as an archetypal holy

---

[73] Wenham 1990.

[74] See Morales 2012b: 130–136 for a detailed analysis of how the deluge narrative is recounted as a reversal of the original acts of creation (e.g. while the separation between the waters is perhaps the fundamental act of creation, their reunification becomes the primary means of the earth's destruction).

[75] Blenkinsopp (1992: 74) e.g. notes that the sons of God and daughters of men episode 'relates a further attempt to break through the barrier separating the divine and human spheres, following the frustrated attempt of the man and woman in Eden to achieve divine status'. See also Hendel 1992: 177; Clark 1971; Oden 1981; Fishbane 1975: 11. Di Vito's (1992) attempt to exclude completely the significance of a distinction and separation between the divine and human realms from the primary history is unconvincing.

of holies upon the summit of the mountain of God, and given that the narrative of the 'world that was' ends in the abyss of waters, it is tempting here to speculate that the narratives between these two poles have also been consciously composed with cultic cosmology in mind:

Tabernacle	≈	Mountain of God	≈	Genesis 2 – 7	
Holy of holies		Summit		Garden (Adam/Eve)	↘
Holy place		Midsection		Eden (Cain/Abel)	↘
Outer court		Base		Nod (sons of God/daughters of men)	↘
Wilderness		Chaos waters		Deluge	

To be sure, the structure of the Sinai narrative (Exod. 19 – 24) stresses the holiness of YHWH precisely by emphasizing the need to set and guard boundaries about Mount Sinai,[76] the mount's threefold division later paralleled by the tabernacle's.[77] It would not be so unusual, then, for the primeval narratives to emphasize the same threefold boundaries in relation to Eden's mount.

More unreservedly, we may affirm that the history of the first cosmos, beginning with the garden of Eden and ending with the waters of destruction, narrates the gradual (and geographical) displacement from the face of God (located in the archetypal holy of holies); and that this ever-eastward estrangement is effected by YHWH himself (in response to human transgression), driving Adam out of the garden, driving Cain east of Eden, blotting out (*'emḥeh*; 6:7; 7:23) humanity from the face of the earth.[78] This movement away from God, once more, is a steady movement from abundant life to death.[79] That movement is significant inasmuch as life and death,

---

[76] Chirichigno 1987.

[77] Rodriguez 1986.

[78] One may also note as widely received regarding Gen. 1 – 7: (1) that the primeval narratives are fundamentally about boundary crossing (probably, human–divine breaches), (2) boundary maintenance along grades of holiness is key to priestly theology and (3) the tabernacle was modelled after the cosmos, specifically as an architectural mountain of God. Other points may be adduced which I hope to bring forward in another work.

[79] The movement from life toward death is none other than from holiness toward an unclean state – holiness and life are one. Cf. the chart in Wenham 1979: 177, n. 34. His extra categories of 'camp' and 'outside camp' are necessitated *after* the deluge and may be explained with reference to the Noahic covenant. God has promised not to destroy the earth again by floodwaters. Because earth-space is unclean, however, tabernacle-space must be created, presenting the ideal: a congregation able to access the outer court (inclusive of the converted Gentiles); the unclean 'outside the camp' category exists contrary to the ideal because of God's promise not to destroy the earth with floodwaters/Sheol when it becomes unclean.

along with the need to separate them ritually, comprises the fundamental distinction at the heart of priestly theology and cultic law.[80] Upon humanity's first transgression, the world outside Eden's gates steadily became the realm of death – any human breach into the divine sphere would therefore involve the (ritually dangerous) mixture of death and life.[81] The Israelite priests' highest duty and danger, therefore, was the maintenance of this primary boundary.

Given the cosmos/tabernacle homology, the theology of Genesis 1 – 7, particularly regarding the divine Presence in the cosmos, will be seen to inform the theology of Leviticus, regarding the divine Presence within the tabernacle. In relation to the cultus, for example, one finds that sin increasingly pollutes the sanctuary so that, eventually, if the sanctuary is not purified by a purification offering (*ḥaṭṭā't*), and ultimately through the annual Day of Atonement, it will be abandoned by God and be destroyed, along with the sinners.[82] This pattern is precisely what we have encountered in relation to the cosmos: while the deluge constituted a resubmerging of the earth in the chaos waters, yet from the perspective of the renewed earth the waters were rather waters of purification. As Benno Jacob discerned rightly, the deluge was only judgment for the living creatures, but for the earth it was 'a bath of purification which washes away its pollution and restores its purity (Num. 35:33ff)'.[83] Along the same lines, Frymer-Kensky writes, 'The idea of pollution was such an important part of Israel's worldview that its Primeval History, its story of origins, was also seen as a story of cosmic pollution and purgation.'[84] This idea, in accord with the narrative's use of the word *māḥâ*, 'to blot/wipe out by washing' (Gen. 6:7; 7:4; 7:23 [twice]), and which is used also for the 'washing away of sins' (cf. Ps. 51:2, 9; Prov. 6:33; Isa. 43:25; Jer. 18:23; 44:22), is significant in the light of the cosmos/tabernacle homology. Indeed, one scholar has even made the suggestive observation that, as on the Day of Atonement, all living things emerge from the ark/tabernacle reconciled with God (8:21 – 9:19).[85] The general

[80] Wenham 2003: 93; Carmichael 1976.

[81] In the cultic sphere the holy (= life) and the unclean (= death) cannot mix. See Jenson 1992: 48–52.

[82] Milgrom 1976a. This theology may serve to understand *ḥaṭṭā't* in Gen. 4:7 as 'purification offering'.

[83] Jacob 2007: 60; cf. McCarthy 1984: 76–77.

[84] Frymer-Kensky 1983: 399.

[85] Harper 2011: 56. Harper (55) also argues that *kpr* (cover/pitch) in the ark narrative (Gen. 6:14–16) may have evoked the rich cultic overtones of atonement, especially as the ark 'becomes the place of mercy and ransom when the waters cover over and atone for the violence of the world'. This remark is strengthened by the liturgical calendar

picture that emerges through the primeval history, therefore, is that of a cosmos constructed as a tabernacle, with a defiled (priestly) humanity driven ever eastward as punishment for sin. Moreover, because humanity's sin had also defiled the tabernacle itself (i.e. the cosmos), the earth needed to be purified.[86]

In the next section we will find that the longing for Eden continues to play a major thematic role in the Pentateuch's narrative, defining the hope of the patriarchs and elucidating the meaning of the tabernacle cultus.

Universal History

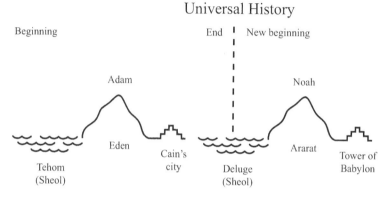

The patriarchal history, from Canaan to Egyptian exile: Genesis 12 – 50

It is within the movement of Genesis 1 – 11 broadly that we must come to understand the call of Abram in Genesis 12:1–3, with the fivefold promise of 'blessing' (*brk*) he receives serving in a manner to overcome the five 'curses' (*'rr*) distributed throughout Genesis 3:1 – 11:26.[87] More narrowly, it is within the immediate context of the tower of Babylon story, with the motives of permanence, divine access and name, that

employed for the narrative inasmuch as the ark rested upon the Ararat mountain in the most sacred cultic month of Tishri, within which the Day of Atonement would be observed – and specifically on the same day on which the tabernacle was set up and dedicated in the wilderness (Gen. 8:13; Exod. 40:2) (Blenkinsopp 1976: 283–284; McEvenue 1971: 59; Mathews 1996: 385). From a cultic perspective, the deluge might be categorized as a ritual of restoration, a return to the founded order of creation – precisely the essence of the Day of Atonement ritual (Gorman 1990: 61; 1993: 48–50; Nelson 1993: 55–59).

[86] Like the cosmos, Israel's tabernacle would also be defiled by sin and need to be cleansed so that, as with the deluge, the Day of Atonement would be known as the day of judgment, the comprehensive purification that ushered in a new year.

[87] See Leder 2010: 82–83.

one can perceive the grandeur of the divine promise to plant Abram's people in the land where they might dwell securely in the divine Presence once more, along with the promise to make his name great. Indeed, the verse directly following the tower story (Gen. 11:10) begins with the genealogy of Shem, the son of Noah whose name means 'name', and whose lineage leads to Abram, to whom YHWH promises, 'I will bless you and make your name [*šēm*] great' (12:2). The antipode to the tower of Babylon will be revealed to Shem's descendants: the tabernacle, God's ordained means of being approached.[88] Humanity's rebellious 'let us make for ourselves a name' by ascending into God's abode (Gen. 11:4) will give way to God's 'let them make for me a sanctuary' (Exod. 25:8) as he descends to make his dwelling among Israel. Once in the land of promise, the tabernacle would eventually yield to the temple, the place in which God would cause his 'name' to dwell, magnifying his glorious renown among the nations – this, the fuller counterpart to Babylon's ziggurat.[89] This antithesis is already represented by Abraham, for at Babylon the builders promoted their own name, while Abraham built altars and proclaimed the name of God.[90] Here it is worth underscoring that Abram was called out of Ur *for the sake of the nations* who had been scattered from the Presence of God. It is the return from *this* exile, itself a reflex of humanity's expulsion from Eden, for which God covenants with Abram. Shem's genealogy and the use of the keyword 'name' bind Abram's call to the tower of Babylon episode. Abram himself was called out of exile in Ur as part of God's plan to reverse the exile of the nations. As already intimated, the theology regarding the temple will emphasize Mount Zion as the goal of the nations' pilgrimage, an emphasis linked deeply with Abraham (Gen. 12:3; 22:18).

Turning now to an overview of the patriarchal history (Gen. 12 – 50), we notice that the movement of gradual alienation continues, God's dealings with his people characterized as 'from afar'. Correlated to this growing distance, the role of Eden within the narrative – the *longing* for Eden – is not diminished along the way. Rather, the

---

[88] Interestingly, Gen. 9:27b of Noah's blessing ('may he dwell in the tents of Shem'), where 'he' may possibly refer to Japheth, is paraphrased in *Jubilees* (*c.*200 BC) as 'may the LORD dwell in the dwelling place of Shem' (Charlesworth 1985: 69). *Targum Neofiti* also understands the passage this way, reading, 'may the Glory of His *Shekinah* dwell in the midst of the tents of Shem' (McNamara 1992: 80–81). This idea corresponds well with the midrashic insight that links the temple's being built in Shem's territory with his being a high priest (Zlotowitz 1977: 179).

[89] Berman 1995: 57–81; Deut. 12:5, 11; 14:23.

[90] Ibid. 63; cf. Gen. 12:8.

progress toward inheriting Canaan is nothing less than a groping toward the Edenic Presence of God. While the chronological movement from Abraham to the sons of Jacob will be characterized by a gradual distancing from the experience of God's Presence, yet Abram's initial movement toward the Promised Land – *westward* from Ur – is characterized as an incipient return to Eden. Indeed, the 'road from Haran to the land of Canaan symbolizes the return of humanity to Eden and to God. Abraham and the promised land provide the counterpoint and answer to Adam and the Garden of Eden.'[91] This idea finds expression in a key moment, when the land is pledged to Abram by YHWH in Genesis 13. The account begins with Abram's going up out of Egypt, one of several foretastes in his life of Israel's later experience. The drama intensifies, however, as strife develops between his and Lot's herdsmen, for their possessions, flocks and herds had accumulated to such an extent they could not dwell together any longer. Here, in a gesture akin to his offering up of Isaac, Abram offers up the land by giving Lot first choice of pasturage, agreeing to part ways in the opposite direction.[92] This peace-making deference that risked losing his claim to a portion of the land of inheritance was also an act of loyal faith in YHWH's provision. As for Lot's choice, we read:

> Lot lifted his eyes and saw the whole valley of the Jordan, that it was well watered – before YHWH destroyed Sodom and Gomorrah – just like the garden of YHWH, as the land of Egypt when you approach Zoar. (Gen. 13:10)

A parallelism in Isaiah makes the connection between the garden of YHWH and Eden obvious:

> > He [YHWH] will make her wilderness like Eden,
> >   her desert like the garden of YHWH.
> > > > (Isa. 51:3)

Serving the apparent interests of his own flocks and herds, Lot chose the well-watered valley that happened to be *outside Canaan*,

---

[91] Och 1995: 233.

[92] See also Vogels 1975. Helyer's (1983) analysis, emphasizing the theme of Abram's heir over that of land, does not diminish the relevance or prominence of the land (but rather complements it). YHWH's response to Abram links both together (Gen. 13:14–17). See Rickett's (2011) discussion on the land theme in ch. 13 as linked to Abram's call in ch. 12.

outside the promises of God – the land of preservation over the land of promise. Aside from the double reference to Sodom's exceeding sinfulness and consequent destruction, the narrative unveils Lot's failure by another telling phrase (13:11): 'Then Lot chose for himself all the valley of Jordan, and Lot journeyed east.' The immediate result of his choice – indeed, the essence of the choice itself – was further displacement to the east, away from God's Presence. The next verse marks the contrast clearly:[93] 'Abram dwelt in the land of Canaan, but Lot dwelt in the cities of the valley and pitched his tent as far as Sodom.' Given the echoes here of Cain who, driven east of Eden, founded a city, we are probably to see Lot's eastward journey and dwelling in the cities of the valley as an (albeit unwitting) association with the line of Cain. Chapters 18 and 19 of Genesis, wherein the same messengers announce the birth of the promised son for Abram's wife, Sarah, and the destruction of Sodom epitomized by Lot's wife, present a reversal of Genesis 13: Sarah's aged, withered womb becomes fertile even as the once well-watered Sodom is turned into an ash heap, Lot's wife into a pillar of salt.[94] Contrary to appearances, perhaps, the good life was to be found in Canaan because that was where God's Presence – the source of life – would be found.[95] This idea is already latent at the opening of the narrative in Genesis 13, as Abram had returned from Egypt specifically 'to the place of the altar which he had made there at the beginning' (v. 4). This second altar, located between Bethel and Ai, had been built by Abram to 'call upon the name of YHWH' and thus to renew the divine engagement that had yielded the first altar – narrated in the previous verse (v. 7) – which he had built to commemorate YHWH's first appearance within the Promised Land, an appearance defined by YHWH's declaration 'To your descendants I will give this land' (Gen. 12:7–8).[96] Throughout the patriarchal age, altars were built only within the bounds of the Promised Land and may have symbolized miniature versions of the 'mountain of God'.[97] Typically marking a theophany encounter,

[93] The x-qatal construction of the Hebrew stresses the contrast ('And it was Abram who dwelt in Canaan').

[94] N. Levine 2006.

[95] That this promise is uppermost in Abram's thinking is evident in the intervening chapter where, doubtful of a son being born to aged Sarah, he cries out to God, 'Oh, that Ishmael might live in your Presence [lepāneykā; 'before your face']!' (Gen. 17:18).

[96] There is a good case that YHWH appeared *only* within the Promised Land, as Gen. 12 does not use the term *r'h* until Abram arrives in Canaan. See Adams 1996: 61–63.

[97] Perhaps the clearest parallel between the altar and the mountain of God is found in Exod. 24:4, where Moses builds an altar at the foot of the mountain and twelve

altars established a primitive sanctuary site, and became tokens of the Presence of God,[98] as well as foretastes of God's dwelling in the Jerusalem temple – for 'the altar is a shrine or house of God'.[99] Abram's return in Genesis 13, then, is not merely to the land, but to the source and heart of the promise of land – to YHWH himself. Lot's choice, accordingly, took him outside the bounds not merely of the Promised Land but of the promised Presence of God. More particularly, Abram's altar and tent are located on a mountain, with Bethel (house of God) on the west and the city of Ai (ruin, heap of rubble) on the east (Gen. 12:8). These untypically precise details are not gratuitous, but serve rather to continue the east–west motif, and the cultic theology of the divine Presence. Eastward of God's sanctuary stands the city of man in ruins. Similarly, the eastward cities of Lot's choice, Sodom and Gomorrah, will end in ruins. Miller notes the parallel relationship of three paired stories in the first half of Genesis: Cain builds a city east of Eden; the tower builders build a city east of Noah's ark; Lot chooses the cites east of Abram's altar.[100] 'In all three of these pairs, Eden – Cain, Noah's ark – Babel, and Abram's altar – Lot, the common structuring parallel includes the sanctuary image and the eastward departure toward a false garden which is a city bound for destruction.'[101] These stories, then, are of a piece with the archetypal pattern of cultic cosmology discussed earlier in this chapter, and which reflects the broad movement of the book of Genesis.

---

pillars according to the twelve tribes of Israel. The twelve pillars surrounding the altar represent the twelve tribes surrounding Mount Sinai, and the consuming fire and smoke on the altar would parallel the description of God's Presence atop Sinai (v. 17). Also, Ezekiel's description of the altar (43:15) includes the phrase *har'ēl*, which, especially given the structural shape itself, is probably to be understood as 'mountain of God' (Albright 1920; Levenson 1994: 92–93). This altar is referred to as a tower in the Talmud (*Sukkah* 49a) and likened to the stairway of Jacob in a midrash (*Gen. R.* 68.16 to Gen. 28:12). As a 'mountain of God', the altar would essentially signify the Presence of God, along with the means of approaching his Presence. See also Kristensen 1968: 106–107; Albright 1953: 147–150; Levenson 1994: 90–99; Morales 2012b: 232–243.

[98] Haran 1985: 16–17. The so-called law of the altar in Exod. 20:22–26 probably serves as an adequate depiction of worship practice in the patriarchal age.

[99] Vos 1975: 69. G. K. Beale (2004: 102) similarly states that 'patriarchal shrines both recalled the original temple in Eden and anticipated the tabernacle and temple'. See also Fishbane 1975: 14.

[100] Miller 1996: 117–118. He notes (117) e.g. that both the tower of Babylon and the Abram–Lot stories use the same verb pair: YHWH 'descends' (*yrd*) to 'see' (*r'h*) before he leaves Babylon and Sodom in ruins.

[101] Ibid. 118.

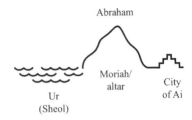

The ruins found east of the sanctuary become a theological *topos* for the gesture away from the divine Presence (cosmos, centre or life) toward chaos and death symbolized by the ruins. Also highly significant, though not emphasized by Miller, is the locale of these stories along the map of redemptive history: Eden–Cain's city at the primordial beginning of the world; Noah's ark–Babylon at the beginning of the new world after the deluge; Abram's altar–Sodom at the beginnings of Israel after the scattering of the nations.[102] The alternative between God's house and the city of man, I suggest, is eschatological – rooted in the beginning of time (*Urzeit*), it foreshadows the end (*Endzeit*), summarizing two alternative paths: life versus death, cosmos versus chaos, entrance into God's Presence versus exile away from God's Presence. These things in mind, the Abraham cycle ends with a significant remark as it tells of Abraham's last act before his death and burial:[103] 'Abraham gave all that was his to Isaac. But to the sons of the concubines that belonged to Abraham, Abraham gave gifts and while he was still living he sent them away from Isaac his son – eastward, to the land of the east' (Gen. 25:5–6).

Having considered one portion at length, I will summarize merely the broad movement of the rest of the patriarchal history here, in relation to the divine Presence. Abraham, we find, experienced infrequent visitations from God, and Jacob even fewer.[104] One such

---

[102] Och's (1995: 233) comments here are apropos: 'God's call to Abraham is formulated in words and arts reminiscent of the original cosmic creation. In both instances, creation entails an initial state of chaos out of which the created object emerges through acts of separation and differentiation. With Abraham, the original chaos is now applied to human existence, as Abraham is commanded to separate himself from all the ties and bonds which connect him to the chaotic confusion of human life after Babel.' Given these parallels, Eliade's (1987: 28, 30, 173) thesis that altar building is tantamount to founding a world is suggestive, the altar being an *imago mundi*.

[103] Securing the covenant promises to his seed through Isaac alone as the child of promise (see Rom. 9:7–8), Abraham sends away his children 'according to the flesh' to the land of the east. When *the* promised Child is born, however, they will return from the east to share in his blessings (cf. Matt. 2:1).

[104] Vos (1975: 69) notes e.g. that in 'the life of Isaac the theophanies all but disappear'.

encounter, however, is most noteworthy. In Genesis 28 Jacob encounters God through a dream and is given a vision of a stairway whose 'summit reached to the heavens' (v. 12). Even as the name so coveted by the tower builders was denied them and freely given to Shem's line, so now the essence of the building project, access to the abode of God through 'the gate of heaven', is vouchsafed as well. Upon waking, Jacob acknowledges that 'YHWH is in this place' and the city is named 'house of God' (bêt-'ēl). 'And he feared, saying, "What a fearful place is this! This is nothing less than the house of God, this is the gate of heaven!"' (Gen. 28:17).

The stairway beheld by Jacob, then, may be understood as the inner reality of the whole sacrificial cultus, which it foreshadows. Rabbi Bar Kappara's comments on this passage in *Genesis Rabbah* 68.12 display a similar interpretation:

> *And behold a ladder* symbolizes the stairway; *set up on the earth* – the altar, as it says, *An altar of earth thou shalt make unto Me* (Exod. 20:21); *and the top of it reached to heaven* – sacrifices, the odour of which ascended to heaven; *and behold the angels of God* – the High Priests; *ascending and descending on it* – ascending and descending the stairway. *And behold, the Lord stood beside him* (28:13) – *I saw the Lord standing beside the altar* (Amos 9:1).[105]

Another interpretation of Genesis 28:12, also found in *Genesis Rabbah* 68.12, has the ladder representing Sinai, with the angels alluding to Moses and Aaron,[106] a justified link inasmuch as the tabernacle cultus itself represents the mountain of God architecturally, continuing the Sinai experience for Israel. This encounter at Mount Bethel also brings to the fore the prominence of mountains in general throughout the patriarchal history,[107] not the least of which is Mount Moriah, upon which the culmination of the Abraham cycle takes place.[108] The binding of Isaac on Mount Moriah in Genesis 22 contains cultic terminology clustered together elsewhere only for the ordination of the Levitical priests (Lev. 8 – 9) and for the Day of Atonement (Lev. 16), and probably served to prefigure the entire cultic economy – even as the foundation story for the Jerusalem temple.[109] Also highly

---

[105] *Midrash Rabbah: Genesis* 1939, 2: 625.
[106] See Heijne 2010: 313, n. 794.
[107] Cf. Beale 2004: 100–102.
[108] See e.g. the analyses of Bergen 1990; Doukhan 1993; Fokkelman 1989.
[109] Walters 1987; cf. 2 Chr. 3:1.

significant, YHWH had called upon Abraham to offer up Isaac specifically as an ascension offering (*'ōlâ*), the same as that offered up by Noah at the foundation of the newly cleansed world. We will return to Genesis 22 when we consider Mount Zion in chapter 7.

Moving forward, by the time we come to the twelve sons of Jacob, the experience of God appears to be through 'parabolic' dreams and providence alone.[110] Indeed, the chronological movement from Abraham down to Jacob's sons is mirrored by the geographic movement from Canaan down to a grave in Egypt, the last verse of the book reading as follows:

> Joseph died . . .
>   and they embalmed him,
>   and he was placed in a coffin
>   in Egypt.
>   (Gen. 50:26)

From a variety of angles, then – from Eden to the waters of the deluge (chs. 1–7); from Eden to Babylonian exile (1–11); from Eden to the grave of Egypt (1–50) – the trajectory of the book of Genesis is from fullness of life to death, and that in relation to alienation from the Presence of God. The book of Exodus, as we will consider in the next chapter, narrates how Israel is reborn out of this grave and ushered into the divine Presence, reversing the movement of Genesis.

---

[110] These dreams, in other words, are not comparable to Jacob's, through which he had encountered and communicated with God.

Chapter Three

Returning to Eden: Exodus, the narrative context of Leviticus

As the fiery glory of YHWH fills the tabernacle at the end of the book of Exodus, the drama of redemptive history thus far comes to a culminating pinnacle. There is even a sense where one could read Genesis 1 to Exodus 40 as a complete narrative, a story about being expelled from God's Presence in Eden, then, finally, being brought back into that Presence *through the tabernacle cultus* – a story about Paradise lost and regained. Fittingly, the tabernacle and its furnishings are pervaded by Edenic imagery. The tabernacle narrative crowning Exodus 40, then, not only forms a bookend with the creation account(s) of Genesis 1 – 3, both pertaining to life in the Presence of God, but, further still, the tabernacle cultus is presented as a mediated resolution to the crisis introduced in Genesis 3 with humanity's expulsion from Eden.

That culmination in mind, the broad movement of the book may be grasped through two wordplays. First, the lives of God's people will be transformed from slavery to worship, both words utilizing the same Hebrew verb *'ābad*, which may be translated judiciously in both cases as 'serve'. This transformation of *'ābad* may also reflect a reversal of its former change from Adam's worship (*'ābad*) in the garden of Eden (Gen. 2:15) to his toiling (*'ābad*) outside it (Gen. 3:23). On this reading, Israel as a new humanity is being restored to the primary purpose of being made according to the image and likeness of God. The second wordplay in Exodus is related to the first: the service of the sons of Israel will be transferred from building cities of storage (*miškān*) to building the tabernacle (*miškān*), the house of God.[1] Here there is some irony inasmuch as the king of Egypt's title Pharaoh means literally 'The Great House'. At issue then is whom Israel will serve, and the nature of

[1] Leder 1999: 21.

that service.[2] Will it be slavery to Pharaoh in the house of bondage (Exod. 20:2) or the worship of YHWH in the house of God? This forking path is fundamental to the narrative plot and theology we traced in Genesis: Does Israel long to dwell with God in his house or would God's people rather continue building the city of man? Set against waiting for a mediated return to Eden through the tabernacle cultus stand Cain's city and the Babylonian tower imaged in the building of Egypt's empire. Through the vacillating eyes of Lot – the cities of the plain, or Abram's altar – we perceive the drama of Exodus most deeply.

Structurally, Exodus may be outlined broadly as two halves dealing with the exodus out of Egypt (1 – 15) and the Sinai covenant (16 – 40), with Moses' song of the sea (15:1–21) serving as the fulcrum between the two. Thematically, the two halves are related to the knowledge of YHWH and the Presence of YHWH, respectively. Divine revelation and divine Presence are coordinated concepts,[3] the steady estrangement from God developed in Genesis having led also – necessarily – to humanity's darkened understanding of God, that is, to a profound ignorance of God. This twofold problem will be remedied for Israel in reversed order: a knowledge of YHWH will be gained as he reveals himself through the exodus deliverance (Exod. 1 – 15); then, Israel will be brought into his tabernacling Presence through the Sinai covenant (Exod. 16 – 40).

Alternatively, we may posit a threefold division as follows, corresponding to the threefold cosmogonic pattern: (1) through the waters (2) to the mountain (3) for life in God's Presence:

Part 1	Exodus out of Egypt (1:1 – 15:21)	*through the waters*	15 chapters
Part 2	Sinai covenant (15:22 – 24:18)	*to the mountain*	10 chapters
Part 3	Tabernacle (25 – 40)	*for life in God's house*	15 chapters

The major headings of this chapter will follow the threefold outline above as we probe how the book of Exodus develops the theme of Israel's being brought into God's Presence as a new humanity, along with how that theme itself drives the plot onward into Leviticus. As we will see, the movement out of Egypt and into God's Presence at Sinai is not merely geographical, but profoundly spiritual – Israel must be transformed, set apart, through the exodus.

---

[2] See also Leder 2010: 95; Och 1995: 235–236.
[3] For a development of this theme in the New Testament, see Macaskill 2013.

Redeemed through the waters: Exod. 1:1 – 15:21

While the book of Exodus opens initially with God's people enjoying his primordial blessing, being fruitful and multiplying and filling the land (1:7; cf. Gen. 1:28), the scene quickly changes as a new Pharaoh arises who did not know Joseph. He sets taskmasters over the sons of Israel to afflict them with harsh burdens, forcing them to build cities of storage (1:11). With a recall of the conflict prophesied in Genesis 3:15, he also attempts to destroy their sons.[4] Israel's bondage thus becomes the context for the exodus. Of prime significance here is what this divinely orchestrated providence is meant to convey about the nature of re-entering God's Presence. Israel's groaning under bondage and Pharaoh's ever-hardening heart combine for a highly particular theological drama: humanity must be redeemed from bondage – from death itself – before it can be brought into life with God. This theology would be rehearsed daily through the tabernacle (and later temple) cult inasmuch as any approach to the divine Presence demanded the shedding of blood.

Redemption and the knowledge of YHWH

As already noted, Israel's departure from Egypt and journey to Sinai were not merely a journey across geography: the exodus was a revolution. Exiled from God's Presence in Eden and suffering his absence through history, humanity had lost grossly the knowledge of God. Consequently, the major theme of the first half of Exodus is not liberation, but rather the knowledge of YHWH.[5] The revelation of YHWH pulsates at the core of Moses' encounter at the burning bush (Exod. 3:13–15; 6:2–3), and Pharaoh's arrogant question sets up the knowledge of YHWH as the context for the drama: 'And Pharaoh said, "Who is YHWH, that I should obey his voice to release Israel? I do not know YHWH, nor will I release Israel"' (Exod. 5:2; cf. 1:8).

Israel's deliverance thus becomes subordinate to the knowledge of YHWH in the sense that YHWH will deliver the Israelites only in such a way as to reveal himself, his glory. By demonstrating his control of nature (e.g. through hail, flies, boils, darkness, etc.), YHWH also manifested his supremacy over the gods of Egypt.[6] The deliverance would lead to a knowledge of him, not only amidst Israel but among

---

[4] That the pharaoh would have had a serpent on his headdress strengthens the allusion to Gen. 3:15.

[5] Eslinger 1991; 1996; cf. Zimmerli 1982.

[6] See e.g. Currid 1997:104–120.

the Egyptians and beyond: 'And the Egyptians shall know that I am YHWH, when I stretch out my hand on Egypt and bring out the sons of Israel from among them' (Exod. 7:5).

The signs and wonders receive their impetus and momentum in this divine self-revelation (7:5, 17; 8:10, 22; 9:14, 29–30; 10:2), as does the final overthrow at the sea (14:4, 18), culminating in a paean of praise:

> Who is like you among the gods, O YHWH?
> Who is like you, majestic in the sanctuary,
> Feared-One in praises, working wonders!
> (Exod. 15:11)

Release from captivity apart from the knowledge that wells up into this acclamation of YHWH's holiness would have been no deliverance at all. Here three points are relevant. First, the signs and wonders worked in Egypt are to be understood within a *theology of creation*, revealing YHWH as Creator.[7] Egypt is steadily de-created until Pharaoh's hosts are submerged in the waters of chaos, whereas Israel emerges from those waters re-created. Israel's praise on the other side of redemption, then, is similar to that of the angelic host on the other side of creation (Job 38:4–7) – YHWH has acted in history and they have tasted of his glory. The categories of creation and chaos are, of course, that of life versus death – the antipodes at the heart of Israel's cultic system. Secondly, as with the exile and new exodus in the book of Ezekiel, YHWH's deliverance of Israel reveals a knowledge of himself *universally* – published among the nations. And so we later find that even a harlot in Jericho has come to know something of him: 'I know that YHWH has given you the land . . . for we heard how YHWH dried up the water of the sea before your face when you came out of Egypt . . . YHWH your God, he is God in heaven above and on earth beneath' (Josh. 2:9–11).

Thirdly, knowledge of YHWH is linked inseparably to his dwelling among his people. Note the development of thought in the following divine utterances:

> I will take you for myself to be my people, and I will be your God. Then you will know that I am YHWH your God who brings you out from under the burdens of the Egyptians. And I will bring

---

[7] Fretheim 1991a: 106–107; 1991b. Creation theology, moreover, is inseparable from cultic or temple theology.

you into the land which I swore to give to Abraham, Isaac and Jacob; and I will give it you as a heritage: I am YHWH. (Exod. 6:7–8)

I will dwell among the sons of Israel and will be their God. And they will know that I am YHWH their God who brought them up out of the land of Egypt that I may dwell among them. I am YHWH their God. (Exod. 29:45–46)

The covenant relationship within the land that defines the knowledge of YHWH in the former passage is, in the latter, expressed as life with God through his tabernacling Presence – tasted already in the wilderness. Klein goes further, stating that the recognition formula ('they will know that I am YHWH') summarizes 'the theological goal of the entire book'.[8] In sum, through the exodus deliverance the nations were to know YHWH as the maker of heaven and earth who had re-created a new humanity (Israel) in order to fulfil his original purpose, opening a way for humanity to dwell in his Presence. Under the shadow of the Babylonian tower the nations scattered in exile would behold a wonder: *Israel redeemed to dwell with God.*

Redeemed by the blood of the Lamb

In order to grasp better the nature of Israel's deliverance ('through the waters' in the cultic paradigm), we will now consider briefly the event that 'lies at the very heart of the exodus story', the Passover sacrifice.[9] It is striking that amidst the epic narration of Israel's redemption from bondage there should suddenly come a chapter of cultic legislation, instituting Passover as an annual celebration (Exod. 12) and thereby marking its central significance. As the culminating sign resulting in the release of the Israelites, the death of the firstborn had been foreshadowed already in YHWH's instructions to Moses for his opening confrontation with Pharaoh: 'Thus says YHWH: "Israel is my son, my firstborn. So I say to you, let my son go that he may worship me. But if you refuse to let him go, indeed I will kill your son, your firstborn"' (Exod. 4:22–23). While on previous occasions God had made a distinction between the Israelites and the Egyptians, Israel had to be redeemed for this final sign, and then this redemption from death was to be celebrated annually at Passover in commemoration of the whole exodus deliverance – as the final provocation the

---

[8] Klein 1996: 271.
[9] Alexander 1995: 16.

tenth sign *coincides* with the deliverance from Egypt. The redemption of Israel's firstborn sons from death, in other words, represents the redemption of Israel (God's firstborn son) from Sheol (Egypt). This idea fits well with our general cultic picture of Israel as a new Adam being delivered through the waters of death and conveyed to the mountain of God.[10] The Passover sacrifice, moreover, develops a highly significant aspect of this paradigm: deliverance through the waters requires a ransoming; it is redemption.

The theology of Israel's redemption is brought out by the three distinct elements of the Passover ritual found in Exodus 12:6–11, 21–22, related to atonement, purification and consecration, respectively: (1) the slaying of a lamb or young goat as a sacrifice, (2) the smearing of its blood on the doorposts and (3) the eating of its meat.[11] Apart from the slaying of the lamb, it is evident that the firstborn sons of Israel would have died, no less than those of the Egyptians. The sacrifice therefore involved the concept of substitutionary atonement, the animal's death being regarded as 'in the stead of' the firstborn male within each Israelite household, atoning for sin.[12] Early Jewish interpretation, such as the *Mekilta deRabbi Ishmael*, Pisba' 7 and *Exodus Rabbah* 15.11, links the Passover sparing of the firstborn son with the near-sacrifice of Isaac in Genesis 22.[13] The book of *Jubilees* even has the redemption of Isaac take place on the date of Passover as its original commemorative event (17:15; 18:3, 18–19).[14] Some rabbinic texts, such as *Targum Neofiti* to Leviticus 22:27, understand all sacrificial lambs to be symbolic of Isaac, including the daily morning and evening ascension offerings (*Lev. R.* 2.11). This insight

[10] While the analogy between Adam and Israel is biblical, and recognized in rabbinical literature, the dissimilarities are as important as the similarities in this analogous relationship. Israel is not in a covenant of works relationship in any sense, though the covenant of grace always involves conditions. Furthermore, Adam was not given a sacrificial cultus, that is, a means of forgiveness, in the garden, whereas one of the gifts of the Mosaic covenant was the system of continual reconciliation revealed in Leviticus.

[11] Alexander 1995: 6–8, 16–18; 2009: 127–135. This citation generally comprehends the ensuing explanation of the three points.

[12] As a redemption from death, Israel's firstborn males whether of animals or humans belonged wholly and utterly to YHWH and needed to be sacrificed to him. For the firstborn sons of Israel, however, God commanded the Israelites to redeem them by the substitute sacrifice of a lamb commemorating the redemption of Passover (Exod. 13:11–16). Later the Levites would be claimed by YHWH, their lives of consecrated service received in place of the firstborn males from the other tribes of Israel (Num. 3:11–13).

[13] Cf. Lyonnet and Sabourin 1970: 261–267.

[14] See also Levenson 1993: 173–199.

corresponds well with understanding the binding of Isaac as a foundation narrative for the Jerusalem temple cult. More to the point, having the substitution of the ram for Isaac as an ascension offering at the root of Israel's cult enables us to understand that cult essentially in terms of typology – a point I will develop in a subsequent chapter.

Secondly, as blood manipulation was often utilized for ritual purgation, the smearing or sprinkling of the blood upon the lintel and doorposts of the house seems to signify the purification of those within. Likewise, since hyssop is also commonly associated with ceremonial purification in the Pentateuch (Lev. 14:4, 6, 49, 51–52; Num. 19:6, 18), use of the hyssop for striking the lintel and doorposts with blood strengthens the interpretation of Passover as a cleansing ritual for the household. The need for cleansing is expressed well in the psalm associated with David's repentance:

> Purge me with hyssop and I shall be clean;
> Wash me and I shall be whiter than snow.
> (Ps. 51:7)

The application of the blood on the lintel and doorposts may also be related to the theology of the gate liturgy inasmuch as Ezekiel 45:19 has the priests applying blood to the temple's doorposts and gateposts. In any case, the analogy between Israel and house, priest and temple serves to bring out the priestly nature of the nation as a whole.

Finally, eating the lamb was also an essential part of the Passover rite, as evidenced by its detailed instructions (12:8–11, 43–47). As the regulation for burning the remaining portions in fire indicates, the sacrificial meat was holy, making those who ate it holy as well (12:10). The entire Passover ceremony – along with the redemption it commemorates – had Israel's consecration to YHWH as its goal. Indeed, all three of its elements make the Passover celebration remarkably similar to the consecration of the Aaronic priests in Exodus 29 and Leviticus 8, which also involved sacrificing, blood smearing and the eating of holy meat. Through the Passover ritual each Israelite household functions in a priestly manner and Israel itself is being prepared to become 'a kingdom of priests and a holy nation' (Exod. 19:6).[15] Indeed, through the Passover rites 'the whole nation became a priesthood for one day'.[16] Relevant here, Middleton likens the

---

[15] Alexander 2009: 129.
[16] Gray 1925: 374.

human vocation as *imago Dei* in Genesis 1 to Israel's vocation as a
royal priesthood among the nations – an insight possibly related to the
'*ābad* wordplay discussed earlier, with Israel being delivered to fulfil
humanity's original vocation.[17] The importance of this consecration
in relation to the theme of dwelling in the divine Presence is brought
out in the following quote from Alexander:

> If they [the Israelites] are to live in the presence of God, they must
> regain the holy status humanity had prior to the disobedience of
> Adam and Eve. The Passover ritual performs this function in the
> historical context of the Israelites coming out of Egypt and
> becoming God's people at Mount Sinai.[18]

The goal of redemption

Deliverance for the sake of worship

For our purposes, we note that the end or goal of Israel's redemption
is nothing other than the goal of creation. God's people are delivered,
in other words, for the same reason humanity had been created: *to
dwell with God in the house of God*. This goal of worship is unmistak-
able throughout the dialogue between God and Pharaoh mediated
by Moses, terms such as 'worship/serve' ('*ābad*), 'celebrate/hold a
feast' (*ḥāgag*), 'sacrifice' (*zebaḥ*), 'ascension offering' ('*ōlâ*), 'worship/
prostration' (*ḥāwâ*) being employed in clear purpose statements. In
Exodus 4:22–23, for example, YHWH directs Moses to tell Pharaoh,
'Israel is my son, my firstborn. So I say to you, send out my son that
he may worship me,' and in 5:1, again, 'Send out my people that they
may hold a feast [*ḥāgag*] to me in the wilderness' (see also 3:12, 18;
4:31; 5:3; 7:16; 8:1, 20, 25–28; 9:1, 13; 10:7–11, 24–26; etc.). All these
statements find a preliminary fulfilment in the worship at Mount Sinai
described in Exodus 24, the first verse of which reads, 'Now to Moses
he [God] said, "Ascend to YHWH, you and Aaron, Nadab and Abihu,
and the seventy elders of Israel, and worship/bow-before-me [*ḥāwâ*]
from afar."' Israel's deliverance, therefore, followed the cosmogonic
pattern identified previously: through the waters of the sea, brought
to the mountain of God, for life in the divine Presence.[19] In the next
two sections I will endeavour to deepen our understanding of this
pattern.

[17] Middleton 2005: 90.
[18] Alexander 2009: 129.
[19] Moses, as Israel's mediator, had also undergone this pattern: through the waters
of the Nile, to the mountain of God, for worship (Exod. 2 – 3).

The song at the sea

Moses' song at the sea (Exod. 15:1–18),[20] containing Israel's history in microcosm and its theology *in nuce*, yields in my estimation *the* biblical theology of sacred writ, and, significantly, it traces the cultic geography of the cosmogonic pattern. While not the precise centre of the book of Exodus, the song has justly been referred to as the book's narrative hinge or fulcrum as well as its theological summary.[21] Structurally, the first half of the song celebrates YHWH's victory through the sea (vv. 1–10), culminating in the ascription of his incomparability (v. 11), while the second half prophesies YHWH's shepherding of Israel by his *ḥesed* to his holy abode, planting them upon the mountain of God (vv. 13–17), and concludes with the ascription of his eternal reign (v. 18).[22] In many ways, verse 13 may be considered a summary of Israel's redemption:

> You in your fealty-love [*ḥesed*] will lead forth the people
>> you have redeemed [*ga'al*];
> You will guide them in your strength to your holy pasture.

This hope of being brought to God's dwelling place is elaborated upon in verse 17:

> You will bring them,
> You will plant them, on the mountain of your inheritance,
>> the foundation of your enthronement that you made,
>>> O YHWH,
>> the sanctuary, O Lord, established by your hands.

Noting the threefold emphasis on the mountain of God as the journey's ultimate *end* for Israel enables us to see this as the goal toward which the liturgy has been moving.[23] Beginning with the depths of the sea and ending upon the heights of the mountain sanctum, the song

---

[20] The literature on this song is extensive. See Bender 1903; Cross and Freedman 1955; Cross 1973; Coats 1969; Muilenburg 1996; Russell 2007; J. W. Watts 1992: 41–62.

[21] M. Smith 1997: 183; Russell 2007: 45–47.

[22] The first half of the poem, narrating Israel's journey between the walls of the threatening sea, is therefore mirrored by the second half, narrating Israel's journey between the walls of the threatening nations (oft likened to the tumultuous sea), and YHWH's incomparability (v. 11) is mirrored by his kingship (v. 18). Thematically, v. 11 constitutes the centre and apex of the whole song (Freedman 1974: 185; Fischer 1996: 35; Burden 1987: 51; Patterson 2004: 48).

[23] Muilenburg 1966: 248–249. Including v. 13's reference, J. D. W. Watts (1957: 377) rightly understands a fourfold emphasis.

traverses cosmic architecture,[24] through the cosmogonic pattern portraying YHWH's mountain as the goal of Israel's redemption. Propp's suggestion, therefore, that the song could with equal justice be called the 'Song of the Mountain', is correct and perhaps even preferable.[25] Understandably, the precise identification of the song's mountain is a matter of scholarly debate, with the referent often understood as Mount Sinai, the land of Canaan, the sanctuary at Gilgal, or Jerusalem / Mount Zion, among other locales. The cosmic description of God's abode, however, seems to point to the heavenly reality (fore)tasted, as it were, by each particular historical mountain in redemptive history – precisely the experience of the mountain of God as cosmic mountain, sanctified by the divine Presence. Goldin, moreover, contrasts the attributes of this song's sanctuary with Solomon's words regarding the temple 'which *I* have built' (1 Kgs 8:27, 43), concluding that

> according to the Song at the Sea, if one is to speak of a *mkwn lshbtk* [place of your abode], of a *mqdsh* [sanctuary], there is no mistaking the hands which made and established it: *mkwn lshbtk* You made, O Lord, *mqdsh*, O Lord, Your hands established. The poet clearly knows that there is a *mkwn lshbtk*, a *mqdsh*, not of Solomon's making. And it was toward that non-Solomonic sanctuary that God had in love led the people He redeemed.[26]

Furthermore, Solomon's prayer at the dedication of the temple clearly acknowledges the functional correlation between the heavenly reality and the earthly copy when he states, 'when they pray toward this place, then you hear from the place of your dwelling, from heaven' (1 Kgs 8:30, 49; etc.). The ambiguous nature of the mountain, then, stems precisely from the fact that a cosmic mountain is in reference, the heavenly reality represented and experienced through the various mountains of Israel's history.[27] Indeed, as the context of this redemptive history opens, the application or significance changes: within the book of Exodus Sinai is the probable referent; within the Hexateuch it is the Promised Land; within the broader Hebrew Scriptures Jerusalem's Mount Zion; within the New Testament the mountain is identified,

[24] Propp 1999: 571; de Souza 2005: 130.
[25] Propp 1999: 562. 'Indeed, the Song is as much a song of God's holy mountain as it is a song of a sea' (Meyers 2005: 122).
[26] Goldin 1971: 45–46. See also 2 Sam. 7:13; 1 Kgs 5:5; 6:1–2, 14–15; 7:51; 9:1.
[27] Cross 1973: 142.

finally, as the heavenly Zion of the new earth – the new Jerusalem. To be sure, the prophetic corpus, proclaiming as it does a new exodus journey to an Edenic Zion, already gestures toward the new Jerusalem. The language of being 'planted' itself evokes Eden imagery where the righteous are likened to trees planted in the house of God (Pss 1; 52:8; 92:12–13).[28] From a purely historical perspective, the language of being planted in God's own abode cannot be satisfied apart from the hope revealed in John's Apocalypse – a hope held out before Israel already in this song, reiterated through the 'pattern' (*tabnît*) upon which the whole cultic system is founded (Exod. 25:9), and embraced in the liturgy (cf. Ps. 23:6). The hope – and divine promise – expressed in Exodus 15:17 is anchored behind the heavenly veil, penetrating beyond Eden's cherubim to a life of joy and feasting in the house of God.

Cosmogonic pattern

There is a sense where, bracketed by the waters of the Nile (Exod. 2) and the sea (Exod. 14), waters of death in both contexts, Egypt itself is pervaded by the symbolism of Sheol, the watery abode of death.[29] Elsewhere in Scripture both Egypt and Pharaoh are likened to the monsters of the chaos sea, Rahab and the dragon or Tannin and Leviathan (cf. Isa. 30:7; 51:9–11; Pss 97:4; 89:10).[30] In Ezekiel 29:3 we read:

> Speak and say, 'Thus says the Lord YHWH:
> "Behold, I am against you,
> O Pharaoh, king of Egypt,
> O great dragon who lies in the midst of his Nile,
> Who has said, 'My Nile is my own;
> I have made it for myself.'"'

A few chapters later in Ezekiel (32:2) Pharaoh is likened to 'a dragon in the seas, bursting forth in your rivers, troubling the waters with your feet and fouling their rivers'. Some scholars see this mythological identification at play in the Exodus narrative, particularly in chapter 7, where the first sign (vv. 8–13) has Aaron's rod turning into

---

[28] Cf. Propp 1999: 570.

[29] Skilled in the art of mummification, Egypt was the land of the dead. This idea feeds into the Israelites' sarcasm: 'Is it because there were no graves in Egypt that you have brought us to the wilderness to die?' (Exod. 14:11).

[30] See e.g. the entries on 'cosmology' and 'monsters' in *DBI*, 171–172, 562–565.

a *tannin*, a 'dragon-gobbling dragon', and the next scene (vv. 14–18) appears to portray Pharaoh as 'a huge mythical reptile wallowing in the river'.[31] Against the backdrop of cultic cosmology it is as if Israel was delivered from the chamber of death in the depths of the sea (and from the sea monster embodying that kingdom) and then conveyed to God's abode upon his holy mountain. Given this movement, it is not surprising that scholars have correlated the deliverance out of Egypt precisely with the movement of lament and thanksgiving psalms.[32] The movement from the waters to the mountain, then, is a movement from death to life,[33] reversing that of the primeval history in Genesis 1 – 7. Emerging from these waters, Israel as God's firstborn son (Exod. 4:22–23) find themselves, as Adam and Noah before, brought to the holy mountain of God, and then to the cultic gates of Eden, the tabernacle.

Brought to the mountain of God: Exod. 15:22 – 24:18

Sinai, mountain of God in the wilderness, at Israel's beginning

As already considered when looking at the structure of the Pentateuch in chapter 1, Mount Sinai as mountain of God dominates the Pentateuch, Israel arriving at its base in Exodus 19, remaining there to the end of Exodus, throughout the book of Leviticus, and up until the departure narrated in Numbers 10.[34] Even the journey to Sinai, moreover, lies within its shadow and deals primarily with the question of whether or not 'YHWH is among us' (Exod. 17:7).[35] Mount Sinai stands, quite literally, at the centre of the wilderness journey, with six stations between Egypt and Sinai, and six stations following Sinai to the plains of Moab.[36] Ever afterward Israel would be defined as the people who had gathered about Mount Sinai, constituted thereby as a cultic community (*'ēdâ*).[37]

---

[31] Guillaume 2004: 232, 235.

[32] Westermann 1981: 259–260; Plastaras 1966: 49–57; Leder 1999: 23.

[33] Cf. Polak 1997.

[34] In Exod. 18 – 40 alone, the term 'mountain of God' and its synonyms are used some forty times in what amounts to 'clear theological usage' (Carpenter 1997: 107).

[35] Propp (1987: 59–61) e.g. argues persuasively that 'rock' (*ṣûr*) refers to Horeb and must denote 'mountain'.

[36] Clifford 1984: 113.

[37] B. W. Anderson 1986: 464.

Who shall ascend the mountain of YHWH?

The dominant attribute of Mount Sinai is its holiness,[38] brought out in a variety of ways by the narrative – chiefly by the fear-inspiring descriptions of the theophany associated with it. Mount Sinai is utterly holy because the unapproachable glory, the thunderous and fiery Presence of God, has descended upon its summit. That holiness is also brought out by the many warnings against approaching or even touching the mount (19:12–13, 21, 23–24; 24:2); by the tripartite division of the mount into bands of holiness (top, 19:20; 24:12, 16–18; midsection, 19:24; 24:1–2, 9–15; base, 19:12, 17); and the need to maintain these boundaries;[39] by the need for consecration (19:10–11, 14–15, 22); and, in addition to all these precautions, by the need for a mediator (19:3; etc.). Once more, then, the question of the gate liturgy naturally arises, 'Who shall ascend the mountain of YHWH?' And that question is answered in no uncertain terms: Moses – and Moses *alone* – may ascend the mountain of God. As mediator Moses is consistently described as the one – again, the only one – who is able to ascend. The arrival at Sinai in Exodus 19 immediately contrasts Israel, who 'camped before the mountain' (v. 2), with Moses, who 'ascended to God' (v. 3).[40] Further on we read, 'YHWH descended upon Mount Sinai, on the summit of the mountain [*'el-rōš hāhār*]. Then YHWH called Moses to the summit of the mountain [*'el-rōš hāhār*], and Moses ascended [*wayya'al*]' (Exod. 19:20).

Immediately following this astounding statement we read what will become a typical prohibition, for the people not to presume to draw near (vv. 21–25), for 'the people are not able to ascend [*la'alōt*] Mount Sinai'. Their inability to ascend into the divine Presence highlights the one who *is* able to do so. In Exodus 20:21 we read a similar summation: 'So the people stood afar off, but Moses drew near to the dense darkness there [i.e. summit of Sinai] where God was.' Returning to Exodus 24 and to the consummation of the covenant in worship, although one reads of Aaron, Nadab and Abihu along with the seventy elders of Israel as being upon the mountain, yet God's call comes to Moses in a particular way that is not as obvious in English translation: 'Now to Moses he said "Ascend to YHWH"' (v. 1) – 'you-ascend' being masculine singular. In the next verse a threefold prohibition follows, according to the mountain's three zones of holiness:

[38] Dozeman 2009: 411, 433–434.
[39] Chirichigno 1987.
[40] For the exegetical basis of this point, see Morales 2012b: 219–231.

> And Moses alone may draw near to YHWH,
> but they [the elders, Aaron and his sons] must not draw near,
> and the people are not to ascend with him.

Then from the midpoint of the mountain, after the elders, Aaron and his sons see, as it were, the feet of God through the sapphire-like clear pavement above (presumably, looking up through or into the cloud of glory on the summit), YHWH calls to Moses, 'Ascend to me on the mountain and be there' (v. 12), and we read, 'Moses ascended into the mountain of God' (v. 13b). Ever higher, the narrative follows him: 'Moses ascended into the mountain, and a cloud covered the mountain' (v. 15). Then, in a scene of profound wonder, we read:

> Now the glory of YHWH dwelled [*wayyiškōn*] upon the mountain of Sinai, and the cloud covered it six days. And on the seventh day he called to Moses out of the midst of the cloud. The appearance of the glory of YHWH was like a consuming fire on the summit of the mountain in the eyes of the sons of Israel. So Moses entered into the midst of the cloud and he ascended the mountain. And Moses was on the mountain forty days and forty nights. (Exod. 24:16–18)

Here we find the familiar 6 + 1 pattern of creation. Moses, as an Adam upon the mountain of God, enters the fire of YHWH's glory on the seventh day.[41] Justly, Exodus 24 has been described as a going 'back to Eden'.[42] For forty days and nights, Moses abides in the fire without being consumed – a foretaste of Israel's destiny, first pictured by the burning bush (Exod. 3; cf. Isa. 4:5–6; Zech. 2:5). In the light of this scene Isaiah's rephrase of the gate liturgy question is fitting, driving us to the inner significance of the ascent into the mountain of God:

> Who among us shall dwell with the consuming fire?
> Who among us shall dwell with the everlasting burnings?
> (Isa. 33:14)

---

[41] 'Thus the seventh day is not only the day of rest from labor, but at the same time it is the day when God and creatures meet within the fire' (Lohfink 1994: 130). Och (1995: 238) notes how the encounter between God and Israel at Sinai is a return to beginnings, re-enacting the original encounter between God and humanity at Eden: 'God has created a new people to stand before Him at Sinai as Adam stood in His presence at Eden . . . God's call to Moses to ascend the mountain is preceded by a period of six days, which alludes to the six days of cosmic creation.'

[42] Hilber 1996: 185.

Once more, the answer of Exodus resounds: Moses alone.

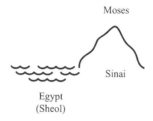

Moses

Sinai

Egypt
(Sheol)

Moses the mediator

As mediator between God and Israel, Moses is able to ascend whereas
the people may not, *and* he is able to descend whereas God may not
(for the same reason the people cannot ascend, lest holy YHWH
consumes them). The mountain thus becomes the symbol for approaching God in worship, the stage for this mediation: Moses ascends in
order to represent the people to God; Moses descends in order to
represent God to the people.[43] While keeping up with the ascents and
descents of Moses is one of the main challenges of the Sinai narrative,[44]
the mere fact of his doing so itself draws us to the theological heart
of the narrative: the need for a mediator. The closest parallel to Moses
thus far in the Pentateuch would be the angels (or 'messengers')
ascending and descending the stepped mountain (with YHWH
standing above) in Jacob's vision at Beth-el, the House of God (Gen.
28:12–13).[45] Moreover, chapters 19 and 24 appear to have been designed
as complimentary pictures of this mediation, each chapter containing
a sevenfold use of the stem *dbr* (to speak, word), along with a sevenfold
use of *yrd* (descend) in chapter 19 counterbalanced by a sevenfold use
of *'lh* (ascend) in ch. 24.[46] Thus construed, in chapter 19 Moses
is primarily presenting God to Israel, whereas in chapter 24 he is
presenting Israel to God in the covenant ratification ceremony that
would ever afterward serve as the paradigm for Israel's cultus, the inner
dynamic of Israel's worship.

[43] Cf. Chirichigno 1987: 460; Hauge 2001: 29, 31.
[44] Niccacci 1997: 217.
[45] After Moses, as we will see, this mediation of ascent and decent will be taken up
by the priests, whose service for the earthly liturgy is commonly paralleled in ancient
Jewish tradition to that of the angels in the heavenly liturgy.
[46] Sarna 1991: 150; cf. Hilber 1996; Sprinkle 1994: 17–29.

Moses' role as mediator comes to its fullest expression in chapter 33 of Exodus – arguably the highest point of tension and resolution in the book – as Moses intercedes for the Israelites who have just committed idolatry by making and worshipping a golden calf. With good reason Wenham notes how the golden calf narrative abruptly and without warning plunges 'into the greatest crisis in divine–human relationships since the flood',[47] for the sin of Israel and the divine judgment it incurs are described in similar terms to the flood narrative. YHWH says the people have 'corrupted' (*šiḥēt*) themselves and have turned aside with haste from 'the way' (*haderek*) that he had commanded them (Exod. 32:7–8), even as the flood generation had become 'corrupt' (*nišḥatâ*), having corrupted 'his [YHWH's] way' (*darkô*) on the earth (Gen. 6:12). Indeed, God's resolution is the same: as he had destroyed the flood generation and started over with Noah, so now he suggests that he will destroy Israel and start over with Moses (Exod. 32:10). The literary structure of Exodus, moreover, brings out the crucial nature of this event, for the golden calf apostasy occurs in Exodus 32, in the middle of the tabernacle account. The instructions for the tabernacle are given in Exodus 25 – 31 and the construction of the tabernacle is recounted in Exodus 35 – 40. Underscoring the heinousness of Israel's sin more deeply, there is a Sabbath legislation *inclusio* formed with the end of Exodus 31 and the beginning of Exodus 35, the ultimate purpose of the tabernacle being Sabbath union and fellowship with God. The Mosaic covenant is likened to a marriage relationship elsewhere in Scripture (cf. Isa. 54:5; Jer. 3:20; Ezek. 16; Hos. 2), with YHWH's wooing Israel in the wilderness. Borrowing that analogy, it is as if the narrative builds momentum as it moves from courtship to betrothal in the covenant ratification ceremony of Exodus 24; then, on the threshold of consummation, Israel commits adultery on the nuptial night:

golden calf idolatry (32:1–24)

Sabbath legislation (31:12–18)   Sabbath legislation (35:1–3)

tabernacle instructions (chs. 25–31)   tabernacle construction (chs. 35–40)

Especially given the context of sacred space and time, Israel's making of the golden calf to symbolize God's Presence, parodying ironically the making and purpose of the tabernacle in Exodus 25:1–9,[48] merits the immediate and unreserved vengeance of God. And yet the

[47] Wenham 2003: 77.

[48] Ibid.

golden calf episode is not actually positioned at the literary centre of the tabernacle account; rather, the crisis it creates ushers in the central focus, namely the intercession of Moses as mediator between God and Israel in Exodus 33. Leading up to Exodus 33 and highly significant for later considerations regarding the Day of Atonement, the day after Israel's sin Moses had declared to the people (Exod. 32:30), 'You have sinned a great sin! Now therefore I will ascend to YHWH. Perhaps I can make atonement for your sin.'

Having ascended Sinai's summit, Moses then offers himself in Israel's stead (v. 32): 'Now if you will forgive their sin – but if not, blot me out, I pray, from your scroll which you have written!' The phrase 'blot out', from *māḥâ*, happens also to have been the term used for God's intention to blot out humanity (*hā'ādām*) from the face of the land (*hā'ădāmâ*) in the flood narrative (Gen. 6:7), heightened all the more by Moses' added explanatory 'from your scroll'. He is in effect calling upon God to forgive Israel by obliterating him instead. Here the essential nature of intercession is manifest: this profound gesture of atonement unveils the inner meaning of Moses' role as mediator. Mediatory intercession is not merely prayer in the sense of 'making requests', but a plea that is also an act of self-giving, that flows from self-sacrifice. YHWH's response, bridging into chapter 33 through resumptive repetition, is that his Presence will not go with Israel into the land. YHWH goes on to promise that his angel (or 'messenger') will drive out the Canaanites, Amorites, Hittites, Hivites and Jebusites, ensuring that the people enter the land flowing with milk and honey (33:3); only, YHWH himself will not go with them. Moses, however, will have none of this, and it is critical to discern why this is so. This proposition brings us to the heart of God's promises to the patriarchs, as well as to the centre of biblical theology. Were these promises primarily about the land, as some suggest? Here God guarantees land entry, and yet Moses refuses (Exod. 33:15): 'If your face does not go, then do not make us ascend from here.' What is the land if bereft of God's Presence, if it will not become a new Eden in which Israel may enjoy life in fellowship with God? Meditation on the choice put before Moses brings recognition of Cain's city, the tower of Babylon, Lot's choice, Esau's shallow contentment – all examples of seeking satisfaction eastward of the flaming sword. So God tests Moses, sifting his heart and discerning its inward motivation and desire: Will he, after all, be willing to rest the matter short of its fundamental goal? No, Moses forsook neither the treasures of Egypt nor the repose of Midian merely to establish another nation among the scattered lot of Babylon's tower – better God's Presence in the wilderness than his absence in the land. Land, then, is not the core of the patriarchal promises, but life in the land *with God*.

Thus the primary issue of Exodus 33 and Moses' mediatorial work comes into focus: *the Presence of God*, particularly his tabernacling Presence, amidst Israel. Having made a golden calf to symbolize God's Presence, Israel is now threatened with the loss of the divinely ordained symbol of his Presence, the tabernacle. After tasting the house of God through the descriptive instructions in Exodus 25 – 31, the narrative unexpectedly plummets into an unthinkable possibility, that the tabernacle will not be built at all – no longer necessary since God will not accompany Israel. Here, then, we find the dramatic height of the book, the focal point of its narrative tension and resolution. The logic of the literary structure, with Moses' mediation occurring between the instructions and the construction of the tabernacle, now becomes manifest: apart from Moses' mediation, there is no tabernacle; there is no new cosmos filled with the glory of YHWH. And so Moses wrestles with YHWH in an exchange that focuses upon his accompanying Presence ('face') among Israel:

YHWH:	My face will go with you . . . (v. 14)
Moses:	If your face does not go with us, do not make us ascend . . . (v. 15)
YHWH:	You cannot see my face, for man cannot see me and live . . . (v. 20)
	My face will not be seen (v. 23)

Ultimately what is vouchsafed is the *cultic* Presence of God, an assurance of his nearness in a manner that nevertheless preserves divine freedom.[49] Whether or not Newing is correct in positioning Exodus 33 and the theme of YHWH's promised Presence as the chiastic centre and rhetorical pinnacle of Genesis to Joshua,[50] the theological centrality of the divine Presence and of Moses' mediatorial work in relation to it cannot be overstated. Indeed, as Newing also points out, the heart of Exodus 33 is verses 7–11, an idealized description of YHWH's meeting with Moses face to face in the tabernacle of meeting. This intimate friendship between YHWH and Moses is the life of Moses' mediatorial work of intercession – and, consequently, that friendship is also the life of Israel. Moses' mediation

---

[49] Brueggemann 1979; cf. Brueggemann 1976; Terrien 1978: 138–152. Brueggemann notes three word pairs, demonstrating a shift from Moses' request of *visibility* to God's concession *via audibility*, working out a way to give *assurance* of God's Presence without *certitude*: glory vs. goodness, face vs. back, see vs. proclaim (Brueggemann 1979: 56).

[50] Newing 1985.

resolves in chapter 34 not only with his descent from Mount Sinai with a new set of tablets, the covenant having been renewed, but also with the somewhat mysterious observation that his face had become radiant from God's Presence. His face shone such that even Aaron, and all Israel with him, was afraid to draw near to him. Moses, therefore, veiled his face when not addressing the people with God's words, unveiling it whenever he entered the Presence of YHWH. While the Hebrew word used for Moses' veil (*masweh*) differs from that of the tabernacle veil (*pārōket*), scholars have nevertheless long noted the analogy at play.[51] Moses has been transfigured by his face-to-face friendship with YHWH, a foretaste of the reality signified by the twelve loaves of the Presence basking in the light of the *měnôrâ* lampstand. Yet to the degree that even God's reflected glory must be veiled from Israel, Israel's knowledge and experience of God – revealed through Moses' mediation – is consequently limited (cf. 2 Cor. 3:7–18).

Tabernacle, life with God: Exodus 25 – 40

Constructing the house of God

While the mass of repetitive material on the instructions and construction of the tabernacle, comprising thirteen of the remaining sixteen chapters of Exodus, may be deemed tedious according to modern sensibilities, yet from the ANE perspective this concentration manifestly brings one to the heart – indeed, to the drama itself – of the narrative.[52] This material is better appreciated by having in mind the psalmist's meditation on the blessedness of dwelling in the house of God:

---

[51] Brueggemann 1994: 954; Enns 2000: 587; Janzen 1997: 262–263. Philpot's (2013) caution here is appropriate, even if, perhaps, he underestimates the function of an *intended* analogy – even Aaron, the future high priest, is afraid to draw near (*ngš*) to Moses (v. 30). Though Enns (2000: 587) states he is 'uncomfortable pressing the matter too far', he nevertheless writes that within 'the broader context of Exodus, we may think of Moses' veil functioning in a similar way to the veil or curtain in the tabernacle. Just as the people could not enter the Most Holy Place to behold God's glory, now they cannot behold the glory of God reflected in Moses. He had, therefore, become the embodiment of the tabernacle; his role as mediator has reached a level and depth not yet attained.' Brueggemann (1994: 954) posits the movement of the divine Glory from Mount Sinai (Exod. 24:15–18) to the tabernacle (Exod. 40:34) *via* Moses' mediation (Exod. 34:29–35).

[52] Enns 2000: 506.

How lovely is your tabernacle [*miškān*], O YHWH of hosts!
My soul longs, yea, faints for the courts of YHWH;
my heart and my flesh sing for joy to the living God.
Even the sparrow has found a home,
   and the swallow a nest for herself,
   where she may lay her young,
near your altars, O YHWH of hosts,
   my king and my God.
How happy are those who dwell in your house,
   ever praising you.

(Ps. 84:1–4)

With the yearning to 'dwell in the house of YHWH for ever' (Ps. 23:6), the tabernacle, constructed according to the pattern of the heavenly reality, becomes a taste of heaven. The instructions for the tabernacle and detailed descriptions of its furnishings function so as to offer the hearers a tour of God's house, removing the veil from what YHWH showed Moses within the cloud (Exod. 25:9). In the same way the boundaries of Canaan described in Numbers 34:1–15 served to stir Israel's longing for life in the land beyond the wilderness; and in the same way the symbolic survey of the New Jerusalem in Revelation 21:9 – 22:5 serves to stir our hearts for the life of the new earth, so the description of the tabernacle and its furnishings is meant to convey the blessed lot of the redeemed who will find themselves abundantly satisfied with the fatness of God's house (Ps. 36:8).

As we turn to consider now, the experience at Sinai as mountain of God will give way to another reality as this approach to God in worship is carried on through the tabernacle as a portable mountain of God.[53] The ultimate goal of Israel's redemption is to have nothing less than God dwelling amidst his people – that, as we will consider later, is the essence of the covenant. In saving Israel through the exodus out of Egypt, therefore, God had declared:

Let them build me a sanctuary that I may dwell in their midst. . . . I will dwell amidst the sons of Israel and I will be their God. They will know that I am YHWH their God, who brought them up out of the land of Egypt to dwell in their midst – I am YHWH their God. (Exod. 25:8; 29:45–46)

---

[53] The phrase 'portable Sinai' is now widely used with reference to the tabernacle. See e.g. Sarna 1991: 237; Enns 2000: 493, 532; Milgrom 2004: 89; Wenham 2012: 244.

That these lines are programmatic is evident already by the narrative drama beginning with the expulsion from the garden of Eden and leading up to the tabernacle account, but also by the extensive and detail-oriented recounting of the follow-through on these divine commands. The Torah, as instruction on the way of YHWH, becomes a literary journey to the house of YHWH. It would be unfitting, therefore, to stop the journey short at the threshold to the divine abode. Rather, by describing the materials, furnishings, instruction and construction of the tabernacle, the Torah ushers us into God's house for a tour of its splendours.

The tabernacle as cultic mountain of God

To understand the tabernacle as God's abode more deeply, we need to explore how the significance of Mount Sinai gets transferred to the tabernacle. Within the context of Moses' ascent in Exodus 24:16–18, Exodus 25 opens with YHWH's speaking to Moses from within the fiery cloud upon the summit of Sinai on the seventh day, as he unveils the plan for the tabernacle cultus: 'Let them make me a sanctuary that I may dwell among them. According to all that I show you, the pattern [*tabnît*] of the tabernacle and the pattern of all its furnishings, just so shall you make it' (vv. 8–9). As much as I have emphasized the prominence of Mount Sinai within the Penta-teuch, it is necessary here to stress how much of the Sinai narrative is taken up more narrowly with the tabernacle cultus. Berman notes, for example, that virtually every law and commandment listed from Exodus 25 until the consecration of the tabernacle in Leviticus 10 pertain directly to the sanctuary.[54] Exodus 25 – 31 is taken up entirely with the instructions for the tabernacle, chapters 35–40 with the construction of the tabernacle; the whole book of Leviticus is taken up with the tabernacle cultus itself (comprised almost entirely of God's speeches from within the tabernacle), some even propos-ing the book to be a literary tour of God's dwelling place;[55] and Numbers 1 – 10 may be summed up adequately within the context of preparations for dismantling the tabernacle before marching onward.[56] Indeed, inasmuch as the Sinai narrative aims at the book of Leviticus,[57] we may also state – and much more aptly – that it aims at the tabernacle cultus. But let us go further: the creation account

[54] Berman 1995: 40.
[55] Douglas 1999a.
[56] C. R. Smith 1996: 18–19.
[57] Knierim 1985: 405.

of Genesis 1:1 – 2:3, along with the garden of Eden narrative of Genesis 2:4 – 3:24, and all the subsequent drama leading up to this point, has set its aim upon the tabernacling Presence of God. It is when, in fact, one sees the prominence of Sinai in all its fullness, that the remaining step – to transfer that significance from Sinai to the tabernacle cultus – becomes apparent.

There is, moreover, a significant phrase that serves to transition from the revelation at Sinai in Exodus 24 to the tabernacle instructions in Exodus 25 – 30. While God's arrival at Sinai had been consistently described by the verb 'descended' (*yārad*) throughout chapter 19, in 24:16 we read rather that God's glory 'dwelled' (from *šākan*) upon the mountain, precisely the mode of divine Presence that will be continued through the tabernacle, as emphasized by its name: *miškān*. This key verb is then employed to frame the section on tabernacle instructions, transforming Exodus 24:16 into something of a preface to the tabernacle cultus:[58]

> Let them make for me a sanctuary so I may dwell [*šākantî*] among them. (Exod. 25:8)

> I will dwell [*šākantî*] among the sons of Israel, and will be their God. They shall know that I am YHWH their God, who brought them up out of the land of Egypt for the purpose that I may dwell [*lĕšākĕnî*] among them. I am YHWH their God. (Exod. 29:45–46)

The purpose of the tabernacle, then, will be to perpetuate the Sinai experience of engagement with God – YHWH's dwelling in the midst of Israel being the very essence of the covenant.[59] Because the tabernacle is an architectural embodiment of the mountain of God, the transfer of God's Presence from Sinai to the tabernacle yields other links and correspondences between them. Commentators, at least since Ramban in the Middle Ages, have noted the similarity between Mount Sinai and the tabernacle, first in relation to their tripartite divisions whereby the holy of holies (and the high priest's sole access) corresponds to the summit, the holy place (accessed by the priesthood) corresponds to the second zone partway up the mountain, and

---

[58] Berman 1995: 216–217.
[59] Note e.g. how the covenant formula (particularly formula A, 'I will be God for you') is welded to the tabernacling Presence in Exod. 29:45. For the variations of the covenant formula, see Rendtorff 1998.

the outer court with the altar (accessed by the people) corresponds to the base of the mountain, also with an altar.[60] Secondly, aside from the districts of holiness common to both Sinai and the tabernacle, each one also becomes the locus of divine speech:

And YHWH called to him [Moses] *from the mountain* [*min-hāhār*], saying . . . (Exod. 19:3)

And YHWH called to Moses . . . *from the tent of meeting* [*mē'ōhel mô'ēd*], saying . . . (Lev. 1:1)

Relevant to this point, the entire book of Leviticus is woven together by divine speeches proceeding from within the veil of the holy of holies. A third similarity shared by Sinai and the tabernacle is in relation to the tablets of the law, which are given from the summit of Sinai and are then stored in the ark within the holy of holies – the summit's typological counterpart. Fourthly, both the mountain and the tabernacle have altars, so that God is approached through the cultic means of sacrifice. Other parallels could be mentioned, but the chief likeness already noted between Mount Sinai and the tabernacle, the one from which all other correspondences derive, is the Presence of YHWH himself, and this Presence is similarly manifested – portrayed yet veiled – at both Sinai and the tabernacle: through the glory cloud:[61]

And the cloud of glory covered the mountain,
and the glory of YHWH dwelt upon Mount Sinai . . .
(Exod. 24:15–16)

And the cloud covered the tent of meeting,
and the glory of YHWH filled the tabernacle.
(Exod. 40:34)

The encounter at Mount Sinai, the locale of the most vividly described theophany – the black, impenetrable smoke, the consuming fire, the thunder and lightnings, the shofar blast and the quaking – is thus transferred to the tabernacle. While I have discussed the mountain of God according to the paradigm of the tabernacle (i.e. the garden of

[60] Sarna 1991: 105; Enns 2000: 391.
[61] Cassuto 1967: 484; Weinfeld 1981: 504–505.

Eden as holy of holies, etc.), the truth of course is quite the reverse. When the cloud of glory journeys from Mount Sinai to the tabernacle (Exod. 40:34), it is as an act of catechesis: the tabernacle has become *the* mountain of God.

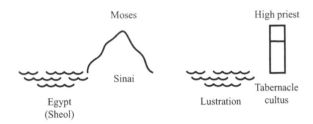

Through the tabernacle cultus, therefore, Sinai is not merely remembered but *relived* – recreated and re-experienced. Berman draws out how the sensory experience of the Sinai theophany, both aural and visual, is perpetuated in the vessels and rites of the tabernacle, noting three objects in particular: the ark, the altar of incense and the altar of burnt offerings.[62] As to the ark, he notes that according to Deuteronomy 5:22 God had spoken the commandments from Sinai, amid the fire, the cloud and the thick darkness, in a *great voice* (*qôl*), and had then inscribed them on the tablets of stone (cf. Exod. 19:16–19; 20:18–21). The ark symbolizes God's *qôl* at Sinai in two ways, as is evident in Exodus 25:21–22:

> You shall put the atonement-cover upon the top of the ark, and in the ark put the [tablets of] testimony which I will give you. There I will meet with you, and I will speak with you – from above the atonement-cover, from between the two cherubim which are on top of the ark of testimony – all that I will command you concerning the sons of Israel.

The ark perpetuates the divine *qôl* at Sinai, first, as a receptacle of the tablets which are a transcript of what had been uttered by the *qôl* at Sinai. This fundamental association is evident in the phrase 'of testimony' ascribed to both: the 'ark of testimony' contains the 'tablets

[62] Berman 1995: 43–52. He (51–52) also notes that these three vessels are highlighted specifically in relation to meeting with God: ark, Exod. 25:22; altar of incense, Exod. 30:6; altar of burnt offering, Exod. 29:42.

of testimony'.[63] Secondly, from the ark God will continue revealing his commandments. The ark, then, is not only the receptacle of the *qôl* from Sinai (v. 21), but the means by which the *qôl* will continue to utter forth the divine testimony (v. 22). The typological correspondence already mentioned between Sinai's summit and the holy of holies is relevant here, with reference to the locale of God's *qôl*.

Grasping the correspondence between the mountain summit and holy of holies is especially vital as we consider the altar of incense. When Moses had ascended Sinai, the 'cloud' (*'ānān*) covered the mountain, and after six days YHWH called to Moses out of the *'ānān* and Moses, we read, entered into the midst of the *'ānān* and ascended the mountain (Exod. 24:15–18). Properly understood, God's glory is manifested by fire. Probably then we are to understand the *'ānān* as a veil covering God's glory, explaining how the cloud was seen by day, but only fire was seen by night (through the cloud). Because it conceals as much as it reveals, the *'ānān* is a powerful symbol for the divine Presence. Berman rightly grounds this function theologically in the words of God to Moses, 'You cannot see my face, for man may not see me and live' (Exod. 33:22).[64] As such, the *'ānān* becomes a symbol both for divine immanence *and* transcendence. More to the point, *because* one may not see God and live, the *'ānān* is a protective screen, a shield, for the one who ascends into the divine Presence. We see this function for the altar of incense, first, in its placement within the tabernacle: 'Place it [the altar of incense] before the veil that is before the ark of the testimony – before the atonement cover that is over the testimony – where I will meet with you' (Exod. 30:6). The altar's incense hereby imparts its fragrance in conjunction with the veil, covering the meeting place of God's Presence. Secondly, within the instructions for the *only* permissible entrance into the holy of holies, and that by the high priest alone on the annual Day of Atonement, the high priest is to take a censer full of burning coals from the altar, along with a fistful of finely beaten sweet incense, and so create a 'cloud [*'ānān*] of incense' in order to cover the atonement cover – the meeting place where God appears – 'lest he die' (Lev. 16:12–13). Clearly, the veil of the curtain must be replaced by the veil of the *'ānān* of incense, lest Aaron – even as consecrated high priest of Israel – see the face of God and perish. Thus Aaron's need for the *'ānān* within

---

[63] Indeed – and this is not noted by Berman – the ark is called 'ark of testimony' only *after* the (tablets of) testimony are deposited within it (albeit, by way of instruction). Exod. 25:21–22 makes this clear, v. 22 being the first use of the phrase 'ark of testimony'.

[64] Berman 1995.

the holiest corresponds well with Moses' need for the *'ānān* at Sinai's summit. 'Only with the protective screen of the *'ānān haketoret*, the symbolic perpetuation of the *'ānān* at Sinai, can the high priest enter into God's Presence.'[65]

Finally, the significant impression of the altar of ascension offering is in relation to its fire. God's glory, once more, is represented by fire. In Exodus 24:17 we read, 'The appearance of the glory of YHWH was like a consuming fire [*'ēš*] on the summit of the mountain in the eyes of the sons of Israel.' Within the context of the covenant ceremony this description of YHWH's glory would naturally correspond to the fire of sacrifice since the ritual entailed Moses setting up twelve pillars around an altar to symbolize the twelve tribes surrounding Sinai – that is, verse 17 conveys that Mount Sinai appeared as a huge altar, with YHWH's Presence on the summit corresponding to the consuming fire. Again, however, the reverse is more to the point: the altar represents the mountain of God ablaze with his fiery Presence. When Moses later recalls the experience, he reminds the people how they had said, 'Now why should we die – for this great fire [*'ēš*] will consume us!' (Deut. 5:25). Moses also calls attention to the fittingness of the fire image; apart from conveying something of God's holiness, it is also an aniconic presence: 'YHWH spoke to you out of the midst of the fire; it was the *qôl* of words you heard but no shape did you see – only a *qôl*' (Deut. 4:12). The implications are spelled out in Deuteronomy 4:15–20: the people are not to act wickedly by sculpting an image in any likeness whatsoever *because* 'you saw no shape when YHWH your God spoke to you at Horeb out of the midst of the fire'. The importance of this image of God's Presence as a consuming fire is evident in other ways. The fire on the altar had originally come forth from YHWH himself at the inauguration of the tabernacle cultus (Lev. 9:24). Because it thus represented his Presence among Israel, the fire was to be kept burning continuously, even when no sacrifices were being offered (Lev. 6:5–6). Also, the ever-rising pillar of smoke from the altar of ascension was the only feature of the cult within view from outside the complex – and from the entrance the altar would have been the central focus.

The tabernacle as a return to Eden

Understanding that Sinai subsumes within its meaning the previous manifestations of the mountain of God, originally Eden's mount, we

[65] Ibid. 48.

can grasp more readily how the tabernacle as an architectural mountain of God was experienced as a mediated return to Eden. (This idea will be strengthened when we examine some of the tabernacle rituals in later chapters, especially the Day of Atonement ritual.) Here it is relevant to recall two points made when considering the creation and Eden accounts in the previous chapter on Genesis. First, there is a homology between the cosmos and the tabernacle. Throughout the Hebrew Bible the cosmos is described as a tabernacle pitched by God, often employing the architectural features of a house (cf. Pss 78:23, 69; 104; Gen. 7:11; Job 9:8; 26:11). We also considered the narrative parallels between the completion of creation (Gen. 1:31 – 2:3) and the tabernacle (Exod. 39 – 40), along with their Sabbath end and function, and the similar language utilized for each ('Wind of God', 'lamps', etc.). Now, given the similar homology between cosmic mountains and temples, the following threefold correspondence may be developed:

Creation	≈	**Mountain of God**	≈	**Tabernacle**
Heavens		Summit		Holy of holies
Earth		Midsection		Holy place
Seas		Base		Outer court

The tabernacle, then, is a cosmos in miniature, and an architectural mountain of God.

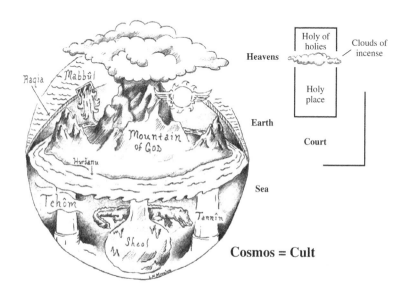

Cosmos = Cult

The second point to rehearse, as established in the previous chapter, is that the tabernacle also corresponds to Eden. Again, I do not intend to retrace the arguments in detail, but rather to recall the more obvious parallels briefly. After Adam and Eve's expulsion from the garden of Eden, YHWH installed cherubim to guard the entrance – specifically to bar access to the tree of life (Gen. 3:24). The only other place within the Pentateuch where one reads of the cherubim is in relation to the tabernacle (Exod. 36:8, 35) and particularly with reference to the holy of holies (Exod. 25:18–22; 26:1, 31; 37:7–9; Num. 7:89). Also, the tree of life in the garden, as with the abundant waters probably symbolizing God's life-giving Presence, appears to find correspondence in the stylized tree – the *měnôrâ* – of the tabernacle. Another parallel is in the terms used to describe the work of the priests within the tabernacle complex and that of Adam within the garden of Eden, 'to worship and guard/obey'. We also noted how both the garden of Eden and the tabernacle are oriented toward the east. Ultimately of course it was the divine Presence that had made Eden the mountain of God, calling forth all of its imagery of abundance, and this Presence is described similarly in relation to the tabernacle, using the verb *hithallēk* (Gen. 3:8; Lev. 26:12). As God's own dwelling, the tabernacle is also a royal palace, a feature suggested by the purple drapes. 'The sequence of metals,' as well, 'from bronze in the outer court, silver round the base of the tent, and pure gold covering the furniture inside the tent, indicated increasing nearness to the divine king.'[66] With reference to the threefold correspondence charted above, Eden should be related to the house of God (the tent structure itself within the courtyard), while the garden of – *within* – Eden should be related more particularly to the holy of holies and mountain summit. In sum, the tabernacle is a cosmos and its holy of holies the garden of Eden upon the mountain of God's clouded, heaven-accessing summit. As the high priest enters the tabernacle, therefore, he travels westward as an ascent of this cultic mountain.

As a divine gift, God's own abode in the midst of Israel must be seen as a revelation of the bosom of God himself, an expression of his deep desire to *be with* humanity. Indeed, the tabernacle has even been called 'a kind of *material "body" for God*',[67] a means by which he might dwell among his people. This purpose, the heart of God, no less of biblical theology, is found as the climax to both sections on

---

[66] Wenham 2003: 76.
[67] Fretheim 1991a: 315.

the *miškān* in Exodus 25 – 31 and 35 – 40. Near the end of the instructions for the tabernacle, YHWH declares:

> So I will consecrate the tabernacle of meeting and the altar. I will also consecrate both Aaron and his sons to minister to me as priests. I will dwell amidst the sons of Israel and I will be their God. They will know that I am YHWH their God, who brought them up out of the land of Egypt to dwell in their midst – I am YHWH their God. (Exod. 29:44–46)

Then, crowning the narrative of the construction of the tabernacle, we read, 'Then the cloud covered the tabernacle of meeting and the glory of YHWH filled the tabernacle' (Exod. 40:34).

The tabernacle as heart of the covenant

The divine desire to dwell with humanity, the goal of both creation and redemption, is the essence of covenant theology – its promissory root, its redemptive-historical vine and its eschatological fruit realized in the new heavens and earth. The covenant formula varies throughout Scripture according to contextual emphasis, and is delineated by Rendtorff as follows:

> Formula A: I will be your God
> Formula B: You shall be my people
> Formula C: I will be your God and you shall be my people.[68]

What however does it *mean* to have YHWH as one's God? What does it mean to be the people of YHWH? The theology and historical movement of the Bible manifests plainly that it is the divine purpose to plant humanity in his Presence that drives and defines these forms. Again, 'I will dwell amidst the sons of Israel *and (so) be their God*,' and 'they will know that I am YHWH *their God*', which is to say, 'that I brought them up out of the land of Egypt so that I may dwell in their midst' (Exod. 29:45–46). Wenham's comment on this passage is helpful:

> According to Exod. 29:43–45 God's real and visible presence in the tabernacle was at the heart of the covenant. 'There I will meet with the people of Israel, and it shall be sanctified by my glory. . . .

---

[68] Rendtorff 1998: 13.

And will dwell among the people of Israel, and will be their God.' After the covenant was broken by the manufacture of the golden calf Moses pleaded with God to renew his covenant: 'If thy presence will not go with me, do not carry us up from here.' (Exod. 33:15)[69]

Moreover, as he prophesies the glories of the new exodus, Ezekiel picks up the language and covenantal pattern of the old exodus, centring it upon God's dwelling (37:26): 'I will cut a covenant of peace with them, it will be an eternal ['ôlām] covenant with them: I will establish [ntn] and multiply them, and I will establish [ntn] my sanctuary in their midst eternally ['ôlām].' Here, by the parallel usage of 'set/establish', the covenant is defined as having the people and God's sanctuary established together. Moreover, the significance of the covenant's being 'eternal' is also defined precisely as – and, indeed, is dependent upon – having God's dwelling in the midst of his people 'eternally'. The next verse (v. 27), probably an allusion to Exodus 29:45, connects God's dwelling among his people to covenant formula C as its basis and reality: 'My tabernacle will be among them, and I will be their God and they will be my people.' As such, the next verse (v. 28) marks the tabernacle itself as a manifestation and visual demonstration of the covenant: 'The nations will know that I YHWH sanctify [mqdš] Israel when my sanctuary [mqdš] is in their midst eternally.' The goal of the new exodus is described in similar terms by Zechariah. In chapter 8 YHWH declares (v. 3), 'I will return to Zion, and dwell [škn] in the midst of Jerusalem . . . the Mountain of YHWH of hosts, the holy mountain.' Then, as he once brought Israel out of Egypt to himself at Sinai, he will now bring his people out of exile to himself in Zion (v. 8): 'I will bring them back, and they shall dwell [škn] in the midst of Jerusalem, and they will be my people and I will be their God in truth and in righteousness.' The parallelism between YHWH and Israel in these two verses describes each as returning to 'dwell [škn] in the midst of Jerusalem', so that their dwelling together, as in Ezekiel, leads into covenant formula C as its explanation (see also Jer. 32:37–41). John's Apocalypse, recording his visions of the new heaven and new earth centred upon New Jerusalem descending out of heaven from God, narrates the final realization of the covenant agenda (Rev. 21:3): 'And I heard a loud voice out of heaven saying, "Behold! The tabernacle [skēnē] of God is with humanity, and he will dwell [skēnōsei] with them,

[69] Wenham 1979: 17–18.

and they shall be his people – God himself will be with them and be their God!"' Here both formula B and A, respectively, are prefaced by a gloss about God's dwelling with his people:

He [God] will dwell with them	→	and they shall be his people
God himself will be with them	→	and be their God

Taken together we have, rather, formula C not only buttressed in a twofold manner with the interpolations on God's dwelling among his people, but also prefaced by it in such a way as to define the covenant's essence: *Behold! The tabernacle of God is with humanity*. Probably, the programmatic phrases concerning the dwelling of God among humanity ought to be considered a separate formula D, whether isolated or in combination with A, B or C – and as *that which defines the other formulas* by way of explanation and elaboration. Suffice it to say that the covenant structure driving redemptive history has one aim: for God's people to be planted on the mountain of God, so they may dwell in his house and gaze upon his beauty for ever. It is, moreover, precisely this aim that generates all of the dramatic tension in the biblical drama, that plummets one into the perplexing dilemma of how a holy God can abide among a sinful people bent upon rebellion, and that lifts up the soul into the mystery of a divine love that opens a way. In short, it is the covenantal purpose of God that necessitates the book of Leviticus and unfolds both the glory of his dwelling place and the rituals required amidst the impending danger suddenly posed to Israel by that Presence. Even the Decalogue must be understood ultimately as the foundational principles for life in the divine Presence;[70] indeed, as the two gifts from Sinai's summit, the Decalogue and the tabernacle are inseparable. Keeping in mind our previous reflection on the coordinate concepts of revelation and Presence, there is a sense where the Decalogue serves to re-present the knowledge of YHWH revealed through the exodus, for the sake of corresponding that knowledge with his tabernacling Presence. This

---

[70] Though every commandment finds its fullest exposition under this purpose and reality of life with God, this is especially manifest in the Sabbath command. Levenson (1984: 288) notes e.g. that the 'two institutions [Sabbath and tabernacle], each a memorial and, more than that, an actualization of the aboriginal acts, are woven together not in a purposeless, mindless redaction but in a profound and unitive theological statement. Sabbath and sanctuary partake of the same reality; they proceed, *pari passu*, from the same foundational event, to which they testify and even provide access. In a cryptic apodictic pronouncement in Leviticus, they appear twice as if they were formulaic pairs: "My Sabbaths you shall observe / And my Sanctuary you are to revere: I am YHWH" (Lev. 19:30; 26:2).'

point is evident in the preface to the Ten Commandments, which of course offers a summary of the exodus: 'I am YHWH your God who brought you up from the land of Egypt, from the house of bondage' (Exod. 20:2). The movement of redemptive history from the Mosaic covenant to the new covenant will therefore involve of necessity the mirrored movement of both God's law and his tabernacling Presence, from an outward to an inward reality – both through the outpouring of the Holy Spirit. Near the close of Leviticus, the hope of realizing the covenant's consummation is held out to Israel once more:

> I will establish [*ntn*] my tabernacle in your midst and
> > my soul will not abhor you.
> I will walk to and fro in your midst,
> > and I will be your God and you will be my people.
> > > (Lev. 26:11–12)

Conclusion

Rehearsing the thrust of this and the previous chapter's labour, the history of the cosmos as narrated in the book of Genesis is one of growing estrangement from the divine Presence, YHWH God dwelling for the most part in his heavenly abode. Now all of the parallels between the tabernacle and the cosmos, between the holy of holies and the garden of Eden, must be brought to bear upon the tabernacle narrative in reverse fashion – for *that* is the point. The height of the wonder that unfolds with the remarkable closing paragraph of the book of Exodus is that for the first time since the primeval flood – since the expulsion from the garden of YHWH – God, through the tabernacle, will dwell amidst humanity. The maker of heaven and earth, who had once walked among humanity in the mists of the olden days before the flood, returns once more – *now* – in history, through a covenant relationship with Israel mediated by Moses. When the glory of YHWH descends upon the tabernacle, therefore, a historic cataclysmic event takes place: the God of heaven in all his thunderous majesty has arrived – the Advent of YHWH – to dwell with his people *on earth*: Eden regained.

A crisis introduced

Tracing the narrative arc from Genesis 1 to Exodus 40, I have endeavoured to unfold the plotline between these bookends pertaining to life in the divine Presence. The closing verses of Exodus 40, nevertheless, are not the end of the drama, but rather the beginning. As high a culmination the building of the tabernacle epitomizes, so deep is the gravity of the problem that reality has now created – and so rich as well the theology this problem will draw out. To delineate this problem and its resolution in relation to the dramatic movement of Leviticus is the object of concern for the next chapter. Here we merely note that, contrary to all expectation fostered by the Exodus narrative thus far, Exodus 40:35 reads, 'Moses was *not able* to enter into the tent of meeting.' Given the tabernacle's role as cultic mountain of God, Moses' surprising inability to enter closes the book with a pointed question: *Who shall ascend the mountain of YHWH?*

Chapter Four

Approaching the house of God: the dramatic movement of Leviticus 1 – 10

Introduction

The tabernacle has a twofold theological meaning. It is first the dwelling of God, YHWH's home, and secondly the tabernacle is also *the way* to God's house, that is, the way to God himself, to engage with him in fellowship. Stated differently, the tabernacle is not only God's house, the place of his Presence, but is the ordained way of approaching the divine Presence – through the cultic system, which includes not only the tabernacle itself but the priesthood, rituals and sacrifices, and the liturgical calendar. This twofold meaning of the tabernacle may be brought out and clarified by its two primary designations: the tabernacle is a 'dwelling' (*miškān*, oft translated 'tabernacle') and a 'tent of meeting' (*'ōhel mô'ēd*) between God and Israel.[1] The distinction is significant; to have the former without the latter voids any hope of fellowship with God, for it cuts off the reconciliation and growth in holiness mediated through the cultus.

Combining the two functions of the tabernacle, the dramatic movement of the book of Leviticus is one of deepening intimacy with God, largely answering the question 'How can Israel *dwell* – have fellowship – with YHWH?' Within the question itself the whole theology of Israel is contained, the holy majesty of God as Creator, humanity's condition of sin and misery, the dire need for redemption

---

[1] Barrois (1980: 33–34), whose view reflects that of critical scholarship in general, presumes two distinct traditions joined by a redactor, but to posit alternative sources for alternative names (foundational as this is for source criticism) is unnecessary; both conceptions of the tabernacle's functions are inseparable, and careful exegesis readily demonstrates the logic of their usage.

and sanctification, and its reformulation becomes the central concern of Israelite worship:

> O YHWH, who may abide in your tabernacle?
> Who may dwell on your holy mountain?
>
> (Ps. 15:1)

The answer will involve sacrifice and obedience, purification and sanctification – both within the transforming Presence of YHWH, who alone is the efficient cause of reconciliation and holiness. As such, Leviticus is about reconciliation between God and humanity through the (temporary and symbolic) means of the tabernacle cultus. Israel's cult is the medium of engagement between YHWH and Israel, bridging the division between sacred and profane – in this sense, it *is* Jacob's ladder.[2] As the culmination of the Pentateuch's primary theme, YHWH has opened a way for humanity to dwell in his Presence. Leviticus serves to explain how that way works: the tabernacle system of worship. Beyond an explanation, Leviticus also probes the *nature* of the way into his Presence, so that the question '*How* can Israel dwell with YHWH?' is understood also to embrace the question of *to what extent*, a grappling with the degree to which Israel may enjoy intimacy – fellowship and union – with God.

With this goal in mind, and returning to the two designations for the tabernacle, we may understand the movement of Leviticus as the drama of how the dwelling of God, the *miškān*, becomes a tent of meeting, an *'ōhel mô'ēd*, for God's people. As will be developed below, the book of Exodus ends with God's dwelling in the midst of Israel. When the glory of YHWH fills the tabernacle (Exod. 40:34), it has indeed become a *miškān*, a dwelling of God – that much of the divine promise (Exod. 25:8; 29:45–46) has been fulfilled in a fitting climax to the book. The covenant relationship established at Sinai, however, calls for far more than the awe-inspiring reality of God's Presence on earth: its chief end is for Israel's engagement with God, humanity's fellowship with the Creator. The drama of Leviticus turns upon this hope, how the *abode* of God can possibly become the *meeting place* between YHWH and Israel.

---

[2] Similarly, Kapelrud (1965: 56) writes, 'in his dream at the cult place of Bethel Jacob dreamed that there was a ladder set up on the earth, and the top of it reached to heaven, and the angels of God were ascending and descending on it (Gen. 28:12). That ladder symbolizes the role of the cult in old Israel.'

As we approach the theme and movement of Leviticus, it is crucial to keep in mind two points. First, while the book is marked out as a separate unit on the macrostructural level, the material is nevertheless meant to be read within the context of its final form within the narrative drama of the Pentateuch. 'Leviticus', as Schwartz writes, 'is the direct continuation of what precedes it at the end of Exodus, and the narrative at the end of Leviticus continues directly into Numbers.'[3] It is this literary framework that enables one to grasp the theology of the various laws and institutions set within it.[4]

The second point derives from the first. While within the book of Exodus scholars widely acknowledge the parallels between the completion of the tabernacle and of creation, along with the tabernacle's rich Edenic imagery and symbolism, yet the significance of those parallels is rarely carried over into Leviticus itself, the very book that unfolds the workings and purpose of the tabernacle cultus.[5] Affirming the tabernacle as a cultic restoration of Eden's garden, the theology and narrative drama of Leviticus become apparent. Exodus 40 closes with a wonder: the garden of Eden planted, as it were, in the midst of Sinai's arid wilderness. Israel's mediator, however, is unable to enter through Eden's gates into the glory of the divine Presence (i.e. Moses is not able to enter the tent of meeting). Here Israel is brought face to face with the fundamental question that has perplexed human civilization across the ages and cultures of history: How does one get back inside, back to, the golden age – back to paradise with God? The legislation of Leviticus, then, is not merely offering tedious ritual instruction; rather, it is narrating a theological story. Leviticus begins with Israel, God's second firstborn son (or second Adam), standing outside the cherubim-guarded entry of Eden. If Moses the mediator may not enter, then how will it be possible for the tabernacle to become a tent of meeting between God and all Israel? With the opening verse, the God who dwells within begins to speak, revealing the way of entry, the way back to the tree of life. To understand Leviticus, then, is to understand the way of YHWH, the path of life.

---

[3] Schwartz 2003: 204.

[4] The divine speeches of Leviticus find their coherence within the wider narrative structure extending from creation to the death of Moses (Nihan 2007: 88–89).

[5] A. C. Leder is a notable exception; cf. Nihan 2007: 89–95.

The narrative drama from Leviticus 1 to 10

Broadly, the first ten chapters of Leviticus contain legislation for sacrifice (chs. 1–7) and the consecration of the priesthood (ch. 8), both delineated logically as prerequisites for the culminating inauguration of the cult, the initiation of the tabernacle system of worship (chs. 9–10). In probing how this section functions within the literary framework of the Pentateuch, however, the opening of Leviticus becomes especially important (1:1): 'And-he-called [*wayyiqrā'*] to Moses, and YHWH spoke to him from the tent of meeting, saying . . .'

The *wayyiqtol* form with which the book begins, and from which it derives its Hebrew title, sets the following legislation within a narrative context.[6] Thematically, the opening *wayyiqrā'* (And-he-called) sets the entire book of Leviticus within the development of God's redemptive dealings, as the following chart illustrates:[7]

YHWH God called to Adam [in the garden of Eden]	Genesis 3:9
God called to him [Moses] from within the bush	Exodus 3:4
YHWH called to him [Moses] from the mountain	Exodus 19:3
YHWH called to Moses from within the cloud	Exodus 24:16
YHWH called to Moses and spoke to him from the tent of meeting	Leviticus 1:1

More particularly for our purposes, the *wayyiqtol* links Leviticus to the narrative context of the *ending* of Exodus, as a continuation of it. We may, therefore, turn to the close of Exodus in order to position the legislation leading up to the inauguration of the tabernacle cultus (Lev. 1 – 10).

As I have already intimated, understanding the closing verses of Exodus 40 – both the height of the wonder they unfold as well as the depth of the problem they present – is essential for grasping the place and function of Leviticus within the story of the Pentateuch, especially so for the first ten chapters of Leviticus. The book of Exodus ends, after all, *without* humanity's actual re-entry into the divine Presence – the story cannot be complete. Rather, Exodus ends

---

[6] In fact, most of Leviticus comprises God's speeches from the tabernacle.

[7] See, similarly, Leder 2010: 120–124, who notes that Lev. 1:1's link to Gen. 3:9 contextualizes the former as addressing the failure of primal humanity to heed God's word. Also significant, this chart brings out the prominent and privileged role of Moses in God's plan of redemption. Notice (1) the trajectory of God's appearance, from the garden of Eden to the tent of meeting (drawing a parallel between the two), and (2) how God's appearance within the cloud serves as the transferring link between Mount Sinai and the tent of meeting (again, drawing a parallel between the two).

in such a way as to transform the entire narrative history of Genesis and Exodus into something of an introduction to the book of Leviticus, even an exposition of the theology of the tabernacle cultus. From a literary perspective a dramatic movement requires either the creating or the resolving of tension. I will argue here that Exodus 40:34–35 creates a tension that propels the content of Leviticus 1 – 10 toward its dramatic resolution.[8]

The instructions for the tabernacle, as we have already seen in the previous chapter, are bookended by God's promise to dwell (*škn*) among his people:

Let them make for me a sanctuary that I may dwell [*šākantî*] in their midst. (Exod. 25:8)

I will dwell [*šākantî*] amidst the sons of Israel and will be their God. And they shall know that I am YHWH their God who brought them up out of the land of Egypt in order to dwell [*lĕšākĕnî*] in their midst – I am YHWH their God. (Exod. 29:45–46)

The event narrated in Exodus 40:34 forms the dawning fulfilment of that promise, *the* narrative event with which the book closes: 'Then the cloud covered the tent of meeting, and the glory of YHWH filled the tabernacle.' This descent of YHWH God into his dwelling place amidst Israel marks a cataclysmic, historic event: for the first time since before the flood, the maker of heaven and earth has a dwelling among humanity. The first function of the tabernacle is manifest: it has become the dwelling (*miškān*) of God. The tension arises, however, in relation to the second function of the tabernacle, as a consequence of the first. Although YHWH God has taken up the tabernacle as his earthly abode, there is as yet no way opened for humanity to approach him safely – much less, to enjoy fellowship with him (which is the intent of the promises in Exod. 25:8 and 29:45–46). Indeed, any appreciation for the magnitude of the new reality created by God's Presence in the tabernacle must lead inevitably to a consideration of the extreme crisis suddenly generated by that reality. This crisis may be defined by the primary designations for the tabernacle: there is as yet no way for the dwelling (*miškān*) of God to become a

---

[8] Cf. Nihan 2007: 89–95. My own emphasis on the narrative role of the tabernacle as a 'tent of meeting' (as distinct from the perspective of it as a 'dwelling') in the following analysis is not found in Nihan's study (though this point may be seen as a development and even completion of his insight).

tent of meeting (*'ōhel mô'ēd*) with him. In Exodus 40:35 we read that Moses 'was not able to enter the tent of meeting' as a result of verse 34, the substance of which is repeated in verse 35b (so as to frame his inability to enter):

> 34: Then the cloud covered the tent of meeting, and the glory of YHWH filled the tabernacle.
> 35: And Moses was not able to enter the tent of meeting, because [*kî*] the cloud rested [*šākan*] above it, and the glory of YHWH filled the tabernacle.

Interestingly, Moses' barred entry is given specifically in relation to the tent of meeting, which is covered by the cloud; while the glory's infilling of the tabernacle is given in relation to the term 'dwelling'. When the glory of YHWH fills it, the tabernacle becomes a dwelling – a *miškān* – indeed. YHWH's Presence, however, is now given as *the* reason (*ki*) for Moses' inability to enter. The tent, in other words, has become a *miškān* but as yet it cannot *function* as a tent of meeting. The terminology appears quite precise. Moreover, Moses' barred entry is a shocking statement as all throughout the narrative of Exodus he alone *is able* to ascend into God's Presence within the clouded summit of Sinai.[9] If Moses is unable to enter the tabernacle, then nobody is able – and yet it is with this dire reality that Exodus closes. YHWH God has taken up his dwelling on earth, but no human being, no Israelite, not even Moses the mediator, is able to approach his abode. As a lead-in to the book of Leviticus, the question of the gate liturgy is, therefore, at the heart of the Pentateuch's theology. Leviticus narrates not only who may enter, but *how* that entrance into the divine Presence is made possible – how God's dwelling may become the place of appointed meeting between God and his people. The book of Exodus ends, therefore, with the climactic infilling of the tabernacle so that it has become, in accord with the promises given in Exodus 25:8 and 29:45, a *miškān* without question. What the book's ending does question, however, is how this tabernacle will come to function as an *'ōhel mô'ēd*. In this manner the tabernacle as divine dwelling (*miškān*) is the height of Exodus, while the tabernacle as meeting place with Israel (*'ōhel mô'ēd*) presents the height of Leviticus. As we will

---

[9] That Moses' inability to enter the tent was deemed a problematic text in Judaism is evident from the proposed solutions offered – see Rashi, Ibn Ezra, Ramban, Rashban and Chizkuni, Sforno, Abarbanel, the Kli Yakar and the Ohr HaChaim, the Malbim and the Netziv, *ad locum.*

see, the tent's function as meeting place will not find a resolution until Leviticus 23 – 25, so that the remarkable statement of the mediator's inability serves a dramatic function: to introduce the book of Leviticus.

To be sure, one might suggest that this matter (of Moses' inability to enter the tent of meeting) is simply what happens whenever a temple is consecrated. After all, we read about a similar situation with the consecration of Solomon's temple in 1 Kings 8:10–11: 'And it happened that when the priests came out of the holy place, the cloud filled the house of YHWH. The priests were not able to stand and minister in the presence of the cloud because the glory of YHWH filled the house of YHWH.' One might also suggest, further, that it is only the artificial division between the books of Exodus and Leviticus that creates this tension at the 'close' of Exodus. In other words, if one continues reading Exodus 40:35 into Leviticus 1:1 seamlessly, then there is no real tension established by the remark about Moses' inability to enter. It is true, in this regard, that the movement from Exodus 40:35 to Leviticus 1:1 follows a pattern similar to what we find earlier in the Exodus narrative. In Exodus 24:15–16, 18 we read:

> Then Moses ascended the mountain, and the cloud covered the mountain. The glory of YHWH dwelt upon Mount Sinai, and the cloud covered it six days. And he called to Moses on the seventh day from the midst of the cloud. . . . so Moses entered into the midst of the cloud and ascended the mountain . . .

Here, then, we find (1) the cloud covering the mountain as the glory of YHWH 'dwells' (*škn*) upon it, and (2) Moses not entering into the cloud until (3) God calls to him. The pattern of approaching the divine Presence on the mountain is thus transferred to its architectural embodiment, the tabernacle (Exod. 40:34–35 to Lev. 1:1):

1. The cloud covers the tent of meeting and YHWH's glory fills the tabernacle.
2. Moses is not able to enter.
3. God calls to Moses.

There is of course an element of truth in these interpretations and we must be careful to avoid false either/or arguments – these insights may rather feed into our suggested reading. Particularly within the narrative context of Exodus, however, neither of these insights deals satisfactorily with Moses' inability to enter the tabernacle. Indeed, because Moses' ability to enter God's Presence as mediator is a major theme of the Sinai narrative, we can see how the Exodus 24 reference above *avoids* any statement about his *not* being able to ascend the mountain or enter the cloud. There is no reason why the same circumvention could not have been employed with the completion of the tabernacle. The unexpected statement of Moses' inability to enter the tent of meeting in chapter 40 must therefore be pressed for its particular function within the narrative.[10] Moreover, the pattern of Moses' awaiting the call of God cannot in fact be read seamlessly from Exodus 40:35 to Leviticus 1:1, since this pattern is interrupted by the insertion of an idealized summary statement in Exodus 40:36–38, serving to round out Exodus as a literary unit. In other words, the book divisions are not artificial. More importantly, whereas we are told in Exodus 24:18 that Moses entered the cloud, we are *not* told in Leviticus 1:1 that he responded to God's call by entering the tabernacle. Finally, the comparison with 1 Kings is not an altogether complete one since, immediately following Solomon's prayer, the priests begin ministering in the temple as he and all Israel offer sacrifices (1 Kgs 8:62–64). In the tabernacle narrative, by contrast, the priests are not merely waiting for the intensity of YHWH's consecrating Presence to diminish (the priesthood itself has yet to be consecrated and installed, and that is part of the point). Rather, the inability to approach God's tent is presented as a problem that needs to be overcome by divinely revealed cultic legislation and a consecrated priesthood to carry out those sacrifices. The tension with which the book of Exodus closes, in other words, is not resolved with the opening verse of Leviticus, but that resolution is nevertheless initiated in Leviticus 1:1 and steadily builds through chapters 1–10. In Nihan's words:

> the book of Exodus closes with a tension that is not resolved. After the completion of Israel's sanctuary, the *'ohel mo'ed*, Moses is *not* allowed inside the tent specifically because the latter is filled with the divine presence, the *kebod Yhwh* (40:35). In other words, although he is present among his people as promised in 25:8 and 29:45, *Yahweh cannot be approached*, even by Moses, and the gap between God and man remains insuperable. After Ex 40, *Lev 1–10 recounts the* gradual *abolishment of this gap*.[11]

---

[10] E.g. one might reasonably conclude that the reality of the divine Presence mediated via the tabernacle is a real Presence not to be trifled with, no less intense – and perhaps more so – than the Sinai experience.

[11] Nihan 2007: 90; emphases original.

Accordingly, within the narrative of the Pentateuch, the remarkable statement of the mediator's inability to enter serves a dramatic function: it introduces the book of Leviticus, *to underscore the necessity of its revelation* of the cultic legislation and personnel ordained by God as *the way* by which Israel may approach YHWH. In other words, Leviticus recounts and theologizes how the *miškān* steadily became the *'ōhel mô'ēd*.

Certainly, from a fundamental understanding of the holiness of God, one may already appreciate the dilemma created by his nearness. Fellowship between God and humanity requires a bridge of communication between two spheres that must be kept absolutely separate: the sacred and the profane, the domain of ultimate life and the realm of death. Nihan is correct, therefore, to trace the drama out with these categories. He notes how, in accord with Aristotle's definition of a plot, the structure of Leviticus 1 – 9 recounts the denouement of the complication stated in Exodus 40:33–35: beginning with YHWH's speech to Moses in Leviticus 1:1, people (Aaron and his sons), then animals and cereals (the first offerings), are transferred from the realm of the profane to the realm of the holy, overcoming this division for the first time in Israel's history with Moses and Aaron's entrance into the tent of meeting in Leviticus 9.[12]

Returning to the point of tension (Moses' barred entry) and recalling the creation–tabernacle parallels, our understanding of the tabernacle as a microcosm becomes central for grasping the significance of what Exodus 40:34 portrays. Moses' completion of the tabernacle is likened to God's completion of the heavens and the earth – it is a new creation. When the Shekinah, the visible manifestation of God's immanent Presence, fills the tabernacle, therefore, the scene represents a new creation filled with the glory of God. As a microcosm, the cloud-covered tabernacle is also a manifestation of the divine will, a foretaste of the new heavens and earth, for 'surely, as I [YHWH] live, all the earth will be filled with the glory of YHWH' (Num. 14:21). Precisely here we are enabled to rearticulate the problem of God's holy and immanent Presence in terms of creation (or cultic) theology: *While the tabernacle represents a new creation filled with the glory of God, there is as yet no new Adam for this new creation.* The book of Leviticus begins to solve this problem, which will take its first nine chapters, as God begins to speak to Moses from the tabernacle, revealing to him the way of approach through (1) the legislation for

[12] Ibid. 90–91.

all of the various sacrifices, and (2) the consecration of the priesthood, especially that of Aaron as high priest. *Anointed to the office of high priest, Aaron will play the role of the new Adam of this new creation within the drama of the tabernacle system of worship.* As my language intimates, it may be helpful to consider the symbolic or representational nature of the tabernacle cultus along the lines of the dramatic plays of a theatre. Shakespeare's Globe Theatre represented a world, a cosmos, whose inhabitants were the actors performing a script. Similarly, Israel's priests represented original (and perhaps renewed) humanity in the cosmos of the tabernacle, and the scripted rituals they performed comprised a drama.[13] To a large extent that drama was most fully enacted on the Day of Atonement, but the rituals performed at the inauguration of the tabernacle cultus in Leviticus 9, summarized in verses 22–24, also comprised a theological drama, variously repeated in Israel's worship. Thus while Moses' new ability to enter the tent of meeting marks Leviticus 9 as the denouement to Exodus 40:35, there is also emphasis upon Aaron's new role as Adam by consecration. 'With the institution of the sacrificial cult, Aaron has gained a new dignity; like Moses, he has become the community's (cultic) *mediator*, a role that will be illustrated in particular in the ceremony of ch. 16.'[14] Demonstrating this new status in a marvellous way, after the inaugural ceremony YHWH begins addressing Aaron directly for the first time (see 10:8–10; 11:1) – a profound honour.

While the next section will examine the drama of the sacrificial system, here I merely note how Leviticus 9:22–24, the climax of chapters 1–10, functions as the resolution to the crisis described in Exodus 40. As stated previously, Moses' inability to enter the tent of meeting has implicit significance for Israel – if he cannot enter, then no one is able to do so. Keeping sight of the goal of the covenant, the tension created by Exodus 40:35 should be understood within the corporate context of YHWH's dwelling with Israel. Set apart as a royal priesthood, Israel's covenantal relationship embodies God's original purpose for humanity. The fundamental question as to *how* Israel will be enabled to draw near the descended YHWH remains. The narrative plot thus unfolds upon the divinely revealed sacrificial cult – this is the medium of communication, the way YHWH has opened for humanity to dwell in his Presence. Perhaps seldom

---

[13] For the priest as representing the redeemed man, see Cheung 1986.
[14] Nihan 2007: 95; emphasis original.

appreciated, *the inauguration of the sacrificial cult in Leviticus 9 establishes a new form of relationship between Yahweh and Israel*.[15] This resolution toward which the narrative has been building since Exodus 40:35 – if not since Genesis 3:24 – is found in Leviticus 9:22–24:

> Aaron lifted his hand toward the people and blessed them, then descended from offering the purification offering, the ascension offering and the peace offerings. Moses and Aaron entered the tent of meeting, and they came out and blessed the people. Then the glory of YHWH appeared [*wayyērā'*] to all the people, and fire came out from before YHWH and consumed the ascension offering and the fat upon the altar. When all the people saw it, they shouted and fell on their faces.

How difficult it is to underscore the wonder being narrated here, as two human beings are given entry into the house of God! Observe, first, how the entrance into the tent of meeting by Moses and Aaron follows the threefold set of divinely appointed sacrifices. Secondly, it is important to note the emphasis upon the corporate experience. The phrase 'the people' occurs four times, at the end of four clauses. The first two uses mark the people as the recipients of divine blessing, and the second two uses, where '*all* the people' occurs twice, focus on their experience of YHWH. While Moses and Aaron are given entrance into the divine abode, clearly the purpose of their doing so is for the sake of the people. Their entrance sanctions all the people to see the glory (*kābôd*) of YHWH. Once more this signals a development, a new stage, in the relationship between YHWH and Israel. While in Exodus 24:17 we read that the 'sight of the glory of YHWH was like a consuming fire on the summit of the mountain in the eyes of the sons of Israel', yet that experience was 'only at a distance and under the veil of the protecting "cloud"', as Nihan remarks, while the experience of Israel *through the sacrificial cult* is more akin to Moses' own in Exodus 24:16, with Leviticus 9:23 marking the first reference to a direct vision of the *kābôd* by the community.[16] As a result of approaching God according to his word (including the consecration of priests, etc.), the inaugural service of worship culminates not only in the blessing of God's people, but *in theophany*, focused upon the altar of ascension offering:

[15] Ibid. 91.
[16] Ibid. 92.

119

> Then the glory of YHWH appeared to all the people,
> and fire came out from before YHWH
> and consumed the ascension offering and the fat
>   upon the altar.
>
> (Lev. 9:23–24)

Earlier, Moses had directed Aaron's activity toward this end: 'for today YHWH will appear to you' (Lev. 9:4), declaring before the people, 'This is the word which YHWH commanded you to do, so that the glory of YHWH will appear to you' (Lev. 9:6). This theophany, therefore, forms the culmination of the narrative, the end for which the cultic legislation had been divinely revealed. God's appearance not only validates the mediation of the tabernacle cultus and the ritual legislation, but his life-giving Presence amidst Israel is their goal. This long-awaited experience, ushering Israel into a deepened relationship with YHWH God, is met with a fitting response by all the people: they shout and fall on their faces. G. A. Anderson underscores the weight of this moment as a fulfilment of YHWH's promise to dwell among Israel and be their God (Exod. 29:45), noting that 'when the daily sacrifices began (Exod. 29:38–42; Lev. 9) *the goal of all creation would be consummated. . . .* The moment of lighting the sacrificial pyre is the very apogee of the Torah.'[17]

With the inauguration of the sacrificial cultus, as YHWH's appearance sends forth the fire of his glory upon the altar of ascension offering, there is a sense whereby YHWH's Presence is maintained by that fire upon the altar regularly, as a cultic Presence – with the altar serving as his meeting place with Israel. The daily (*tāmîd*) service called for the priests to offer up a yearling lamb as an ascension offering, one at the break of day and another at the close of the day (Exod. 29:38–46).[18] In the instructions for this daily service God underscores its function as a meeting between himself and Israel:

---

[17] G. A. Anderson 2001: 22; emphasis original.

[18] The daily service included rituals within the holy place, coordinated with the morning and evening ascension offerings: when the lamps of the menorah would be tended in the morning and evening, sweet incense would also be burned on the altar of incense (Exod. 30:7–8). Probably, the smoke of the incense altar corresponded in some fashion to the pleasing aroma of the ascension offering on the outer altar, both utilizing fine incense. The curious use of the verbal root of ascent (*'ālâ*) to describe the lighting, burning or arranging of the lamps (cf. Exod. 30:8; Lev. 24:2; Num. 8:2–3) probably also serves to relate the menorah lamps to the ascension offering.

This will be a daily ascension offering throughout your generations at the door of the tent of meeting before the face of YHWH, where I will meet you there to speak with you there. There I will meet with the sons of Israel, and it shall be sanctified by my glory. . . . I will dwell among the sons of Israel and will be their God. And they shall know that I am YHWH their God, who brought them up out of the land of Egypt, that I may dwell among them. I am YHWH their God. (Exod. 29:42–46)

Finally, note once more how the designation 'tent of meeting' is used in 9:23 with narrative logic and purpose to describe human entry into God's dwelling, a clear reversal in Exodus 40:35 of Moses' inability to enter the 'tent of meeting' specifically. This is not to say that the dwelling has become the fully functional tent of meeting yet, only that an important step toward this goal has been accomplished.

By way of underscoring a relevant point before concluding, the following question is helpful: What is the difference between God's un-approachability in Exodus 40 and his being approached in Leviticus 9? The answer, fundamentally, is that the problem of the divine Presence amidst a sinful people required *divinely revealed* cultic legislation – in short, God is approached through sacrifice and an ordained priesthood to offer them.[19] To appreciate the need particularly for divine revelation – a point of emphasis throughout – in approaching God, it may be beneficial here to revisit Leviticus 1:1:

'**And he called** (*qr'*) *to Moses*, **YHWH spoke** (*dbr*) *to him* from the tent of meeting, **saying** (*'mr*) . . .'

The impasse with which the narrative of Exodus ended is here overcome by God's speaking. No fewer than three different terms for his speaking (marked in bold print) are woven throughout this verse – without question, the remedy to humanity's estrangement must be revealed by God (in theological terms there can be neither safe nor life-giving access to God apart from special revelation). Notice also the twofold emphasis upon the one to whom this revelation is given (marked with italics) – revelation requires a consecrated mediator. Finally, much of the drama involves the novelty of the place from which God is here said to speak: the tent of meeting (as underlined). Not only has the tabernacle, in a manner of speaking, duplicated

---

[19] See also Hilber 1996: 187.

God's heavenly abode, but steadily the goal for which God speaks will be realized – he will have fellowship with Israel. Through the divinely revealed cultic legislation, the fire that dwells in their midst does not consume Israel.

Understanding the sacrificial cultus (Lev. 1 – 8)

Having traced the narrative drama from Exodus 40 to Leviticus 9 – 10, we will now probe the significance of the cultic legislation set within the context of that movement. As already touched upon, entrance into God's house required sacrifices (chs. 1–7) and a consecrated priesthood to offer them (ch. 8),[20] both regulated by divine revelation. There is, moreover, a sabbatical principle at work, which underlies the entire book deeply, with seven divine speeches conveying the instructions for sacrifice (Lev. 1 – 7), and seven steps commanded for the consecration of the priesthood (Lev. 8),[21] a principle that continues into the final section of the book.

In the following two subsections we will consider the overall order of sacrifices, along with the elements comprising each type of sacrifice, with the aim of reconstructing both the theology and drama of the sacrificial system of worship.

The order and theology of sacrifice

Leviticus 1:1 – 6:7 covers laws for 'ascension' ('ōlâ), 'tribute' (minḥâ), 'peace' (šĕlāmîm), 'purification' (ḥaṭṭā't) and 'reparation' ('āšām) offerings, addressed to the laity, while the rest of chapters 6 and 7 addresses priestly duties in relation to these offerings. The first three offerings (ascension, tribute and peace) taken together and in order present an ideal worship scenario, each voluntary and dubbed an 'iššeh, a 'gift by fire', a sweet aroma to YHWH (Lev. 1:9, 17; 2:2; etc.).[22] The second two offerings (purification and reparation) were expiatory in nature, required as a remedy for particular sins. In practice, one or both of these expiatory sacrifices would precede the

---

[20] Lev. 8 will not be examined in detail, but worthy features include its sevenfold pattern, utilizing the formula 'as YHWH commanded' (vv. 4, 9, 13, 17, 21, 29, 36), and its marking a transition from Moses to Aaron and the priesthood, as is evident from the last occurrence of the formula (see G. A. Anderson 2011).

[21] Balentine 2002: 184.

[22] In the designation 'gift by fire' I have included the two possible derivations of the term, either 'fire' or 'gift'. Though 'gift' has a wider consensus, yet it is nevertheless the case that the appropriation of the 'gift' to YHWH is effected through its being burnt in the altar fire (cf. Kurtz 1998: 150–151).

triad of ascension, tribute and peace offerings. Probably, Leviticus begins with the ascension offering because, as we will return to consider, it may have represented the core, and perhaps even summation, of the entire sacrificial system. There is, in fact, wide variety when it comes to the order of sacrifices listed in different passages of the Old Testament, and some accounts focus on only one offering. Broadly, narratives delineating sacrifices may be subdivided into either an administrative or a procedural order, with the latter reflecting cultic practice.[23] Providing a window into Israel's liturgy, the procedural order is the key for understanding the theology of sacrifice. Leviticus 9 presents us with just such a procedural order of worship – all the more significant inasmuch as it narrates the tabernacle's inaugural service. As a narration of Israel's liturgy, the inaugural service is the culmination of the offerings outlined in the previous chapters, and may help us to understand their theological significance. The whole ceremony is summarized in verse 22: 'Aaron lifted up his hands to the people and blessed them; then he descended from performing the purification offering and the ascension offering and the peace offering.' The preceding narrative in verses 1–21 makes it clear that the tribute offering accompanied the burnt offering (v. 17), collapsed into it for the summary statement, and that this set of offerings took place prior (and prerequisite) to the high priest's blessing of the people. The liturgy, therefore, begins first with the purification (and/or reparation) offering, is followed by the ascension offering (accompanied by the tribute) and then concludes with the peace offering. While there is substantial overlap in the ritual for each of these sacrifices, it is possible nevertheless to isolate their primary significance. What is emphatic for the purification and reparation offerings is the blood manipulation, which underscores expiation, cleansing from sin. The ascension offering was unique in that the entire animal (apart from its skin), rather than just a portion of its meat and fat, was consumed on the altar's fire and transformed into a pleasing aroma, conveying the idea of full consecration. The peace offering was the only offering in which Israelite worshippers partook of the sacrificial meat, along with their family and friends, in a meal of communion

[23] Rainey 1970; B. A. Levine 1965. Rainey (486–487) refers to the order of Lev. 1:1 – 6:7 as didactic, and the order of sacrifices in 6:8 – 7:38 as administrative, as does Kleinig (2003: 35–36), who suggests the first section codifies the regulations for the offerings, while the second ranks them in order of holiness. Rigby's (1980) structural analysis of Israelite sacrifice fits naturally with the order of Leviticus' presentation: the ascension offering is foundational, creating life (with God); the peace offering sustains life (by communion with God); the expiatory offerings restore life.

and fellowship in the Presence of God. The overall logic of the order, then, is expiation, consecration and fellowship, or, in Kurtz's phraseology: justification, sanctification and union (*unio mystica*).[24]

Name of offering:	**Purification**	**Ascension**	**Peace**
Ritual emphasis:	Blood manipulation	Completely burnt up, transformed into smoke	Eating a meal
Meaning:	Expiation →	Consecration →	Fellowship

The goal for Israel is fellowship and communion with God. Because YHWH God is holy, the source of life, however, the requirement for communion with God is utter and complete consecration. Yet before consecration to God can become a possibility, Israel's sins must be dealt with, expiated – only a cleansed humanity may belong to YHWH. The way to God, then, is through a bloody knife and a burning altar. Sacrifice, in keeping with my proposed theme for the Pentateuch, is the way YHWH has opened for humanity to dwell in his Presence. In the next section we will consider this way in more detail.

The cultic journey: ascent into the presence of God

Worship through sacrifice was a journey into the Presence of God, a rite of passage in the sense that the journey involved a process of transformation and consecration.[25] The term 'offering' (*qorbān*) is built from the Hebrew root *qrb*, which means 'to draw near'.[26] Leviticus 1:2 uses this root four times, stating, 'When anyone brings-near [*yaqrîb*] an offering [*qorbān*] to YHWH, you shall bring-near [*taqrîbû*] your offering [*qorbankem*] . . .' While Exodus had closed with the inaccessibility of God in his dwelling, Leviticus opens with divine legislation aimed at allowing Israel to draw near, this approach through the sacrificial cultus. Beyond the other important aspects of sacrifice, then, one must not lose sight of the fundamental goal and reality of Israel's cultus, namely that this way has been opened for humanity to draw near to God. Indeed, the other aspects of sacrifice we will consider serve rather to explain *how* sacrifice enables one to draw near to God. Perhaps first and foremost among these is atonement, for 'the whole sacrificial system serves to atone and finds

---

[24] Kurtz 1998: 160–163.

[25] While the sacrifices of ordination in particular result in new status, all sacrifices in a more general sense involve the boundary crossing of a rite of passage (Leach 1985; Nelson 1993: 55–56).

[26] Similarly, the Hebrew verb *ngš* may be translated as 'to offer', but more precisely means 'to draw near'.

its meaning in the atoning function of sacrifice itself'.[27] Yet, once more, atonement is a *means* to an end, a means to Israel's fellowship and communion with YHWH God. This goal is discernible in the English term itself, 'at-one-ment', indicating reconciliation between God and humanity. While the precise understanding of the Hebrew verb *kipper*, typically translated 'atone', has been complicated by its possible roots and cognates,[28] its scriptural usage implies a twofold meaning: ransom from death and purification from pollution – both functions being involved by varying degrees in atonement, according to context.[29] As the Exodus story recounts, to be brought into the Presence of God at Mount Sinai, Israel had first to be ransomed from death as well as purified from the pollution (sin/uncleanness) of death's realm. Worship through the tabernacle cultus probably involved a re-experiencing of that cosmogonic pattern.

Keeping in mind the basic threefold theological movement of Israel's liturgy, we turn now to walk through the journey of worship according to the six major rites involved.[30]

The presentation rite

Within the context of God's covenant with Israel, including the exodus redemption, an Israelite's public worship at the tabernacle would begin by presenting for the officiating priest's inspection the animal to be sacrificed (Lev. 1:2–3, 10; etc.). This, of course, presumes the prior activity of choosing the domestic animal from one's flock or herd. In the next chapter we will consider cleanness/purity laws, but suffice it to say here that choosing an unblemished, clean animal from one's own flock or herd not only underscored the personal cost involved (for an animal that had been raised, fed and tended at one's own expense), but also facilitated the idea of vicarious substitution.[31] Leviticus

---

[27] Gese 1981: 103.

[28] An Arabic cognate, now generally rejected, suggests the meaning 'cover' or 'hide', an Akkadian and Aramaic root suggests 'wipe off', while the Hebrew noun *kōper*, which probably gave rise to the denominative piel form *kipper*, signifies 'ransom' (R. L. Harris 1961; Feder 2010). Scriptural usage typically signifies the outcome or effect ('purify', 'atone', 'expiate') rather than the manner ('wipe', 'rub', 'cover', etc.).

[29] See Sklar 2005.

[30] Cf. Abba 1977: 134–135; Berman 1995: 116–124; Low 2009. There are some rites, no doubt significant, such as removing the suet, incinerating animal parts outside the camp, etc., which we must bypass in this general treatment.

[31] Klawans (2009: 63–64) suggests that, along with the regular tending of the flock (Ps. 23:1–2; Isa. 40:11; Ezek. 34:15–16), this act of choosing an animal for sacrifice, and thereby exercising sovereignty over life and death, is to be seen as an act in imitation of God.

22:17–28 defines some of the characteristics that made an animal blemished, and thus unfit for sacrifice, among which include its being blind, broken or maimed; having any discharge or scabs; having a limb too long or short; or having testicles that are bruised, crushed or torn.

One should not overlook the pastoral opportunities at this point of presentation. A priest might notice, for example, the slightest indication of disease in the eye of an otherwise healthy-looking animal, but that would nevertheless render the animal dead within months. Was the worshipper seeking to approach God without cost, under the delusion that God could not search the heart? Or had the worshipper been careless in choosing the animal, so as to overlook its inevitable death (a scenario manifesting no less spiritual indolence)? Neither would it take much creativity to imagine the sorts of bribes a priest might entertain to turn a blind eye to unfit animals, nor the abuse a faithful priest might endure in being zealous for God's honour amidst a corrupt and wayward generation. In the post-exilic era, after the temple had been rebuilt, YHWH rebuked the priesthood for offering defiled food on his altar, and admonished the people for failing to reverence him in worship:

'When you offer [*ngš*] blind animals for sacrifice,
  is that not evil?
And when you offer [*ngš*] lame and sick animals,
  is that not evil?
Offer [*qrb*] such to your governor!
  – will he accept you or be favourable to you?'
  says YHWH of hosts.

(Mal. 1:7)

One's approach to God is the surest dissection and deepest revelation of the heart. More than this, the God-ordained approach to himself is the most proficient school for the heart. If Leviticus as the central book of the Pentateuch has anything to teach at all, it is that Israel's theology is hammered out upon the anvil of approaching God in worship.[32] Whether one surveys Israel's understanding of redemption or sanctification, atonement or eschatology, theology-proper or anthropology, every doctrine is oriented to and finds its fullness in humanity's entrance into the divine Presence.

[32] Milgrom (1991: 42) likewise remarks, 'Theology is what Leviticus is all about. It pervades every chapter and almost every verse. It is not expressed in pronouncements but embedded in rituals.'

Part of the theology of the presentation rite is found in the term translated 'without blemish' when applied to sacrificial animals, yet otherwise translated as 'blameless' when applied to human beings: *tāmîm*. An animal's being whole and sound, without blemish, served to symbolize the morally blameless life, a life of whole-hearted submission to the will of God. We have already noted how Noah was called both blameless and righteous (Gen. 6:9), the prerequisite attributes for approaching God's holy mountain (Ps. 15:2); and Abraham was called upon by God to walk before him and 'be blameless' (Gen. 17:1). Understanding the symbolism of the Hebrew cultus would be helped by maintaining a consistent translation of *tāmîm*, an Israelite bringing forward a blameless or whole-hearted substitute by which – or perhaps better, *through* which – to approach the living God.[33] As the holiness legislation in the second half of Leviticus will demonstrate, the *tāmîm* requirement for sacrificial animals in the Levitical approach to God presented the ethical requirement for Israel fully and finally to enjoy the life of communion and fellowship with YHWH held out by the covenant. Indeed, when summarizing the expectation for Israel in the land, and this particularly as opposed to the detestable customs of the Canaanites, Moses says, 'Blameless [*tāmîm*] you shall be before YHWH your God' (Deut. 18:13).

Every time an Israelite sought to draw near to God through sacrifice, the animal he presented was symbolically answering the question 'Who shall ascend the mountain of YHWH?' As God probes the heart for moral integrity, so the priest was to probe the animal substitute for blamelessness, evidenced symbolically by the lack of blemishes or defects. The importance of this cultic symbolism carries through for the entire journey into God's Presence, as will be evident in the next rite.

The hand-leaning rite
After the animal has been presented and has passed the priest's inspection, the worshipper lays his hand on the animal's head, pressing down upon it heavily (Lev. 1:4; 3:2, 8, 13; etc.). The Hebrew verb for this gesture, *sāmak* (from which this rite is dubbed *sĕmikâ*), denotes more than merely laying one's hand upon the animal, but rather means to press down on or lean on with heavy pressure. Leviticus 1:4 reads, 'Then he shall lean [*sāmak*] his hand on the head of the ascension offering, and it will be accepted on his behalf to make atonement for

[33] Trevaskis 2011: 196–207.

him.' The result of this gesture, therefore, is that the animal now stands as a vicarious substitute for the worshipper, with the specific end of making atonement on his behalf – that is, of presenting the Israelite before God, reconciled and accepted.

There have been a variety of suggestions regarding the significance of this hand-leaning rite. Some propose that it signified the transference of sin from the Israelite to the animal, while others believe that it was simply a way of indicating one's ownership of the animal. To address the latter suggestion more briefly, ownership of the animal is an element that deserves emphasis, yet it is a point that would already have been established during the presentation rite – there is no objection to understanding this element as informing the hand-leaning rite, but also no reason to limit the significance to ownership. Regarding the transference-of-sin model, it is true that this gesture finds a parallel in the symbolic transference of sin to the scapegoat on the Day of Atonement (Lev. 16:21). As Low points out, however, the *sĕmikâ* gesture is performed on other occasions as well, such as for the appointment of successors and the consecration of Levites (Num. 8:10; 27:18, 23; Deut. 34:9), which clearly involve no transfer of sin.[34] Moreover, there are also important differences between this rite and that of the Day of Atonement. With regard to the scapegoat, Aaron the high priest (1) lays *both* hands upon the goat, (2) *confesses* over it all the sins of Israel, and then (3) the goat is *led away* into the wilderness to bear away those sins symbolically. As far as we can discern, none of these acts takes place during the *sĕmikâ* rite for other offerings. More importantly, once Israel's sins are symbolically transferred to the scapegoat, it is *not* sent into God's Presence in the holy of holies, but rather away from his face, outside the camp of Israel and into the wilderness as a place of chaos and death.[35] This is because, once the transfer of sin has taken place, the scapegoat is no longer worthy to be brought into the divine Presence. (Much more apt, then, to compare the Israelite's animal with the goat that is actually sacrificed and whose blood is brought into contact with the atonement lid.) Other aspects of the sacrifice suggest that, on the contrary, the sacrificial animal is still regarded as blameless and holy after the hand-leaning gesture. Its flesh, for example, is still considered most

[34] Low 2009: 16.

[35] In relation to the atoning death of the cross, note that Jesus is led outside the gates of Jerusalem to suffer the wrath of God for his people's sins. It is as the resurrected righteous one that he afterwards enters the heavenly holy of holies. In this manner Jesus fulfils the pattern of both goats on the Day of Atonement.

holy and to be eaten in a holy place by a consecrated priest, while the carcass must be incinerated in a clean place, with the one who performs this task requiring no subsequent purification.[36] These objections considered, we can see that transferring one's sins to the animal would defeat the purpose of its being blameless, able to ascend into the heavenly abode of God as a pleasing aroma.

The discussion thus far enables us to focus on the drama of sacrificial worship. The blameless animal is not merely a substitute for the worshipper, but rather a *vicarious substitute*.[37] The Israelite's *sĕmikâ* gesture, leaning his hand heavily upon the animal's head, is 'a dramatic declaration that he is this animal, that it is taking his place in the ritual'.[38] Unable to ascend God's holy mountain of himself, the Israelite will ascend *through* his blameless substitute – the *sĕmikâ* rite establishes this necessary identification.

The slaughter rite

Upon identifying himself with the animal, declaring as it were, 'I am this animal,' the Israelite himself would then ritually slaughter (*šāḥaṭ*) the animal by cutting its throat (Lev. 1:5). The act thus demonstrates a willingness to die to oneself, along with an acknowledgment and submission to the judgment of God that 'the soul that sins shall surely die' (Ezek. 18:20). Once more it is not that the worshipper's sins have been transferred to the animal, making it worthy of death, but rather that the blameless one (with which the Israelite has identified himself) must die – life for life. The inescapable consequence of the worshipper's own sinfulness is death – there can be no atonement apart from death.[39] The identification established through the *sĕmikâ* rite ensures nevertheless that the worshipper is himself 'dying' through the animal's death, accepting its judgment and being delivered through it. In a sense that will not be fleshed out until the ascension of Christ, yet no less legitimate here: God must be approached through death. Returning to the cosmogonic paradigm of the exodus deliverance, we see that Israel was not merely delivered from the waters of death, but through them, dying to the old life-in-Egypt in the process and in preparation for life-with-God in the land of Canaan, even as Noah was delivered through the waters of death, dying to the old creation so as to live to the present one.

---

[36] Gane 2005: 57.
[37] Leach 1985: 145; Janowski 2008: 220–221; Wenham 1995: 77–80.
[38] Wenham 1995: 80.
[39] Bromiley 1949.

Slaughtering the animal represented 'an absolute self-surrender, a self-sacrifice, so entire that no self-regarding element is left in it, i.e., in a death unto self'.[40] How fitting this posture is in relation to the rest of the journey of worship, and to the meaning of the ascension offering in particular, will be evident shortly.

The blood-manipulation rite

The slaughtering technique of slitting the throat ensured the maximal drainage of blood from the animal's body. Precisely here, in collecting and manipulating the blood, the priest's labour would begin in earnest, dashing, tossing, scattering, sprinkling, daubing or pouring out the blood, depending on the particular ceremony involved. Typically, the blood would be applied to one of the sacred objects associated with the sanctuary and God's Presence, whether the altar of ascension (smeared upon its horns, dashed against its side, poured out on its base), the altar of incense within the holy place (smearing its horns), the veil partitioning off the holy of holies (dashed against it or in its direction on the floor) or the atonement lid of the ark within the holy of holies (sprinkled upon it). The significance of the blood rite for atonement cannot be overstated. Leviticus 17:11 states, 'For the soul [*nepeš*] of the flesh is in the blood, and I myself have given it to you upon the altar to make atonement for your souls [*napšōtêkem*]; for it is the blood that makes atonement for the soul [*nepeš*].' While the slaughter rite signifies death to self, it is critical to understand the blood rite in relation to life – indeed, to the worshipper's own life. As the verse above makes clear, the blood represents the 'soul' or life of the flesh. Through the blood manipulation, the soul of the worshipper, identified with the animal in the *sĕmikâ* rite, is being brought into contact with the divine.[41] The blood therefore symbolically conveys the offering up of one's (blameless) life to God. Probably, that blood served as a purging agent as well, a detergent, purifying the sacred objects from the pollution of the Israelite worshipper's sin, and expiating that sin from God's sight.[42] If we consider the twofold understanding of *kipper*, where 'atonement' includes both ransom from death and purification from pollution, we find that the logic to both is unfolded by blood's significance of life.

---

[40] Gayford 1953: 116. The approach to God through Christ in the new covenant requires no less: 'If anyone would come after me, let him deny himself and take up his cross, and follow me' (Matt. 16:24).

[41] Gese 1981: 106.

[42] Gane 2005.

Life ransoms from death, and life wipes away the stain of death. When Israel's uncleanness defiles the tabernacle and its furnishings, therefore, sprinkling, placing or smearing 'life' (blood) upon the horns of the altar of ascension offering, for example, serves to wipe away and obliterate the pollution of death. Understanding the correlation of life with holiness, this basic point, that life obliterates death, appears to be the rationale for why an unclean person must not have contact with the holy – lest such a one dies (Lev. 15:31).

For my purposes, I emphasize here the blood rite of the purification (and reparation) offering, inasmuch as blood manipulation is central to this offering in particular, and I am following the procedural order of sacrifices without repeating the overlapping rites of each offering. Leviticus 4 delineates the procedure for the purification offering. We find that when either the whole congregation sins collectively, or when the high priest, who represents the whole congregation as mediator, sins, then blood must be sprinkled seven times before the veil in the holy place, and put on the horns of the altar of incense in the holy place, with the rest poured out at the base of the altar in the courtyard. When, however, the transgressor is an individual leader or common Israelite, blood is not brought into the holy place but rather is put on the horns of the altar in the courtyard, with the rest poured out on its base. While blood was applied to sacred objects to purify them, the pouring out of blood at the base of the altar was probably done in order to reconsecrate (or sanctify) the altar.[43] It also appears evident that the more significant the sin in relation to the transgressor's status, the more deeply sin's pollution must be purged from the sanctuary. Gane helpfully distinguishes among three types of purification offerings, according to the locale where blood is applied: Outer Altar purification offerings, Outer Sanctum purification offerings and the Inner Sanctum purification offerings of the annual Day of Atonement, the first two kinds accomplishing purgation prerequisite to forgiveness.[44] Upon completion of the purification offering, we read the common refrain

> So shall the priest make atonement [*kipper*]
> on his behalf for his sin,
> in order that he may be forgiven [*nislah*].
> (Lev. 4:26; cf. vv. 20, 31, 35; 5:10; etc.)

[43] Gorman 1990: 81–89. Cf. Lev. 8:15.
[44] Gane 2005: 45–90.

The passive form of the verb for 'forgiveness' affirms that this gift is dispensed as a divine prerogative alone:

> As YHWH's representative, the priest effects purgation by per-forming the ritual, but he has no authority to forgive the [sinner]. This accords with the use of the verb s-l-ch, 'forgive,' elsewhere: it never has a human subject but always refers to pardon granted directly by God, a kind of forgiveness that only God can give.[45]

The goal of the purification offering, then, is expiation for the sake of forgiveness so that the Israelite may be able to proceed to the 'gift by fire' stages of the cultic journey into the Presence of God. Leviticus 17:11 makes clear that 'I myself have given it [the blood] to you upon the altar, to make atonement for your souls': the blood of atonement is a gift of God to humanity and not vice versa. 'Hebrew sacrifice is based upon what God does for man: it presupposes the divine initia-tive in redemption,'[46] which is to say, once more, that Israelite sacrifice must be understood within the context of Israel's covenant relation-ship with YHWH. In summary, this first stage in worship deals with expiation, the removal of sin so that the worshipper may be forgiven and accepted by God.[47] Ultimately, the goal of the blood rite (and the whole sacrificial process) is at-one-ment: reconciliation with God, union with him.[48]

The burning rite

After the animal's blood is manipulated, part or the whole of the animal is burned up and turned into smoke on the altar. The Hebrew verb used for this process of burning, *hiqṭîr*, is a technical term in Scripture for cultic burning, signifying the transformation of the sacrifice into smoke. Whereas *sārap* is used as the general word for burning to destroy in the common spheres of life, *hiqṭîr* refers to the burning that takes place specifically upon the altar fire. The word for incense, *qēṭōret*, shares the same root as *hiqṭîr*, highlight-ing the emphasis on transformation into smoke. In an insightful study, Eberhart notes that all five sacrifices (purification, reparation,

[45] Ibid. 51.
[46] Abba 1977: 133.
[47] While expiation is the emphasis of this first stage, it is important to understand that atonement includes the entire process, the six rites as a whole.
[48] '[T]he rite with blood expresses . . . either the establishment (in covenant-sacrifice) or the restoration (in the sacrifice of expiation) of the union of the chosen people with God' (Lyonnet and Sabourin 1970: 180).

ascension, tribute and peace offerings) share this similar ritual of burning sacrificial material on the altar, a ritual, he suggests, that not only serves to define each sacrifice as an 'offering' – that is, as an 'approach/drawing near' (*qorbān*) to God, but that consequently serves as the climactic rite in worship.[49] How, we might ask, does *hiqṭîr* cause an approach to God? The burning rite transforms the animal's flesh into a 'pleasing aroma' (*rēaḥ-nîḥōaḥ*), transporting it to God's heavenly abode as the smoke *ascends* from the altar.

Once again, though each of the main sacrifices involves a burning element, our focus will be on the ascension offering, the *hiqṭîr* rite par excellence, in which the whole animal was turned into smoke as a pleasing aroma. We will first consider the significant place of the ascension offering in the Bible, then go on to study three aspects of its meaning, which contribute to that significance. It would be difficult indeed to estimate the high significance attributed to the ascension offering in the Bible. This sacrifice is mentioned twice in the book of Genesis, for example, and both times involve momentous occasions. The first instance forms the resolution to the deluge narrative, when YHWH is appeased by the ascension offerings of Noah (Gen. 8:20–21). The second is the final episode in the life of Abraham, when YHWH calls for him to offer up Isaac, in whom the promise of blessing has been invested, as an ascension offering (Gen. 22:1–19). We find a similar case at the conclusion to the books of Samuel, wherein, as YHWH plagues Israel so that seventy thousand men die, the onslaught is finally ended when David offers up ascension offerings on the threshing floor that will later become the site of Solomon's temple (2 Sam. 24:24–25; 2 Chr. 3:1). Given these contexts, Geller's translation of *rēaḥ-nîḥōaḥ* as 'propitiating savor' is fully justified.[50] The climactic role of the ascension offering in each of these narratives underscores vividly its uniquely effective function of appeasing and pleasing YHWH God, a point well worth reflecting upon. Whether quelling the divine wrath after the destruction of the cosmos, or gesturing toward the manner in which the divine promises will be fulfilled through Abraham's seed, or in staying the sword of YHWH after it has slayed thousands of his own people, there is a profound significance attached to the ascension offering, the most costly of all

---

[49] Eberhart 2004. Sacrifices may be summarized in Scripture according to the burning rite. Cyrus' decree, e.g., which called upon the released exiles to rebuild the temple, declared one of the main purposes for doing so was that priests 'may offer sacrifices of pleasing aroma to the God of heaven' (Ezra 6:10).

[50] Geller 1992: 100.

the Levitical sacrifices. We have already had occasion to note, further-more, that the book of Leviticus begins dramatically with God's speech from the tent of meeting, revealing the way for Israel to enter his Presence. Receiving the position of prominence, the legislation for the ascension offering comprises the first divine speech from the newly consecrated tent of meeting. Perhaps the highest measure of the estimation accorded the ascension offering in Scripture may be seen in how the altar in the courtyard takes its name from this offering: it is called specifically 'the altar of the ascension offering' (*mizbaḥ hā'ōlâ*).[51] Even when it is the blood of the purification offering being manipulated, we nevertheless read that it is to be put on the horns of 'the altar of the ascension offering', while the rest of the blood is poured out at the base, again, of 'the altar of the ascension offering' (Lev. 4:25) – the animal having been slaughtered 'at the place where he would slaughter the ascension offering before YHWH' (4:24). Probably this designation for the altar derives from the *tāmîd* or 'daily' ascension offerings, by which the morning and twilight of each day was marked by an ascension offering of a yearling lamb, bookending the day – and all Israel – within the ascending smoke of its pleasing aroma (Exod. 29:38–42; Num. 28:1–8). All other offerings throughout the day were placed upon and constituted additions to the *tāmîd* ascension offering. Moreover, when other sacrifices offer merely a portion of the animal in the *hiqṭîr* rite so that it ascends as a pleasing aroma to God, these should be seen as token ascension offerings. Thus the altar, along with the people of God whose lives are oriented by it, receives its identity and unveils its primary *purpose* in the title 'the altar of the ascension offering'. Ultimately, the altar exists for Israel's cultic ascent to God. In other words, it is the ascension offering that fulfils the *telos* of the altar, and the *telos* of Israel is fulfilled through the altar.

Having considered its significant place in Scripture and in the life of Israel, let us look briefly at three noteworthy aspects of the ascension offering.

First, it is important to recall how the ascension offering's burning rite differed from that of the other offerings: the *whole* animal, not merely a part of it, underwent the burning. As discussed briefly already, the burning of the entire animal conveys the sense of utter consecration – a life yielded entirely to YHWH, in full submission to

---

[51] So labelled seven times in Exodus (30:28; 31:9; 35:16; 38:1; 40:6, 10, 29), seven times in Lev. 4 (vv. 7, 10, 18, 25 [twice], 30, 34), and four times in Chronicles (1 Chr. 6:34; 16:40; 21:26, 29; 2 Chr. 29:18).

his will and in complete obedience to his law. There is, then, an essential element of absolute surrender and total self-dedication involved in the ascension offering, which, however vicarious, must contribute to our understanding of its peculiar influence upon God. It is this gesture of utter consecration, including the fundamental element of atonement underlying it, that alone explains its profound worth in the divine estimation – indeed, as instituted by God himself. In the flood narrative the ascension offerings represented, at the foundation of the newly cleansed earth, an atoned humanity fully given over to YHWH. Similarly, in the Abraham narrative we see God drawing out the means by which his promise to bless the nations will be fulfilled, namely through a seed of Abraham who will be fully consecrated to the will of God. As with the flood narrative so in the account of David's census in 2 Samuel 24: YHWH's just wrath is appeased through ascension offerings, a powerful episode that, combined with Abraham's near-sacrifice of Isaac on Mount Moriah, formed a fitting foundation story to the Solomonic temple. Berman captures well how the Abraham story in particular relates to the ascension offering:

> The word *olah* means 'one that rises,' meaning, within a sacral context, toward God above. . . . God's call to Abraham dramatizes the sense of devotion that we are called upon to feel in our service of God. Our entire being – even our very lives – should be selflessly devoted to God. When an animal is offered as a *korban olah*, it functions in the same way as the ram that was offered in the place of Isaac. It symbolizes our willingness to devote our entire existence to the service of God.[52]

The second aspect is that of transformation. In the burning rite 'the offering is not destroyed but transformed, sublimated, etherealized, so that it can ascend in smoke to the heaven above, the dwelling-place of God'.[53] Through this ritual of transformation, the ascending smoke becomes a visible presentation of humanity's return to God.[54] Since the altar's fire is linked intimately with the glory of God's Presence (Lev. 9:24), this transformation should probably be understood theologically in terms of sanctification, what the New

---

[52] Berman 1995: 123.
[53] Hicks 1953: 13. See also Gayford 1953: 79; Milgrom 1991: 160–161; Low 2009: 27–29; Kurtz 1998: 154–155.
[54] Lyonnet and Sabourin 1970: 169.

Testament will reveal as the Holy Spirit's fire of purgation.[55] Whereas the previous aspect of consecration stemmed from the fact that the entire animal was placed upon the altar, this aspect of transformation is linked more particularly to the altar fire, and to the need for the material to be altered so as to become fitting for the Presence of God. To be sure, the offered-up animal had been blameless and clean. Nevertheless, as Kurtz remarks, the animal

> was not absolutely pure, in comparison, that is, with the holiness of God, to whom it was to be offered as a gift; but only relatively so, in comparison with the unclean, sinful man, whose sanctified self-surrender the surrender of the animal was intended to represent. Although in this relation it was pure and faultless, without sin or blemish, yet with the stamp of the earthly it bore the faults and imperfections of everything earthly. . . . And if anything earthly is to be offered to God, even though it be relatively the most holy and pure, it requires first of all to be purified, refined, and sanctified. The dross must be removed, and the true metal exhibited in its genuine refinement. And that was done by the purification and refinement effected by the fire.[56]

The fire's thoroughly sanctifying transformation of what was already clean and blameless speaks deeply concerning both the nature of God and the manner by which he may be approached. The theology is not far removed from the words that will resound later in Leviticus, 'Be holy for I, YHWH your God, am holy' (Lev. 19:2; cf. 11:44–45; 20:7).[57]

Thirdly, the *hiqṭîr* rite not only transforms the animal into an aroma pleasing to God, but also – by that transformation – causes it to ascend to his heavenly abode. Stated differently, the transformational burning was for the sake of *transferring* the animal, and the worshipper vicariously through it, from the ordinary earthly plane to the divine heavenly realm, to the ownership of

---

[55] Elsewhere I have examined how the altar may have represented the mountain of God in miniature (and thus a temple in miniature), with its fire more particularly representing God (Morales 2012b: 231–243).

[56] Kurtz 1998: 154.

[57] Penetrating beyond a surface-level understanding of Israel's cult, the unity between Lev. 1 – 16 and the so-called ethical dimensions of chs. 17–27 becomes apparent. See Trevaskis 2011.

God.[58] While God's Presence was thought of as residing in the holy of holies of the tabernacle, we recall that this inner sanctum was also understood to be the cultic counterpart to the heavens, so that perhaps, in a way never completely free of tension, both God's nearness and majestic transcendence were kept in view.[59] A similar idea of ascending to heaven *via the sacrificial fire* is found in a curious incident when the messenger of YHWH announces Samson's birth. After Manoah offered up an ascension offering, we read in Judges 13:20 that 'as the flame ascended heavenward from the altar, the messenger of YHWH ascended in the flame of the altar!' As the fundamental offering of Israel's cultus, the ascension offering takes its name from this aspect in particular, underscoring what one might dub the ascension theology at the heart of Israel's worship – and Israel's Pentateuch. If the question of the gate liturgy (*Who shall ascend the mountain of YHWH?*) indeed forms a theological under-current to the drama of the Pentateuch, it is significant that Leviticus itself opens with the ascension offering. Through the *hiqṭîr* rite, the Israelite ascends, ushered into YHWH's Presence with the clouds.[60]

It is this entrance into the heavenly abode that serves to explain the logic of the tribute offering (*minḥâ*), which follows the ascension offering and is typically placed atop it: one approaches the divine Majesty not only utterly purified but with a tribute. This vicarious entrance into God's Presence through the ascending smoke of pleasing aroma also explains the logic – and wonder – of the final rite.

The communion rite

Upon ascending into the heavenly abode of God, the Israelite enjoys the hospitality of the house of God. This aspect of the cultic journey is highlighted by the communion rite of the peace offering, whereby

[58] Nelson 1993: 59–62. He (60) writes that 'the altar fire was a pipeline into the other world, vaporizing a burnt offering, the fat of a communion sacrifice, some grain, or even wine (Num. 15:7), up to Yahweh's domain'. Similarly, Leach (1985: 144) states that the 'fire of the altar is the gateway to the other world, the channel through which offerings can be transmitted to God'.

[59] It may even be the case that the tent itself was in an analogical relationship with the altar, that it was thought of as the house of God (*miškān*) atop the mountain of God (altar), so that this 'ascent' may have been viewed in terms of approaching God's Presence within the *miškān*. One point of exploration would be the possible correspondence between the altar of ascension in the courtyard and the incense altar before the veil.

[60] Fletcher-Louis (1997: 176, 180–186) relates the entrance of the high priest into the holy of holies with the clouds of incense in Lev. 16 to the Son of Man's approach to God in Dan. 7. It is possible that the imagery of the ascension offering relates to both.

the Israelite was given a portion of the sacrificial meat to eat with his family and friends in the Presence of God. In the ANE, as is still the case in various cultures today, friendships were solidified and covenants sealed by a shared meal, and hospitality itself was a serious matter of honour. In the Bible God himself is seen to be the model for what it means to be a host. When brought into YHWH's house, through the way he has opened, the worshipper is treated as a son and prince. In Psalm 23:5, as we considered in the prologue to this book, David declares:

> You prepare a table before me in the sight of my enemies;
> You anoint my head with oil;
> My cup runs over.

Psalm 36 describes the joys of those who find shelter in God's house:

> They are amply sated by the abundance of your house,
> And you give them drink from the river of your delights ['dn].
> For with you is the fountain of life;
> In your light we see light.
>
> (Vv. 8–9)

Rehearsing once more a point made in the prologue, the word 'delights' derives from the same root for Eden. Together with the 'fountain of life', as well as the mention of the 'shadow of your wings' in verse 7 (alluding to the cherubim within the holy of holies), the house of God is portrayed with rich Edenic and temple imagery. Entering God's house is, indeed, much like entering through the gates of Eden; one is fully sated – a token of the satisfaction humanity may find in God himself. We find a similar view of God's house in Psalm 65:4:

> How happy is the man whom you choose [bḥr]
>   and cause to approach [qrb] you,
> That he may dwell [škn] in your courts.
> We shall be satisfied with the good things of your house,
>   your holy temple.

In many ways this happiness describes the history of Israel: chosen by God, caused to draw near to him through the tabernacle cultus, and given the hope of dwelling in his Presence within the house of God.

As the Hebrew designation implies, the meal portion of the peace offering (*šĕlāmîm*) was marked by a renewed sense of fellowship with God and his people, an occasion to celebrate with gratitude. Deuteronomy 12:7, anticipating the worship of YHWH at his designated place in the land, captures the atmosphere of the peace offering well: 'And there you shall eat in the Presence of YHWH your God, and you shall rejoice in all that your hands undertake, you and your households, in which YHWH your God has blessed you.' Since eating may sometimes be connected to rejuvenation, some suggest that YHWH's giving of the meat to the worshipper may also represent the restoration of life,[61] a point that appears to be supported by the psalms referenced above. With the life–death dichotomy underlying the theology of the cult it is probable that all sacrifices were thought of as accessing the life of YHWH. Along these lines it has been suggested that the ascension offering creates life, the peace offering sustains life, while the expiatory sacrifice regains life;[62] in each case the word 'life' may be replaced by 'fellowship with God'. What is worth underscoring lies in the mere suggestion of fellowship with God Almighty. That one may enter the Presence of the consuming fire at all, without immediate condemnation and destruction, is in itself a feat; but to do so not merely to render a tribute (fitting enough) but also to enjoy table fellowship with YHWH is the marvel of the cultus and of Israel's covenant. Indeed, it could be that the word 'sacrifice' (*zebaḥ*) itself, along with 'altar' (*mizbēaḥ*), which is derived from it, has as its central idea the covenantal feast,[63] with *zebaḥ* as 'meal' and *mizbēaḥ* as 'table'.[64] Just here one must be impressed afresh with the *reality* of the divine intent manifested in the creation account, namely that God created humanity for the sake of fellowship and communion. Once more we are brought to the heart of the covenant promise: YHWH aims to dwell among his people, who are brought into his Presence to enjoy him. The reality of the covenant, the central concept of Israel's religion,[65] is this fettering of YHWH and Israel together in a relationship that finds distinct expression in the *šĕlāmîm* feast. As mentioned earlier, this final rite may adequately be labelled 'union', for it, along with the theology of Leviticus as a whole, is

[61] Wenham 1979: 81; Low 2009: 29–30.
[62] Rigby 1980.
[63] Berman 1995: 131.
[64] Its Akkadian cognate *zibu* means 'meal', utilized in contexts of major celebrations and cultic feasts (B. A. Levine 2002: 127).
[65] Abba 1977: 130–132.

but the silhouette of the New Testament's pulsing heart: union with Christ.

The benediction

God's Presence is never neutral; the result of engaging him must ever be either blessing or judgment. Meeting with God through the way he has opened leads to benediction, while approaching YHWH through a manner he himself has not ordained results in judgment. One reason why this is so is because the unclean cannot come into contact with the holy without being destroyed. The way of YHWH, therefore, required the blood of atonement and the burning of consecration, that is, cleansing and sanctification, but all for this end of benediction. Cleansing is for the sake of sanctification; sanctification is for the sake of blessing, found in communion and fellowship with God. YHWH's way is, then, the way of blessing. Indeed, the divine condescension, seeking a lasting habitation among Israel, the establishment of a way of reconciliation and engagement, all this is for the purpose of blessing his people – the will and purposes of God, the paths and laws of God, are for the sake of this benediction. The glory of God *is* humanity's beatitude.

A few points come into focus as a result of the previous statement. First, while I have written of the various rites performed by priests and the laity, as well as humanity's journey into the Presence of God, nevertheless, it is appropriate ultimately to understand Levitical ritual, rather from the divine perspective, as the activity of God. It was, of course, God himself who revealed the cultic legislation to Moses, so that this way may only be understood as his doing. But, furthermore, every stage of the journey into his Presence is marked by his participation: YHWH God himself cleanses Israel through the rite of atonement; YHWH God himself consecrates Israel through the burning of the offerings; YHWH God himself blesses Israel through the upraised hands of the high priest. Secondly, in the inaugural ceremony that established the cultus we find the benediction linked closely with the theophany (Lev. 9:23). The ceremony itself had been for the sake of this 'appearing' of YHWH (9:4, 6), and then the appearance, the theophany, is associated with benediction. The substance of the benediction is found in Numbers 6:23–27, and should be understood as conveying not only spiritual but also creational well-being (vitality, health, bountiful crops, protection from enemies). In this Aaronic blessing, too, benediction is intimately correlated to theophany:

> YHWH shine the light of his face upon you
>   and be gracious to you;
> YHWH lift up his face upon you
>   and give you peace.

The theophany of the inaugural ceremony is ever afterward conveyed ritually through the fires of the altar, a connection buttressed through the link to benediction – the Aaronic benediction, given from before the altar at the conclusion of each daily service, manifested YHWH's face and gracious Presence verbally.[66]

Thirdly, YHWH had already promised this end of blessing for the cultic approach to himself, in the so-called law of the altar found in Exodus 20:24:

> An altar of earth you will make for me, and you will sacrifice on it your ascension offerings and your peace offerings, your sheep and your oxen. In every place where I cause the remembrance of my name I will come to you, and I will bless you.

The triad of altar, divine name and blessing come together when, from the altar of ascension offering, the priest recites the Aaronic benediction, which serves to place YHWH's name upon his people.

Conclusion

Having traced the overall logic of the sacrificial system in a general manner, we may see that Israelite worship was a cultic journey into YHWH's heavenly abode, a journey that entailed the blood of atonement and the fires of consecration, but one that also led to joyous communion and fellowship with God – beatitude. That is the way YHWH has opened for humanity to dwell in his Presence; that is the journey of redemptive history.

The daily service

With the inauguration of the tabernacle cultus in Leviticus 9 the daily morning and evening service begins. The legislation for the daily liturgy, centred on the ascension offering, is given in Exodus 29:38–46 and Numbers 28:1–8, and ran as follows:[67]

---

[66] Kleinig 2003: 218–220.
[67] Cf. ibid. 2003: 39.

1. *The rite of atonement*: the priest, having slain a yearling lamb, would splash the lamb's blood against the altar of ascension offering. YHWH, hereby, cleansed and pardoned his people, as preparatory for meeting with and blessing them.

2. *The rite of intercession*: after washing his hands and feet with water from the basin, the priest would enter the holy place to trim the lamps and to burn incense on the altar of incense. Whether or not the priest would pray during this rite, the texts do not say, yet the ritual act was itself an act of intercession, the high priest bearing the names of the twelve tribes on his shoulders and breastplate into the house of God. With this rite YHWH accepted his people, again as preparatory for meeting with and blessing them. On the Sabbath the priest's duties also included changing the bread of the Presence.

3. *The rite of ascension offering*: the priest, garments suffused by the incense cloud's fragrance, emerged from the holy place to lay the meat and various parts of the lamb upon the altar, along with a tribute offering of flour mixed with oil and a drink offering of wine. This public ascension offering, focused upon the *hiqṭîr* rite of transforming the animal into smoke, was offered up on behalf of Israel, morning and evening, and signified Israel's consecration to God. The offering would create a pillar of smoke, ascending to the heavenly abode of God as a soothing aroma. Through this rite YHWH communicated his approval and met with his people. On the Sabbath two lambs were used for each of the morning and evening services.

4. *The rite of benediction*: finally, the priest would stand before the altar, lift up his hands and bless the people, using the words of the Aaronic blessing to place YHWH's name upon them (Num. 6:22–27). Here, once more, YHWH's meeting with his people through the way he himself had ordained led to Israel's blessing and beatitude.

The inauguration of the daily service marks a significant development in how the dwelling of God becomes the tent of meeting.[68] Indeed, this was the stated goal of its legislation:

---

[68] I have John Kleinig to thank for helping me to see more clearly the important role of the daily service in relation to my thematic approach to Leviticus.

This will be a daily ascension offering throughout your generations at the door of the tent of meeting before YHWH, where I will meet with you to speak with you. And there I will meet with the sons of Israel, and it will be sanctified by my glory. (Exod. 29:42–43)

After YHWH had appeared in glory for the inaugural service, his fiery Presence unveiled by the cloud, that theophany was probably conveyed thereafter *ritually*, through the column of smoke created by the ascension offering. Daily, morning and evening, the way was opened for Israelites to meet with YHWH their God and to receive his blessing. Stage one in the *miškān*'s becoming an *'ōhel mô'ēd* had been reached: YHWH met with Israel daily at the altar.

Another crisis introduced

As with Exodus 40, the culminating narrative of Leviticus 9 yields a new experience of the glory of God. Also comparable to the literary strategy of Exodus 40, however, the following verses (10:1–3) introduce a crisis that will propel the drama of the next section, chapters 11–16. The newly consecrated cosmos, the tabernacle, meant to be the cultic stand-in for the true cosmos polluted by sin, will be defiled by Nadab and Abihu's disobedience, and then be polluted by their corpses. How this crisis provides the context for the book's next movement is the subject of the next chapter.

Chapter Five

Cleansing the house of God: the dramatic movement of Leviticus 11 – 16

Introduction

While chapter 9 of Leviticus closes with the high point of Israel's direct vision of God's glory, chapter 10 immediately reminds us – by the sudden and sobering deaths of Nadab and Abihu – that this new access has also opened a new threat: the cultic bridge of communication between the sacred and the profane also entails the possibility of muddling the division between them. Because this new danger creates the tension that propels the drama from chapters 11 to 16, Leviticus 10:1–3 will be addressed in the following section.

The narrative drama from Leviticus 11 to 16

Leviticus 10:1–3 reads:

> Then Nadab and Abihu, the sons of Aaron, each took his censer and set fire in it, put upon it incense, and drew near before YHWH strange fire, which he had not commanded them. So fire went out from before YHWH and devoured them, and they died before YHWH. And Moses said to Aaron, 'This is what YHWH spoke, saying:
>
>> "By those who draw near me I must be sanctified;
>> and before all the people I must be glorified."'
>
> So Aaron was silent.

Appropriately, Nihan refers to this episode as 'the reversed image to the glorious ceremony of ch. 9',[1] offering the following lines of

---

[1] Nihan 2007: 92–93.

reasoning: Nadab and Abihu's action is described by the narrator as *not* having been commanded by YHWH, deliberately breaking with the pattern of Leviticus 8 – 9, where each ritual sequence concludes with the phrase 'as YHWH commanded' (8:4, 9, 13, 17, 21, 29, 36; 9:7, 10). Secondly, YHWH 'consumes' (*'kl*) Nadab and Abihu as he had formerly consumed the sacrifices in 9:24. A third correspondence is with YHWH's not being 'glorified' (*kbd*) by Nadab and Abihu's unauthorized offering, whereas, after Moses and Aaron's divinely ordained offerings, his glory had appeared before the whole community.[2] Here it is helpful to reflect once more on how the priestly service, advancing the goal of the covenant itself, is for the sake of *corporate* Israel: Nadab and Abihu are consumed because YHWH must be glorified 'before all the people'. In this sense we may say that *both* ceremonies in Leviticus 9 and 10 concluded the same, with God being glorified before the people. Finally, Aaron's silence following the death of his sons contrasts with the community's joyful shout at the conclusion of the tabernacle's inaugural ceremony. Not only are both episodes ironically paralleled, but both also take place on the same day (cf. 10:19), and both 'function together as a complex symbol illustrating the implications of the new relationship with God initiated by the inauguration of the sacrificial cult'.[3] Stated differently, Leviticus 9 and 10 together portray both the blessedness of Israel's access to YHWH, as well as the depth of danger that access has simultaneously created for Israel. Both episodes are necessary to appreciate the implications for Israel's newfound nearness to the divine Presence; either one without the other would preclude emphasis on what is central in regard to Israel's cultus, namely that the *only* way of approaching YHWH is the way he himself has opened by revelation to Moses.[4]

While it is difficult to understand the precise form of Nadab and Abihu's transgression, the nature of their sin – and the main point of emphasis – was in their doing that which YHWH 'had not commanded

[2] Nihan (ibid. 92–93) posits the following chiastic structure:
    Lev. 9:23b: and the glory of Yhwh appeared to all the people
      Lev. 9:24a: fire went out from before Yhwh and consumed upon the altar . . .
      Lev. 10:2a: fire went out from before Yhwh and consumed them
    Lev. 10:3aβ: from before all the people I will be glorified
[3] Ibid. 93.
[4] The two outcomes for the people, life in God's Presence vs. being consumed (death) by God's Presence, may be aligned with the destiny of the two goats on the Day of Atonement, ultimately forecasting the final day of judgment when God will be glorified (both in casting the wicked out of his Presence and in ushering redeemed humanity into his Presence).

them'. As already rehearsed, while YHWH has opened a way for humanity to enter his Presence, the only way to avoid danger is to enter through obedience to his torah, walking *positively* in that way. That said, various indications in the text have led scholars to offer suggestions for the specific sin of Aaron's sons.[5] Inasmuch as YHWH commands Aaron afterward that he and his sons should abstain from intoxicating drink when they enter the tent of meeting 'lest you die' (10:8–11), it could be that his sons were performing their duties while drunk.[6] Others suggest that 'strange fire' probably refers to fire not taken from the altar of ascension offering, which had been kindled directly from YHWH's glory (so as to represent his consuming the sacrifices). A combination of these suggestions is also possible, of course: because Nadab and Abihu were drunk, they were negligent with their duties, appropriating fire from the wrong source. Ultimately, the brothers manifested a lack of the fear of YHWH, which led to their negligence (whatever the form of their disobedience). Within the broader context of the structure of Leviticus, moreover, it appears quite plausible that Nadab and Abihu had attempted to penetrate the Presence of God within the holy of holies. Four lines of reasoning may be offered. First, the description of their action parallels that of Aaron on the Day of Atonement, specifically in their use of censers (Lev. 10:1; 16:12–13). Secondly, Leviticus 16 prefaces the Day of Atonement legislation with a rehearsal of the deaths of Nadab and Abihu, drawing a clear point of application: Aaron himself is not to presume to enter at just any time or in any manner within the veil, lest he die (in like manner to his sons).[7] Apparently his sons were guilty of this very presumption, and Leviticus 16 offers, *for the first time*, torah for the how and when and who of entering the holy of holies. Thirdly, the description of Nadab and Abihu's action in Leviticus 16:1 – namely 'when they drew near [*qorbān*] before YHWH' – fits well with such an interpretation, especially so within the context of chapter 16's ceremony. The fourth line of reasoning pertains to the narrative development of the book: Leviticus 10 creates a new tension that will be resolved by Leviticus 11 – 16, culminating in the Day of Atonement. We turn now to consider this development.

---

[5] For a summary of the history of interpretation, see Milgrom 1991: 633–635; Bibb 2001: 83–87.

[6] Within the context of the tabernacle's being a restored garden of Eden, one may suggest a parallel with the incident of Noah and Ham (Gen. 9:18–25).

[7] B. Schwartz's (2001) attempt to strip the reference to Nadab and Abihu in Lev. 16:1 of all but chronological significance is unconvincing.

The narrative tension created by Leviticus 10 is twofold. First, the sanctuary needs to be restored, cleansed from the corpse pollution resulting from the deaths of Nadab and Abihu.[8] Corpse pollution is the most serious pollution in the cultic system, as well as the most contagious, referred to as the 'father of the fathers of uncleanness' in later rabbinic tradition.[9] Nevertheless, until Leviticus 16 there had been no mention of cleansing the tabernacle from the defilement incurred by the deaths of the priests, whose bodies were removed 'from before the sanctuary' (*mē'ēt pĕnê-haqqōdeš*; Lev. 10:4).[10] In his role as an Adam figure within the garden of Eden Aaron is not allowed even to mourn the deaths of his sons – for anything that smacks of death, or that is contrary to being in the Presence of the source of life, is forbidden. How tragic, then, the almost immediate polluting of the sanctuary by the most serious and contagious defilement possible, death itself. Despite the intervening legislation of chapters 11–15, the urgency of this situation is not lost, since the opening verse of Leviticus 16 immediately brings the reader back to the events of Leviticus 10 – the Day of Atonement ritual is revealed on *the same day* as the deaths of Nadab and Abihu, so that in point of fact the remedy for this grave defilement is revealed immediately. The legislation of Leviticus 11 – 15, therefore, is inserted between chapters 10 and 16, breaking up the narrative for strategic reasons – precisely to add urgency and relevance for the laws of clean and unclean. Because the Day of Atonement ritual became the annual cleansing not only of Israel, but especially of the sanctuary, Gorman rightly labels the ceremony of Leviticus 16 as a ritual of restoration (or refounding, as distinct from a ritual of founding), serving to re-establish or renew the original founded order of creation, community and cult.[11] The Day of Atonement, then, cleanses the tabernacle cultus so as to restore it to the original pristine state of its inauguration in Leviticus 9. From the perspective of the narrative of Leviticus, which connects chapters 10 and 16, it appears that *the original occasion for the revelation of*

---

[8] Kiuchi 1987: 66–85; Milgrom 1991: 635–640; Gorman 1997: 64–65, 94; Jürgens 2001: 299–302; Nihan 2007: 100–101.

[9] Wright 1992a: 730.

[10] Similarly, G. A. Anderson (2001: 24–25, 23) states, 'But no sooner has creation come to closure than its very centerpiece, the tabernacle, was violated. In consequence of this, the Day of Atonement served to set creation aright. . . . It is not until Leviticus 16, the first rite of atonement, that these priestly sins are rectified. Israel's first public penitential moment is motivated by the errors of her cultic beginnings.'

[11] Gorman 1990: 61–102.

this ceremony to Moses was, specifically, to cleanse the sanctuary from the corpse pollution caused by the deaths of Nadab and Abihu.[12] This is not to say, of course, that the resolution of the Nadab and Abihu episode is the *ultimate* purpose of Leviticus 16, as the Day of Atonement is probably already foreshadowed in the description of the atonement lid (*kappōret*) in Exodus 25:17–22, and the theology of this ceremony comprehends the whole of the Pentateuch and the rest of the Scriptures. Rather, Leviticus 10 functions literarily, as noted above, to provide the original *occasion* that led to Leviticus 16, serving to underscore and explore its nature.

The second aspect of tension caused by the incident in Leviticus 10:1–3 relates to the question of how near one may approach the divine Presence. Had Nadab and Abihu attempted to enter within the veil? I have already mentioned various parallels between their actions in Leviticus 10 and the actions of Aaron the high priest in Leviticus 16, making this suggestion plausible. In both narratives priests present an offering of incense (*qĕṭōret*) on a portable censer pan (*maḥtâ*), yet with opposite results. By Aaron's successful entry into the holy of holies, and because incense was often associated with divine presence in antiquity, it appears probable that Nadab and Abihu were indeed attempting to penetrate deeper into God's Presence. This interpretation finds support from the summary description of their attempt, given in Leviticus 16:1 as 'when they drew near before YHWH',[13] given, once more, as a *preface* to the Day of Atonement legislation. Beyond the need to cleanse the sanctuary of profanation through the ceremony revealed in Leviticus 16, the deaths of Aaron's sons also serve to stress the *limits* of the sacrificial cult as it pertains to the mediation it establishes between God and Israel.[14] The cult bridges but does not abolish the distance between God and humanity; being a form of indirect communication, it raises the question of whether or not a direct, personal encounter with God is possible – an issue underscored by Nadab and Abihu's failed attempt.[15] With the instructions for the high priest's annual entrance into the inner sanctum in Leviticus 16, where he encounters God, the tension finds a preliminary resolution.

[12] Nihan 2007: 100.

[13] Ibid. 101–102.

[14] An aspect of this limitation relates to validating the high priest's exclusive privilege to enter the holy of holies with the censer incense, a point similarly found in the narratives of Num. 16 – 17, the theological heart of the book of Numbers.

[15] Nihan 2007: 103–104.

After YHWH appears to the community before the sanctuary, therefore, the question arises as to the limitations on Israel's approach to him. Is there any possibility of a direct, personal encounter with God beyond the second veil of his earthly dwelling? The failed attempt by Nadab and Abihu highlights the limits of Israel's approach to YHWH, while also generating a new crisis, the (recurrent) need to cleanse and restore the tabernacle cultus from defilement. Between the bookends of the crisis provoked in Leviticus 10 and its resolution in Leviticus 16, chapters 11–15 provide legislation for ritual purity, for distinguishing between clean and unclean. 'The account of the death of Aaron's sons in Leviticus 10 thus functions as a highly sophisticated narrative pivot, uniting Leviticus 1–9 and 11–16 and making possible the revelation of a second set of *toroth*.'[16] The bookends of Leviticus 10 and 16, then, provide the interpretative context and dramatic movement for the laws set within. After Leviticus 10:1–7 demonstrates the threat aspect of the new relationship with God initiated by the inauguration of the sacrificial cult, the response of Leviticus 10:8–11 becomes programmatic for the rest of the book of Leviticus:

> Then YHWH spoke to Aaron, saying: 'Wine and strong drink you are not to drink, you, nor your sons with you, when you enter into the tent of meeting, lest you die. It shall be an everlasting statute throughout your generations, that you may distinguish [separate, *habdîl*] between holy and profane, and between unclean and clean, and that you may teach the sons of Israel all the statutes which YHWH has spoken to them by the hand of Moses.'

The solemnity and significance of this passage is underscored in various ways, both by its occasion and by the substance of the speech. It marks the first time YHWH speaks to Aaron directly and the only time he speaks to Aaron alone. Within this context, as C. R. Smith has pointed out, verse 10's purpose clause sets the agenda for the remaining two sections of Leviticus: distinguishing between holy and profane becomes the general subject matter for chapters 17–27, and distinguishing between unclean and clean becomes the subject matter for chapters 11–15, culminating in ch. 16's legislation, which the high priest 'shall do for the tent of meeting which remains among

16 Ibid. 104.

them in the midst of their uncleanness' (v. 16).[17] While the order of the book's content is inverted (addressing first the separation of unclean and clean in chapters 11–15, and then that of holy and profane in chapters 17–27), here it is delineated logically: only after one has distinguished between what is holy and what is profane can one separate further within the category of profane between what is clean and what is unclean. The order of the book's progress, however, appears to be determined by Israel's historical experience, which entailed the gradual movement into God's Presence, proceeding from the status of unclean to clean (within the category of profane or common) and then from clean (profane) to holy.

To summarize the first two movements of the book, this 'analysis suggests that Leviticus 1–10 and 11–16 are organized around the general theme of *the mediation of the divine Presence in Israel in and through the sacrificial cult*; in this broad scheme, the theophany of Leviticus 16, after that of Leviticus 9–10, corresponds to a further stage in a pattern of *gradual intimacy* between Yahweh and Israel'.[18] Just as the book's first section culminated with a theophany, the appearance of YHWH before the people at the altar of ascension offering (9:23–24), so the second section culminates in a theophany, as YHWH appears before the high priest in the cloud above the atonement lid (16:2): 'lest he die, for in the cloud I will appear [*'ērā'eh*] above the atonement lid'. While the book's first movement culminated in a theophany upon the altar of the outer court, the second movement culminates in a theophany upon the atonement lid of the holiest place. Stage two in the *miškān*'s becoming an *'ōhel mô'ēd* has been reached: YHWH meets with Israel's high priest within the holy of holies. The Day of Atonement legislation, moreover, provides for the annual cleansing of God's dwelling from the people's uncleanness – a cleansing necessary for the dwelling to function regularly as the meeting place between YHWH and Israel.

Summary

It may be helpful here to rehearse and restate briefly the first two movements of the book, particularly with reference to the theme of dwelling with God. The following chart presents the dramatic movements of Leviticus thus far, beginning with Exodus, in summary fashion:

[17] C. R. Smith 1996: 24.
[18] Nihan 2007: 106; emphases original.

(1) Exod. 25:8; 29:45 → Exod. 40:34
promise: God's dwelling among Israel/**fulfilment:** divine glory fills God's house
    (2) Exod. 40:35 → Lev. 9:23
    *crisis: no entry into God's house/**resolution:** entry into God's house*
    (YHWH appears)
       (3) Lev. 10:1–3 → Lev. 16
       *crisis: no entry within veil, pollution/**resolution:** entry within veil, cleansing*
       (YHWH appears)

After God indwells the tabernacle in Exodus 40:34, the tension of Moses' inability (and therefore that of anyone else) to enter God's house in the following verse then leads to contextualizing the entire first section of Leviticus (chs. 1–10) under the drama of *how* one may approach God in his house, a question answered dramatically as God begins to speak from the tent of meeting, revealing the sacrificial legislation (chs. 1–7) and directing the consecration of the priesthood (ch. 8), all of which culminates in the inauguration ceremony where Moses and Aaron are allowed entry into the tent of meeting and, when they emerge, God's glory appears outside to all the people. The question then turns on *how near* one may approach God in his house – what is the nature of Israel's relationship with YHWH established by the Mosaic covenant? Lacking the fear of YHWH, Nadab and Abihu attempt to draw nearer to him, perhaps even beyond the second veil, through a way not commanded. Their consequent death serves a twofold function: first, their deaths have polluted the tabernacle (the new creation / garden of Eden), in turn uncovering the need for a way to cleanse and restore the house of God and its cultus regularly; secondly, their failure underscores the boundaries – the limits – of humanity's approach to YHWH through the revealed sacrificial cultus. This twofold tension functions to contextualize the second part of Leviticus (chs. 11–16) under the drama of *how near one may approach God in his house*, along with the further question of *how God's house may be cleansed regularly from inevitable defilement*, both of which find their resolution in the Day of Atonement ceremony – and both of which also speak to the nature of the 'tent of meeting'. We may now consider the chart once more, with the addition of the contextualized material inserted between crisis and resolution, that material functioning as *a means of fulfilment or resolution*:[19]

---

[19] The crises, both of Exod. 40:35 and of Lev. 10:1–3, revolve around the use of the negative particle *lōʾ*, Moses' *not* being able to enter and Aaron's sons approaching the divine Presence in a way *not* prescribed. The legislation then functions to overcome

(1) Exod. 25:8; 29:45 → [tabernacle (25 – 31; 35 – 40)] Exod. 40:34
  (2) Exod. 40:35 → [sacrifices (Lev. 1 – 7) priesthood (8)] Lev. 9:23
    (3) Lev. 10:1–3 → [distinguish between unclean and clean (11 – 15)] Lev. 16

Considering that the divine command for Israel to build a sanctuary in Exodus 25:8 is for the sake of enabling the glory of YHWH dwelling on Sinai (Exod. 24:16–17) to abide with Israel through the tabernacle cultus, it becomes evident how the theophanies of Exodus 24 and 40, Leviticus 9 and 16 form a structuring device.[20] Note as well that the movement from Exodus to Leviticus also involves a general movement from mountain of God to tabernacle, and from Moses to Aaron, the high priest, in a manner replacing Moses as *cultic* mediator. This insight leads us back to the earlier point that while God had used Moses to build the tabernacle as an architectural mountain of God or garden of Eden, there was as yet no new Adam for this new creation. God therefore used Moses to consecrate the priesthood, the actors for this cultic drama, and especially the high priest, whose role was that of Adam.

Under the scheme charted above, the narratives provide a goal for the legislation, a point that will be especially relevant as we probe the third and final movement of Leviticus. Equally important to grasp, the goal itself, toward which the legislation aims, is for a progressively deepened relationship with God.

Understanding the laws on clean and unclean (Lev. 11 – 15)

Once the tabernacle had been established, keeping the sacred space undefiled became a priority. References to the deaths of Nadab and Abihu bookend the laws of clean and unclean (Lev. 10:1–3 – [chs. 11–15] – 16:1–2), adding both urgency and purpose to the legislation. And as already noted, YHWH's only speech addressed to Aaron exclusively serves to introduce these laws, calling him to distinguish between unclean and clean that he may teach such to Israel, and lends gravity to this section of the book (10:10). Furthermore, near the end of the clean/unclean legislation, we read, 'So you shall consecrate the sons of Israel from their uncleanness [*ṭm'*], lest they die in their uncleanness [*ṭm'*] by defiling [*ṭm'*] my dwelling which is

that negation, allowing for Moses' entrance, and for Aaron's experience of the divine Presence within the veil.
[20] See Nihan 2007: 105, n. 137.

in their midst' (15:31). This is, of course, precisely what happens to Nadab and Abihu, serving once more to underscore the laws on clean and unclean within the context of approaching YHWH. Once Nadab and Abihu's fault reveals the dreadful possibility that defiling YHWH's dwelling may lead to death, it is naturally an urgent matter to specify those impurities that pollute the sanctuary.[21] Beyond any other considerations, as we will see, the purity laws must be understood both as springing out of and flowing into the prospect of Israel's ever-deepening relationship with YHWH, facilitating Israel's drawing near to him. After mapping out the conditions of clean and unclean within the cultic system, we will probe their rationale and then consider the function of the purity laws in the life of Israel.

The cultic system mediated between the two realms of common and sacred. However, within the realm of the common a person or object might be either 'clean' (*ṭāhôr*) or 'unclean' (*ṭāmēʾ*), presenting the dangerous possibility that the unclean could come into contact with the holy. Wenham summarizes this threefold categorization in a helpful manner:

> Everything that is not holy is common. Common things divide into two groups, the clean and the unclean. Clean things become holy, when they are sanctified. But unclean objects cannot be sanctified. Clean things can be made unclean, if they are polluted. Finally, holy items may be defiled and become common, even polluted, and therefore unclean. . . . Sanctification can elevate the clean into the holy, while pollution degrades the clean into the unclean. The unclean and the holy are two states which must never come into contact with each other. . . . According to Leviticus, then, sacrificial blood is necessary to cleanse and to sanctify. Sacrifice can undo the effects of sin and human infirmity. Sin and disease lead to profanation of the holy and pollution of the clean. Sacrifice can reverse this process.[22]

The following table, based on Wenham's, charts out the cultic system's threefold division, created by its two major boundaries, separating the holy from the common and the clean from the unclean.

---

[21] Milgrom 1991: 1011.
[22] Wenham 1979: 19–20, 26.

The cultic system's threefold division may be further refined by understanding the categories of holy and common in relation to the *status* of persons, places, objects and time, whereas clean and unclean refer rather to the *condition* of persons, places or objects.[23] For our purposes, what is important to grasp is that the condition of clean derives its value within the spectrum of movement toward YHWH, as the prerequisite for crossing the common–holy boundary. As is evident in Leviticus 15:31, Israel's uncleanness posed a two-pronged problem. First, attempting to approach the divine Presence while unclean risked immediate death for the Israelite. This consequence is integral to the overall message of Leviticus, 'that holiness is more powerful than impurity, that life can conquer death'.[24] Be that as it may, if the accumulated uncleanness contracted by the tabernacle was not remedied ritually, then a second problem would unfold, namely Israel would be threatened with the loss of its highest blessing and reason for existence: YHWH God would abandon his dwelling among them. As we will come to see more deeply in the next chapter, YHWH's Presence was the source of Israel's sanctification – apart from his cleansing, Israel would then bear their own guilt and suffer the threats of the covenant.

An alternative designation for clean and unclean is purity and impurity, though as the broader concept I will retain the clean/unclean terminology.[25] Fundamentally, *ṭāhôr*, 'clean' or 'pure', is the basic requirement for being in the divine Presence, as manifested even by the ark in the holy of holies, which had been overlaid with 'pure' (*ṭāhôr*) gold (Exod. 25:11). *Thus to be clean means to be fit for the Presence of God, while to be holy means that one belongs to God.* Something that is holy must remain exclusively in God's realm (sacred space), living for his will alone, or else be destroyed so as to prevent common or profane usage. Through covenantal relationship with YHWH, the

[23] Averbeck 1997b: 481.
[24] Milgrom 1991: 639.
[25] Wenham 1979: 20.

normal status of Israel was clean; that of the priesthood was holy, having YHWH himself for a heritage. The (holy) priests were to facilitate the relationship between holy YHWH and (clean) Israel, a relationship that would steadily make Israel, and eventually the nations as well through Israel, holy. This point reveals – and, indeed, follows from – a more significant reality: God's purpose and activity in the world is to cleanse and sanctify, while the purpose and activity of Satan and the sinful nature is to profane and pollute. God's ways are the paths of life, while the ways of the corrupt lead to death.

Turning now to consider the rationale for the clean/unclean laws, we begin with a basic breakdown of the clean/unclean legislation:

- Distinguishing between clean and unclean animals (ch. 11).
- Cleansing after childbirth (ch. 12).
- Diagnosing skin (and other surface) diseases as unclean (ch. 13).
- Cleansing skin (and house) diseases (ch. 14).
- Diagnosing and cleansing of unclean bodily discharges (ch. 15).

Remembering that the discussion of animals in chapter 11 is in relation to Israel's diet, essentially constituting food laws, Gorman is correct in discerning that each set of instructions has to do, for the most part, with bodily boundaries.[26] While apparent exceptions include instructions about garments, containers and houses, yet these may be perceived primarily in terms of their being a threat to the human body's contracting of uncleanness. A plausible arrangement of this material is as follows:

A   Uncleanness within the body (food) (ch. 11)
  B   Bodily discharges (blood flow of childbirth) (ch. 12)
A' Uncleanness on the body's surface (skin diseases) (chs. 13–14)
  B' Bodily discharges (various scenarios) (ch. 15)

Though the literature on this legislation is extensive and varied,[27] it is

[26] Gorman 1997: 68. To be sure, animals had already been distinguished as either clean or unclean in the primeval age (Gen. 7:2) *before* the divine allowance of eating meat. This distinction related rather to God's 'diet', as it were, the altar being his table (Gen. 8:20). The analogy between Israel's diet and sacrifices (God's eating) will be addressed below.

[27] A sampling of which, apart from the general commentaries, includes Gispen 1948; Douglas 1966; 1972; Neusner 1975; Carmichael 1976; Wenham 1981a; Wenham 1983; Frymer-Kensky 1983; Budd 1989; Firmage 1990; Wright 1992a; Hanson 1993; Douglas 1993; Whitekettle 1996; Wright 1996. For the sake of brevity I will not rehearse and assess the various other proposals that have been offered as the rationale for the purity laws (cf. Hartley 1992: 142–147; Budd 1989: 282–290).

possible nevertheless to offer sound, if general, affirmations regarding the rationale for the clean/unclean laws.

Life and death

The contrast between life and death is at the heart of the clean/unclean laws.[28] Understanding YHWH to be the fountain of life, the spectrum between life and death may be mapped out spatially, with life and ordered cosmos at one end, and death and chaos at the other end. The nearer one approaches YHWH, the closer one gets to life in abundance. Conversely, the further one is driven from YHWH the more deeply death and chaos are experienced. Keeping in mind how the tabernacle is an architectural mountain of God and model of the threefold cosmos, the holy of holies corresponds to the clouded summit of the mountain, the heavenly abode of God. As the place of God's Presence, the holy of holies represents the uttermost source of life. At the opposite end of the spectrum is the wilderness, which corresponds to the unruly waters surrounding the mountain, underneath which lies Sheol, the realm of chaos and death. What is clean may be brought into God's Presence at the entrance of the tabernacle (the courtyard before the altar). Before drawing nearer to him, however, the clean person, animal or object must be sanctified, made holy, so as to belong to YHWH. Broadly, what is unclean lies closer to the death/chaos extremity, and what is clean is closer to the life of YHWH; beyond the status of clean is that of holy, and then most holy, which is nearest to YHWH, who is himself absolute life (holiness).

With this cultic map in place we can begin to understand the rationale for why some animals, objects or people are classified as either clean or unclean. One leading idea, argued by Douglas,[29] is that the notions of wholeness and normality served as the primary distinction between clean and unclean. Wenham, however, rightly subsumed these helpful categories under the more fundamental opposition between life and death, noting that while childbirth, menstruation and sexual intercourse would surely have been considered normal, yet they still caused uncleanness because each involved the loss of life liquids, barring people from worship until they recovered from such loss:

> God, who is perfect life and perfect holiness, can only be approached by clean men who enjoy fullness of life themselves. The unclean

[28] Milgrom 1991: 766–768, 1000–1004; Carmichael 1976; Wenham 1983.
[29] Douglas 1966.

are those who in some way have an aura of death about them in that they manifest less than physical wholeness.[30]

Many of the unclean animals are associated with death in some fashion, whether in being carnivorous predators or scavengers, living in caves (tombs), or, like pigs, by being associated with underworld deities in pagan worship.[31] Along these lines, creatures that demonstrate some abnormality within their class (like fish without scales) are considered further from the wholeness of an ordered cosmos in terms of life. Similarly, in relation to humans, certain physical defects preclude a descendant of Aaron from serving as high priest since he represents original or restored creation and 'must be perfect as a man, if he is to be a priest'.[32] Various conditions such as skin diseases make Israelites unclean because it brings them into the realm of death. When Miriam became leprous, Aaron prayed, 'Please do not let her be as one dead, whose flesh is half consumed . . .' (Num. 12:12). The leper pronounced unclean, therefore, is required to go into mourning, dishevelling his hair, rending his clothes and being exiled outside the camp of Israel (Lev. 13:45–46) – in essence, such a person 'experienced a living death'.[33] Many of the discharges of bodily fluids (such as blood or semen), along with the womb shortly after childbirth, may be correlated with loss of life, rendering one unfit to be in the Presence of fullness of life. Because the wilderness represents chaos and death, Sheol, all that severely smacks of death is driven into the wilderness and away from the Presence of God.

The need to separate life from death, the unclean from the holy, also helps to explain why, for example, the high priest must never have contact with death, corpses defile, and a young goat is not to be cooked in its mother's milk. Depending on the severity of uncleanness, the ritual remedy may be a mere matter of washing and waiting until evening or it may require purification offerings, the person remaining unclean for seven days, or even being banished from the camp of

[30] Wenham 1983: 434. An alternative explanation is that the clean/unclean laws are based upon the common priestly exhortation to imitate God: since God neither dies nor has sexual relations, these characteristics are unfitting for his Presence (Wright 1992a: 739; Frymer-Kensky 1993: 189; Klawans 2001: 142–143).

[31] Sprinkle 2000: 649. Averbeck (1997b: 483) notes that there are no unclean plants; so animals that chew the cud are by nature vegetarian, while scavenger and predatory animals/birds are eliminated from this category.

[32] Douglas 1966: 51.

[33] Wenham 1979: 201.

Israel.[34] Uncleanness, then, 'seems to have cast the shadow of death over its bearers'.[35] Since major impurities not only pollute but endanger, atonement (*kipper*) is appropriate, as the unclean person needs not only to be cleansed but also to be ransomed from the realm of death.[36] While contracting uncleanness was a movement from life towards death, the purification rituals were understood as a movement from death towards life, typically involving symbols of life (blood and water). Inasmuch as obedience to the torah of YHWH was itself the path of life, the calling to distinguish between life and death flowed out of and into Israel's covenant relationship:

> See, I have set before you today life and good, death and evil. . . . I call as witnesses against you today heaven and earth: life and death I have set before you, blessing and cursing. Now choose life that both you and your descendants may live. Love YHWH your God, obeying his voice and clinging to him, for he himself is your life and your length of days; so that you may dwell in the land which YHWH swore to your fathers, to Abraham, Isaac and Jacob, to give them. (Deut. 30:15, 19–20)

God's holiness and sin's pollution

The poles of life and wholeness versus death and chaos may also be understood within the correlation of life with holiness and death with sin. The deaths of Nadab and Abihu, which bracket the clean/unclean laws, are set within the context of God's holiness. Indeed, Moses interprets their deaths to Aaron by relating YHWH's word that 'by those who draw near to me I must be regarded as holy' (Lev. 10:3), an admonition that permeates the atmosphere of the Day of Atonement ceremony as Aaron himself approaches God within the holiest place of the tabernacle.

On the one hand, even though serious moral offences render one unclean, yet the *ritual* uncleanness discussed in Leviticus 11 – 15 cannot be equated with sin simplistically.[37] Situations that render one

---

[34] See Averbeck's (1997b: 485) delineation of regular, irregular and severe uncleanness.

[35] Kugler 1997: 14.

[36] Sklar 2008.

[37] Moral impurity should be distinguished from ritual impurity. Ritual impurity is impermanent, sometimes contagious, may defile the courtyard altar, and, while requiring cleansing, does not require forgiveness; moral impurity requires atonement (sometimes being cut off or death), defiles the land, along with the innermost areas of the sanctuary, but is not contagious (cf. Hayes 2006: 746, 748–749).

temporarily unclean, such as contact with a carcass, sexual intercourse, childbirth or a skin ailment, are not regarded as moral offences against God. And even though sometimes the remedy involves a purification offering (also dubbed 'sin offering'), the text is quite clear in distinguishing the uncleanness rituals of chapters 11–15 from that of the purification offering for sins detailed in chapters 4 and 5. In Leviticus 4 and 5 we read the common refrain 'So the priest shall make atonement for him, and it shall be forgiven him' (4:20, 26, 31, 35; 5:6, 10). In the clean/unclean laws of Leviticus 11 – 15, however, one finds instead 'So the priest shall make atonement for her and she will be clean' (12:8), or 'So the priest shall make atonement for him who is to be cleansed before YHWH' (14:31), demonstrating that the status of unclean is not one that necessarily calls for the forgiveness of sin. A woman's periodic flow of blood, then, is not considered a moral failure or transgression of God's law, requiring forgiveness. On the other hand, there is what Sprinkle has adequately described as a 'strong analogy between "unclean" and "sin"'.[38] He goes on to explain that the Day of Atonement cleanses from both sin and uncleanness, and the Pentateuch regularly describes immoral acts and iniquities – murder, adultery, idolatry – as unclean. The prophets make this correlation as well. Isaiah, who himself cried out, 'Woe is me, I am ruined – for I am a man of unclean lips!' (6:5), proclaims YHWH's call to moral cleanness:

> Wash yourselves, make yourselves clean;
> Put away the evil of your doings before my eyes.
> Cease to do evil . . .
>
> (Isa. 1:16)

Gispen notes how often the prophets call for inward cleanness, suggesting that the main purpose of the clean/unclean laws is to teach Israel to abstain from the dirtiness of sin, that uncleanness came into the world because of sin.[39] Such cleanness of heart becomes a divine promise and an object of hope for Israel:

---

[38] Sprinkle 2000: 653; cf. Gane 2010: 8–9. Neusner (1975: 24) regards uncleanness as 'a metaphor for sexual misdeed, idolatry, or unethical behavior' and says that cleanness 'was compared to sexual purity, service to one God alone, and correct action. These metaphors were natural in the context of the cult, which above all else signified holiness and produced the right relation to God.'

[39] Gispen 1948: 193–196.

Then I will sprinkle clean water upon you,
　and you shall be clean.
From all of your uncleanness and from all of your idols,
　I will cleanse you.

(Ezek. 36:25)

To summarize, while in Leviticus 11 – 15 uncleanness is not flatly
or immediately equated with particular sinful acts, it is nevertheless
treated as being generally or ultimately the result of sin: uncleanness
represents the pollution of sin. Contact with a carcass results in
uncleanness, therefore, not because such contact is in itself a sin, but
because death and mortality are the result of sin. Precisely here the
correlation between holiness and life/wholeness is critical. Physical
imperfection, disruptions, deformities and maladies, though not considered sinful in themselves, nevertheless still reflect sin's damage and
pollution of the earth, and therefore require ritual cleansing.

One can readily see how the notion that sin defiles would accord
with the theology of sacred space intrinsic to the cultic system. Reflecting upon the tabernacle's function as a microcosm, however, also
provides an interpretative key to the early narratives of Genesis, as
we have already seen. The deluge, for example, not only served to
judge sinners, but also to cleanse (at least figuratively) the cosmos
from sin's pollution. Indeed, YHWH's retreat to the heavens afterward
may be explained according to the continuing prospect of the earth's
pollution by sin – for man's heart had yet remained evil continually.
It is for this very reason that a sacred space, the tabernacle, had to be
constructed and consecrated in order for YHWH to dwell amidst
Israel. And this, once more, is at the core of the drama of Leviticus:
a sacred bubble has been set within a sea of uncleanness; how now
may any Israelite, when even his lungs are polluted, enter this sphere?
And how may this sphere be kept clean continually? It is important
to understand, moreover, that while for Israel the status of clean was
the normal state, yet this status was never to be taken for granted (as
an ethnic right or otherwise). Rather, it was the direct result of its
covenant relationship with YHWH – cleanness was a result of Israel's
divine redemption and consecration. Here Wenham's impression that
the cleansing of the leprous man (Lev. 14) may have been informed
by Israel's original cleansing is suggestive. He notes, for example, the
parallel between the Passover ritual in Exod. 12 and how hyssop was
also used to sprinkle blood upon the man healed of leprosy (14:6–7),
so that there is a sense in which an unclean Israelite would be restored

or resanctified by a process similar to Israel's original cleansing and sanctification – he 'had to be born again into the community by blood and water (cf. John 3)'.[40]

We will appreciate the covenantal facet of cleanness more deeply in the following section, but here it is worth reflecting on the instructive nature of the cleansing process. Ritual uncleanness served not only to bear witness to the widespread pollution of sin, but also, by contrast, to the infinite holiness of Israel's God, and, therefore, to the need for cleansing as a prerequisite to entering into his Presence. Fundamentally, a person declared unclean is one who was 'not allowed to appear in the Presence of Yahweh, to partake of the divine service'.[41] More than this, 'human beings, by virtue of being part of this sin-cursed, fallen world, are "unclean" or "contaminated" and are not automatically eligible to approach God';[42] in other words, the *normal* condition of (sinful, fallen) humanity is uncleanness. From this perspective, the clean/unclean legislation manifests its consistency with, and reinforcement of, the theology of the gate liturgy: *Who shall ascend into the mountain of YHWH?*

Israel and the nations

What has been mentioned in relation to humanity's basic unfitness for the divine Presence would also be true of Israel apart from the covenant with YHWH. Within the covenant relationship, however, which had been preceded by the blood both of redemption (at Passover) and consecration (sprinkled at Sinai), Israel's normal status became that of being clean, while the nations had been left in their state of uncleanness. God's electing love – and redemptive purpose – had therefore created the dichotomy of Israel (clean) and the nations (unclean), which, being all of a piece, may be coordinated with the previous contrasts: life versus death, holiness versus sin, Israel versus nations. When YHWH had separated Israel from the nations, he purposed to separate Israel from the sinfulness of the nations – the pollution of idolatry, for example – so that, eventually, as a royal priesthood, Israel might serve as a mediator between holy YHWH and the unclean nations. Rather than ethnicity, it is the uncleanness of sinfulness that informs Israel's call to be separate from the nations: 'Do not make yourselves unclean [*tm'*] by any of these things [i.e. sexual immorality]; for by all these the nations have become unclean

---

[40] Wenham 1979: 27.
[41] Gispen 1948: 190.
[42] Sprinkle 2000: 652.

[*ṭm'*], which I myself am casting out before you' (Lev. 18:24). The identification of the nations with uncleanness is especially evident in the symbolism of the food laws, whereby Israel is associated with clean animals while the nations are associated with unclean animals:

> You shall not walk in the customs of the nation that I myself am casting out before you, for they commit all these things, and therefore I abhor them. But I have said to you, 'You shall inherit their land, and I will give it to you to possess, a land flowing with milk and honey.' I am YHWH your God, who has separated you from the peoples. You shall therefore distinguish between clean animals and unclean, between unclean birds and clean, and you shall not make your souls detestable by beast or by bird, or by anything that creeps on the ground, which I have separated from you as unclean. You shall be holy to me, for I YHWH am holy, and have separated you from the peoples that you might belong to me. (Lev. 20:23–26)

This passage marks the clearest explanation of the *function* of the food laws.[43] Just as God had separated Israel from among the peoples, so Israel was to distinguish between clean and unclean animals in relation to eating (edible vs. inedible). Every meal served as a reminder of God's election of Israel out of the nations, but also of Israel's call to keep themselves separate from the uncleanness of those nations – to be a holy people. The food laws thus became a sign of Israel's identity and calling, a wall of separation between Israel and the nations. Israel had been chosen of God and cleansed, and so possessed, with his dwelling in their midst, fullness of life; the Gentiles were still exiled from the divine Presence, unclean and in the realm of death. When Jesus' atonement and gift of the Spirit yield true cleansing for both Jew and Gentile by faith, therefore, the food laws, which served to symbolize and foster the distinction between them, will be done away with (see Acts 10 – 11).

Clean and unclean within the cultic system

Having considered the dichotomies of life and death, God's holiness and sin's pollution, Israel and the nations, it remains for us to discern

[43] I am distinguishing between the function (or theological purpose) of the food laws and the rationale. The basis for qualifying an animal as clean or unclean I would define as the rationale (i.e. the life vs. death dichotomy), whereas the purpose for making distinctions (however informed or random their basis) is to inculcate Israel's need to be separate from the nations' paganism.

how these poles were unified in the tabernacle cultus. Following the dramatic movement of the book, we can see how the concerns of pollution and God's holiness, which through the deaths of Nadab and Abihu bracket the clean/unclean laws, are shaped specifically with reference to *approaching* God's Presence. Before chapters 11–15, Nadab and Abihu die for drawing near to YHWH unlawfully; after the clean/unclean legislation, Aaron as high priest will draw near to YHWH within the holy of holies. The grades of unclean, clean and holy must therefore be understood within a spectrum of movement, symbolically mapped out upon the graded space of the tabernacle cultus.[44]

	Cosmos		*Cultic cosmos*
Humanity in relation to YHWH		**Animals**	**Space**
Holy	Priests	Sacrificial	Tabernacle
Clean	Israel	Clean	Camp
Unclean	Gentiles	Unclean	Wilderness

The vertical movement should be understood in relation to concentric circles: Israel was chosen out of the Gentiles, and cleansed; then the Levites, and Aaron's line in particular, were chosen out of Israel, and sanctified for sacred service. Across the horizontal plane we can see that the tabernacle cultus formed a microcosm of the cosmos, with animals (and birds) serving as substitutes for clean and unclean people.[45] Perhaps most important for our purposes is that only what is clean may become holy. From one's own (clean) flock, for example, the Israelite would choose a sheep to set apart (make holy) for sacrifice. A Canaanite or Moabite, therefore, could not belong to God without first becoming clean within Israel's covenant relationship with YHWH. Equally significant, it was God's will that *all* Israel become holy. Having conveyed Israel from the status of unclean, among the nations, to that of clean in relationship with himself, God purposed to sanctify his people to be his own treasured possession. This goal had been voiced by God during the opening revelation at Sinai:

---

[44] It is the nature of the case that this table cannot be exact, inasmuch as there is overlap between cosmos and cult (note e.g. the status of priests). See also the charts in Wright 1992a: 738, 740; Wenham 2003: 92.

[45] Mary Douglas (1966: 41–57; 1972), from an anthropological approach, has demonstrated the close analogy between humans and animals in ancient Israel's culture.

> You yourselves have seen what I did to the Egyptians, and how I bore you on wings of eagles and brought you to myself. Now, therefore, if you will surely obey my voice and keep my covenant, then you shall be to me a treasured possession among all peoples; for all the earth is mine. And you shall be to me a kingdom of priests and a holy nation. (Exod. 19:4–6)

Deeper fellowship with God, then, was the goal of holiness, and the clean/unclean laws were set within the context of pursuing holiness. This point may be seen in the function for the dietary laws given in Leviticus 11:44–45, for example, which utilizes the root 'holy' (*qdš*) five times. We will reflect further on the programme of Israel's sanctification when considering holiness in the next chapter, but here it is worth emphasizing once more the integrating principle of the cultic *approach* to YHWH God. The gradations of unclean, clean and holy were embodied not only by the sacred space of the tabernacle, but also by the divisions of people, animals and even materials co-ordinated with them. Yet while the separation established by these boundaries was firm, it would be a mistake to assume that they created a static system. On the contrary, the sacrificial cultus was fundamentally about crossing boundaries; and the gradations rather created a graduated path of holiness, leading into the divine Presence.[46] Even the distinction between Israel and the nations, and this set within the context of life and holiness, with their counterparts of death and pollution, must be understood as subservient to the goal of fellowship and communion with God. The attainment of this goal, which required Israel's own holiness, may be grasped through a dynamic revealed in the clean/unclean laws, namely that while the clean status is inactive (as in non-contagious), both holy and unclean are dynamic (as in contagious), tending to extend their spatial dimensions.[47] Herein the wide panorama of potentiality opens up: either a holy Israel in a holy cosmos enjoying communion with holy YHWH, or else a defiled Israel and defiled tabernacle/land abandoned by YHWH.

Approaching YHWH God, then, is the integrating element of Israel's cultic system. This means that, above all else, to be unclean is understood fundamentally as being excluded from the Presence of YHWH, while being made clean means becoming fit for his Presence. Here, finally, is the reason why being clean matters, and why becoming

[46] Cf. Abrahams 2006: 423; Whitekettle 1996: 379.
[47] Liss 2008: 342.

unclean was a cause for distress. Israel's covenantal gift was the Presence of YHWH in their midst. Ritual uncleanness, barring one from worship at the tabernacle, was a reminder that all of life was oriented around the reality and nature of I AM WHO I AM, the source of life, wholeness and holiness, and that sin and its pollution, if not expiated and cleansed, would eventually lead to death, to permanent exile away from his Presence.

This movement towards and away from God brings us back to the parallels between the tabernacle and Eden. With the Eden narratives serving to inform the symbolism of the cultus, including its rituals, being clean may have been understood in terms of admittance to Eden, while being banished from Israel's camp would have been a sort of 'reenactment of the fall, when Adam and Eve were expelled from Eden. . . . As Adam and Eve experienced a living death when they were expelled from Eden, so every man who was diagnosed as unclean suffered a similar fate.'[48] Given the tabernacle's Edenic symbolism, along with Israel's inability to enter at the close of Exodus, it is at least suggestive that the book of Leviticus begins with how specifically 'ādām may approach YHWH (1:2), recalling Adam's expulsion from the garden of Eden.[49] The analogy between Israel's exile from the land and that of Adam from the garden has long been acknowledged in ancient rabbinical interpretation and is a commonplace in scholarship today.[50] What has, perhaps, been less recognized is how the clean/unclean legislation may have played out that drama ritually on a regular basis in the life of Israel.

Approaching the divine Presence, along with the sacrificial cultus to facilitate it, however, was itself a means to the end of communion with YHWH God. Here the mysterious relationship between Israel and the tabernacle merits further contemplation. Milgrom famously described the dynamic between Israel and the tabernacle along the lines of Oscar Wilde's *The Picture of Dorian Gray*, the tabernacle serving as a spiritual barometer measuring the people's spiritual condition:

> sin may not leave its mark on the face of the sinner, but it is certain to mark the face of the sanctuary . . . the sinner may be unscarred

[48] Wenham 1979: 201, 213; cf. Wright 1992a: 739.

[49] Trevaskis 2011: 93–106, 199–200. The term 'ādām is rarer than nepeš and 'îš for conveying 'man' or 'person'. Kiuchi (2007: 61) suggests that 'ādām carries the nuance of post-fall humanity.

[50] See Postell 2011.

by his evil, but the sanctuary bears the scars and, with its destruction, he too will meet his doom.[51]

While its finer points require assessment and critique, Milgrom's view is helpful in bringing out the cultic correlation – one is tempted to say 'spiritual bond' – between Israel and the tabernacle, inviting further exploration. For example, although that bond is revealed negatively with regard to Israel's impurities causing the defilement of the tabernacle, might not the direction be reversed, causing the sanctification of Israel? This is precisely what we will find when considering holiness in the next chapter, that God through the sanctuary (and the Sabbath) purposes to make Israel holy. The bond, then, is a two-way street, which must be coordinated with the overall movement of the clean–unclean spectrum. Yet might this dynamic analogy between Israel and the tabernacle point us more deeply into the purposes of God as expressed in the covenant formula 'I will dwell in your midst'? Beyond the pollution of sin, what might it mean that the *people's* uncleanness was manifested as a defilement of God's *dwelling*? One wonders, then, if the thought might ever have entered the mind of an ancient Israelite, that the tabernacle itself gestured toward a mystery so profound that the light of human intellect cannot fathom its depths (2 Cor. 6:16; Eph. 2:19–22; 1 Peter 2:4–10).

Leviticus 16: the Day of Atonement

Without question, the Day of Atonement was at the heart of Israel's calendar and life.[52] It is also, as we considered in the opening chapter, the structural and thematic centre of the Pentateuch,[53] the literary summit to which and from which the narrative drama ascends and descends. Indeed, the high priest's narrated entry within the veil of God's house is, for the reader, an entrance within the inner sanctum of the Pentateuch's theology,[54] the keystone of the cultic system of forgiveness of sins.[55] After the expulsion from the garden of Eden, this entrance into the tabernacle holy of holies presents the nearest human approach to God's Presence. As such, the Day of Atonement

[51] Milgrom 1976a: 397–398.
[52] The literature on this topic is extensive; recent works include Stökl Ben Ezra 2003; Gane 2005; Hieke and Nicklas 2012.
[53] See also Kalimi 2012: 75–76; Hartley 2003a: 55.
[54] Cf. Geller 1992.
[55] Seidl 1999.

is dubbed a *šabbat šabbātôn* (Lev. 16:31; 23:32), a Sabbath of solemn rest or, with the LXX translation, 'the Sabbath of Sabbaths', a high estimation reflected in the rabbinical title *yoma*, '*the* day'.[56] On this most solemn day the Israelites were called upon to 'afflict' (*'nh*) their souls, typically understood as expressing repentant sorrow by fasting, in accord with the day's cultic rites, which may be adequately understood in terms of a heightened and intensified purification offering. Reference to the purification offering frames the account of the high priest's duties, which begin with the purification offering's blood in verse 3 and end with his adding the fat of the purification offering(s) to the ascension offerings in verse 25 – in effect, binding the various activities into one 'purification offering of purgation'.[57]

To summarize the annual ceremony briefly, the Day of Atonement ritual involved two pairs of offerings: a purification and ascension offering for the high priest Aaron and his priestly house, and a purification and ascension offering for all Israel. Both purification offerings were offered first, however, and then both ascension offerings were offered afterward. An elimination rite with a scapegoat took place in between these two sets of offerings, and should be seen as completing Israel's purification offering.

The high priest would bathe and put on simple (though holy) linen clothes to sacrifice both of the purification offerings first, purging the inner sanctum, the tent of meeting and the altar with blood. The central focus of the ceremony, the height of its tension and drama, was the high priest's entrance into the holy of holies. Having placed within the holy of holies a censer full of burning coals and much finely ground sweet incense to create a cloud, screening his eyes from God's glory,[58] the high priest would sprinkle the bull's blood (from his own purification offering) upon the atonement lid of the ark eastward and then seven times before it. After casting lots to designate which goat would be sacrificed (as Israel's purification offering) and which would serve to carry away Israel's sins, he would offer the goat upon which YHWH's lot fell and complete the inner sanctum's purgation with its blood. A similar process was carried out in the holy place, probably applying blood to the incense altar and then seven times before it. Finally, the high priest would purge the altar of ascension offerings by daubing its horns with the mixed bloods of the bull and goat, and then sprinkle the altar itself seven times to reconsecrate it. After purging

56 Stökl Ben Ezra 2003: 15–17.
57 Gane 2004: 276; cf. Milgrom 1976b.
58 Hertz 1988: 156.

the inner and outer sanctums and the altar, the high priest would bring the live goat and press both hands upon its head, confessing all of Israel's 'wickedness' or 'guilt' (*'ăwônōt*), 'transgressions' (*piš'êhem*) and 'sins' (*ḥaṭṭō'tām*) so as to transfer Israel's culpability entirely upon this goat (Lev. 16:21),[59] which would then be led out to the wilderness by an appointed man. The high priest would then bathe again and put on his ornate garments to offer up both of the ascension offerings, adding, finally, the fat from the purification offerings. The Day of Atonement includes, then, three main rites that are interwoven as one ceremony:[60] an *entrance rite*, of the high priest into the inner sanctum; a *cleansing rite*, of the tabernacle cultus; and an *elimination rite*, of the people's sins into the wilderness.

The following sections provide an approach to the Day of Atonement ceremony particularly within the narrative context of Leviticus and within that of the Pentateuch. The significance of this day's rites will be probed in relation to the following three themes: cleansing the tabernacle (and people) of God, approaching the divine Presence and re-entering the garden of Eden.

Cleansing God's house

The Day of Atonement was the day of purgation: the tabernacle and its furnishings, the high priest and the priesthood, and all the Israelites were purged from Israel's uncleanness, atonement being made by the high priest for Israel's sins. Consequently, this festival was understood both as a day of judgment and a day of reconciliation.[61] Cleansing God's house of the pollution caused by Israel's uncleanness was the main focus of the ceremony, with the ultimate purpose of maintaining God's tabernacling Presence in their midst.[62] The double use of the root for 'clean' (*thr*) in Leviticus 16:30 underscores the chapter's function as the culmination of the clean/unclean laws of chapters 11–15, as well as how those laws and the Day of Atonement are set within the fundamental goal of abiding with YHWH: 'For on this day, he [the high priest] will make atonement for you to cleanse you from all your sins. Before YHWH, you will be clean.'

---

[59] Rightly, Hartley (2003a: 58) sees the heaping of these terms as encompassing 'the entire spectrum of human sinning, from blunders to premeditated wrongs'.

[60] See Rodriguez 1996.

[61] One would be hard-pressed, therefore, to find a more suitable background for the prophetic 'Day of YHWH', which otherwise appears without introduction or explanation (cf. Amos, Joel).

[62] Wenham 1979: 228.

As already developed at length, both the Nadab and Abihu tragedy *and* the Day of Atonement legislation occur on the same day, the latter given as a response to the former. Leviticus 16 begins with a resumptive repetition, mentioning the deaths of Aaron's sons so as to bring the reader back to the story, which has been paused. By splitting these two events that took place on the same day, and inserting the clean/ unclean legislation between them, the inserted laws receive their proper importance and purpose contextually. This scheme also deepens our understanding of the Day of Atonement as a cleansing rite. Nadab and Abihu defiled the tabernacle through corpse pollution, not to mention by their transgression. Such an incident cannot but immediately manifest the sobering reality hitherto not thought of – their deaths stand merely as the initial example that served to identify the ongoing threat of the tabernacle's defilement. The laws of clean/ unclean serve in a manner to identify the various other ways in which the people's uncleanness posed a problem. Inserting those laws before the Day of Atonement legislation demonstrates that this ceremony is not a specific and merely occasional response to a particular incident, but rather that this purification ceremony will be the regular resolution to Israel's uncleanness and defilement of the tabernacle.

The Day of Atonement legislation narrates the cleansing of God's house from the inside out, a movement that may be traced according to the purification offerings' application of blood.[63] First, God's earthly throne room, the holy of holies, is purged through the blood sprinkled on the atonement lid and before the ark. The instructions of Leviticus 16:14 call for an eastward (*qēdĕmâ*) sprinkling of the atonement lid, which presumably required the high priest to stand west of the ark. The movement of purgation then continues eastward from the ark with the cleansing of the holy place and then the altar in the courtyard. From the courtyard the live goat continues the eastward movement in carrying off Israel's sins and culpability to an uninhabited place in the wilderness.[64] The Day of Atonement, therefore,

---

[63] Gane 2004: 279.

[64] Gane (ibid. 272–273; emphases original) distinguishes what is purged from the tabernacle (impurities) from what is transferred onto the live goat (moral faults): 'From the sanctuary he [the high priest] removed *physical ritual impurities*, inexpiable rebellious sins, and expiable sins (16:16), but on the live goat he placed *culpabilities*, inexpiable rebellious sins, and expiable sins (16:21).' Milgrom (1976b; 1991: 1043–1044), following the Mishna (*m. Šebu.* 1.4–7), suggests the sanctuary was purged from impurity/pollution by the sacrificed goat, while Israel was purged from sins, the cause of impurity, by the scapegoat. Rodriguez (1996: 285–286) finds no such distinction, stating that the same sin and impurity removed from the sanctuary are then eliminated by the scapegoat. Cf. Adu-Gyamfi 2013: 6–7.

reverses the presumed steady movement of uncleanness toward the tabernacle throughout the year. Moreover, while the individual Israelite who with true contrition had offered purification offerings throughout the year had indeed been forgiven already, the Day of Atonement, beyond atoning for transgressions and sins which had not been remedied (through ignorance or rebellion), also served to cleanse Israelites from the stain of their sins, beyond forgiveness.[65] The Day of Atonement fittingly consummates the start of the new year, which had been signalled by the shofar blasts ten days earlier: God's house in microcosm has been cleansed, and Israel's sins have been expiated out into the wilderness.

Before turning to the next section, a further observation is worthy of mention. With the tabernacle being a microcosm of the cosmos, its rituals, including those of the Day of Atonement, should be related to the reality of the cosmos. This idea is already embraced in principle by those who find the cleansing of the tabernacle to comprise something of a cultic counterpart to the cleansing of the cosmos that was accomplished through the flood. Especially in the light of the covenantal promise, however, one needs also to underscore the future-oriented aspect of the Day of Atonement ceremony. The cultic drama of the microcosm's cleansing points prophetically to a Day of Atonement not enacted on the cultic stage but rather upon its counterpart, the cosmos as true house of God. Within the purification ritual for the tabernacle the analogical link between the tabernacle and cosmos unfolds a promise for the purification of the cosmos. This idea merges naturally with understanding the Day of Atonement *eschatologically* as a drama of the day of judgment – the final cleansing and entrance into God's house, along with the final expulsion from his Presence. Stated differently, *the drama of the tabernacle's defilement by the sin and corpse pollution of Aaron's sons mirrors the drama of Adam's own transgression and defilement of the cosmos*. The questions that surface naturally and urgently in Leviticus in relation to the tabernacle as God's house had already surfaced in relation to the garden of Eden narrative: What can be done? Is all lost? The answer provided in Leviticus through the Day of Atonement on the stage of the cultic drama, therefore, provides the answer for the cosmos as house of God as well – there must be a Day of Atonement for the cosmos. Ultimately, this annual purgation reiterates the need for a full and final cleansing – one that cannot be threatened or undone – for the covenant

[65] Büchler 1967: 263; Gane 2004: 278.

promise of humanity's communion and fellowship with God to be realized.

Approaching the divine presence

We have already considered how Nadab and Abihu's deaths may be understood as a failed attempt to approach YHWH within the veil, so that Aaron's entrance on the Day of Atonement may be seen as the counterpart, as the God-ordained way of approach. The movement of the book of Leviticus, as well as the covenant between YHWH and Israel it expresses, is one of deepening intimacy with God, deepening access to divine life. Alongside the objective of purifying the tabernacle and Israel, then, one should not lose sight of the complementary theme of approaching the divine Presence. Not only is the annual cleansing necessary so that God may continue abiding among his people, but the ceremony itself represents humanity's closest encounter with God possible in this stage of history – perhaps the nearest approach into his Presence since the expulsion of Adam. 'I will appear in the cloud', YHWH had declared, 'above the atonement lid' (Lev. 16:2).

Using a censer to create a cloud of incense smoke, shielding his eyes from beholding the divine glory, the high priest entered the holy of holies, the cultic counterpart to the heavenly throne room of God. The divine access attempted by the ziggurat builders, constructing its summit into the heavens, was here vouchsafed to Israel through an ordained and consecrated mediator, the high priest, and this on one day alone annually. Pouring full double-handfuls of finely beaten sweet incense onto the pan of burning coals (Lev. 16:12–13), the high priest indeed entered 'heaven' with the clouds. This being the case, when during the exile the prophet Daniel envisions an Adam-like figure approaching God's throne with the clouds of heaven we are probably to understand this as a priestly image,[66] a point to which we will return in a later chapter. In the following section we will consider the approach to God more fully within the context of the Pentateuch's overarching Eden narrative.

Entering Eden

Beyond its setting within the dramatic movement of Leviticus, the Day of Atonement should also be understood within the narrative drama of the Pentateuch broadly and thematically, as the storyline

---

[66] Fletcher-Louis 1997.

has unfolded from Genesis 1 to Leviticus 16.[67] My survey of Genesis and Exodus in previous chapters entailed a journey from Eden as the mountain of God in the beginning to Ararat as the mountain of God in the end-and-new beginning, then on to Sinai as the mountain of God at Israel's beginning, and, finally, to the tabernacle as the mountain of God in Israel's cult. This facet of the tabernacle, common among the temple ideologies of the ANE,[68] whereby the tabernacle/ temple represents an architectural embodiment of the mountain of God, will prove especially helpful for understanding the theology of the Day of Atonement. It should be underscored, however, not only that 'Leviticus exploits to the full an ancient tradition which makes a parallel between Mt. Sinai and the tabernacle,'[69] but that the tabernacle symbolizes the archetypal mountain of God, with Eden near its summit. If Genesis may be adequately labelled 'the longing for Eden', and Exodus 'the return to Eden', then Leviticus may similarly be subtitled 'entering the garden of Eden', especially with reference to Leviticus 16 as its central chapter.

Adam had been rested in the garden of Eden near the summit of the mountain of God. Upon his transgression he and the woman were exiled out of the garden, east of Eden, and YHWH God set cherubim, along with a swirling flaming sword, on the eastward gateway to guard the way to the tree of life. Thereafter, this life of God was, presumably, mediated to Adam's family through a cultic approach at the gateway. The primeval history of Genesis, however, narrates the steady eastward descent of humanity away from the face and abode of God. Once the way of YHWH had been corrupted, the history comes to a close amidst the waters of destruction, the path away from God being one away from life toward death, from cosmos to chaos.

Understanding the Day of Atonement within the narrative context of the Pentateuch, however, not only entails knowing the Eden storyline of Genesis, but also perceiving just how the tabernacle cultus sets the stage for the liturgical drama of Eden's re-entry. It is fitting,

---

[67] As it turns out, some of the Yom Kippur *Sedrei Avodah* poems (some dating perhaps to the second temple period), typically include an account of creation, the history of humanity from Adam to Aaron and a description of the high-priestly ritual on the Day of Atonement (cf. Stökl Ben Ezra 2003: 59–64), in essence following the same theological pathway I am proposing. While we assume the Pentateuch's literary and theological coherence, source critics nevertheless often regard Lev. 16 as the culmination of P's narrative, which begins in Gen. 1. Rarely, however, is the Pentateuch's *storyline* taken into account for understanding the Day of Atonement ceremony.

[68] Lundquist 2014.

[69] Douglas 1999a: 59.

therefore, to rehearse briefly how the tabernacle represented the mountain of God, and how the high priest functioned within that tabernacle stage as an Adam figure.

Tabernacle as cultic mountain of God
In previous chapters we have considered the parallels between the tabernacle and Eden as the mountain of God, noting also its parallels with Mount Sinai. This significance of the tabernacle, that it functions as the mountain of God within the cultus, should be given its just influence upon any consideration of the meaning of priestly ritual in Israel, perhaps especially so with reference to the Day of Atonement ceremony. Once more it is the Eden narrative itself that provides the liturgical drama and logic for the tabernacle cultus. Rehearsing rather briefly, then, a sketch of the parallels that link the tabernacle to the Eden narrative, we recall the following correspondences developed earlier: the divine Presence within the tabernacle is described in terms similar to his Presence in the garden of Eden; the veil partitioning off the holy of holies was woven with cherubim just as cherubim had been stationed to guard entry into the garden of Eden; priestly duty within the tabernacle is depicted with the same verbs used for Adam's duties within the garden; just as the tabernacle is constructed along a threefold graded system of holiness in relation to accessing God's Presence, so Eden as mountain of God established boundaries of holiness related to God's Presence. Taken together, these correspondences served as catechism for Israel, fusing the narrative theology of sacred writ with the ritual theology of approaching YHWH in worship. Within the context of the Pentateuch the tabernacle is a lush garden paradise, the mountain of God with the garden of Eden upon its summit – the way to YHWH God. The holy of holies corresponds to the summit of God's mountain, and so to the garden of Eden found there. Walking westward, therefore, from the courtyard toward the sanctum was a movement toward God, representing Israel to him – an *ascent* into the summit of the architectural mountain of God. Walking eastward from the sanctum toward the courtyard was a movement away from God, representing him to Israel – and a *descent* from the cultic mountain of God.

It is perhaps necessary to emphasize here that the establishment of the tabernacle cultus did not by any means re-establish humanity's pre-expulsion intimacy with God in the garden of Eden. Rather, it appears that Israel's situation may be likened to that of Adam and his family after the expulsion, who lived just outside the garden's gateway and approached his Presence there through divinely revealed cultic ritual. After the nations were scattered eastward, far removed from the face of God, Israel lived as near to life as is possible in a post-expulsion world. Moreover, Israel, within their covenant relationship with God, had the prospect of regaining that life – and the tabernacle cultus, its sacrificial legislation and rituals, along with its priesthood, served to mark out that pathway.

High priest as cultic Adam

The symbolism of the tabernacle as microcosm and Edenic mountain of God cannot be disassociated from the priesthood any more than the creation account can be disassociated from humanity's role within it. As J. A. Davies asks, 'What impression was conveyed to the Israelite community as day by day they saw their priests, dressed in their finery, enter God's house to attend upon him and to enjoy his company in the surroundings of an ideal world?'[70] Taken together, the tabernacle and priesthood constituted something of a celestial globe, as it were, within Israel's midst, a renewed humanity dwelling with God in a consecrated cosmos. Within this sphere the Adamic identity of the high priest in particular is fundamental to the Pentateuch's cultic theology – he functioned as a true or second Adam within the restored Eden of the tabernacle.[71] As such the high priest, exalted above his brothers as the one 'upon whose head the anointing oil was poured and who was consecrated to wear the garments' (Lev. 21:10), is the only one dubbed 'messiah' in the Pentateuch, *hakōhēn hammāšîaḥ* (Lev. 4:3, 5, 16; 6:22). Now the ritual that, within the priesthood, set the high priest apart – indeed, the function and purpose of his anointing – was his exclusive annual entry into the holy of holies.[72] The Day of Atonement was an *entrance rite*, and the messiah's office – his labour and mission – was defined by that entry.

The gate liturgy: Day of Atonement as garden of Eden entry

The Day of Atonement involved, first and foremost, an *entrance rite*, of the high priest into the inner sanctum. As Nihan observes, 'The gradual restitution of the divine presence in Israel's sanctuary is thus structured on the model of an ancient Near Eastern ritual of temple entrance, which finds its climax in the great ceremony of Lev. 16.'[73]

[70] J. A. Davies 2004: 150.
[71] Fletcher-Louis 2004: 96; 2006: 159.
[72] Cf. B. A. Levine 1965: 311.
[73] Nihan 2007: 614.

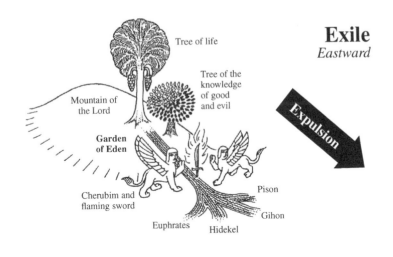

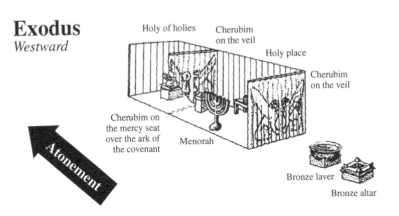

Once more, the tabernacle was not merely the earthly house of God, but the *way* to God – the way of YHWH. Now, keeping in mind the parallels between the garden of Eden and the tabernacle, one may discern readily how the entrance into the holy of holies, 'the archetypal priestly act',[74] comprised a liturgical drama: the annual re-entry into the garden of Eden. On the Day of Atonement Adam's eastward expulsion from the garden of Eden was reversed as the high priest, a

[74] Nelson 1993: 148.

cultic Adam, ascended westward through the cherubim-woven veil and into the summit of the cultic mountain of God. Furthermore, this drama of the garden's re-entry had a theological plot and purpose, as Parry observes, 'Thus, he [the high priest as Adam] returns to the original point of creation, where he pours out the atoning blood of the sacrifice, reestablishing the covenant relationship with God.'[75]

In many ways, our literary journey thus far has been for the sake of understanding the theology of the illustration above.[76] Here, then, at the heart of the Pentateuch we find an answer to the question *Who shall ascend into the mountain of YHWH?* The one able to ascend is the Adam-like high priest, with blood, on the Day of Atonement. *This* is the way YHWH has opened for humanity to dwell in his Presence. As noted in the opening chapter, atonement is the central doctrine of the Pentateuch:

```
FRAME: 'And YHWH said to Moses . . .' (16:1)
            A. Aaron should not go into holy of holies any time he wishes
               (16:2)
                B. Aaron's sacrificial victims, special vestment (16:3–4)
                  C. Sacrificial victims provided by people (16:5)
                      D. Aaron's bull, goat for sin offering, goat for Azazel
                         (16:6–10)
A. Genesis            E. Aaron sacrifices bull (16:11–14)
  B. Exodus             F. Goat sacrificed as sin offering (16:15)
     X. Leviticus – ch. 16 →    X. Atonement (16:16–20a)
  B.' Numbers            F.' Goat sent to wilderness (16:20b–22)
A.' Deuteronomy        E.' Aaron's closing activities (16:23–25)
                      D.' Goat for Azazel, Aaron's bull, goat for sin offering
                         (16:26–28)
                  C.' People rest and humble themselves (16:29–31)
                B.' Anointed priest officiates wearing special garments
                   (16:32–33)
            A.' Anointed priest makes atonement once a year (16:34)
FRAME: 'As YHWH commanded Moses . . .' (16:34)
```

Within the narrative progression, then, atonement, along with its elements of purification and ransom, is that which enables the *return* to YHWH God, a *reversal* of Eden's expulsion. The Pentateuch, therefore, unfolds the *Levitical* way YHWH has opened for humanity to dwell in his Presence, a way characterized by the drama of the cultus, and serving merely as a pattern and analogy for the cosmos. The New Testament, as we will see in chapter 8, declares – most fundamentally

[75] Parry 1994: 135.
[76] The illustration is by Michael P. Lyon, Typography of Eden and Temple.

– the *new* and living way for entering and abiding in YHWH's Presence, a way finally to be experienced within a new cosmos.

The expulsion of the live goat

Part of the high priest's duties on the Day of Atonement included taking two young goats and presenting them before YHWH at the tent of meeting's doorway, to cast lots for them: one designated for YHWH and the other for *'ăzā'zēl*. The high priest would sacrifice the goat whose lot fell for YHWH, using its blood to purify God's house. Upon the head of the second goat he would lean both hands, confessing over it all the guilt and rebellion of Israel, and then an appointed man would lead the goat, symbolically loaded with Israel's sins, out into the wilderness. Here we are concerned with this second goat, utilized for what may be called an elimination rite. The term 'azazel' is problematic, and has defied scholarly consensus with regard to its meaning.[77] There are four main suggestions as to its significance, with some variety within each: (1) azazel may refer to a demon (or to a god of wrath, perhaps even expressing YHWH's own displeasure via an alter ego), (2) azazel may refer to a place, a rocky precipice or the uninhabited wilderness, (3) azazel may simply mean 'utter destruction', (4) azazel may signify 'the goat that is sent away'. Rather than weighing in on the merits and weaknesses of each proposal, I will focus on discerning the significance of the rite itself within the theological drama of the cultus. Whatever the precise import of the term 'azazel', the basic significance of the azazel rite is not difficult to discern – the second goat is used to placard the removal of Israel's sins and guilt.[78] In keeping with that understanding, I will refer to the live goat by its traditional ascription 'scapegoat', along with 'azazel goat', as I make the following two points.

First, the scapegoat's role should be understood in conjunction with that of the goat that is sacrificed. As an elimination rite the azazel goat ritual is often probed in isolation, from a redactional and/or comparative religion approach. Within the context of Leviticus 16, however, the rite is fully integrated as part of one complete ceremony, associated particularly with the young goat that is sacrificed. For example, while two rams are also used on the Day of Atonement, as ascension offerings for the priestly house and for Israel respectively,

[77] Aside from commentaries, see e.g. Cheyne 1895; Feinberg 1958; Ashbel 1965; Tawil 1980; Wright 1987: 31–74; Grabbe 1987; Wright 1992b; Janowski 1995; Levy 1998; Douglas 2003; Pinker 2007.
[78] Hoffmann 1906: 444; Wenham 1979: 235.

yet these two animals are not brought together in the same fashion as are the two goats. The text is quite careful to portray the goats as a set: the high priest takes them both from the congregation of Israel, presents them both together before YHWH at the door of the tent of meeting, and then casts lots for them both. The instructions for the high priest in Leviticus 16:5, moreover, refer to both goats together as a single purification offering:[79] 'He will take from the congregation of the sons of Israel male goats as a purification offering.' To be sure, the expulsion rite is not an offering in the technical sense. Nevertheless, in removing sin, the scapegoat's function fits the precise significance of *ḥaṭṭāʾt* as 'purification',[80] and, combined with the blood manipulation of the sacrificed goat, completes the picture of atonement. Indeed, there is historical precedent for understanding these goats to be identical in appearance, and chosen expressly because of this likeness,[81] as if it were one goat accomplishing two different aspects of atonement – purification and expiation, cleansing from sin's pollution and the removal of sin's guilt.

Secondly, the expulsion rite should be understood within the context of the tabernacle's cultic geography. That the scapegoat symbolically carries away Israel's sins is plain enough. The significance of the wilderness as the scapegoat's destination, however, is rarely appreciated. Rudman, a notable exception, understands the wilderness as analogous to the waters of chaos, a place of non-creation, so that in removing sin from Israel, the azazel-goat removed chaos from creation.[82] This goat, as D. Davies put it, 'passed from the realm of ordered society, from the holiness of the tabernacle into the chaos, into the symbolic nothingness which obtained outside the community of God's people'.[83] What remains is to fit that understanding of the wilderness within the complex of the tabernacle's Eden symbolism. Upon the summit of the mountain of God the garden of Eden stands as the apogee of life and cosmos; the wilderness forms the precise antonym and polar opposite: death and chaos. One may discern this relationship, for example, in the prophecy of Isaiah 51:3 (cf. Ezek. 36:35):

---

[79] Cf. Kaufmann 1947: 571–572.

[80] Milgrom 1990: 1018.

[81] E.g. *m. Yom.* 6.1 states, 'The two goats of Yom Kippur, it is a mitzvah that they be equal in appearance, height, value and be bought at the same time.' See the earliest extant sources delineated by Stökl Ben Ezra (2003: 29, n. 53).

[82] Rudman 2005. Note how the wilderness is described in terms of the waters of chaos in Deut. 32:10 (*tōhû*; cf. Gen. 1:2).

[83] D. Davies 2009: 394–395.

> For YHWH will comfort Zion,
> > he will comfort all her desolate places;
> He will make her wilderness like Eden,
> And her desert like the garden of YHWH . . .

This cultic geography receives its bearings in relation to YHWH: the holy of holies represents his Presence as the fountain of life, while the wilderness represents the furthest remove from his face and is thus the place of darkness and death. Now it is of peculiar interest that the two goats of the Day of Atonement proceed in opposite directions, one journeying into the garden of Eden via its lifeblood and the other away from YHWH, to the wilderness loaded with Israel's sins. Moreover, as both goats begin together at the doorway of the tent of meeting, their movement may be tracked along an east–west alignment, movements coordinated with the early narratives of Genesis in relation to God's Presence. Here it is worth emphasizing that the goats, as one symbol, stand *for the sake of* Israel: the sacrificed goat conveying Israel favourably into the inner sanctum vicariously, the led-away goat conveying Israel's sins away from the face of God. Broadly, then, the scapegoat signifies *expulsion* (from Eden, within the cultic geography established by the tabernacle).[84]

It is not difficult to see how this separation of the two goats could be readily perceived as portraying a final separation – a day of judgment in the ultimate sense.

Excursus: Adam's fall

I have now traced the Pentateuch's narrative from Genesis 1 to Leviticus 16, from Adam's descent of the Edenic mountain of God to the high priest's ascent of the cultic mountain of God. From this vantage point of Leviticus 16 it may be helpful now to take a westward glance back to a previous question regarding Adam. Noah upon the summit of the Ararat mountain had offered up ascension offerings, an atonement at the foundation of the new beginning; the patriarch Abraham was called to the summit of Mount Moriah to offer up Isaac

---

[84] This point evades typical scholarly debate over whether the scapegoat may be said to prefigure Christ or Satan, etc. As a symbol for expulsion (and ultimate perdition), it is analogous to Israel in exile, the final damnation of the reprobate, including that of Satan, and the exile suffered by Jesus Christ on behalf of his people upon the cross.

as an ascension offering; after the golden calf apostasy Moses had ascended Mount Sinai to offer himself up as an atonement for Israel; and now we have found that the annual divinely ordained ascent into the summit of the cultic mountain of God was for the express purpose of making atonement by the Adam-like high priest. The weight of these examples, which may justly be defined as a pattern, must bear upon our understanding of what Adam should have done when he was faced with the transgression of the woman. Is it possible the narrative leans toward the possibility of Adam's offering himself up as an atonement for the sake of the woman? The question becomes more relevant when we consider the following points: (1) that Adam was 'one flesh' with her, (2) the later gestures of atonement throughout Genesis (and the Pentateuch), (3) that Adam is put forth as the archetypal high priest dwelling within the archetypal holy of holies.

As to the first concern, it is worth probing the function of Genesis 2 in the light of the woman's sin in Genesis 3. In Genesis 2:18 YHWH God had described Adam's aloneness as 'not good' (*lo'-ṭôb*), a significant statement within the context of his repeated affirmations of good with regard to every aspect of creation in Genesis 1. This lack is eventually resolved with the creation of the woman, so that chapter 2 ends with Adam's declaration 'This is now bone of my bone and flesh of my flesh,' and so on, in verse 23, while the final verses, verses 24–25, reiterate the one-flesh status of a man and his wife. Now within this arc from lack to resolution we find an odd reference in verses 19–20, namely that God brought before Adam every beast of the field and every bird of the air, but 'for Adam there was found no helper suitable to him'. In communicating the basic incompatibility of humans and animals this passage drives a stake into the heart of the Levitical cultus – for 'it is not possible for the blood of bulls and goats to take away sins' (Heb. 10:4). As we have noted with reference to the dietary laws and to the tabernacle cultus in general, animals stand as substitutes merely for the *drama* of the cultus, as established and therefore accepted by God. However, the converse is also taught by the text, positively: blameless Adam was the only true substitute possible to atone for the woman's sin. Indeed, one may argue that the woman's origin takes this catechism one step further: she was brought forth from Adam amidst a divinely imposed sleep. Historically, the church has understood the atonement of Christ's death as that of the last Adam who accomplished precisely what the first Adam had failed to do, an idea possibly reflected already in the Gospel of John

(19:33–34), where, amidst the sleep of death upon the cross, Christ's side is opened for the creation/redemption of his bride, the church.[85]

Secondly, the failure to make some gesture of atonement within the garden of Eden appears to linger throughout the narrative of the Pentateuch, seeking fulfilment. Several factors suggest such a reading. At the heart and literary centre of the Pentateuch, as we have already seen, Adam's failure finds cultic fulfilment on the Day of Atonement, as the high priest ascends into the architectural garden of Eden with the blood of atonement. We have also already noted the pattern of atonement upon mountain summits. As something of the father of humanity, Noah's first act after the flood is to offer up ascension offerings upon the Ararat mount as an atonement; Abraham is called to offer up Isaac as an ascension offering upon Mount Moriah, and so on. But also, in more subtle ways, the narratives demonstrate a divine solicitation of just such a gesture of atonement. God's testing of Abraham is, perhaps, obvious enough. Less appreciated is the role of Judah in what is often dubbed the Joseph story (Gen. 37 – 50), the centre of which focuses upon Judah's intercession before Joseph, the longest and most impassioned speech in Genesis, noted by scholars for its persuasive eloquence,[86] wherein he offers himself in the stead of his brother Benjamin (44:32–34; cf. 43:9). It is this act, as emphasized by the narrative, which triggers Joseph's self-disclosure and the story's reversal.[87] Similarly, when Israel faced God's impending wrath after worshipping the golden calf, Moses ascended Sinai's summit and offered himself as an atonement (Exod. 32:30–35). As these examples demonstrate, whether or not YHWH will accept such an act is not the point – indeed, in the latter three cases there was no final implementation – but rather the gesture itself underscores the mystery of the divine purpose. So with Adam's fall, the theological possibility of his standing as an atoning substitute (intriguing as it is) is not at issue, but rather what sort of response would have been fitting as the son of God, as the father of humanity, as the woman's husband?

Finally, the previous two points should be considered within the context of the tabernacle and priestly imagery woven throughout

---

[85] See Daniélou 1960: 48–56. Jesus then awakes (resurrects) in a garden, calling Mary 'woman', she mistaking him for a gardener (John 19:41; 20:14–15). John's narrative reflects an Adam theology already evident in the Pauline epistles (cf. Rom. 5:12–21; 1 Cor. 15:21–22).

[86] Cf. Wenham 1987: 425.

[87] There are, in fact, significant links between the Joseph story and the Day of Atonement, discerned already in *Jub.* 34.17–18 (*c.* second century BC; see J. M. Harris 1996; Carmichael 2000).

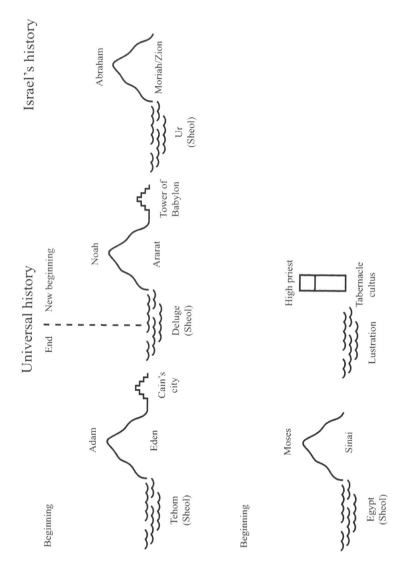

the Eden narrative. Adam is portrayed as the archetypal high priest dwelling in the archetypal holy of holies. Arguably, the original audience would have seen readily Adam's omission: What work, after all, does the high priest perform the only time he is allowed within the holy of holies, if not the work of atonement? Returning to Leviticus 16, one may surmise the Day of Atonement called upon both memory and faith: memory, a looking back to the first Adam's failure and expulsion from the divine Presence in Eden; faith, a looking forward to the remedy for that expulsion, to the last Adam's re-entry into God's abode with his own blood for atonement. Atonement is at the heart of the Pentateuch, because atonement is the doorway to life with God. The theme of YHWH's opening a way for humanity to dwell in his Presence, as I have suggested throughout this work, advances the main storyline of the Pentateuch, enabling one to discern the logic and beauty of Leviticus' central position within that context. As the next chapter will endeavour to demonstrate, while atonement is the doorway to life with God, that life itself is possible only through holiness – to dwell with God humanity must be holy.

Chapter Six

Meeting with God at the house of God: the dramatic movement of Leviticus 17 – 27

Introduction

By chapter 16 of Leviticus the tabernacle cultus is complete from the perspective of basic legislation: the way of approach through sacrifices mediated by a consecrated priesthood has been revealed, as well as the means for restoring the cultus regularly after it has become defiled. This newly opened access to God, however, is not the goal of the covenant; it is, rather, a means to the end of life with God. To a large degree, then, the second half of Leviticus deals with this prospect of life with God, including the implications for the people who have YHWH dwelling in their midst, who are being cleansed and consecrated through YHWH's Presence in the tabernacle cultus. Also, while it is true that the basic legislation for the tabernacle cultus is complete, nevertheless further legislation is necessary, particularly in relation to Israel's calendar – the annual festivals must be divinely appointed. Though, increasingly, the idea of sacred time has become elusive in modern culture, we have already seen that it is key to understanding the creation account, woven into the cosmos itself. One might ask, for example, what good it is to have a sanctuary-like cosmos (sacred space) with a priestly humanity (sacred status), apart from appointed times of fellowship with God (sacred time). Similarly, without appointed Sabbaths and festivals for fellowship with God, the tabernacle, along with its priesthood and rituals for drawing near, would have no *telos* or purpose. The tabernacle, after all, was meant by God to be a tent of *meeting*. As we will see, the final third of Leviticus resounds with the festive gatherings of Israel's calendar – a sure signal that the dwelling of God has indeed become the tent of meeting between Israel and God.

Approaching the third section of Leviticus, one does not find any narrative introducing an obvious crisis to propel the story's movement onward. The main reason for this is that the crisis caused by the deaths of Aaron's sons requires *both* the second and third sections of Leviticus for full resolution. This point is evident from the programmatic statement we have already considered in Leviticus 10:10 – the divine response to the tragedy, in other words, not only encompassed chapters 11–15 (distinguishing 'between unclean and clean', culminating in ch. 16), but also chapters 17–27 (distinguishing 'between holy and profane'). To be sure, the atonement ceremony of Leviticus 16 had cleansed the sacred space from defilement and allowed for a deeper entrance into the divine Presence by the high priest. But the deaths of Nadab and Abihu had also unveiled more clearly both the utter holiness of God and the severe limitations of the cultic – or *any* – system to neutralize the reality of his holiness.[1] The only effective and lasting safeguard in God's Presence must necessarily be authentic holiness; hence chapters 17–27 of Leviticus. This is not to say, however, that there is no dramatic movement from the central high point, the Day of Atonement ceremony, to the end of the book. When approached through the unifying theme of Israel's gradually deepening relationship with YHWH, the final section of Leviticus will be found to possess the weightiest drama, and to hold out the most intimate manner of life in the divine Presence possible. Now that a way to cleanse and renew the tabernacle cultus has been established in Leviticus 16, the prospect is opened for that tabernacle cultus to *function* as the regular place for Israel's appointed meetings with God – it is now ready to function as the tent of meeting, the *'ōhel mô'ēd* in the life of Israel. As a *consequence* of the Day of Atonement Israel is now able to *participate* in God's holiness – a prospect with a view to full and lasting communion with YHWH God.

This work has proposed that the literary movement of the book of Leviticus lies in the drama of how God's dwelling (the tabernacle) becomes Israel's meeting place with God (the tent of meeting) – that is, how the *miškān* becomes the *'ōhel mô'ēd*. This goal, as we will see in due course, is portrayed symbolically in Leviticus 24:1–9. I will begin therefore by probing the cultic symbolism of the lampstand and bread of the presence in Leviticus 24:1–9, and then, positioning that account within the overall movement of Leviticus, I will endeavour to demonstrate that it functions as the heart of the book's resolution.

[1] See G. A. Anderson 2015.

Because, in general terms, the third section of Leviticus runs from chapter 17 to 27, one may ask legitimately why I am focusing upon Leviticus 24 as the culmination to the third movement (and, indeed, as the culmination of the whole threefold movement of Leviticus). Briefly, the subdivisions to this third section yield the holiness laws of chapters 17–22, followed by the appointment of sacred times in chapters 23–25. Leviticus 26 then *applies* the entire revelation of Leviticus 1 – 25 with covenant promises and threats, a sure sign that the book's final movement has already been accomplished, while scholars widely consider Leviticus 27 an appendix. After Leviticus 23 – 25 has demonstrated that the dwelling has become a tent of meeting, that covenantal gift of God is applied in the life of Israel. Therefore, in accord with the literary strategy of the book's first two movements, we are aiming to probe how the inserted legislation of chapters 17–22 relate to the resolution of the third movement in chapters 23–25. Leviticus 24, as we will see, is at the heart of chapters 23–25, and in many ways summarizes symbolically the goal of the entire cultic system.

The symbolism of the lampstand and bread of the Presence

In this section my goal is to make the case that the lampstand shining upon the bread of the presence offers a symbolic picture of the Sabbath: Israel basking in the light of God's blessed presence, mediated by the cultus:

> Then YHWH spoke to Moses, saying: 'Command the sons of Israel to bring you pure oil of beaten olives for the light, to make the lamps burn/ascend [*lĕhaʿălōt*] continually [*tāmîd*]. Outside the veil of the testimony, in the tabernacle of meeting, Aaron will tend it from evening until morning before YHWH continually [*tāmîd*]; it will be an everlasting statute in your generations. He will tend the lamps on the pure [gold] lampstand before YHWH continually [*tāmîd*].
>
> 'And you will take fine flour and bake twelve loaves with it. Two-tenths of an ephah will be in each loaf. You will set them in two piles, six in a row, on the pure [gold] table before YHWH. And you will put pure frankincense on each pile, so that it may be on the bread for a memorial, a fire-gift to YHWH. Sabbath by Sabbath he will tend it before YHWH continually [*tāmîd*], from the sons of

Israel as an everlasting covenant. And it will be for Aaron and his sons, and they will eat it in a holy place, for it is most holy to him from the fire-gifts of YHWH, an everlasting statute.' (Lev. 24:1–9)

The lampstand and bread of the presence in Numbers 8:1–4

Before attempting to discern the meaning of the cultic ritual as described in Leviticus 24:1–9, it may be helpful first to rehearse the significance of the similar account in the book of Numbers, which we considered in the prologue. Numbers 8:1–4, we saw, narrates YHWH's instructions through Moses for Aaron to arrange the lamps of the candelabra in the holy place so that they beam their light forward, upon the twelve loaves of bread (representing Israel) on the golden table. This scene portrayed symbolically much the same as the priestly benediction found in Numbers 6:23–27, namely the blessed light of God's face shining upon his people, as mediated through the priesthood. Numbers 6:23–27 and 8:1–4 present the blessing of God upon the people of God, mediated by the priesthood of God. The arrangement of the holy place in Numbers 8:1–4, therefore, portrays the ideal of Israel basking in the light of the divine Presence. The symbolism of Leviticus 24:1–9 will be found to be consistent with that of Numbers, with however the added emphasis upon sacred time, and particularly that of the Sabbath.

The lampstand and bread of the presence in Leviticus 24:1–9

Turning now to Leviticus 24:1–9, we will consider the text's two sub-divisions – verses 1–4 pertaining to the lampstand, and verses 5–9 pertaining to the bread – together as one complete portrait. Both sections highlight Aaron's duties (vv. 3–4, 8–9), the people's contribution to the ritual (vv. 2, 8) and contain requirements referred to as everlasting statutes (vv. 3, 9). Both sections, furthermore, emphasize the continual nature of these requirements through the use of the Hebrew word *tāmîd* (continually, continuity). While the tending of the lampstand is a daily *tāmîd*, evening and morning, yet the renewed arrangement of the fresh bread with the addition of incense is per-formed as a weekly *tāmîd*, specifically on the Sabbath, and is dubbed an everlasting covenant.[2]

---

[2] The bread, with the addition of pure frankincense as a memorial, is also said to constitute an *'iššeh*, a gift by fire to YHWH (v. 7). As their due, the priests receive the bread that was removed and are to eat it in a holy place (v. 9).

Roy Gane's study, though treating the bread ritual alone, makes two observations useful for our purpose. First, as the only offering designated 'an eternal covenant', the bread of the presence uniquely symbolizes the relationship between YHWH and his people.[3] Rightly, he associates the twelve loaves with the twelve tribes of Israel, suggesting that even the division into two piles of six supports this understanding (cf. Exod. 28:9–12; Deut. 27:11–13). I would suggest once more, however, that, in order to symbolize the covenant relationship, the bread of the presence in verses 5–9 should be read in the light – literally – of the lampstand ritual (vv. 1–4). In fact, the original instructions for the lampstand in Exodus 25:37, quite similar to those found in Numbers 8:1–4, make the inclusion of the table of shewbread *normative* for the lampstand's symbolism: 'You shall make seven lamps for it, and then arrange its lamps so that they shine light in front of it.'

Secondly, Gane affirms that the changing of the bread on the Sabbath defines its meaning in terms of Sabbath (and creation) theology, noting that the Sabbath itself is referred to as an 'eternal covenant' and 'a sign' between YHWH and Israel (Exod. 31:16–17).[4] Now given that the menorah is made up of seven lamps, which require the evening and morning *tāmîd*, it could be that a cosmological symbolism links this ritual with the bread *tāmîd*, focusing on the Sabbath in particular.[5] Along similar lines Poythress writes that the seven lamps correlate

with the general symbolism for time within Israel. The heavenly bodies were made in order to 'serve as signs to mark seasons and days and years' (Genesis 1:14). The whole cycle of time marked by the sun and moon and stars is divided up into sevens: the seventh day in the week is the Sabbath day; the seventh month is the month of atonement (Leviticus 16:29); the seventh year is the year of release from debts and slavery (Deuteronomy 15); the seventh of the seven-year cycles is the year of jubilee (Leviticus 25). Fittingly, the lampstand contains the same sevenfold division, symbolizing the cycle of time provided by the heavenly lights.[6]

[3] Gane 1992. See also Hoffmann 1971, 2: 212.

[4] Gane 1992. Inasmuch as Exod. 16 also involves Israel, bread and the Sabbath (note the emphasis on the bread's being fresh on the Sabbath, vv. 24–27), its relationship to Lev. 24 is worth exploring.

[5] Ruwe (1999: 324–325) e.g. believes the menorah may be associated with the sevenfold structure of Gen. 1.

[6] Poythress 1995: 18–19.

Just as the creation account establishes the evening and morning of days for the sake of the Sabbath, the daily *tāmîd* of verses 1–4 of Leviticus 24 similarly establishes a rhythm of days for the sake of the Sabbath *tāmîd* in verses 5–9. Already, then, one may discern the profound homology between cosmos and cult: just as the cosmos was created for humanity's Sabbath communion and fellowship with God, so too the cult was established for Israel's Sabbath communion and fellowship with God. 'Sabbath by Sabbath' (*bĕyôm haššabbāt bĕyôm haššabbāt*), as verse 8 has it, the twelve loaves of bread are renewed in the light of the lampstand. This cultic drama, I propose, symbolizes the ideal Sabbath, the twelve tribes of Israel basking in the divine light, being renewed in God's Presence Sabbath by Sabbath.

Leviticus 24:1–9 within the context of chapters 23–25

We turn now to investigate the significance of Leviticus 24:1–9 within the context of chapters 23–25. Leigh Trevaskis has convincingly argued that Leviticus 24:1–9 presents the ideal of Israel paused in worship before YHWH, on the sabbatical occasions described in chapters 23 and 25 that frame it.[7] He notes that chapters 23 and 25 are united by two common themes, the first of which is a concern for calendric time. Israel's annual feasts are delineated in chapter 23, emphasizing their dates in particular. This stress on calendric time is especially evident when compared with the enumeration of feasts in Numbers 28 – 29, which devotes more attention to the prescribed offerings than to their appointed times. Chapter 25, establishing the (seventh year) land Sabbath (vv. 1–7) and the (fiftieth year) jubilee Sabbath (vv. 9–55), is also clearly concerned with calendrical time.

The second common theme uniting both chapters, as noted by Trevaskis, is a sabbatical principle. The two Sabbaths detailed in chapter 25 are apparent enough, yet the same is also true for the appointed feasts of chapter 23: there are seven major festivals, seven days of rest, several festivals occurring on the seventh month, every seven years being a sabbatical year, and there is a grand sabbatical year after the seventh of the seven-year cycles. As Jay Sklar remarks, this structure 'brings a Sabbath feel to the entire year and thus a constant reminder of the covenant the Sabbath signifies'.[8] J. H. Kurtz, in his classic nineteenth-century work on the sacrificial worship of the Old Testament, expressed a similar sentiment:

---

[7] Trevaskis 2009; cf. Walton 2001b: 302–303.
[8] Sklar 2014: 277.

The peculiar character of the Mosaic festivals was expressed *formally* in their being regulated as much as possible by the number seven, as the stamp of the covenant of God with Israel . . . and *materially* by their being separated from the labours, toils, and cares of everyday life for the sanctification and consecration of the whole man to purposes of religion and the worship of God.[9]

Since we have already noted how the *tāmîd*s of the lampstand and the bread of the presence both underscore the element of time in a way similar to the creation account, focusing upon the Sabbath, it seems Leviticus 24:1–9 fits well within the thematic context of chapters 23–25 and, as a cultic symbol, certainly appears to capture the ideal for Israel's sacred convocations, which are themselves rooted in the Sabbath.[10] Indeed, the introduction (Lev. 23:1–4) to the festival legislation bookends the Sabbath (v. 3) with dual references to the appointed feasts of YHWH (*mô'ădê yhwh*) and the holy convocations (*miqrā'ê qōdeš*):[11]

And YHWH spoke to Moses, saying, 'Speak to the sons of Israel and say to them:

"The appointed feasts [*mô'ădê*] of YHWH which you are to proclaim as holy convocations, these are my appointed feasts [*mô'ădāy*].

"Six days shall work be done, but the seventh day is a Sabbath of solemn rest, a holy convocation. You shall do no work. It is a Sabbath to YHWH in all your dwellings.

"These are the appointed feasts [*mô'ădê*] of YHWH, the holy convocations, which you shall proclaim at their appointed time [*mô'ădām*]."'

(Vv. 2–4)

[9] Kurtz 1998: 342; emphases original.

[10] Gorman (1997: 127) also makes the observation that 'Leviticus 23 divides the year into two parts by placing emphasis on the activities of the first month and the seventh month. The two-part division of the year reflects the two-part division of the day – day and night. Two seven-day observances are also required, one in the first month and one in the seventh month. In addition, seven holy convocations are identified in the calendar (vv. 7, 8, 21, 24, 27, 35, 36).' If valid, the twofold and sevenfold nature of the annual feasts comports well with the lampstand and bread *tāmîd*s, respectively.

[11] Cf. Baumgarten 1966: 278, who notes a similar phenomenon in the summation toward the end of the chapter (vv. 37–38), pointing out how this Sabbath 'intrusion' had led to the rabbinic query 'What place has the Sabbath in the chapter dealing with the festivals?' (*Sifra ad locum*).

What the insertion of the Sabbath accomplishes in Leviticus 23:1–4 is likewise accomplished by the insertion of Leviticus 24:1–9 between chapters 23 and 25. 'Once we have recognized the notion of the "Sabbath" to be an important thread running through Lev. 23–26,' writes Warning, 'one must admit that this keyword – occurring twice in 24:5–9 – may have prompted the ancient author to place this pericope here.'[12] The lampstand shining its light upon the twelve fragrant loaves is a symbol of the covenant,[13] the covenant itself signified by the Sabbath – Leviticus 24:1–9 *is* a picture of the Sabbath. We may therefore conclude that Leviticus 24:1–9, as a cultic symbol, is the theological heart of chapters 23 to 25.

Leviticus 24:1–9 and the blasphemer tale (24:10–23)

Since understanding the unity of chapter 24 as a whole will be helpful toward considering the structure of Leviticus below, the relationship between 24:1–9 and 24:10–23 must be addressed briefly.[14] Building on the work of Bibb,[15] Trevaskis explains the function of the blasphemer story in verses 10–23 as serving as something of a foil to the cultic ideal expressed in verses 1–9, in effect extending the ideal holiness of the community represented in the ritual (vv. 1–9) to every aspect of life in the camp/land – even to the sojourner (vv. 10–23).[16] His fine analysis may be buttressed by reflecting upon the tale's emphasis on the sacred 'name' of YHWH, noted three times (vv. 11, 16 [twice]). Recalling now that the Levitical blessing of Numbers 6:23–27, in which YHWH's face is made to shine upon Israel, is formally characterized as 'placing my name upon them' (v. 27), we may see how Israel's Sabbath by Sabbath basking in the divine Presence sanctifies the community particularly by placing the sacred name upon them. Significantly, Leviticus 22 closes with legislation concerning the divine name in terms quite similar to that of the Sabbath: neither the 'holy' name nor the 'holy' Sabbath is to be 'profaned',

[12] Warning 1999: 94.
[13] It is fitting, then, and perhaps a part of the symbolism, that Moses, who brought the twelve tribes into the divine Presence within the Sinai covenant, is the one who first brings the twelve loaves into the light of the lampstand (vv. 5–7). Cf. Trevaskis 2009: 303; Leithart 2014.
[14] Typically, scholars explain Lev. 24:10–23 as a rather obvious interpolation that, perhaps, maintains structural balance with the Nadab and Abihu narrative (10:1–7) yet without manifesting any coherence with its literary context. See e.g. Milgrom 2008: 2082. For a review of some of the textual difficulties inherent in the blasphemer story, see Hutton 1999.
[15] Bibb 2005: 210–215.
[16] Trevaskis 2009.

because it is 'YHWH who sanctifies you' (22:32–33; cf. Exod.
31:13–14). Kamionkowski (2009) understands the name as expressing the holy bond that binds God and Israel together, serving as
a 'portal' or meeting place between the divine and human, and
concludes that the sojourner's blaspheme was a sort of penetration
(*nāqab*) into the divine sphere akin to an unwelcome entry into the
holy of holies, a relevant analogy as we will see in the next section.[17]
Here, however, it is worth pointing out that the chapter's general
movement progresses in focus from the community's innermost heart
(vv. 1–9) to its outermost edges (vv. 10–23), in terms of location
(holy place vs. outside the camp), identity (Israel vs. association
with Egypt) and actions (life vs. death), a movement that mimics
the pattern followed on the Day of Atonement.[18] Along with the
sanctuary, the Sabbath and the divine name are the major sancta
that can be desecrated by Israel.[19] Its placement within the Decalogue,
moreover, affirms a primarily *cultic* purpose for the divine name
(Exod. 20):

- No other gods but YHWH (v. 3).
- No idols/likeness for YHWH (vv. 4–6).
- Hallowing the divine name (v. 7).
- Sabbath (vv. 8–11).

While the first and fourth commands pertain to the proper object and
time of worship, the second and third commands may be regarded
together as relating to the proper manner of worship. God had given
Israel his name for the sake of invoking him in worship, a spiritual
Presence contrasted with that of idols. Shortly after the Decalogue,
the divine name is contrasted with idols once more: 'You shall not
make anything to be with me – gods of silver or gods of gold you
shall not make for yourselves. . . . In every place where I record
my name I will come to you, and I will bless you' (Exod. 20:23–24).
Von Rad is, therefore, correct in saying that as 'the very heart of
the cult of ancient Israel' the divine name theologically 'takes the

[17] Kamionkowski 2009.
[18] Rooke (2015: 167) also notes, 'Indeed, in Lev. 22:32–33 there is a specific association of Egypt with profaning the name of God, when via Moses God tells the
Israelites, "You shall not profane my holy name, that I may be sanctified among
the people of Israel; I am the Lord, I sanctify you, I who brought you out of the land
of Egypt to be your God: I am the Lord."'
[19] Nihan 2007: 99; cf. Wright 1992a: 735; Kleinig 2003: 11–12.

place which in other cults was occupied by the cultic image'.[20] In giving them his name, YHWH had given Israel himself, along with the ever-present help and benediction such access to his Presence opened – the utmost being his divine Presence in worship by invocation.[21] The holiness section of Leviticus is laced with warnings against profaning the divine name (see 18:21; 19:12; 20:3; 21:6; 22:2, 32), and these should be understood primarily within the context of the name's cultic usage. The sacred name was given chiefly as the means by which to invoke God's Presence on the Sabbath, and its profanation in the second half of Leviticus 24 marks a clear contrast with the portrait of the first half. If we understand God's name as something of a sanctuary outside the sanctuary, related to the light of his countenance, then the literary placement of the blasphemer story obtains coherence.[22] The shift from cult (vv. 1–9) to community (vv. 10–23) in Leviticus 24, moreover, offers in microcosm the general movement of the book of Leviticus from cult (chs. 1–16) to community (chs. 17–27),[23] a movement to which we now turn our attention.

The dramatic movement of Leviticus 17 – 25

In this section I will position Leviticus 24:1–9 within the final movement of Leviticus, considering how it functions to portray symbolically that the *miškān* has now become an *'ōhel mô'ēd* indeed. Once more this finale requires understanding the promises and threats of chapter 26 as the *application* of chapters 1 to 25, a sure signal that the basic content has been covered.[24] We proceed, therefore, with the supposition that chapters 23–25 (with Lev. 24 as their heart) form the climax to the dramatic movement of the book, a climax that is both festive and jubilant.[25]

---

[20] Von Rad 1962: 183.

[21] Kleinig 1992.

[22] In Deuteronomy the place where Israel will approach God in the land is characterized as the place where he chooses 'to put his name' for his dwelling place (see 12:5, 21; 14:24; 16:2).

[23] Cf. Bibb 2005: 210–215; Trevaskis 2009: 307–312.

[24] Ch. 27 should probably be regarded as something of an epilogue or appendix (though no mere afterthought), which, in a similar fashion to the book of Deuteronomy, keeps the book from ending with covenant threats/curses (see Hartley 1992: 479; C. R. Smith 1996: 30; Nihan 2007: 94).

[25] This is the case whether one restricts the 'feasts' section to chs. 23–25 or, with Zenger (1999), to chs. 23–26.

The terms miškan and 'ōhel mô'ēd

A preliminary discussion of the terms 'dwelling' (*miškān*) and 'tent of meeting' (*'ōhel mô'ēd*) is necessary at the outset. Is it legitimate to make much of terms that may otherwise appear to be used synonymously (as translated e.g. by the LXX and Vulgate)? No doubt some scholars would not concede such a nuanced use of terms, even at the level of redaction. Historically, source-critical scholarship has maintained that after incorporating the designation 'tent of meeting' from earlier sources (E and J, or possibly D), the Priestly writer used the terms *miškān* and *'ōhel mô'ēd* indiscriminately, without any intended difference in meaning.[26] Several factors, however, suggest that the possibility is at least worth exploring. First, etymologically, of course, there is a clear difference of emphasis in both terms, even though they have the same referent. *Miškān* highlights the tabernacle as God's dwelling place, the earthly copy of his heavenly abode; while *'ōhel mô'ēd* underscores the tabernacle as the place designated for Israel to meet with God at the appointed times.[27]

Secondly, at least *some* of the time, the Pentateuch does appear to use each of these terms in a manner that is sensitive to their etymological nuance. While my approach to the overall dramatic movement of Leviticus presents a major scenario (in relation to Exod. 40:34–35), yet just such a careful and deliberate use of these terms appears also in Exodus 25:9 – 33:7. Within this section Exodus 25:9 – 27:19, which for the most part contains instructions for making the various furnishings and curtains of the tabernacle (and courtyard), utilizes *miškān* exclusively (nineteen times). Exodus 27:20 – 33:7, however, which includes instructions regarding Aaron's garments and the cultic functions within the tabernacle, utilizes *'ōhel mô'ēd* exclusively (seventeen times). Here it is perhaps significant that this section begins with Exodus 27:20–21, constituting the first use of the term *'ōhel mô'ēd* in the Pentateuch, by relating the daily *tāmîd* of the lampstand. Indeed, the transition from the former section to the latter is marked by the only occurrence of the term *'ăbōdâ*, 'service', within Exodus

---

[26] See e.g. Haran 1985: 272.

[27] Cf. Averbeck 2003: 807–827. Haran (1985: 269) notes the fundamental distinction between these two terms (God's 'abode' vs. the place to which he comes at 'the appointed time'), but only at the source level (as a distinction between the P and E tents), asserting that P uses both terms indiscriminately. This assessment has not gone unchallenged, however. Sommer (2001: 56), for example, has affirmed P's intended difference in these terms, suggesting they manifest a tension between two orientations toward divine presence within P itself. On either approach the point stands.

25 – 27 (27:19), manifesting the shift in focus from the tabernacle's construction/equipment to its cultic function.[28] Moreover, since Exodus 25 – 31 is widely attributed to P,[29] a literary approach to the material seems probably to have more potential for explaining word choice than a merely source-critical one. In a three-part study of the usage of these two terms in Exodus 25 – 40 Hendrix concludes that the expressions *miškān* and *'ōhel mô'ēd* are discrete and specific rather than interchangeable, and that most analyses of this text have lacked sensitivity to the distinction between these two terms, which he explains as follows: in Exodus 25 – 40 *miškān* is used within the context of constructing the tabernacle as a transient dwelling place, whereas *'ōhel mô'ēd* is used when the context is the tabernacle's cultic function.[30] A few decades earlier Kearney had already observed as much, in relation to the first (Exod. 25:1 – 30:10) of the seven speeches that comprise chapters 25–31:

> Most of it separates readily under two general headings: the Dwelling and its furnishings (25:8–27:19) and the priesthood of Aaron (27:20–29:42). One clear distinction between these two parts is in the name of the sanctuary: *mishkan* ('Dwelling') in the first and *'ōhel mô'ēd* ('Tent of Meeting') in the second. 'Tent of Meeting' is an apt name in this second section, where the redactor builds climactically towards a continuous sequence of cultic 'meetings' with God (cf. 29:38–43). The divine establishing of the Aaronide priesthood is a proximate preparation for these 'meetings' and, most significantly, at the beginning and within the conclusion of this second part, there is mentioned Aaron's care of the lamps (27:20–21; 30:7–8). This 'inclusion' was of major importance to the redactor, for he allowed abrupt transitions in the text in order to achieve it.[31]

My suggested significance for Leviticus 24:1–9 corresponds well with Kearney's two insights here, making sense of the use of *'ōhel mô'ēd* in 27:20 – 29:42 and explaining why the inclusion of Aaron's care of the lamps (27:20–21; 30:7–8) was of such 'major importance' since it portrays symbolically the goal of the covenant as it is expressed and experienced through the tabernacle cultus. Although this topic

---

[28] Averbeck 2003: 810.
[29] See e.g. Childs 2004: 529–537.
[30] Hendrix 1992a; cf. 1991; 1992b.
[31] Kearney 1977: 375.

requires (and merits) its own separate study, the case for an undiffer-entiated use of *miškān* and *'ōhel mô'ēd* is inconclusive and contested, while that for a logical use of these terms according to their etymology appears strong, at least in some sections of the Pentateuch. This point leaves open the possibility we have been pursuing, namely that the difference in these terms is key to the drama of Leviticus. That drama, we recall, began with the crisis introduced at the end of the book of Exodus (40:34–35), wherein we read that when the tabernacle had become God's dwelling, filled with his glory, Moses 'was not able to enter the tent of meeting'.

Meeting with God at the house of God

The theme of Israel's increasing intimacy with YHWH through the sacrificial cultus is set within the drama of how the *miškān*, God's dwelling, becomes the *'ōhel mô'ēd*, the meeting place between Israel and God. We observe, then, that the first two sections of Leviticus as I have delineated them, approaching God's house (chs. 1–10) and cleansing God's house (chs. 11–16), do not satisfy the significance of the term *'ōhel mô'ēd*. These sections do, however, serve as necessary preliminaries before the tabernacle can function as a 'tent of meeting'. And, indeed, as we will see, chapters 23–25 (symbolized by 24:1–9 as their centre) have this precise function as their subject. For this final section of Leviticus I will present four lines of reasoning that support understanding Leviticus 24:1–9 as symbolizing the goal of the *miškān*'s becoming an *'ōhel mô'ēd*. We will consider the theme of sacred time with which this third section closes, how that theme relates to *'ōhel mô'ēd* terminology, how my proposal fits the overall narrative strategy discerned in the previous two sections, and how my proposal corres-ponds with the literary structure and theme of Leviticus.

The theme of sacred time

Keeping in mind the cult and cosmos homology, Vogels makes two relevant points regarding the fourth-day creation of the heavenly lights in Genesis 1:14–18,[32] which we considered briefly when studying the creation account. First, the word for 'light' or 'luminary', *mā'ôr*, is rare; elsewhere in the Pentateuch it always refers to the lamps of the tabernacle lampstand. Secondly, the chief function of the heavenly lamps is for the sake of the *mô'ădîm*, a word better translated as 'cultic festivals' rather than 'seasons [of nature]'. Significantly, we also noted

---

[32] Vogels 1997; see also Rudolph 2003.

Vogels's point that the singular *môʿēd* refers 135 out of the 160 times it appears in the Pentateuch to the 'tent of *meeting*', with the vast majority of the other cases referring either to the 'fixed time' of a cultic festival or simply being a synonym for the 'festival' itself.[33] The creation account, let us recall, is structured by a Sabbatical principle, opening with a seven-word sentence, containing seven paragraphs with seven days, and climaxing on the seventh day of divine rest. The first, middle and last days all deal with time: the period of a day (day 1), the heavenly lamps for marking annual cultic festivals (day 4), and the weekly Sabbath (day 7).[34] The catechism is clear: the cosmos was created to be the meeting place between God and humanity, specifically on the appointed days of meeting, which are built upon the Sabbath.

Understanding the tabernacle as a mini-cosmos, one would expect a similar purpose for its construction, and such is indeed the case (cf. Exod. 31:12–17).[35] The goal is for the tabernacle to become an *ʾōhel môʿēd*, the place where Israel meets with God Sabbath by Sabbath. If we understand this as the end toward which the narrative has been leading, then we can discern the dramatic significance of chapters 23–25 of Leviticus.

Terminology

Just here it is critical to consider the *ʾōhel môʿēd* terminology. The word *môʿēd* is built from the root *yʿd*, meaning 'to appoint, meet'. For this reason Haran discussed the original significance of *ʾōhel môʿēd* as the place to which YHWH comes 'at an appointed time'.[36] That this function of the tabernacle, far from being incidental, is essential to its purpose may be seen from the programmatic statement in Exodus 29:42–43 (cf. 25:22; 30:6, 36), which contains a threefold use of the root *yʿd*:

---

[33] Vogels 1997: 164–165.

[34] Weimar 2002: 836; Vogels 1997: 164, n. 4, 176–178; Gorman 1993: 52–53.

[35] See the parallels between the cosmos and tabernacle in relation to the Sabbath in Kearney 1977; Weinfeld 1981.

[36] Haran 1985: 269. The typical source-critical approach to *ʾōhel môʿēd* is to presume it to have derived from the E (elohist) source, which never used 'tabernacle' or 'tent of the pact', and understood God's appointed meetings as sporadic visits – he never 'dwelt' in the tent (i.e. the tent was never a *miškān*) as exemplified in Exod. 33:7–11. In line with Israel's steady immersion into the experience of Moses, however, it seems more probable that Exod. 33:7–11 forecasts the prospect of the *miškān*'s becoming an *ʾōhel môʿēd* between Israel and YHWH, in a similar fashion to Moses' tent here – a development, moreover, that would not negate the tabernacle's *miškān* aspect.

The daily ascension offering shall be throughout your generations at the door of the tent of *meeting* [*mô'ēd*] before YHWH, where I will *meet* [*'iwwā'ēd*] with you to speak with you there. And I will *meet* [*nō'adtî*] with the sons of Israel and it shall be sanctified by my glory.

Klein observes that the term 'meet' is at the heart of this 'summary paragraph, which articulates the central significance of the whole institution of the tabernacle'.[37] This usage, moreover, is not an isolated instance. 'There I will *meet* [*wěnō'adtî*] with you,' YHWH says with reference to the atonement lid in the instructions for the ark in Exodus 25:22; 'where I will meet [*'iwwā'ēd*] with you', again referencing the atonement lid, in Exodus 30:6; and 'in the *'ōhel mô'ēd* where I will meet [*'iwwā'ēd*] with you' in Exodus 30:36 – all passages that have the making of the tabernacle and the establishment of the cult in view. In Exodus, moreover, the people of God become the *'ēdâ*, built from the same root, the cultic community appointed to meet with him.[38] Finally, the root *y'd* not only designates the place to meet with God and the people who will meet with him, but, as we have already had occasion to notice, it designates the times appointed to meet with God, the *mô'ădîm*. Leviticus 23, being a chapter concerned with cultic festivals, is itself defined by its sixfold use of *mô'ădîm* (vv. 2 [twice], 4 [twice], 37, 44).[39] The *'ēdâ* meets with God at the *'ōhel mô'ēd* for the *mô'ădîm*. Just as the Sabbath marks the time for the bread to be renewed under the light of the lampstand, so too the Sabbath marks the time for Israel to convene, a *miqrā'-qōdeš* (23:3), as a sacred assembly for fellowship and communion with YHWH.[40]

Returning now to the dramatic movement of Leviticus, what greater affirmation can be given to demonstrate that the sanctuary has finally become the tent of *mô'ēd* than these chapters calling Israel to gather about the sanctuary *specifically for* the *mô'ădîm*? Once more I suggest that the goal of the tabernacle, in harmony with that of the cosmos,

[37] Klein 1996: 268. While Klein (269–270) does not investigate the significance of the alternative terms for the tabernacle further, his following remark is suggestive: 'God's mere presence in the tabernacle is important, but God also promises to meet with Moses or the whole of Israel in order to communicate with them his will (25:22; 29:42; 30:6, 36); that is, his presence becomes active and engaging, setting obedience as a consequence of divine presence. The tabernacle is called the "tent of meeting" in Exodus more than thirty times.'

[38] See B. W. Anderson 1999: 86, 107; von Rad 1962: 233–234; G. Davies 1999: 144.

[39] Nevertheless, it is the Sabbath that serves as the unifying principle for Lev. 23, as well as for chs. 23–26; see Hui 1990: 147–151.

[40] Ibid. 1990: 148, 151–154.

is portrayed symbolically in Leviticus 24:1–9. We have already noted the correspondences between the lamps of the menorah and those of the cosmos, along with the Sabbath *tāmîd* and the seventh day. In short, all the necessary elements of Genesis 1:1 – 2:3 are found in Leviticus 24:1–9 for the sake of presenting a cultic picture of Israel's basking in the renewing light of God's Sabbath-day Presence – a beautiful, theological symbol for the significance of the tabernacle cultus as it has unfolded in Leviticus. Just as the creation account narrates the founding of both cosmos and the Sabbath or sacred time,[41] so Leviticus narrates the founding of the tabernacle and the Sabbath or sacred time. More importantly, the message of Leviticus is that the Sabbath/*mô'ădîm* convocations with God for which the cosmos was created (but which had been frustrated through the latter's defilement) may finally take place through Israel's cult. *The unfulfilled purpose for which the cosmos was created may now be realized through the tabernacle cultus of Israel.* Inasmuch as Leviticus 23 – 25 describes festive pilgrimages to God's house, along with the redemption and rest entailed in the jubilee legislation, these chapters form a fitting celebratory resolution, signalling what the tabernacle has become for Israel: a tent of meeting-with-God.[42]

Narrative strategy

My suggestion for the true resolution to the third section of Leviticus yields a narrative strategy similar to the previous two sections. Once more, while there is no apparent new crisis propelling the movement from ch. 17 to chapters 23–25, we are to understand these chapters as a further answer to the original Nadab and Abihu crisis, as several scholars have noted.[43] YHWH's response to Aaron after the tragedy – again underscored all the more as it is the *only* time he speaks exclusively to the high priest – is programmatic for the rest of the book (10:10): 'that you may distinguish between holy and profane [chs. 17–27], and between unclean and clean [chs. 11–16]'.

That understood, we find that the arc from Leviticus 16 to chapters 23–25 contains the insertion of holiness legislation, which is

---

[41] Cf. Gorman 1993: 51.

[42] This is especially the case if the MT is revocalized, as many would have it, so that the pilgrimage festivals referenced in Exod. 23:17, 34:24 and Deut. 16:16 are 'to see the face of YHWH' rather than 'to appear before the Presence of YHWH'. See G. A. Anderson 2009: 163–164.

[43] Cf. e.g. C. R. Smith 1996: 24.

appropriately contextualized by chapters 23–25 and their emphasis upon the Sabbath (and sanctuary). Bracketing the bulk of the book's third section we find the following words repeated verbatim (Lev. 19:30; 26:2), which link the Sabbath with the sanctuary:[44] 'You will keep my Sabbaths and reverence my sanctuary: I am YHWH.' The narrative logic of the inserted legislation becomes plain upon considering that Sabbath engagement with God in his sanctuary is not only the *goal* of holiness, but also the regular *means* for Israel to become holy, as is evident from Exodus 31:13: 'Surely my Sabbaths you shall keep, for it is a sign between me and you throughout your generations, that you may know that I am YHWH who sanctifies you.' God's Presence in the tabernacle is the source of sanctification, while Israel's sacred calendar prescribes the occasions for entering his sanctifying Presence. It is the light of YHWH's countenance that sanctifies, and this is experienced particularly on the Sabbath, the 'sanctuary in time' and 'beachhead of holiness in the world'.[45] Time was the first object of sanctification in Scripture and, indeed, marks the only use of the term 'holy' (*qdš*) in Genesis (2:3),[46] because it is the time set aside for setting humanity apart to God. Understanding holiness from the angle of Israel's cult, holy means belonging to God. Entering into the Sabbath regularly, Israel was steadily to grow in its calling of belonging to God. It is not incidental, then, that the third section of Leviticus parallels the emphasis upon time found in Genesis 1:1 – 2:3.[47] Leviticus 16, which not only caps the second section (chs. 11–15) but also serves as the pivot for the book's two halves, begins the concern with time. The annual day of purgation was not only central to Israel's sacred space, by entrance into the holy of holies, but was also central to Israel's sacred time, as the focus of the cultic calendar,[48] the subject of chapters 23–25. The Day of Atonement legislation opens with Aaron's being forbidden to enter the inner sanctum 'at just any time' (v. 2), and then is rounded off with what marks, somewhat surprisingly, the book's first mention of the Sabbath (v. 31). After the holiness legislation, chapters 23–25 then mark a significant spike in the use of *šbt* (occurring twenty-six times in these

---

[44] For more on this link, cf. Berman 1995: 10–19. Ruwe (1999: 103–120) sees these bookends as establishing the basic two topics for this section of Leviticus: chs. 17–22, sanctuary; chs. 23–25, Sabbath. Nihan (2007: 478) refers to the two coordinates of holiness: space and time.

[45] Firmage 1999: 110.

[46] Cf. Heschel 2003: xvi–xvii.

[47] Wagner (2009: 314–315) has also argued that chs. 23–25 deal with 'sacred times'.

[48] J. A. Davies 2004: 162.

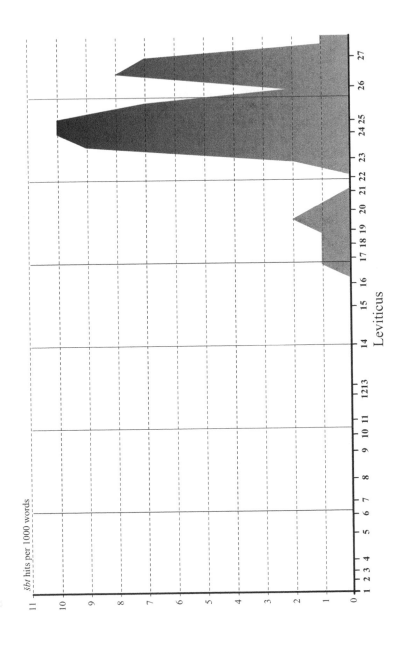

chapters) as reflected in the table on p. 202.[49] Since the Sabbath is the sign of Israel's covenant with God, and since like the cosmos the tabernacle cultus was established for Sabbath-day engagement with God, it is no wonder that Leviticus 26 applies the covenant in terms of the Sabbath (*šbt* occurring nine times in this chapter).

Clearly, the book of Leviticus closes with a major emphasis on sacred time, and particularly, as with the creation account, on the Sabbath day. When the Sabbath is understood as the appointed time for Israel's engagement with God, it will be seen to have the same purpose and function as the sanctuary itself – the Sabbath and the tabernacle cultus are coordinated gifts to Israel, through which God gives himself to humanity.

Literary structure and theme of Leviticus

My focus upon Leviticus 24:1–9 finds confirmation in the literary structure of the book.[50] Various scholars have noted that chapters 8–10, 16 and 24 of Leviticus relate and allude to one another self-consciously, a significant phenomenon for the book's structure. Smith points out, for example, that Leviticus 16 begins by alluding to the deaths of Nadab and Abihu (10:1–3), and it also ends by indicating that the Sabbath legislation applies equally to both native and sojourner (16:29), which then forms part of the resolution to the blasphemer story (24:22).[51] Bibb notes the remarkable parallels between the blasphemer's execution and the scapegoat ritual in Leviticus 16, including the laying of hands on their heads and their bearing away iniquity.[52] My approach, once more, requires a holistic reading of Leviticus 24 (vv. 10–23 read as an extension of vv. 1–9),[53] as well as understanding Leviticus 24 as central to the concern of chapters 23–25. In fact, the connections with Leviticus 16 include

[49] Accordance Bible Software 10.2.0 (OakTree Software, Inc., 2013). The root *šbt* occurs forty times in Leviticus. For the table I have removed the use of this root in 2:13 ('not allow the salt of the covenant to be *lacking*') as not pertinent.

[50] For some of the issues involved with Lev. 24 in relation to the book's structure, see Master 2002.

[51] C. R. Smith 1996. Even if one disagrees with Smith's understanding that all three pericopes are 'narratives' (i.e. including the Day of Atonement legislation), the point that there is intertextuality among chs. 8–10, 16 and 24:10–23 stands nevertheless.

[52] Bibb 2005: 213–214; see also Trevaskis 2009: 310. Taking Kamionkowski's previous analogy (2009: 75), we may posit that the blasphemer story entails an elimination rite for the community with respect to the name, whereas the Day of Atonement is an elimination rite for the community with respect to the sanctuary.

[53] May it be the case that vv. 1–9 have reference to the sacrificial goat, whose blood is brought into the divine Presence, while vv. 10–23 allude to the scapegoat who is driven away from God's face?

prominent references to the Day of Atonement in the chapters that frame Leviticus 24 (cf. Lev. 23:26–32; 25:9).[54] Understanding Leviticus 24 as the climactic resolution to the book's third section (and, indeed, to the book itself), therefore, corresponds well with the structural significance of the narrative in 24:10–23, as noted by various scholars.[55]

We turn now to consider how this structure correlates to the major theme of Leviticus. In accord with Nihan's study, the basic theme of Leviticus is Israel's gradual initiation by YHWH himself into the requirements of the divine Presence.[56] This initiation takes place in three successive stages, each concluding with a reference to the divine Presence: Leviticus 9 – 10 marks YHWH's appearance to the community before the sanctuary; in Leviticus 16 he appears to Aaron within the veil of the inner sanctum; and Leviticus 24 portrays the goal of both the covenant and the tabernacle cultus, Israel basking in the Sabbath light of YHWH's countenance within the outer sanctum.[57] Leviticus 26, with its covenantal promises and threats, serves as an application to the whole book, an appeal based upon the gift of the tabernacle cultus, *which has now come to function as a tent of meeting between Israel and God.* I will consider Leviticus 26 later on in this chapter, but here merely remark that the main promise alludes to YHWH's permanent Presence outside the sanctuary, Eden-like, as a promissory prospect of the covenant (26:12); and the main threat alludes to a primeval-like expulsion from his Presence in exile (26:33). To grasp the nature of the covenant promise it is critical to understand that the prospect of Leviticus 26:12 is altogether contingent upon the steadily increasing holiness of Israel that may be realized only through

---

[54] Trevaskis 2009: 310. Sanders (2009: 193, nn. 104, 105), who affirms Lev. 16 as the book's thematic and structural centre, notes how this ceremony corresponds to the Sabbath on a microscopic level (being described as a *šabbat šabbatôn*) and to the jubilee year on a macroscopic level.

[55] Douglas 1999a: 195–217; C. R. Smith 1996; Luciani 2005: 98–305. Nihan (2007: 550, 616) considers Lev. 10:10–23 a major interpolation outside the coherent structure of chs. 17–26.

[56] Nihan 2007: 108–110.

[57] Nihan misses the significance of Lev. 24, finding in Lev. 26:12 the resolution to the book's third movement. However, Lev. 26:12 forms a *prospective* blessing rather than an accomplished stage. Moreover, connecting the points from Lev. 16 directly to 26 tends to overlook the intervening accomplishment and denouement that occur in chs. 23–25, neglecting what the tabernacle *has become* since Lev. 16 – what it *now is* for Israel even before the fulfilment of 26:12. Finally, Lev. 26, with its covenantal promises and threats, forms an application to the whole book, so that one must find the third section's resolution before ch. 26. Nihan's insight into the significance of the divine promise in 26:12 is nevertheless validated – and even strengthened – when positioned rather to function as the concluding application to the whole book.

Israel's full and regular embrace of the *'ōhel mô'ēd* Sabbath engagement with God, as portrayed in chapters 23–25. Once more the relationship between God and Israel established by the covenant is full of potential that may be realized only through regular and sincere Sabbath engagement with God through the tent of meeting.

In the light of the literary structure of Leviticus the full significance of Leviticus 24:1–9 becomes apparent: it constitutes a *cultic* theophany within the holy place – a ritual or symbolic theophany. In retrospect we can see that each of the three theophanies of Leviticus takes place within the context of worship, mapped on Israel's calendar, and within one of the three areas of sacred space so that the *entire* tabernacle complex is encompassed: (1) on the tabernacle's inauguration upon the eighth day (of Nisan, New Year) at the altar in the courtyard, (2) on the Day of Atonement (the 'Sabbath of Sabbaths') in the holy of holies, and (3) on the Sabbath, regularly, in the holy place. The structure can be summarized as below.[58]

	CRISIS	[Inserted legislation]	RESOLUTION	*Divine presence*
Exod. 40 to Lev. 9 – 10	No entry into God's house (Exod. 40:35)	Laws of sacrifices and consecration of priesthood (Lev. 1 – 8)	Entry into God's house (Lev. 9)	Public theophany before the *'ōhel mô'ēd* on eighth day (Lev. 9:23)
Lev. 11 – 16	Tabernacle polluted; limits of approach to YHWH (Lev. 10:1–3)	Laws of clean/unclean (Lev. 11 – 15; cf. 10:10)	Tabernacle cleansed; YHWH approached within the inner sanctum (Lev. 16)	Theophany inside the inner sanctum of *'ōhel mô'ēd* on Day of Atonement (Lev. 16:2)
Lev. 17 to 23 – 25	Second response to Nadab and Abihu event (Lev. 10:1–3)	Laws of holy/profane (Lev. 17 – 22; cf. 10:10)	Israel's Sabbath assemblies at God's house produce holiness (Lev. 23 – 25)	Cultic theophany inside holy place of *'ōhel mô'ēd* on Sabbath (Lev. 24:1–9)
Covenantal application: Lev. 26	Promises and threats: either primeval-like Presence (26:12) or primeval-like exile from Presence (26:33)			

[58] For the book's third movement there is no mention of YHWH's 'appearing' (*r'h*) as there is for the first two theophanies (Lev. 9:23; 16:2). This inconsistency, however, (1) remains an issue in Nihan's scheme as well, who proposes Lev. 26:12 as the third theophany, and (2) may be explained by its nature as a cultic or symbolic theophany.

Adding the final dramatic stage of Leviticus to my previous chart yields the following movements:

(1) Exod. 25:8; 29:45 → [tabernacle (25 – 31; 35 – 40)] Exod. 40:34
  (2) Exod. 40:35 → [sacrifices (Lev. 1 – 7) priesthood (8)] Lev. 9 – 10
    (3) Lev. 10:1–3, 10 → [unclean and clean (11 – 15)] Lev. 16
      (4) Lev. 10:1–3, 10 → [holy and profane (17 – 22)] Lev. 23 – 25

While Exodus 40 yields a consecrated tabernacle, filled with YHWH's glory, the second, third and fourth movements mark stages, from the realm of the profane to that of the sacred, along Israel's gradual initiation into full life in the divine Presence. Israel's gradual *consecration* to YHWH, therefore, means their growing *intimacy* with him. From the perspective of God's Presence the broad movement can be traced from YHWH's appearing to the entire community outside the sanctuary in the courtyard (altar of ascension), to his appearing to Aaron within the veil of the holy of holies (atonement lid), and finally to his cultic Presence within the holy place (lampstand, bread of the Presence). Structured by these references to the divine Presence, the narrative's progress can be outlined as below.

(1) Exod. 25:8; 29:45 → Exod. 40:34
promise: God's dwelling among Israel/**fulfilment:** divine glory fills God's house
  (2) Exod. 40:35 → Lev. 9:23
  *crisis: no entry into God's house/**resolution:** entry into God's house*
  (YHWH appears in courtyard)
    (3) Lev. 10:1–3 → Lev. 16
    *crisis: engagement with God, pollution/**resolution:** entry within veil, cleansing*
    (YHWH appears in holy of holies)
      (4) Lev. 10:1–3 → Lev. 23 – 25
      *crisis: engagement with God, profane/**resolution:** meeting with God, holy*
      (YHWH appears in holy place)

With the cultic calendar revealed, establishing the set times for Israel to meet with YHWH at the tabernacle, Leviticus has now covered the categories of sacred space, sacred status and, here, sacred time. Stage three, the final stage, in the *miškān*'s becoming an *'ōhel mô'ēd* has been reached: YHWH meets with Israel at the appointed sacred times, weekly and annually. As we will go on to see below, Leviticus 26 sets forth the covenantal prospect of Israel's enjoying God's Presence in a manner that yet goes beyond the bounds of the cultic meetings with God portrayed in chapters 23–25.

Conclusion

In conclusion, the symbolic significance of Leviticus 24:1–9 for which I have argued, that it portrays the ideal of Israel's basking in the light of YHWH's Sabbath Presence, forms a fitting and climactic resolution to the book's thematic movement and literary strategy, also validating the chapter's structural significance. Whereas the book of Exodus ended with Israel's mediator being unable to enter the *'ōhel mô'ēd*, the book of Leviticus ends with a lengthy and festal portrayal of Israel's sacred assemblies at the sanctuary to commune and fellowship with God – it ends, in other words, with a fully functioning *'ōhel mô'ēd* in the life of Israel. While the book's first half establishes the regular cleansing and maintenance of God's house, the second half focuses upon how his house will function as a meeting place with Israel – and this as the goal and means of Israel's holiness. One might therefore describe the movement of Leviticus justly as 'from cult to community', or from the *miškān* to the *'ōhel mô'ēd*.

Understanding Israel's call to holiness (Lev. 17 – 22)

Commentators have long noted the transition from cultic matters in Leviticus 1 – 16 to the more ethical, communal matters related to the prospect of life in the land dealt with in Leviticus 17 – 27.[59] While the cultic context never fades from view, it is the case that the second half of Leviticus addresses a wider range of social and moral issues, from sexual immorality and idolatry, to murder, incest and, more positively, what it means to love one's neighbour. The laws describe a life that fits with YHWH's holy nature and that may be defined adequately as one of justice and love.[60] As we will observe below, however, *both the context and the purpose of these laws have the worship of YHWH as their focus* – and so may also be considered cultic. My concern in this section is more general in nature, endeavouring to consider the legislation of Leviticus 17 – 22 particularly with regard to the logic of its placement within the third movement of the book.

---

[59] While dealing primarily with the logic of the inserted laws of chs. 17–22 within the overall third movement of Leviticus, particularly in relation to chs. 23–25, I will nevertheless also address Lev. 26 (and, to a lesser extent, 27) in this section.

[60] Dumbrell 2002: 47.

Broadly, the first part of this legislation (chs. 17–20) deals with matters pertaining to the Israelite laity, while the second (chs. 21–22) gives rules for the priesthood. After a brief word regarding the individual subsections of these chapters, I will, under four headings, pursue a theological understanding of Israel's call to holiness.

The transition to matters of life beyond the boundaries of sacred space is sensed already in Leviticus 17 wherein the sacrificing of animals *outside* the tabernacle is prohibited. Clearly, what takes place through the sacrificial cultus has implications and demands for life outside the cultus. Because, for example, animal blood is YHWH's provision for ransom at the price of life, Israel is to display a high regard for life (and atonement) by not consuming blood (17:10–12). Implicit in these commands is the desire to guard Israel against idolatry (vv. 5–7).

While there appears to be a logical ordering to the social morality legislated in chapters 18–20, beginning with marriage and moving outward to one's relationships with family members, countrymen, resident aliens, the poor and infirm, and so on,[61] the primary object of concern, once more, is *cultic*, guarding the pure worship of YHWH God. Chapters 18 and 20 are written in parallel so as to frame chapter 19, both dealing with prohibitions against various sexual offences and idolatry. By contrast, chapter 19 offers positive rules and is unified by the Decalogue, with all ten commandments being either alluded to or quoted.[62] This central chapter may be summarized by its own centre, the admonition to 'Love your neighbour as yourself' in 19:18.

Leviticus 21 – 22 addresses matters specifically related to the priest-hood, detailing restrictions related to mourning, marriage, physical defects and sacrificial animals. The aim of this legislation, as discerned by the references bookending this section, is to keep God's holy name from profanation (21:6; 22:32), which may be understood alternatively as maintaining the purity of the cultic approach to God.

The only source of holiness: the presence of YHWH God

Israel's call to holiness may be grasped in a twofold manner. First, the *need* for Israel's holiness is rooted in the essential nature of God – in his own utter holiness. Since God is 'infinite, eternal and unchangeable' in holiness, as the catechism has it, then if there is to be any intimate relationship with him, that is, if the goal of the covenant and

---

[61] Hertz 1988: 488.
[62] Wenham 1979: 264; Kaiser 1994: 1131.

telos of creation will ever be realized, Israel's character must steadily be conformed to YHWH's. Secondly, the *source* of Israel's holiness is – and could only ever be – God himself. While Israel is called to keep laws, therefore, yet doing so did not make the people holy but rather prepared them to be made holy by YHWH's Presence.[63]

Given these realities, it is not surprising that the chapters on holiness may be divided up by variations of the formulas 'I am YHWH' (18:2, 4–6, 21, 30; 19:3–4, 10, 12, 14, 16, 18, 25, 28, 30–32, 34, 36–37; 20:7), 'Be holy for I, YHWH your God, am holy' (Lev. 19:2; 20:26) and 'I am YHWH who sanctifies you' (20:8, 24; 21:8, 15, 23; 22:9, 16, 32). As expressive of his character, YHWH's name is also emphasized (20:3; 22:2, 32), along with warnings regarding its profanation (18:21; 19:12; 20:3; 21:6; 22:2).[64] If we understand that glory refers to his outward manifestation, and holiness to YHWH's inner nature,[65] then, though perhaps somewhat simplistic, the progress of Leviticus moves ever more deeply into the knowledge of YHWH, from the fires of his glory (Lev. 1 – 16) to the character of his holiness (chs. 17–27), along with the corresponding – and *reciprocal* – requirements (cultic and ethical) for Israel. Returning to the point, it is the reality of the *miškān* itself, of God's dwelling amidst the camp of Israel, that holds the prospect for Israel's holiness. Even as the tabernacle was consecrated by YHWH's Presence, so too Israel would be consecrated through their Sabbath by Sabbath basking in his Presence. This prospect, as we have seen, entails the *miškān* of God becoming an *'ōhel mô'ēd* between God and Israel, precisely the point of Leviticus. Without God's cultic Presence there can be no sanctification whatsoever.

True holiness: belonging exclusively to YHWH

YHWH God, as the only utterly holy being, is himself *the* source of holiness. The process of Israel's becoming holy ('sanctification'), therefore, entailed becoming more and more like God, which may also be understood in terms of belonging, ever more deeply, to him. While Israel had been consecrated to YHWH through the covenant at Sinai, called to be a priestly nation, yet on a practical level it was the Levites (and especially Aaron's house) who were holy while the rest of Israel had the status of being clean. From a cultic perspective one may readily discern that the difference between a clean and a holy

---

[63] Hartley 2003b: 425.
[64] Wenham 1979: 22.
[65] Dumbrell 2002: 47.

object (whether an animal or an Israelite) was that the latter had been transferred to the realm of YHWH's ownership. In terms of daily life, to be holy means to live in full submission to the will of God, for the sake of the purposes of God – to belong completely to him. This goal had been set out in Exodus 19:4–6:

> You have seen what I did to the Egyptians, and how I bore you on eagles' wings and brought you to myself. Now therefore if you will indeed obey my voice and keep my covenant, then you will be to me a treasured possession [*segullâ*] above all people – for all the earth is mine. And you shall be to me a kingdom of priests and a holy nation.

While we cannot develop the argument here, Israel's own enjoyment of God as well as their mission from God to the nations was contingent upon this one goal of holiness, of Israel's becoming a treasured possession of God. Let us consider now the parallel prohibitions of chapters 18 and 20 within the context of the programme for Israel's becoming God's special belonging.

First, Leviticus 18 – 20 begins with a strong polemical thrust,[66] against Israel's following the statutes of the nations:

> You shall not do as is done in the land of Egypt,
>   where you once dwelled,
>   and you shall not do as is done in the land of Canaan,
>   where I am bringing you.
> You shall not walk in their statutes.
> My judgments you shall do, and my statutes you shall keep,
>   to walk in them – I am YHWH your God.
>
>   (Lev. 18:3–4)

As a prologue, this programmatic statement contrasts the evil statutes of the gods of Egypt and Canaan, as prohibited in chapters 18 and 20, with the good statutes of Israel's God, as put forth in ch. 19.[67] While YHWH's statutes lead to long life in the land, those of the gods of Egypt and Canaan will lead to the land's vomiting the Israelites out. Secondly, and as Douglas has discerned, the rationale for the prohibitions of chapters 18 and 20 are most readily explained within

---

[66] Wenham 1979: 250.
[67] Douglas 1999b: 343.

the context of the *religious practices* of Egypt and Canaan (see the table below).[68]

Chapter 18 prohibitions	Chapter 20 prohibitions
vv. 16–18 Incest	vv. 11–21 Incest
v. 19 Menstrual uncleanness	v. 18 Menstrual uncleanness
v. 20 Adultery with neighbour's wife	v. 10 Adultery with neighbour's wife
v. 21 Devoting children to Molech	vv. 2–5 Devoting children to Molech
v. 22 Homosexuality	v. 13 Homosexuality
v. 23 Bestiality	vv. 15–16 Bestiality
	vv. 6–8 Mediums, wizards
	v. 9 Cursing father or mother
vv. 24–30 'For all of these abominations the men of the land did, who were before you, so the land became defiled; lest the land vomit you out, when you defile it, as it vomited out the nation that was before you.'	v. 22 'You shall therefore keep all my statutes and all my ordinances, and do them, that the land where I am bringing you may not vomit you out. You shall not walk in the customs of the nation which I am casting out before you.'

To quote Douglas:

> The formality of the context cannot be overlooked. The contrast with Deuteronomy 27 shows that the anathemas in Leviticus 18 and 20 are not laws about everyday affairs. They say nothing about marriage, inheritance, divorce, or choice of marriage partners. They are not concerned with wrong conduct in family life so much as with breach of covenant. These are laws about faithfully worshipping the only Lord God and about defilement by idolatry. The verses start with Egypt and Canaan, referring with loathing to Egyptian and Canaanite cults. Both supporting chapters mention Molech worship; the second one denounces mediums and seers. . . . The pure and noble character of the Hebrew God is contrasted with the libidinous customs of the false gods.[69]

Fundamentally, this insight means that the holiness laws of chapters 18 and 20 are essentially cultic in character, prohibiting the vile customs that characterize the cults of the nations. Already the relationship between this material and that of the Sabbath-centric material in Leviticus 23 – 25 begins to surface – a relationship we will explore in the next section.

---

[68] Ibid. 344–346.
[69] Ibid. 346.

Secondly, and with respect to the opening of these chapters once more, the divine wisdom of the wilderness setting is worthy of reflection: the wilderness is neither 'Egypt where you dwelt' nor 'Canaan where I am bringing you' (Lev. 18:3), both lands polluted by the uncleanness of sexual immorality and idolatry. The wilderness is the necessary no man's land where YHWH can fashion a new nation after himself.[70] Bringing them into the wilderness, the place of non-creation, God recreates Israel as a new humanity at the primal mountain of God, an idea in accord with the liminal stage of a rite of passage.[71] Since the nations have become corrupted and have turned aside from the way of YHWH, the paths of life – in accord with the life of YHWH himself – cannot be learned or deduced from nature or the wisdom of the peoples, but must be revealed: 'my judgments you shall do, and my statutes you shall keep' (v. 4). The holiness legislation, moreover, is not merely a practical code of conduct as much as a manifesto of Israel's identity as those who belong to YHWH:[72] 'And you shall be holy to me for I YHWH am holy, and have separated you from the peoples, that you should belong to me' (Lev. 20:26). As explained by this verse, chapters 18 and 20 serve to *separate* Israel from the detestable religious customs of the nations, while chapter 19 sets out the life that accords with Israel's cultic access to YHWH's presence – for the sake of *belonging* to him. The geographical separation of Israel from the nations *via* the wilderness aims at the more fundamental religious separation from them, so as to establish Israel as a nation belonging to YHWH.

Finally, the theme of belonging to YHWH is the appropriate place to touch on Leviticus 27 briefly. Not only does this final chapter serve to keep the book from ending negatively with the divine threats of Leviticus 26,[73] but it also serves to bring out the theme of redemption. Chapters 25 and 27 are marked by the only uses of the root for 'redemption' (*gā'al*) in the book of Leviticus, seventeen and twelve times respectively; and, while the term itself is not used in ch. 26, the theme of redemption is nevertheless present, looking back to Israel's redemption out of Egypt (26:13) and forward to Israel's redemption

---

[70] It is in this sense that the prophets can describe the wilderness as the place of Israel's betrothal to YHWH (cf. Hos. 2:14).

[71] The three phases of a rite of passage entail (1) the act of separation from a social structure or cultural condition, (2) a marginal state, described as 'liminal', and (3) reincorporation into a new social structure (Gennep 1960: 15–25).

[72] Rooke 2015.

[73] Hartley 1992: 479.

out of exile (26:44–45).[74] Out of this reality, that Israel has been redeemed by and therefore already belongs to YHWH, the book closes with the topic of the free-will dedication of one's self and/or one's belongings to God, 'reclaiming for God that which is, or those who are, already God's', in the making of special, uncoerced vows 'out of love for and gratitude to God'.[75] The redemption of such persons and belongings, then, both imitates the activity of God and reminds the Israelite of the high cost of redemption, along with the gravity of what it means to belong to YHWH.[76]

How precisely – by what *process* – Israel was steadily to grow in holiness, in belonging to God, is the subject of the next section.

The pursuit of holiness: the dynamic between cult and holiness

In the light of Israel's need for engagement with God it is to be expected that chapters 17–27 of Leviticus should deal thoroughly with holiness. In fact, this section's emphasis on holiness, saturated with repeated uses of the term 'holy' and its derivatives, has led some scholars to label it the holiness code (H), presumably the work of a holiness school later incorporated into the final form of Leviticus and the Pentateuch by priestly redactors (P).[77] Once the narrative logic and flow of Leviticus in its final form are appreciated, however, resorting to complicated theories of composition becomes unnecessary. It is probably an anachronism, moreover, to assume that ancient Israel discerned a sharp category distinction between cultic and ethical requirements.[78] Besides, many moral concerns, such as murder, sexual abominations and idolatry were also, as Wenham points out, causes of uncleanness, polluting the offender, sanctuary and land – that is, they were also a matter of cultic concern.[79] In any case, the simplistic opposition between the *cultic* holiness of Leviticus 1 – 16 (P) and the *ethical* holiness of Leviticus 17 – 26 (H) has recently been questioned, inasmuch as the latter regulations may be seen plausibly as making explicit what is implicit in the theological symbolism of

---

[74] C. R. Smith 1996: 29–30.

[75] Ibid. 30.

[76] The redemption price, furthermore, ensured that all of God's people could be involved in the stewardship of his house (Kleinig 2003: 595).

[77] I. Knohl (2007), however, posits the holiness code as a later addition to the priestly source. Note that, because ch. 27 of Leviticus is typically regarded as an appendix, it is not usually considered part of the holiness code.

[78] Cothey 2005; Brueggemann 2005: 678.

[79] Wenham 2003: 95; cf. Frymer-Kensky 1983.

the former.[80] Ritual purity and ethical conduct, once more, are mutual obligations that have a reciprocal relationship. Indeed, and certainly from the perspective of Israel's covenant relationship with YHWH, the cultus (typological and provisional as it is) both demands and directs the worshipper to the yearned-for reality, *the life* with YHWH God that only absolute and comprehensive sanctification can enable.

The progression, then, from cult in the first half of Leviticus to community in the second is not only natural and logical, but also necessary – the *purpose* of the cult is to sanctify Israel to YHWH. So whereas the root for holy (*qdš*) is typically restricted to cultic objects and personnel in Leviticus 1 – 16, it is an expected development to find it applied to ordinary Israelites amidst everyday life in chapters 17–27, a designation no longer applied merely to the priesthood but to the entire congregation of Israel, albeit *prospectively*.[81] What, however, is not typically appreciated sufficiently is that the holiness of Israel (chs. 17–27) is in fact the goal and *programmed consequence* of the cultus of Israel (chs. 1–16). Here we need simply to reflect once more on the nature of Israel's sanctification, having YHWH God as the source of holiness. Though analogies are of limited value, the following comparison may be helpful: just as basking in the sun's light brings colour, warmth and health to the body, so basking in God's Presence brings holiness, that is, gradual sanctification. The programme for Israel's sanctification was not founded merely upon a set of laws, but rather was rooted in the regular cultic entrance into God's Presence. Because, fundamentally, worship is entering God's Presence, drawing near to God through the way he has opened, Israel's holiness was contingent – in an absolute sense – upon their Sabbath engagement with God. Leviticus establishes a reciprocal relationship between cult (chs. 1–16) and community (chs. 17–27), but the starting point and priority in this cycle is the way YHWH has opened for his people to dwell in his Presence through the cult – a regulated entrance that results in blessing, holiness and life, rather than in judgment and destruction. It is critical, then, to reflect on the immediate purpose of the tabernacle cultus as enabling Israel to draw near to YHWH God. We noted in chapter 4 that the term 'offering' (*qorbān*), built from the Hebrew root *qrb* and signifying 'to draw near', is utilized four times at the opening of Leviticus: 'When anyone brings-near [*yaqrîb*] an offering [*qorbān*] to YHWH, you shall bring near [*taqrîbû*] your

---

[80] See e.g. Trevaskis 2011.
[81] Knohl 2007: 185; Meyer 2013; Kugler 1997: 16.

offering [*qorbankem*] . . .' (Lev. 1:2). It is this startling reality, that Israel may draw near to the Maker of heaven and earth, that has been opened by YHWH himself through the sacrificial cultus that unravels every theological knot, and confirms both the literary coherence and the spiritual sublimity of Leviticus. To the degree that Israel submitted to that programme of worship, to that degree they would be made to ascend by marked stages of holiness to the face of God. Israel was to pursue holiness by pursuing God.

What remains now is to see how the broad movement and relationship between Leviticus 1 – 16 and 17 – 27 is reasserted in a climactic way in the third movement of the book: there is a reciprocal relationship between Leviticus 23 – 25 (positively, the Sabbath-centred appointed times of worship and liberation) and Leviticus 17 – 22 (negatively, the denial of the cultic practices of the nations; life of love and justice). Indeed, central to this finale is Leviticus 24, which, as we have seen, itself mirrors this dynamic relationship between Sabbath/cult (vv. 1–9) and the rejection of (Egypt-related) blasphemy, as it pertains to the community (vv. 10–23). Again Sabbath engagement with God was not only the goal of holiness, but was also the means to that holiness, the Levitical way in which Israel was to become God's treasured possession and, thereby, his servant to the nations. Leviticus unveils the programme for this astounding agenda through the twin gifts from the summit of God's mountain: torah and tabernacle cultus.

The goal of holiness: communion and fellowship with God

By this point in our study of Leviticus it is clear that the goal of holiness is union and fellowship with God. As we have seen, the final dramatic movement of the book, given in chapters 23–25, expresses that goal in the festal gatherings of Israel at the tent of meeting, with God's Sabbath-day Presence at their heart. Yet, as truly significant and wondrous as this final development is, we are nevertheless justified in asking whether or not the covenant may have gestured toward any further intimacy with God. Bluntly stated, will there be life with God *beyond* the cultus? It is when we consider the height of the Levitical approach to God, as the high priest ascends within the veil to the summit of the cultic mountain of God on the Day of Atonement, cleansing both God's house and God's people so that Israel can meet with God Sabbath by Sabbath, when we consider this blessed new reality, that *the* question emerges and imposes itself persistently: Is this access to the divine Presence the *end*? Is it the full extent (expressing, therefore, the *limits*) of humanity's restoration to YHWH

God? Here the function of Genesis 2 – 3 and the garden of Eden within the narrative leading up to the book of Leviticus must be brought into account. While the tabernacle mediates something of the life of Eden to Israel, the question nevertheless remains: Will humanity ever be able to experience such unhindered life with God again? Does the dire necessity to separate between holy and profane, which so characterizes existence after the expulsion, mean that humanity may only ever come to fellowship with God through the veil? These considerations lead us to reflect ever more deeply upon the central question of this work:

> O YHWH, who may abide in your tent;
> who may dwell on your holy mountain?
> (Ps. 15:1)

To be sure, the answer, which relates as much to how as to who, lies in the question, for the ascription of the mountain as holy – and this because it is YHWH's own abode, set apart to and for him – determines that the one who would dwell on this mountain of God, in this Eden, must also be holy, set apart utterly to and for YHWH. This need for and promise of holiness for God's people, as we have seen, underlies the dynamic relationship between Israel's cultic access to God and the holiness legislation, as well as the profound hope that pervades Leviticus.

What, then, is the further hope held out for Israel's relationship with YHWH, beyond that which is enabled through the Levitical cultus? Intriguingly, amidst the forking paths of blessing and curse assured by God for Israel's faithfulness or apostasy in Leviticus 26, we find the following promise embedded:

> I will set my tabernacle among you
>   and my soul will not abhor you.
> I will walk to and fro among you;
>   I will be your God and you will be my people.
> (Vv. 11–12)

Here, and as we will consider in the next chapter, the forking paths amount to the ones taken by the alternative goats on the Day of Atonement: either more deeply into the divine Presence, into life itself, or else further away from God into darkness, chaos and death. In other words, Israel's ultimate blessing or curse is described in terms of *progressive nearness* to or *progressive estrangement* from the divine Presence. This progressive nearness or estrangement is dependent upon whether or not Israel pursues the relationship with YHWH established by the covenant – 'pursues' because divine fellowship and union are promissory, a buried seed full of potentiality that, like all relationships, must be nurtured and so brought to fruition. The promissory nature of the covenantal relationship means not only that it is progressive and organic, but also that it has a *telos*, a culmination.[82] As the culmination of the list of blessings, YHWH promises not only to set his tabernacle in the midst of Israel (the hope of Exod. 25 – 40), but that he will even walk in their midst – a statement, Nihan posits, that clearly goes *beyond* the previous one.[83] He also notes that the terminology of 26:12 is actually reminiscent of descriptions found in the primordial period before the deluge (Gen. 1 – 5), where the distance between God and humanity was less clearly marked and where certain privileged ancestors are said to have walked with YHWH. More importantly, the language may also recall life with God in the garden of Eden (Gen. 3:8). On this interpretation, '*the ultimate blessing of Lev. 26 considers nothing less than the restoration, in Israel, of the relationship between God and man that existed before the Flood*, thus connecting the conclusion of Leviticus with the beginning of Genesis'.[84] In retrospect, this promise must be seen as the only theological development possible. Indeed, both creation (Gen. 1 – 3) and redemption (Exod. 15:17) prohibit the resting of hope upon anything less than genuine communion and fellowship with God within the temple of creation itself. Moreover, the tabernacle's having a clearly typological nature, patterned (*tabnît*) after the heavenly abode of God (Exod. 25:9; etc.) and representing a microcosm, along with its system of animal substitution, all stamp the ritual drama of its cultus with the impress of both a catechetical and promissory function – and marking it, therefore, as provisional.

At issue now is the logical progression from the dynamic relationship between the holiness legislation (chs. 17–22) and the Sabbath meetings with God (chs. 23–25) to the promise of Leviticus 26:12. Phrased as a question, what is the necessary requirement, beyond the

---

[82] This progression toward a *telos* in humanity's relationship with God unifies the covenants of redemptive history. Alternatively, when covenants are seen as establishing flat, static relationships (legal or otherwise), a disunity among them (and redemptive history) surfaces that is not warranted by Scripture.

[83] Nihan 2007: 106.

[84] Ibid.; emphases original.

blood-work of Leviticus 1 – 16, for humanity to live Eden-like, face to face with YHWH? As already touched upon, the inescapable, unalterable condition is holiness. Either for humanity to enter so as to abide in God's house or for God to come out of his house, as it were, to commune openly with humanity – in either case, humanity (and the cosmos as the stage and temple for this fellowship) must be holy. Without holiness no one will see YHWH (cf. Heb. 12:14). Especially at this point it is important to stress the defining context of holiness legislation: *it is for the sake of fulfilling the covenant relationship*, of fulfilling the divine longing for fellowship with humanity, that YHWH says, 'Be holy because I, YHWH your God, am holy' (Lev. 19:2).[85] The allusion to the covenant formula, to YHWH's being Israel's God, undergirds the call to holiness with the potentiality that is the heart of the covenant itself, the hope of dwelling with God. Justly then one might characterize the divine goal and labour of redemptive history in terms of *making holy* – the complete and utter sanctification of both cosmos and humanity, which, as with the tabernacle and priesthood, are inseparable.

This analysis fits well with Nihan's understanding that Leviticus 26:12 brings a new development, closing with a promise that goes beyond the mediation of the sacrificial cult to an even more direct form of engagement between God and humanity. This prospect becomes possible because the holiness previously reserved for God, his sanctuary and priests in Leviticus 1 – 16 is now being vouchsafed to the community of Israel in the second half of Leviticus.[86] Having learned the distinction between clean and unclean (chs. 11–15), and having been entirely purified (16), the prospect of Israel's full consecration to God (17–25) yields the promise of YHWH's permanent Presence outside the sanctuary, returning humanity to the golden age before the flood.[87]

To clarify, the holiness delineated in chapters 17–27 is held out by way of *prospect*, rooted and mandated by the divine nature, 'You *shall be* holy, for I YHWH your God *am* holy' (19:2), a prospect that culminates in the promise of Leviticus 26:12. Wenham captures this reference's promissory nature well when he writes:

> But if [the people of Israel] obey, they can expect to enjoy the highest of all divine blessings, his personal presence. 'I shall walk

---

[85] See also Lev. 11:44–45; 20:7; Isa. 53:8; 1 Peter 1:16.
[86] Nihan 2007: 106–107.
[87] Ibid. 108.

among you and become your God, and you will become my people'
(v. 12). All that was initially promised in the Sinai Covenant (Exod.
19:5–6) will then prove true in reality.[88]

Three points are in order. First, it is important to keep underscoring
the role of chapters 23–25 as the programme of holiness, both the
end and means for Israel's holiness: Sabbath by Sabbath worship is
God's established path to the promise of Leviticus 26:12. Ultimately,
Israel's destiny would be determined through their habit of worship
– the forking paths are cultic, either the ordained approach to YHWH
or apostasy. Secondly, it is the new covenant that will finally push
Israel through to this covenantal *telos* – this is therefore an organic
progression, aligned with the original goal set forth in the Mosaic
covenant. In other words, the goal of the new covenant is no different
from the goal of the old covenant, though the new covenant will
supply the indispensable means to this end. The Day of Atonement
ritual set within the tabernacle, which was created after the pattern
of the true abode of God, pointed to the antitype, to the work of
atonement necessary for cleansing both cosmos and humanity. Nevertheless, we must maintain, thirdly, that holiness was a real possibility
through the way opened by YHWH in Leviticus, and so, although
inseparable from the person and work of the Son (which undergirded
all reconciliation throughout Israel's history), the goal set forth in the
Mosaic covenant was indeed a real goal with true potential.[89] One
point alone is needed to establish the reality of the promise held out
in Leviticus 26:12 (as well as the reality of Israel's culpability in not
attaining it), namely that the divine Presence in their midst was itself
a *real* presence – all else follows from this, given our understanding
that God's Presence is the source of sanctification. Since it is his
Presence that sanctifies, and since he had established his dwelling
among them, along with the sacred occasions on which to meet with
him through the tent of meeting, Israel's failure to be consecrated
cannot be anything other than a sincere and culpable failure, a breach
of covenant, true apostasy. Edenic life with God would not be attained
apart from the diligent use of the cultic life with God he had revealed.
Leviticus stands as the divinely revealed programme for Israel's

---

[88] Wenham 1979: 18.
[89] One may think of the sacrificial cultus as establishing a system of credit: the
Israelite received true spiritual goods (including forgiveness) through the purification offering, e.g., but the real payment of the accumulated debt awaited the Son's
crucifixion.

holiness, a calling through which Israel, as Servant of God, would bring the way of YHWH to the nations, and would experience communion and fellowship with God.

Adding the prospective reality held out as a covenantal promise in Leviticus 26:11–12, the following movements unfold:

(1) Exod. 25:8; 29:45 → [tabernacle (25 – 31; 35 – 40)] Exod. 40:34
(2) Exod. 40:35 → [sacrifices (Lev. 1 – 7) (8)] Lev. 9 – 10
(3) Lev. 10:1–3 → [unclean and clean (11 – 15)] Lev. 16
(4) Lev. 10:1–3 → [holy and profane (17 – 22)] Lev. 23 – 25
(5) Lev. 26 → [covenantal promises and threats] Rev. 21 – 22

In sum, Israel was given the covenantal prospect of Edenic life with God, contingent upon holiness. The simple programme for that holiness was the Sabbath by Sabbath entrance into the divine Presence. As Israel regularly basked in the light of his face through the tabernacle cultus, YHWH would increasingly sanctify Israel. This programme of sanctification, of course, entailed avoiding the cultic abominations of Egypt behind them and of Canaan before them; rather, it called for Israel, as with Moses' face, to reflect the light of his countenance among the nations.

Chapter Seven

Establishing the earthly house of God: from Sinai's tabernacle to Zion's temple

Introduction

In this chapter we will explore how the cultic theology of Leviticus pervades and gets developed in the rest of the Old Testament. As we approach the next major mountain in Israel's history, we will first round out the Pentateuch with a brief look at Numbers and Deuteronomy – fitting, since these books are set within the context of Israel's pilgrimage to Mount Zion.

The book of Numbers narrates Israel's initial failure to enter the land due to unbelief, in dreadful fear of the Canaanites (Num. 14). That unbelief is then dissected by the literary and theological centre of the book, in Numbers 16 – 17, where three episodes are narrated in which, ultimately, Aaron's prerogatives as high priest are challenged (16:1–40, 41–50; 17:1–13). The last rebellion was resolved by depositing twelve staffs representing the twelve tribes of Israel by the ark in the tabernacle. The symbolism is strengthened inasmuch as the staffs were taken from the leaders of each tribe, and had each one's name written upon them, but also because the Hebrew word for 'staff' (*maṭṭeh*) happens to mean 'tribe' as well.[1] On the next day, while the other rods had remained dry wood, Aaron's rod had budded with blossoms and ripe almonds, as if it had been grafted to the menorah, which was a stylized almond tree (Exod. 25:31–40).[2] This life-out-of-death symbol served as God's vindication of Aaron as the designated mediator. Drawing near to God through Aaron would lead to life. Doing so apart from this anointed priest would lead to death:

---

[1] See Wenham 1981b.
[2] Here it is a curious observation that Exodus, Leviticus and Numbers each has the ascent into God's Presence at the centre (Exod. 19; Lev. 16; Num. 17).

'Surely we die, we perish, we all perish' (Num. 17:12). The question of the gate liturgy, then, is at the heart of Numbers: *Who shall ascend the mountain of YHWH?* The high priest alone may ascend into the summit of the architectural mountain of God, the holy of holies. For our purposes, these episodes underscore an important point: while the Israelites were too fearful to enter the land of Canaan (although this entrance had been divinely vouchsafed to them), yet they had no trepidation over entering the holy of holies – that is, they had no fear of YHWH himself. Indeed, because Israel did not fear YHWH they would fear their enemies. Most fundamentally, Israel does not appear to comprehend the significance of what has taken place through the tabernacle cultus, that God the Maker of heaven and earth now truly resides in the midst of the camp, and how that divine Presence has escalated the prospect for Israel, either for abundant life or judgment and death. This failure and unbelief, moreover, makes a mockery of the whole trek to Mount Zion, bound up as it is with the goal of dwelling with YHWH. Ironically, although they desired, out of self-assertion and revolt, to enter the holy of holies, they did not yearn sufficiently for that life with God in the house of God in Zion.

Nevertheless, the overarching theme of the book is YHWH's steadfast love, as demonstrated by his resolute commitment to bring his people into the land – he has chosen to bless, and not curse, Israel. Numbers 22 – 24 recounts how the Moabites hired paganism's most famous prophet, Balaam, to curse the Israelites. Given the unbelief, disobedience and rebellious grumbling of Israel, the reader surely expects God to make full use of this opportunity to curse his people. Yet when from the mountain peak of Peor Balaam gazed down at Israel encamped by their tribes, the Spirit of God came upon him, causing him to see and declare a wonder:

> How lovely are your tents, O Jacob!
> Your dwellings, O Israel!
> Like palm groves that stretch out,
> like gardens by the riverside,
> Like aloes planted by YHWH,
> like cedars beside the waters.
> (Num. 24:5–6)

By God's Spirit, Balaam saw what Israel would not acknowledge: that with YHWH God, the fountain of life, in their midst through the tabernacle, their encampment had become the garden of Eden. The point, again, is fundamental for the existence of Israel: the true gift is YHWH himself – better to be vagabonds in the wilderness with YHWH than to be established in the land as a nation without him. What Israel does not acknowledge through unbelief, Balaam declares in the power of the Spirit of YHWH.

The book of Deuteronomy presents the farewell sermons of Moses, integrated with the Decalogue, which he applies by pleading with Israel to choose life instead of death (30:11–20). The forking paths of the covenant – life and blessing versus death and curse – are brought to bear once more, represented as two mountains: Gerizim (life) and Ebal (death) (chs. 27–30; 11:29). As with the promises and threats of Leviticus 26, it is crucial to understand these paths cannot be reduced simplistically to obedience versus disobedience in the sense of a merely political relationship, analogous to the suzerain–vassal treaties of the ANE. Israel is called to love YHWH and to walk faithfully in his ways, including the regular Sabbath-by-Sabbath entry into his Presence, a relationship generally portrayed with household terms (father–son, husband–wife).[3] Once more, drawing ever nearer to YHWH would lead to abundant life, while departing from his path would lead ever more deeply into death.

Given the theology of the gate liturgy, whereby it is the righteous who are delivered through the waters to the mountain of God, it cannot be insignificant that Moses states three times emphatically that Israel's entry into the land is *not* because of the people's righteousness (9:4–6). In a profound sense, rather, Israel's entry appears to be linked in Deuteronomy with Moses' death, which casts its shadow over the entire book – every mention of Israel's entry presumes the mediator's death.[4] Indeed, it has even been suggested that Moses is portrayed as a suffering mediator whose death outside the land is, to some extent, vicarious for Israel.[5] Especially since much of the high priest's role as mediator is patterned after Moses, it may be we are to understand Moses' death as the paradigm for the high priest's death. The high priest's work of atonement culminated in his own death, which 'purged the land of the blood guilt associated with violent death and allowed those convicted of manslaughter to leave the cities of refuge and

[3] The covenant formula ('I will be your God and you will be my people, and I will dwell in your midst') resonates rather with ancient marriage and adoption formulas, representing the most intimate of personal relationships (Sohn 1999).

[4] Olson 2005.

[5] Von Rad 1962: 294–295.

return home (Num. 35:28, 32)'.[6] As their mediator, Moses, finally through his own death, enables Israel to enter the land of their inheritance. This entrance, moreover, is for the sake of life in God's Presence:

> But the place where YHWH your God chooses, out of all your tribes, to put his name there for his dwelling place, that is the place you are to seek and there you shall go. . . . And you shall rejoice before the face of YHWH your God, you and your sons and your daughters, your male and female servants, and the Levite who is within your gates (since he has no portion nor inheritance with you). (Deut. 12:5, 12)

Zion, mountain of God as Israel's inheritance

> Great is YHWH, and to be praised exceedingly in the city
>   of our God, in his holy mountain.
> Beautiful in elevation, the joy of the whole earth
>   is the Mountain of Zion on the farthest sides of the north,
> in the city of the mighty king. God is in her citadels,
>   he is known as her stronghold.
>
>   (Ps. 48:1–3)

Much of the flow of sacred history can be traced as the movement from Sinai, where Israel was consecrated to God in the wilderness, to Zion, as Israel inherited the land of Canaan.[7] Just as Israel had been delivered through the waters of the sea and brought to Mount Sinai, the same pattern is repeated for the mountain of God in the land: Israel is led through the waters of the Jordan River and brought to Mount Zion. Inheriting the traditions and legacy of Sinai, Mount Zion became *the* mountain of God for Israel,[8] the mountain that will eventually be exalted over all the earth, transformed into Eden. Creation, kingship, temple, Eden, Sabbath, victory and inheritance, blessing to the nations, all these concepts converge upon the significance of Zion. In the following subsections I will show how Zion develops the biblical theology of Leviticus: dwelling with God.

---

[6] Wenham 2008: 54.
[7] Clifford 1972: 98; Cohn 1981: 3.
[8] Levenson 1987: 89–96; Clifford 1972: 113–117, 154–155.

Blessing to the nations: Zion as Abraham's mount of worship

The earliest gesture toward Zion in the Pentateuch, aside from Eden's mountain, is found in the narrative of Abraham's near-sacrifice of Isaac in Genesis 22 – under the name Moriah.[9] Recalling that the original context of the Abraham narrative was the divine intent to reverse the tower of Babylon judgment on the nations (cf. Gen. 12:3), the mysterious event at 'the mountain of YHWH' (v. 14) is portrayed as the dramatic confirmation of the covenant, especially with regard to the central promise that through Abraham's seed 'all the nations of the earth will be blessed' (v. 18). Within the context of Genesis 1 – 11 the blessing to the nations to be worked out in sacred history cannot be relegated to a generality, but rather should be understood in relation to humanity's expulsion from God's Presence – as a restoration to dwelling with God in the house of God.

The divine oath by which the promises have been confirmed is linked inseparably to the cultic significance of the test (vv. 16–18). YHWH had called upon Abraham to take his son, in whom all the promises were invested, and to offer him up as an ascension offering. In the ensuing history of Israel God would reveal to David this same mount as the chosen place whereupon, Abraham-like, David would build an altar to offer up ascension offerings (2 Sam. 24). As the Chronicler records it, God sent fire out of heaven upon the altar of ascension offering, so that David responded (this time, Jacob-like), 'This is the house of YHWH God, and this is the altar of ascension offering for Israel!' (1 Chr. 21:26; 22:1). Immediately, David contracted masons from among the resident aliens (*gērîm*) to secure hewn stones for building the house of God. In 2 Chronicles 3:1 all of these theological lines are brought together: 'Now Solomon began to build the house of YHWH at Jerusalem on Mount Moriah, where he had appeared to David his father at the place that David had established on the threshing floor of Ornan the Jebusite.'

It is difficult to miss the international associations with Zion and the temple here, given the labour of the resident aliens and the Jebusite's threshing floor, not to mention the role of Hiram, king of Tyre (2 Chr. 2:3, 11). More importantly, 2 Chronicles 3:1 and Genesis 22 are the only two places where Moriah is mentioned in the Old

---

[9] Regrettably, lack of space precludes our investigation of the relationship of Melchizedek/Salem to the cultus of Zion/Jerusalem (cf. Ps. 110).

Testament.[10] This locale, therefore, along with the terminology of YHWH's 'appearing' to David (the root of which underlies the name 'Moriah'), links the theologically climactic episodes in the lives of Abraham and David to the temple of Solomon. Upon building the temple, Solomon's fifth petition at its dedication ceremony lays special stress on the nations:[11]

> When a foreigner who is not of your people Israel comes from a distant land for the sake of your name – for they shall hear about your great name and your mighty hand and your outstretched arm! – when he comes to pray toward this house, you, hear in your heavenly abode and grant all for which the foreigner invokes you. In this way all the peoples of the earth will know your name and fear you, as does your people Israel, and they will know this house, which I have built, is called by your name. (1 Kgs 8:41–43)

From the beginning (Gen. 12:3), then, Zion has had the nations within its compass and *telos*, a reality developed by the prophets who envision the nations streaming to Zion in celebration of the feast of Booths (cf. Isa. 2:1–4; Mic. 4:1–5; Zech. 14:16–21).

The theological connections we have probed comport well with understanding Genesis 22 as a foundation story for the Jerusalem cultus.[12] One implication following this observation is that the worship of ancient Israel at Solomon's temple was founded upon a last-second sleight of hand, wherein the son of promise had been replaced by a ram, a substitution that had been supplied and approved by God himself for the cultic system. As discussed in the Passover section of chapter 3 of this book, there is a rich history of rabbinical interpretation on this point, clearly demonstrating that the sparing of Isaac was understood deeply as the sparing of Israel, relevant for the entire sacrificial system. Here two points are in order. First, there is no validation for understanding that this allowance for animal substitution had somehow negated Israel's calling to become completely consecrated to God – that was Israel's destiny and mission, for the sake of the nations, a calling itself solicited by the theology of the sacrificial cultus. Secondly, within

---

[10] Ancient Jewish interpretation also understood this mount to be where Adam was created. Cf. *Gen. R.* 14.8.

[11] Berman (1995: 71–72) is probably correct in observing that this function of the temple as a symbol for God's acclaim among the nations reaches its apex with the visit from the queen of Sheba (1 Kgs 10:4–9), although this scene highlights rather Solomon's wisdom and reign broadly more than it does the temple in particular.

[12] Walters 1987.

the episode of Genesis 22 there is a clear shift from Abraham's obedience to YHWH's provision, and this not merely of the ram. At the centre of the narrative Abraham himself redirects dramatic expectations to God, saying, 'My son, God will provide for himself a lamb' (v. 8). Then, at the resolution to the action, he names the mountain according to this still future-oriented expectation, 'YHWH will provide' (*yhwh yir'eh*), an expectation that had apparently become common currency ('as it is said to this day, "In the mount of YHWH it shall be provided,"' v. 14). Ancient Jewish interpreters had even understood the Passover legislation, whereby the lamb or young goat had replaced the Israelite household's firstborn son (representing Israel as God's firstborn son), as a token fulfilment of this expectation. In sum, the theological inheritance of Solomon's temple on Zion includes the promise of blessing to the nations, through an utterly consecrated Israel, an Israel whose mission is defined in terms of the sacrificial cultus.

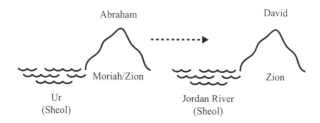

Permanence: Zion as YHWH's chosen habitation

YHWH's choice of Zion for his dwelling place appears to have been an eternal election. As we have just rehearsed, it is the place to which he led Abraham for the near-sacrifice of Isaac, as well as the place, generations later, he revealed to David in order to quell the divine wrath through sacrifice. Far from having an incidental role, YHWH's chosen place is central to both stories. The books of Samuel have the corresponding movement from tabernacle to temple as their theme, beginning with the scandalously debased sanctuary at Shiloh (1 Sam. 1 – 3; cf. Judg. 21) and concluding with David's purchase of the divinely revealed temple site.[13] The height of Israel's history then culminates in the transfer of the ark to the temple and Solomon's temple-dedication ceremony in 1 Kings 8, his sevenfold petition affirming the mediatorial role of the temple at both a cosmic and an

---

[13] Dumbrell 2001: 45.

international level, as *the* channel of communication between heaven (God's true abode) and earth (humanity's abode).[14] In retrospect, the exodus deliverance is understood to have had Zion – standing for the whole land of Canaan – as its goal:

> He made a path for his anger;
>> he did not spare their soul from death,
> but gave their life over to the plague,
>> and destroyed all the firstborn in Egypt . . .
> But his own people he caused to go forth like sheep,
>> and guided them in the wilderness like a flock.
> He led them on safely, so that they did not fear,
>> but the sea overwhelmed their enemies.
> And he brought them to his holy border,
>> this mountain which his own right hand had acquired.
>> (Ps. 78:50–54)

The theology, hopes and expectations bound up with Mount Zion are extolled in Israel's liturgy and by their prophets, with particular emphasis upon its being the mountain of YHWH's permanent choosing: Zion is YHWH's resting place (*měnûḥātî*) for ever (Ps. 132:13–14; cf. 152:1; 78:69), for he loves Zion (Ps. 78:68) and has built his house there (Ps. 87:2) – he has singled out Zion (Ps. 68:17) and dwells in her midst (Ps. 46:6); Zion is YHWH's holy mountain (Jer. 31:23), the joy of the whole earth (Ps. 48:3), the perfection of beauty (Ps. 50:2) and the cornerstone of the new creation (Isa. 28:16).[15] As the people of YHWH, Israel's own history is, of course, joined to this divine election of Zion – the place of his rest has become the place of Israel's promised rest, as Solomon declares plainly at the temple-dedication ceremony (1 Kgs 8:56), 'Blessed be YHWH, who has given rest to his people Israel, according to all that he had spoken. Not one word has failed of all his good word, which he spoke by the hand of Moses his servant.' Moses had indeed already noted this correspondence between Israel's land of rest and YHWH's chosen mount:

> But you shall seek the place where YHWH your God chooses out of all your tribes to put his name for his dwelling [*šiknô*], and there you will go . . . for as yet you have not come to the rest and

---

[14] Cf. Knoppers 1995.
[15] Childs 1962: 85.

inheritance which YHWH your God is giving you. When you cross over the Jordan and dwell in the land which YHWH your God is giving you to inherit, and he gives you rest from all your enemies round about you, so that you dwell in safety, then there will be the place where YHWH your God himself chooses to make his name dwell [*šakkēn*]. (Deut. 12:5, 9–11)

The prohibition (Deut. 12:7–8, 13–14) of other places underscores both YHWH's choice of Zion (in a similar fashion to Gen. 22 and 2 Sam. 24) and Israel's profound association with that choice.

In 2 Samuel 7, which relates the covenant with David, YHWH himself connects David's desire for temple-building with his people's rest:

I will appoint a place for my people Israel, and will plant [*nṭ'*] them, that they may dwell in a place of their own and not be shaken any more; nor shall the sons of violence afflict them any more, as in the beginning.

This language brings us back to the hope of Israel expressed in the Song of the Sea, perhaps *the* summary of Israel's story and the drama of redemption:

You will bring them in and plant [*nṭ'*] them on the mountain
    of your inheritance,
  in the place you made for your abode, O YHWH,
  the sanctuary, O Lord, that you have established with
    your hands.

(Exod. 15:17)

I will return to the Davidic covenant below, but here observe that because the temple, particularly in the transition from the tent-dwelling of God, would symbolize the permanence of Zion, David was proscribed from building it due to his being a 'warrior who has shed blood' (1 Chr. 28:3). That is, it was more fitting for a son of David who represented the stability of *dynamic succession* to build the temple than for David himself, who represented the conquest leading to that rest and stability,[16] to do so, a point that Solomon himself, whose name derives from *šālôm* (peace), appears to understand (1 Kgs 8:17–20).

---

[16] See Berman 1995: 73–75.

Ultimately, every attribute of Zion derives from its being YHWH's chosen habitation – Zion is secure and inviolable, the source of the river of life and abundance, the locale of the Davidic king's throne, the place to which the nations will pilgrimage in worship of YHWH, the foundation of the new creation and focus of Israel's eschatological hopes.

The temple: Zion as the city of David

An inexorable movement drives the narrative of 1 and 2 Samuel, a destiny toward which its leading character, David, gravitates: the founding of Zion and the site of the temple. The One of Sinai will be known as the One who dwells in Zion. A step toward that goal is reached when David conquers Jerusalem: 'David took the stronghold of Zion; that is, the City of David' (2 Sam. 5:7; cf. 1 Kgs 8:1). As the gloss indicates, Jerusalem or Zion is, expressly, the City of David – of the One who will reign on YHWH's behalf. Just as previous mountains in sacred history have been associated with particular individuals and covenants (Adam with Eden, Noah with Ararat, Moses with Sinai), so Zion is associated with David and the covenant made with him. The bond between David and Zion may be seen in Psalm 132, where the psalmist seeks blessing for Zion based upon YHWH's remembrance of David and vice versa: YHWH will not turn from his covenant with David 'because [kî] YHWH has chosen Zion; he has desired it for his dwelling place' (v. 13). More deeply, there is also a decisive bond between YHWH and the king who will reign on his behalf; because YHWH has chosen Zion for his permanent dwelling, his chosen king must also be established there – it is 'the city of the great [divine] king' (Ps. 48:2) and so of his son, the vice-regent, as well (Ps. 2:6–7). The divine choice of both Zion and David are brought together in 2 Chronicles 6:6 (cf. 1 Kgs 8:16):[17] 'I have chosen [wa'ebḥar] Jerusalem that my name may be there, and I have chosen [wa'ebḥar] David to be over my people Israel.'

That Zion and David are paired by divine election is found elsewhere, as in Psalm 78:68–70:

> But [YHWH] chose the tribe of Judah,
>   Mount Zion which he loves.
> And he built his sanctuary like the heights,
>   like the earth which he has founded for ever.

---

[17] Probably, as a correction to haplography, 1 Kgs 8:16 should be emended to match 2 Chr. 6:5–6 verbatim.

> He chose David his servant,
> and took him from the sheepfolds . . .

This bond is forged and sealed through the Davidic covenant.

As we will see, the covenant with David establishes nothing less than the goal of redemptive history; through it God further reveals *how* he will bring forth the life with Israel solicited within the Sinai covenant. As we turn to 2 Samuel 7, where the substance of the Davidic covenant is found, it may be helpful here to touch upon ancient Israel's understanding of house(hold). The words for 'house(hold)', 'build', 'stone' and 'son' are related by sound in Hebrew, and the latter three may even derive from the same root,[18] a point that leads to rich wordplay in the Bible. Just as a 'house' (*bayit*) is 'built' (*bānâ*) with 'stones' (*'ăbānîm*), so a 'household' (*bayit*) is 'built' (*bānâ*) through one's 'sons' (*bānîm*).[19] Now in response to David's desire to build a *bayit*-house for God (2 Sam. 7:1–3), YHWH responds:

> YHWH declares to you that YHWH will make for
> you a *bayit*:
>
> 'When your days are fulfilled
> and you lie down with your fathers,
> I will raise up your seed after you,
> who will spring forth from your body,
> and I will establish his kingdom.
> He it is who will build a *bayit* for my name.
> I will establish the throne of his kingdom for eternity.
> I will be his father, and he will be my son.'
> (2 Sam. 7:11b–14a)

The *bayit* David would like to build for God is a house. YHWH, however, honours David even while denying him his desire: YHWH, rather, will build David a *bayit*. Not only does YHWH reverse roles, but he also escalates the building project from a *bayit* made with stones to a *bayit* made with living stones, sons – from a *bayit*-as-house to a *bayit*-as-household. This point is clear from the reference to David's seed, the establishment of his kingdom, and even to his son's being regarded as YHWH's son (*bēn*). YHWH will build David an enduring

---

[18] See Gesenius 1888: 142.
[19] Presumably, one's daughters would go on, through marriage, to help build another's house.

royal household: a dynasty. Finally and climactically, through this *bayit*-as-household, David's seed or YHWH's son will build a *bayit* for YHWH's name. In this manner the *bayit* for YHWH is utterly dependent upon YHWH's own faithfulness to build a *bayit*-as-household for David – YHWH will, in a sense, build himself a *bayit* through David's household. Just here it is especially critical to grasp well the significance of the third *bayit*: Does it refer to a house or a household? To facilitate discussion, the threefold use of *bayit* may be outlined as follows:

1. David desires to build a *bayit* (house) for YHWH.
2. YHWH will build a *bayit* (household) for David.
3. One from David's household or YHWH's son will build a *bayit* (?) for YHWH.

If one accepts *bayit* number 3 as 'house', then YHWH is merely asserting that, in place of David, it will be David's son who will build a temple for God. Given, however, that YHWH had already transfigured the term *bayit* from a house of stones to one of living stones (sons), can it really be the case that on this third and climactic usage he is reverting to the sort of house David had originally desired to construct? Not only would such an understanding seem somewhat paltry by comparison but, further, YHWH had already undermined this option with his initial response (vv. 4–7). On the other hand, understanding *bayit* number 3 as 'household' accords well with the statement that David's seed will be considered YHWH's son. In retrospect the glorious fulfilment will prove this twofold option to have been a false either/or, as David's son, the stone the builders rejected, becomes the chief cornerstone in the house of God – a dwelling for God's Spirit comprising living stones (cf. Ps. 118:22; Eph. 2:19–22; 1 Peter 2:4–10). God's people are destined to be both the house and household of God.

This reality will leave its impress upon Solomon's temple, voiced with his own tongue: 'Will God indeed dwell on earth? Look! Heaven and the heaven of heavens cannot contain you – how much less this house which I have built!' (1 Kgs 8:28).

Excursus: kingship in ancient Israel

Properly conceived as grounded in God's own kingship, Adam's reign began before his fall away from communion with God. On the sixth day he had been commissioned by God to fill and subdue the earth, and to rule over the creatures (Gen. 1:27). It should be underscored that this commission was given, once more, *before* the fall into sin and misery, precisely within the context of man in union with God – that is, given to man as bearer of the image of God (Gen. 1:26), created both to fellowship with God and to mediate the blessed reign of God over all the earth. The theology here is twofold. First, Adam was to gather up all creation into the seventh-day praise and adoration of God, which is what it means to 'rule and subdue'. He was charged to set apart ('sanctify') creation increasingly until the whole earth would be holy, filled with the abiding glory of God. Secondly, there is no blessing to be enjoyed, be it ever so marginal, that does not derive from the reign of God – that is the joy of what it means to *be subdued*, especially so after the expulsion from life with God. To summarize, the commission bestowed upon Adam entailed that his kingship would be in the service of his priestly office, namely that he would rule and subdue for the sake of gathering all creation to the Creator's footstool in worship, for the liturgical declaration 'YHWH reigns.' The Sabbath consummation was the heart and goal of the sixth day's commission to rule.

Once we understand the original function of Adam's kingship, we are in a better place to assess this agenda throughout the rest of the Old Testament. God's reign is universal, and from the beginning his plan of redemption aimed at all the families of the earth, never over-looking that He 'shall inherit all the nations' (Ps. 82:8). Here the role of Genesis 1 – 11 as a prologue to Israel's narrative cannot be over-emphasized, for Israel's own identity and sacred calling spring from this universal context and are ever determined by it. As we have seen, after the nations were scattered into exile from the tower of Babylon, God called out Abram in Genesis 12, promising that through him 'all the families of the earth will be blessed' (v. 3). This promise was later reiterated to Abraham: 'in your seed all the nations of the earth shall be blessed, because you have obeyed my voice' (Gen. 22:18; cf. 18:18); it was then vouchsafed to Isaac (26:4), and then onward to Jacob as the father of the twelve tribes of Israel (28:14). Coupled with this promise one may discern the undercurrent of kingship: Abram had been promised that 'kings will come from you' (Gen. 17:6), and a genealogy is followed that will blossom forth into the line of David. Eventually, through Israel a king would arise to gather the nations back into the Presence of God.

Israel, moreover, was brought into covenant fellowship with God at Sinai in order to live as a priestly kingdom and holy nation (Exod. 19:6); that is, to be a light to the Gentiles. The parallel defining attributes 'priestly' and 'holy' must be understood in the sense of being set apart to YHWH God *for the sake of* the nations; Israel was to be a mediator between God and the nations. This sacred calling had much more to do with being subdued than with subduing other peoples. Israel needed to be consecrated and sanctified, transformed into the servant of God for the sake of the world, to glorify God before the nations. Psalm 67, one of many psalms calling on the Gentiles to praise God, declares plainly that Israel received mercy and even the priestly blessing so that God's way would be known on earth, that his salvation would encompass the nations. Through Israel's early period, however, 'there was no king in Israel', which meant 'everyone did what was right in his own eyes' (Judg. 21:25). In other words, without one to incarnate God's reign, Israel would persistently fall away into apostasy. Israel needed to be subdued before they could be a light to the Gentiles.

Upon the installation of David as king of Israel the commission became a divine charge to a human king once more. Psalm 2, probably used during Israel's coronation ceremonies, is instructive on this point. In the midst of the raging nations YHWH declares, 'As for me, I have set my king on Zion, my holy mountain' (v. 6). The king then professes the divine decree 'YHWH said to me, "You are my son; today I have begotten you. Ask of me, and I will make the nations your heritage, and the ends of the earth your possession"' (vv. 7–8). The phrase 'my son' draws us once again to Adam, and to another facet of the theology of kingship.

In a unique sense Adam may be called the firstborn son of God (begotten *and* made). Luke's genealogy of the Messiah, for example, brings us back to Seth as 'the son of Adam', then on to Adam as 'the son of God' (Luke 3:38; see Gen. 5:1–3). Formed from the dust of the ground and conveyed to Eden's garden, the summit of God's holy mountain, Adam became 'son of God'. As YHWH's firstborn, then, Adam's inheritance was as wide as his commission: the whole earth – for mine are 'the cattle on a thousand hills', declares YHWH God, 'the world and its fullness are mine' (Ps. 50:10–12). Adam possessed, in other words, the inherent right to rule and subdue all the earth on his Father's behalf and for the sake of his Father's glory. Here an often neglected point merits underscoring: although Noah may be portrayed as something of a new Adam within the newly cleansed cosmos, yet *he was never commissioned to rule and subdue*, an omission all the more significant inasmuch as he was, like Adam, called to 'be fruitful and multiply, and fill the earth' (Gen. 6:1). The divine right of kingship was withheld until the rise of David. As redemptive history progresses, Israel then becomes, as it were, God's second firstborn son. Recall here the particularity of the words Moses was to speak at his opening confrontation with Pharaoh: 'Thus says YHWH: "Israel is my son, my firstborn. So I say to you, let my son go that he may worship me. But if you refuse to let him go, indeed I will kill your son, your firstborn"' (Exod. 4:22–23; cf. Hos. 11:1).

Returning now to Psalm 2, David as head of Israel and by divine promise (2 Sam. 7:14) could be considered God's son in a special sense, evidently receiving the mantle of Adam as a *function* of his office. By his anointing, David inherited Adam's role as 'son of God' and king of the earth. 'I will make him my firstborn,' says God, 'the highest of the kings of the earth' (Ps. 89:26–27). It is important to understand that *only as such* does David receive the promise to rule and subdue the nations. David's commission was to spread the will and reign of God over the earth – his enemies were not merely political or personal, but the enemies of God, kings who had set themselves against YHWH and his anointed. In reality, however, the goal of subduing Israel would prove quite enough. Worse still, it was Israel's kings themselves who led God's sheep astray into perverse rebellion and heinous idolatry. The exile was inevitable.

Yet, remarkably, within the context of Israel's apostasy, God promised to raise up a Davidic Servant who would not only lead the tribes of Jacob through a new exodus, but who would also be given 'as a light for the nations, that my salvation may reach to the end of the earth' (Isa. 49:6). This same Servant, we go on to read, would suffer God's judgment in bearing the sins of many, that as an exalted priest he might 'sprinkle many nations' (Isa. 52:13 – 53:12; cf. 1 Peter 1:1–2). Having atoned for the sins of his people, this coming Messiah – the last Adam, the seed of Abraham, the true Israel, the greater David, the suffering Servant, *the* Son of God – would ascend on high to reign from the heavenly Mount Zion, from the right hand of God the Father. The commission of Matthew 28:18–20, then, is but the embrace of the inheritance promised in Psalm 2 (and Dan. 7). Yet this kingship is in the service of a priestly office, to usher God's people into his Presence through the veil of torn flesh and shed blood. Through his outpoured Spirit the Messiah reigns to subdue and summon all creation to the adoration of his Father (1 Cor. 15:24–28).

Davidic kingship, then, is (1) rooted in YHWH's kingship and (2) an inheritance of Adam's role as son of God. In reality, all three offices of anointing (prophets, priests and kings) possess an Adamic role, and are oriented by the mountain of God. Indeed, as to the Adamic role, it is possible to comprehend the progress of redemptive history according to what we may call 'God's three sons': Adam was the first firstborn, who functioned as prophet, priest and king. Secondly, God created a corporate firstborn son, Israel. (Due to humanity's estate of sin and misery there was a separation of powers, as it were, with the distribution of the offices of prophet, priest and king among the members of Israel distinctly.) Finally, as the last Adam and true Israel, *the* Son of God dawned, as prophet, priest and king, now conforming humanity to himself as the image and likeness of God. As to the offices being oriented by the mountain of God, we have already observed in a previous chapter how the high priest's office is focused upon and validated by his annual entrance into the summit of the architectural mountain of God, the holy of holies, on the Day of Atonement (Lev. 16). Similarly, kings were enthroned upon God's holy mountain, and prophets were sent from it. The king, at his coronation, was installed upon God's holy mountain, reigning from the earthly Zion as a reflection of YHWH's reign from the heavenly Zion (Ps. 2). And to become a servant of YHWH, a prophet had first to encounter him at the mountain of God and then be sent forth from it as a messenger (Isa. 6; Exod. 3:1–10). Since all three offices are cultic, functioning distinctly for the same divine goal, one may see how kingship in ancient Israel accorded with what I have argued to be the Pentateuch's major theme: the Davidic king reigned to shepherd humanity to the house of God upon the mountain of God.

Conclusion: Zion as the Eden of Israel's end

In marked contrast to the failure of the rebellious tower builders in Genesis 11:1–9, the unified narrative of Genesis 12 to 1 Kings 8 presents the first cycle of sacred history as culminating in Israel's inheritance of permanence and rest, obtained through divine grace and faithfulness. Moreover, while the tower builders had sought to make a name for themselves, Solomon builds a house for YHWH's name. And, instead of being the place from which the nations were scattered, Zion is the place to which the nations will stream. The contrast in Genesis, then, between Eden and Babylon is reasserted as the forking path always before Israel, the choice between two cities with antithetical desires and destinies: Zion (as Eden) versus Babylon. Especially as the holy mountain awaiting Israel's restoration from exile, Zion increasingly becomes identified with motifs originally associated with Eden.[20] The renewal YHWH will bring about upon the eschatological new exodus will cause the land to burst forth in fruitfulness so that it will be said, 'This land that was desolate has become like the garden of Eden' (Ezek. 36:35). Indeed, YHWH will comfort Zion:

> He will set her wilderness like Eden,
> and her desert like the garden of YHWH.
> Joy and gladness will be found in it,
> thanksgiving and the voice of song.
>
> (Isa. 51:3)

Zion as *the* mountain of God – chosen by YHWH as his dwelling for ever – becomes the city Israel awaits, the haven that is heaven itself, and the place to which the redeemed among the nations will be gathered, having been ransomed from the dominion of death. The mountain of God in the beginning has indeed become the mountain of God at the end.[21] 'Zion has become Eden'.[22]

> Now it shall come to pass in the latter days, that the
> mountain of the house of YHWH shall be established
> as the summit of the mountains,
> and shall be exalted above the hills.
> And all nations shall flow to it.
> Many peoples shall walk and say,
> 'Come, and let us ascend the mountain of YHWH,
> to the house of the God of Jacob.
> He will teach us his ways so that we may walk in his paths.'
> For out of Zion shall go forth the torah,
> and the word of YHWH from Jerusalem.
> He shall judge between the nations, and rebuke many people.
> They shall beat their swords into plowshares,
> and their spears into pruning hooks.
> Nation shall not lift up sword against nation;
> neither shall they learn war any more.
>
> (Isa. 2:2–4)

---

[20] Cf. e.g. Levenson 1976: 25–36; Dumbrell 2001: 24–25, 95–95, 134; Stager 1999; Fishbane 1998: 116–120.
[21] Clifford 1984: 123.
[22] Childs 1962: 87.

Exile and restoration

Two movements, either toward or away from the divine Presence upon the sacred mountain, define every movement and prophetic expectation in the Hebrew Bible. Robertson,[23] for example, has justly described the message of the prophets as summarized in relation to the movement of exile and restoration, a significant pattern that may even be seen to have shaped the canon of the Old Testament.[24] The journey toward the mountain of God may be labelled an exodus (or entrance), and being driven away from the mountain of God may be dubbed an expulsion (or exile), among other terminology used. As these contrasting movements are oriented by God's Presence, they are cultic movements. In Leviticus 26 two paths – and therefore two journeys – are put before Israel, life versus death. The path of YHWH culminates in the promise of verses 11–12:

> I will make my dwelling [miškānî] in your midst
> and my soul shall not abhor you.
> I will walk in your midst. I will be your God
> and you will be my people.

The path of idolatry and apostasy, however, culminates in the threat of verse 33:

> I will scatter you among the nations
> and unsheathe the sword after you.
> Your land will be desolate and your cities a waste.

Ultimately, these two paths may be understood according to the alternative treks of the two goats on the Day of Atonement – either into the Presence of life in the house of YHWH, or ever more deeply into the realm of death and chaos. Each of these two movements, as we will see, includes a set of motifs, comprising a complete picture. For example, one always *ascends* to the land of God's mountain and always *descends* from it.[25] In the following subsections I will sketch the outlines of the paradigms for exile and restoration as a fleshing out of Israel's cultic theology.

---

[23] Robertson 2004: 453–498.
[24] Koorevaar 2014.
[25] Cf. Talmon 2001: 111.

Exile

While the gate liturgy for approaching the mountain of God requires righteousness and blamelessness to make one fit for ascent (Pss 15; 24:3–5), the opposite gesture of expulsion from God's mountain results from one's being unfit, due to unrighteousness, and may be considered an anti-gate liturgy.[26] The Bible contains various examples of divine expulsion upon *hybris*, particularly as the pride that presumes to ascend into God's Presence. Broadly, expulsion from the mountain of God involves terms such as 'to send out' (*šālaḥ*), 'to cast out' (*šālak*), 'to drive out' (*gāraš, nādap, nāhag*), 'to banish' (*nadaḥ*), 'to scatter' (*pûṣ, zārâ*), 'to be brought down or caused to descend' (*yārad*), and involves a downward movement from the heights of the mountain summit/house of God toward the depths of Sheol (pit, waters, ground or earth) or to be devoured by fire (destroyed, perish).

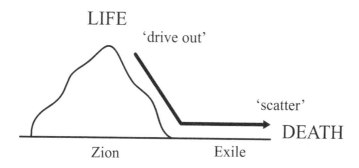

Jonah 2:1–3 serves as an example of this movement:

> But Jonah prayed to YHWH his God from within the fish, and he said, 'I cried out in my distress to YHWH, and he answered me. Out of the belly of Sheol I cried, and you heard my voice. For you cast [*šalaḥ*] me into the deep, into the heart of the seas, and the river surrounded me, all your billows and your breakers passed over me.

[26] Thus the conditions for entrance into the land/house of God are the same as for abiding in it as well as the basis for expulsion from it (cf. Jer. 7:1–16; 16:10–15). This ethical requirement, however, should not obscure the fact that it is YHWH who casts out and brings in (both often expressed in the hiphil); the former in judgment, the latter in redemption.

Relating this passage to Ezekiel 28:8 ('They will cast you down to the pit, and you will die the death of the defiled in the heart of the seas'), Callender says, 'the primal human is cast out of the divine habitation into Sheol, an image both of expulsion and of death, the same fate, essentially, as that of the first couple in Genesis'.[27] Israel's exile is itself linked to the primal expulsion out of Eden through intertextuality in the Hebrew Bible, a comparison richly mined throughout the history of Jewish interpretation.[28]

Beyond the primal expulsion narrated in Genesis 3:22–24, three other examples in the biblical literature are of note: Genesis 11:1–9; Isaiah 14:13–16; Ezekiel 28:1–19.[29] The Isaiah and Ezekiel references, prophetic oracles, entail the presumptuous 'ascending not simply mountains in general but the "mountain of God"',[30] and the Genesis 11 reference probably involves an attempted ascent into the divine abode through ziggurat construction.[31] Beginning with the tower of Babylon narrative, the *hybris* of building a ziggurat by which to ascend into heaven – for its 'head/summit is in the heavens' (v. 4) – ends with judgment and exile, a scattering over the face of the earth (v. 8).[32] Here the scattering language includes not only a descent but also an outward movement so that, as we will see in the next section, restoration to God's Presence will require both a gathering of those who were scattered and their being shepherded back to God's mountain. Because the outward movement is away from the Presence of God, it corresponds to Sheol, the realm of death.

In the Isaiah oracle the king of Babylon, who aspires to be enthroned upon God's mountain, says, 'I will ascend to heaven / . . . I will also sit enthroned on the mount of assembly on the farthest sides of Zaphon' (v. 13), but is rather, in poetic justice, brought down to Sheol, the 'farthest sides' of the Pit (v. 15). Similarly, in Ezekiel's oracle the king of Tyre, set upon the 'holy mountain of God' (v. 14), also described as 'Eden, the garden of God' (v. 13), is as a profane thing cast 'out from the mountain of God' because he was filled with 'unrighteousness' (*hamas*)[33] and sinned (v. 16). Some have noted how

---

[27] Callender 2000: 189.

[28] Cf. Morris 1992; Bovell 2004; Postell 2011.

[29] On these passages in relation to expulsion, see Cohn 1981: 33–34; Talmon 1978: 441–442.

[30] Cohn 1981: 33.

[31] Cf. e.g. Walton 1995.

[32] Cf. Clines 1997: 75, 149, n. 22.

[33] Interestingly, this is the same term for the offence that brings on the deluge (cf. Gen 6:11, 13).

the king's creation is portrayed in Adamic and priestly terms, as is his judgment (v. 18): being turned to 'ashes' for 'defiling your sanctuaries' – an image 'suggestive of the expelled primal human as an excommunicated priest'.[34] In Leviticus 21:23 the blemished priest is denied approaching the altar lest he 'profane my [YHWH's] sanctuaries'. As Cohn's summary implies, the imagery of ascent to or abiding upon the sacred mount – that is, the imagery of the gate liturgy – serves as the basis for the lament:

> The attempts of foreign kings to scale the mythological mountain of God meet with disastrous results. Similarly, foreign kings cannot ascend Zion, Yahweh's chosen mountain. Only the descendant of David reigns on Zion (Ps. 2.6); foreign kings flee in fright (Ps. 48:5–7).[35]

These three passages, then, involve a casting down or out of the mount of God (or a ziggurat presumably replicating it) because of sin, specifically *hybris*. These expulsions, once more, echo the primal expulsion of Genesis 3 as something of a gate liturgy in reverse.

Also, and aside from the primal exile of humanity from the tower of Babylon and the judgment on the kings of Babylon and Tyre already considered, other examples of this movement may be found in the prophetic judgments against the nations,[36] whose paradigmatic sin is also self-exaltation.[37] In Ezekiel 29, for example, Egypt is judged for its *hybris*, for exalting (*nāśâ*) itself above the nations (v. 15; cf. v. 3) so that YHWH declares, 'I will scatter [*pûṣ*] the Egyptians among the nations and disperse [*zārâ*] them throughout the countries' (v. 12), utilizing language strikingly similar to the exile of Israel (cf. Ezek. 11:16).[38] Not only so, but the reverse movement (to which we turn next) is also divinely promised to Egypt:

> Yet, thus says YHWH God, 'At the end of forty years I will gather [*qābaṣ*] the Egyptians from the peoples among whom they were scattered. I will return [*šûb*] the captives of Egypt and cause them to return [*šûb*] to the land of Pathros, to the land of their origin, and there they shall be a lowly kingdom.' (Ezek. 29:13–14)

---

[34] Callender 2000: 89.
[35] Cohn 1981: 39.
[36] See Vogels 1979: 82–113.
[37] Robertson 2004: 168.
[38] Vogels 1979: 89.

Perhaps the chief example of exile is that of Israel's southern kingdom, from Mount Zion to Babylon. The exile movement away from God's Presence may be seen in the following:

- The expulsion from Eden (Gen. 3:22–24; 4:9–16).
- The deluge (Gen. 6 – 7).
- The scattering from the tower of Babylon (Gen. 11:1–9).
- The driving out of the Canaanites before Israel (cf. Deut. 4:38; Lev. 18:24–28).
- The casting down of the kings of Babylon and Tyre (Isa. 14:13–16; Ezek. 28:1–19).
- The exile of Israel into Assyria (cf. 2 Kgs 17; etc.).
- The exile of Judah into Babylon (cf. Deut. 4:23–28; 28:64; etc.).

Each of these various historical occasions of the exile movement is analogous to the others, often involving similar terminology and, for our purposes, theology. The prospect of Israel's expulsion from the land is repeatedly compared to the driving out of the Canaanites – if Israel defiles the land with idolatry and immorality as the Canaanites did before them, then they too will suffer a similar expulsion (see Lev. 18:24–28; Deut. 4:38). Like the builders of the tower of Babylon, Israel will be scattered to the furthest ends of the earth from the life of YHWH:[39]

> And YHWH will scatter [*pûṣ*] you among the peoples, and you will be left few in number among the nations where YHWH will drive [*nāhag*] you. And there you will serve gods, the work of men's hands, wood and stone, which neither see nor hear nor eat nor smell.
> YHWH will scatter [*pûṣ*] you among the peoples from one end of the earth to the other end of the earth. (Deut. 4:27–28; 28:64)

Furthermore, as already mentioned, exile is the path on which the live goat is driven on the Day of Atonement, bearing the sins and uncleanness of Israel into the wilderness, the place of non-creation and chaos

---

[39] W. Brueggemann (2005: 435) notes, 'Israel is "scattered" (*pûṣ*), a new term in Israel's Yahwistic vocabulary, of which Yahweh is characteristically the active subject. Israel is scattered to the winds, away from the promised place, and away from its resources for identity. Exile is indeed the complete defeat, loss, and forfeiture of life with Yahweh.' D. J. A. Clines (1976: 505) notes how exilic Israel would have read the scattering of the nations (Gen. 11) in the light of its own diaspora. Cf. the language of Deut. 4:27; 28:64; Isa. 8:7–8; 17:12–13; 24:18–19; 54:9; Jer. 18:17; 21:13–14.

– death. Understanding the analogy among these historical exiles allows one to go beyond the debates, for example, as to whether or not the scapegoat is fulfilled by Jesus Christ or by Satan.[40] In becoming the sin-bearer for his people, Jesus suffers exile upon the cross, descending 'into hell' as the Apostles' Creed phrases it, and so fulfilling, in a manner, the scapegoat's cursed path. Upon the day of judgment, however, all the ungodly will be cast into the lake of fire for the eternal exile. These instances of exile may be added to our previous list:

- The Day of Atonement scapegoat driven into the wilderness (Lev. 16:10).
- The crucifixion of Jesus Christ (Mark 15:33–34).
- The final casting out into darkness, the second death (Ps. 1:4–5; Rev. 20:11–15).

The cultic theme of the Pentateuch, therefore of *YHWH's opening a way for humanity to dwell in his Presence*, demonstrates not only how the cultic approach to YHWH in worship itself becomes a foretaste of the final and lasting entry, but also how the forsaking of such access becomes a foretaste of the final exile. Israel's historical exile was the result of forsaking the joys and privileges of the Sabbath entrance into YHWH's Presence.

Restoration

Israel had descended into Egypt, portrayed as Sheol, so that the exodus out of Egypt was an ascent to Sinai, the mountain of God in the wilderness. This cosmogonic pattern is then repeated for Israel's entrance into the land, to Zion, the mountain of Israel's inheritance:

> But when you cross over the Jordan [*through the waters*] and dwell in the land which YHWH your God is giving you to inherit, and he gives you rest from all your enemies round about, so that you dwell in safety, then there will be the place YHWH your God chooses to make his name abide [*to the mountain*]. There you shall bring all that I command you: your ascension offerings, your sacrifices, your tithes, the heave offerings of your hand, and all your choice offerings which you vow to YHWH [*for life in the divine Presence*]. (Deut. 12:10–11)

[40] See e.g. Levy 1998.

After the exile, the reverse gesture of restoration is essentially that of the cosmogonic pattern, and applies the following terminology: being 'brought back, returned or gathered' (*bô*, *šûb*, *qābaṣ*), 'set, placed' (*śûm*, *nātan*), 'rested' (*nûaḥ*), 'planted' (*nāṭa'*, *šātal*) upon the mountain of God so as 'to stand' (*qûm*), 'sojourn, abide' (*gûr*), 'dwell' (*yāšab*, *šākan*) there, and involves an upward movement of 'ascent' (*'ālâ*). Entrance (ascent) and expulsion (descent) are not merely primal, related to the beginning, but are ultimately telic gestures, related to the end.

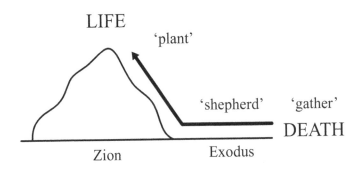

The hope of Israel, as we have had occasion to observe already, is expressed precisely in terms of the entrance paradigm, in the Song of the Sea:

> You in your loving-kindness [*hesed*] will lead forth
>   the people you have redeemed;
> You will guide them by your strength to your holy
>   habitation . . .
> You will bring them in [*bô*] and plant them [*nāṭa'*]
>   on the mountain of your inheritance,
>   In the place, O YHWH, you have made for your
>   own dwelling,
>   The sanctuary, O Lord, which your hands have
>   established.
>
>   (Exod. 15:13, 17)

This song describes Israel's deliverance within the framework of the archetypal journey: through the waters to the mountain for life in the divine Presence. There are two images here, furthermore, that call for brief consideration: that of a shepherd leading his flock to his mountain abode, and that of being planted like a tree upon that mountain (i.e. dwelling in YHWH's house). The first is a metaphor of journey, the second of arrival. As to the journey image, Psalm 23 gives us, perhaps, the best-known meditation on the assurance expressed in Exodus 15. YHWH is the shepherd who sustains his sheep through the wilderness, feeding and guarding them by his 'loving-kindness' (ḥesed) along the paths of righteousness. This image is also utilized by the prophets to describe the return from exile:

> I will return [šûb] Israel to his pastures, and he will feed on Carmel and in Bashan, and his soul shall be satisfied upon Mount Ephraim and in Gilead. (Jer. 50:19)

> I will gather [qābaṣ] the remnant of my sheep from all the lands where I have driven them and will return them [šûb] to their pastures, and they shall be fruitful and increase. (Jer. 23:3; cf. Zeph. 3:19; Ezek. 39:27; Mic. 2:12; 4:6)

As Widengren has shown,[41] this theme of gathering scattered peoples, which recurs in prophecies of salvation, was a common part of the royal ideology of Mesopotamia; though while noting the sheep imagery, he failed to link this theme with the king's role as shepherd. In Israel this role is an aspect of the eschaton and is dominated by YHWH as king and shepherd, but also appears to be delegated to the Messiah as the Servant of YHWH (cf. e.g. Ezek. 34:23; 37:24; Isa. 49:5–6), naturally, since the king reigns as 'son of God'. Moses, who encountered YHWH while tending sheep (Exod. 3:1–2), fulfils this role as he leads Israel through the waters to the mountain of Sinai:

> Your way was in the sea,
>   your path in the mighty waters,
>   though your footsteps were not perceived.
> You led like a flock your people,
>   by the hand of Moses and Aaron.
>   (Ps. 77:19–20)

---

[41] Widengren 1984.

This exodus pattern of entrance, *the cosmogonic pattern*, is significant since Israel's return from Babylonian exile will be prophesied in terms of a new exodus. Returning to Psalm 23, the end of the journey is the mountain of YHWH's temple, so that the psalmist confesses, 'I will dwell[42] in the house of YHWH for ever.' That is to say, YHWH himself, dwelling with him, is the *telos* of the paths of righteousness – 'to the mountain' means to himself. As some have observed, Psalm 23 may be read with reference to the new exodus whereby, instead of the covenant curses the (new covenant) blessings will pursue God's people as he brings them into the land once more, where YHWH will host them with the fatness of his house.[43]

The second metaphor, of arrival, found in the words 'you will bring them in and *plant* them on the mountain' (Exod. 15:17), is expressed well in Psalm 1, where we are instructed that the one who meditates upon the torah of YHWH will be like a tree 'planted' (*šātal*) by streams of living water, an allusion to the garden of Eden upon the holy mountain of God. Again, this is an eschatological image (as it is in the Song of the Sea), for the ungodly will be 'driven away' (*nādap*) like chaff, unable 'to stand' (*qûm*) in the judgment, but YHWH knows the way of the righteous – indeed, he leads them on this path as their shepherd.[44] This hope, nevertheless, is often expressed as the present condition of those who trust in YHWH, planted specifically in the house of God:[45]

> But as for me,
> I am like a green olive tree in the house of God.
> (Ps. 52:8)

> The righteous will flourish like a palm tree;
> he shall grow like a cedar in Lebanon.

---

[42] Cf. *BHS* n. C for emending *šûb* to *yāšab*. LXX has *katoikein*.

[43] Cf. Isa. 55:1–3; Freedman 1980; Barre and Kselman 1983.

[44] As such, shepherding is a positive metaphor for guiding God's flock to his mountain. Thus YHWH's judgment upon the shepherds of Israel was precisely because, rather than guiding them to himself (expressed most fully in guiding them to his mountain for worship), they 'scattered' (*pûṣ*) the sheep away. Jer. 23:1–2: '"Woe to the shepherds who destroy and scatter [*pûṣ*] the sheep of my pasture!" says YHWH. Therefore thus says YHWH God of Israel against the shepherds who feed my people: "You have scattered [*pûṣ*] my flock, driven them away, and not attended them. Look at me – I will attend to you for the evil of your doings," says YHWH.' Cf. Jer. 10:21; Ezek. 34:5–6, 12. As an example of the eschatological use of this paradigm near the end of the Second Temple period, see Rev. 21:27 (cf. 21:7–8; 22:14–15; Matt. 25:34, 41).

[45] The eternal planting of the righteous as trees of life is a theme developed richly in the literature of the Second Temple period; on this see Lanfer 2012: 60–63.

> Those who are planted in the house of YHWH
> shall flourish in the courts of our God.
>
> (Ps. 92:12–13)

Similarly, God's people are called 'oaks of righteousness' and 'the planting of YHWH' in Isaiah 61:3. As mentioned earlier, Balaam's inspired vision in Numbers 24, once again, describes the Israelites as trees planted in the garden of Eden:

> How lovely are your tents, O Jacob!
> Your dwellings, O Israel!
> Like palm groves that stretch out,
> Like gardens by the riverside,
> Like cedars beside the waters.
>
> (Vv. 5–6)

Because of God's Presence in their midst, even in the arid wilderness, Israel lives in paradise.

In the ANE the tree was a common metaphor for the king and his kingdom,[46] a symbol found in the Bible as well (cf. Ezek. 31; Dan. 4). If we understand the 'man' of Psalm 1 as having primary reference to the king, the first psalm functions rather like the kingship law of Deuteronomy 17:14–20, holding out a promise for the kingdom,[47] with the tree imagery marking Psalm 1 to be as much about kingship as Psalm 2. The anointed king, representing Israel, must fulfil righteousness so that his kingdom may be planted upon the mountain of God, to flourish and prosper.

In summary, restoration to God's Presence means that those who were scattered must be gathered; then, as the flock of God, they are shepherded to his abode at the mountain of God where they will be planted so as to bask in the life-giving light of his Presence. The prospect of gathering the scattered people of God is forecasted already in Deuteronomy 30:3: 'Then YHWH, your Lord, will return [šûb] you from your captivity and have compassion on you, and he will again gather [qābas] you from all the peoples, among whom YHWH, your God, has scattered [pûs] you.' To dwell with God in his house defines the yearning and hope of Israel, as well as the goal of their restoration.

---

[46] Widengren 1951.

[47] See e.g. Grant 2004. For the psalms concerning individuals as having reference to the king, see Eaton 1976.

This exodus movement toward God's Presence may be seen in the following:

- The entrance into the garden of Eden (Gen. 2:8, 15).
- Resting of the ark upon the Ararat mount (Gen. 8:4).
- Israel's going into Canaan (cf. Deut. 12:10).
- Pilgrimage to Zion for worship at the Solomonic temple (Pss 15; 24).
- The new exodus return of Judah (and the nations) to Zion (Deut. 30:3).[48]
- The Day of Atonement sacrificed goat whose life is brought into the holy of holies (Lev. 16:15).
- The ascension of Jesus Christ into heaven (Luke 24:50–53).
- Entrance into the New Jerusalem (Ps. 1:3; Rev. 21 – 22).

Exile and restoration in the history of Israel

The theology of the gate liturgy serves as a paradigm for Israel's history, unfolding the essence of the exile and the restoration.[49] Reduced to a basic archetypal movement, the prophets threaten Israel with death in the form of exile from God's Presence in Zion; and they promise Israel life afterward in the form of restoration to God's Presence in Zion. The prophets use a variety of images to express the reality of exile, each conveying something of the depth of this judgment. Jonah, representing Israel, had been exiled to Sheol, cast into the deep, an experience that was meant to form within him a new sympathy for the plight of Assyria, which, as we will consider, was analogous to his situation. Sometimes the exile is spoken of as the levelling of Mount Zion (Mic. 3:12). With Hosea, the expulsion is portrayed in terms of household imagery and the separation of husband and wife, Gomer the adulteress being driven out of the house. This plight is coloured further by the names of her children: Lo-Ammi, 'not my [YHWH's] people', and Lo-Ruhammah, 'no mercy [from YHWH]'. To be exiled is, in other words, to become as one of the Gentile nations – far from God, without his mercy, not his people. Again these are all distinct attributes of the same realm, the realm of death – *the exile was 'the death*

---

[48] See also Jer. 50:19; 23:3; Zeph. 3:19; Ezek. 39:27; Mic. 2:12; 4:6.

[49] Indeed, 'more than one third of all the occurrences of *pûṣ* are used in reference to the exile. Thus "scattering" clearly constitutes divine judgment against Israel' (Kaminski 2004: 32).

of deaths' for Israel.[50] This understanding is most vividly rendered in Ezekiel's vision of the valley of dry bones (Ezek. 37). While some prophets, such as Amos and Micah, speak in more literal and historic terms, merely proclaiming exile into Assyria and Babylon, respectively, the other images serve to explain the theology of exile, that exile from God's Presence means death for Israel. Charting the few examples I have offered will enable us to probe this theology further:

Zion, *life with God*	Israel's exile	Nations, *death apart from God*
Jonah	→	Sheol
Amos	→	Assyria
Hosea	→	Gomer driven out of house (separation)
		Lo-Ammi (not my people)
		Lo-Ruhammah (no mercy)
Micah	→	Babylon
Ezekiel	→	Valley of dry bones

The first point to make is that when we understand the theological significance of the exile as death, then we may understand the significance of the restoration as resurrection, precisely the theology of Ezekiel 37. Hosea also describes restoration as resurrection:

> From the hand of Sheol I will deliver them;
> From death I will redeem them.
> Where, O Death, are your plagues?
> Where, O Sheol, is your sting?
>
> (Hos. 13:14)

We are probably to understand the same imagery in Hosea 6:2, which declares, 'After two days he will revive us; on the third day he will raise us up that we may live before his face,' a reference we will examine in the next chapter. Returning to the point, our grasp of the nature of the restoration deepens simply by reversing the images of exile: from Sheol to the mountain of God; from Assyria and Babylon to Zion; from separation to the redemption of matrimony; from homeless bastard children to adoption within the household of God – from death to resurrection life. Secondly, in entering the realm of death and becoming 'not my people', Israel truly joined the plight of the nations.

---

[50] The quote is from the title of K. J. Turner's book *The Death of Deaths in the Death of Israel* (2011), who argues that as a theological concept in Deuteronomy exile represents the death of Israel.

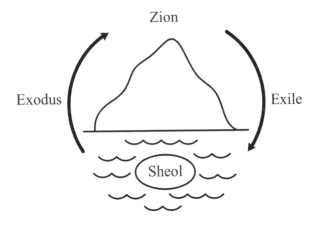

Indeed, Israel's history (Gen. 12 to 2 Kgs) mirrors that of humanity (Gen. 1 – 11), for both begin in God's Edenic Presence and both end with Babylonian exile:

Nations (Gen. 1 – 11):   From Eden mountain of God to the tower of Babylon scattering and exile

Israel (Gen. 12 to 2 Kgs):   From Zion mountain of God to the Babylonian scattering and exile

Here it is crucial to hold fast to the purpose of Abraham's calling and Israel's election: the ultimate restoration of the nations. For when God promised to restore Israel, who had become 'not my people', we

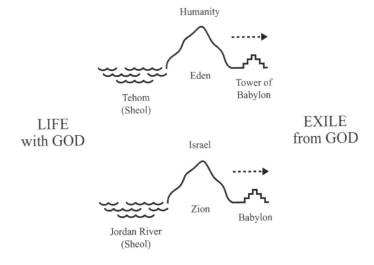

find that this restoration from 'not my people' to 'my people' will include a remnant of the nations who, of course, were also 'not my people', a point developed by Paul in Romans 9:22–26.[51] Israel becomes as one of the Gentile nations, entering into the stark plight of the nations, even death itself, ultimately as part of God's plan to redeem the nations. This redemption will be made possible because Jesus Christ, as second Adam and true Israel, will suffer the profound exile – from the heights of the heavenly Zion to the depths of Sheol, entering into the plight of humanity and Israel's exile from God, in order ultimately to lift them up with himself, through his own restoration to the Father by his resurrection and ascension.

In essence, the prophesied restoration was portrayed as a recapitulation of Israel's sacred history, a pattern that can be delineated as follows:[52]

(1) exodus redemption → (2) consecration → (3) consummation of
                        by covenant   the inheritance

This pattern aligns well with my cosmogonic pattern: through the waters (exodus redemption), to the mountain (consecration by covenant), for life in the divine Presence (consummation of inheritance). In short, the prophets declared there would be *a new exodus*. This new exodus would require a new Passover of redemption and lead to a new mountain of God from which a new covenant would be inaugurated, a new covenant yielding the gifts of torah and the tabernacling Presence – both in a revolutionary transforming manner. The new exodus would also create a newly consecrated Israel and culminate in inheritance of the land. Given that the first epoch of sacred history ended in exile, the recapitulation involves an escalation of God's activity – indeed, this new exodus of redemption is understood as ushering in the new heavens and new earth, bringing history to its destined culmination. 'This salvation, this second exodus from the bondage of sin and the power of Sheol', writes Ninow, 'surpasses by far the first exodus experience and leads into the eschatological redemption.'[53]

It would not be unjustified to claim that New Testament theology may be formulated as new exodus theology. Often, however, the exodus themes drawn out of the New Testament are restricted to parallels with the historical exodus out of Egypt, neglecting entirely

---

[51] See Robertson 2004: 205–206.
[52] Phythian-Adams 1947.
[53] Ninow 2001: 213.

the new exodus themes prophesied of the restoration. While lack of space precludes their development here, one finds various new exodus themes of the prophetic literature taken up by the apostolic writers. The restoration will involve the following:

- The visitation of YHWH himself, preceded by an Elijah-like messenger.
- The full and final redemption/ransom and cleansing of God's people from their sins.
- The reunion of the northern kingdom of Israel and the southern kingdom of David.
- All the nations participating in the deliverance – that is, an international exodus.
- A Davidic shepherd as the new Moses to lead the new exodus.
- A new covenant.
- The Spirit of God poured out abundantly upon his people.
- The torah put within his people's hearts.
- God's dwelling established among his people.
- A widespread knowledge of YHWH God.
- Peace established among the nations under the rule of the Davidic shepherd.
- The earth transformed into Eden.

Reduced to two great expectations, the new exodus dawns with the messianic Davidic shepherd and the outpouring of the Holy Spirit – all the other aspects of the restoration result from these. A careful reading of the prophetic material will bear out that all hope for true restoration was divinely anchored upon the work of these two persons. The *one goal* of the new exodus, however, is but the original *telos* for creation, the redemption of Israel, and the heart of the covenants made with

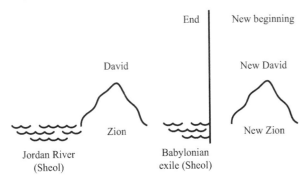

his redeemed people: for YHWH God to dwell amidst humanity in union and fellowship – to be their God and they his people.

Needless to say, the historical return from exile did not usher in the new heavens and new earth, nor was it an exodus to make the previous one out of Egypt pale by comparison. As to the rebuilt house of God, many of the elderly priests, Levites and leaders of Jerusalem wept as they recalled the greater splendours of Solomon's temple (Ezra 3:12–13) – and, most devastating, the glory of YHWH never returned to the second temple. These considerations, along with the manifest lack of renewal in the hearts of the Jewish returnees, served to foster the understanding that Israel was indeed still in exile, still awaiting the glorious new exodus, an apocalyptic expectation that would lead the flock of God to the heavenly Jerusalem, the heavenly Mount Zion.[54] It is possible, moreover, to discern already in the prophets a prediction that the promised restoration would take place in a twofold manner, by a physical return from Babylon followed by a spiritual return – *the* new exodus. In Isaiah, for example, Gentry discerns the following symmetrical outline as part of a larger structure:

C Promises of Redemption (42:18–44:23)
    1. Release (42:18–43:21)
    2. Forgiveness (43:22–44:23)
C' Agents of Redemption (44:24–53:12)
    1. Cyrus: Liberation (44:24–48:22)
    2. Servant: Atonement (49:1–53:12) –
      Third, Fourth Servant Songs[55]

According to this literary plan, there are two distinct aspects of restoration: first, the release of Israel (42:18 – 43:21) paralleled to the agent of that release, Cyrus (44:24 – 48:22); and secondly, the spiritual redemption (43:22 – 44:23) accomplished by the Servant (49:1 – 53:12). More plainly, part of the book of Daniel addresses this precise issue of post-exilic expectations, informing the faithful community that while there would be a return to Judea after Jeremiah's prophesied seventy years, the full restoration would not come for another 'seventy weeks' of years, or 490 years (Dan. 9), during which four world kingdoms would dominate before the kingdom of God was inaugurated by the Son of Man figure (Dan. 7). The parallel imagery in Daniel 2

---

[54] Cf. Schmidt 1983: 219–220; Terrien 1978: 402–403.
[55] Gentry 2007.

pictures the Son of Man or kingdom of God as a stone that, after crushing the colossus (four kingdoms), grows into a mountain – an image that not only illustrates the principle of the kingdom's humble origins and steady growth, but also conveys the profound mystery of the divine will in cultic terms. The Davidic stone will be rejected and then exalted as the chief cornerstone in God's temple (Ps. 118), growing into the cosmic mountain of God – into the abode of God, the temple. It may also be argued that Ezekiel's vision of dry bones contains the principle of a two-stepped process of restoration inasmuch as the resurrection takes place in two stages: first the bodies come together through his prophesying (37:7–8), and then they are made to live through the *rûaḥ*, the wind/breath (vv. 9–10), a reality directly linked to the outpouring of the Spirit (v. 14). Israel's historical return from Babylon to form a nation once more was a resurrection of sorts – a feat for the nations to behold. But the fact of the matter is that Israel, while reconstituted as a body, had remained without the Spirit of life, arguably the central promise of the new exodus. Finally, the statement in Hosea 6:2 also accords with a two-staged restoration: 'After two days he will revive us; on the third day he will raise us up.'

While exile meant death for Israel theologically, it took the uneventful return from Babylon, laced with hardship and a stumbling back into the former sins, to drive the point home: Sheol was not merely a characteristic of life in Babylon, but of Israel's national heart – Israel was dead spiritually, in darkness. The return to Judea served only to clarify both the diagnosis and the prophesied remedy. Upon the outpouring of the Spirit – and only then – would Israel become the new Israel, the Israel that had been resurrected from Sheol and ushered into the heavenly abode of God.

Conclusion

The cultic approach to YHWH not only evoked the primordial access to Eden's mountain, so as to taste the purpose and essence of life, but it was also telic, expressing Israel's deepest hope. The yearned-for goal of Israel's life, experienced regularly *through* the cult, is YHWH's mountain abode – indeed, upon the holy mount YHWH shall be seen (cf. Gen. 22:14). To gaze upon his splendour, upon his face – this one thing is both the end and the fount of Israel's most profound longings and doctrines. This is the end and substance of biblical theology.

Given the paths we have trodden, one is led to affirm that the history of redemption, along with all of its narrative drama, is driven by one theological theme: *YHWH's opening a way for humanity to dwell in the divine Presence*. This journey through the waters to the mountain of God, to dwell with YHWH in his house, is expressed in the cosmogonic pattern as the purpose of creation, in the exodus pattern of deliverance as the purpose of redemption, traced through the history of Israel, relived and renewed through the temple cultus, and, ultimately, it formed the paradigm for all expectation – the *end* of the journey for the redeemed among Israel and the nations: eternal life with God in the house of a new heavens and earth, the Edenic Mount Zion. The end is life lived within the radiant glory of his face, the reality of the Sabbath day's cultic theophany within the holy place.

Look! The angel who spoke with me came forth, and another angel came forth to meet him and said to him, 'Run, speak to the young man saying this, "As villages without walls so will Jerusalem be inhabited, because of the multitude of humanity and animals in her midst.

"For even I," declares YHWH, "will be for her a wall of fire all around and I will be the glory in her midst. . . .

"Sing and rejoice, O daughter of Zion! For look! I come and I will dwell in your midst," declares YHWH. And many nations will be joined to YHWH in that day, and they shall be my people. I will dwell in your midst . . .

"Thus says YHWH, 'I will return to Zion and will dwell in the midst of Jerusalem, and Jerusalem will be called the city of truth, and the mountain of YHWH of hosts – the holy mountain.'"' (Zech. 2:3–5, 10–11; 8:3)

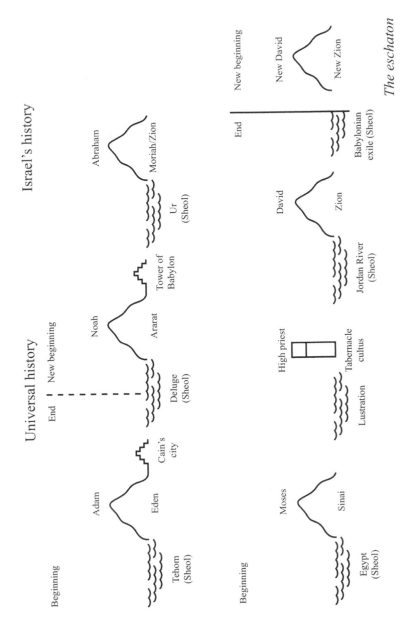

Chapter Eight

Entering the heavenly house of God: from the earthly to the heavenly Mount Zion

And certainly for this reason Christ descended to us, to bear us up to the Father, and at the same time to bear us up to himself, inasmuch as he is one with the Father.

(John Calvin)

Introduction

When upon the summit of Mount Sinai, shrouded by the thick black cloud, Moses had been emboldened to pray, 'Please, show me your glory!' (Exod. 33:18), he was pleading for the ultimate goal and function of the temple: to see the face of God. To behold the glory of God is the purpose of the human soul, the latent potential of those created in his image and likeness. The soul's capacity, however, must be developed; the soul must be cleansed and sanctified – the pure in heart will see God (Matt. 5:8). This work of cleansing and sanctification is also a function of the temple, for the sake of mediating an ever-deepening relationship with, and revelation of, God. These two functions of the temple have a reciprocal relationship: the sacrificial cultus is the way to YHWH, providing the cleansing needed for entering his Presence; the tabernacle is also the abode of God, where he is encountered, an engagement that is itself sanctifying and transfiguring. The temple is, therefore, humanity's end as well as the means – the way – to that end.

Now while the Levitical way of approaching God had set out the goal, yet it could not bring humanity to its destined end. As we have considered in previous chapters, the Levitical system undergirding the tabernacle and later temples was a typological and temporary – *though real* – means of engagement with God. The temple was a model of the cosmos; its atonement rituals cleansed the model but not the cosmos itself. The high priest was an Adam figure by office but not in reality: he represented YHWH by office but not in himself. As the author of Hebrews is at pains to demonstrate, the blood of bulls and goats could not truly take away sins; the need to offer sacrifices continually was but a reminder of the Levitical system's inability finally to cleanse and sanctify once and for all – that is, the Levitical way could not bring humanity into 'perfection', to its destiny in beholding God (10:1–10). The high priests of the Levitical priesthood, moreover, needed to offer sacrifices continually for their own sins, while *death* prevented them from continuing their ministry of mediation (11:20–28) – a most telling failure. If the high priest himself could never reach the goal of perfection in life with God, how could the objects of his mediation hope for better? Plainly, 'if perfection was possible through the Levitical priesthood,' the author of Hebrews asks, 'what further need would there be for another priesthood?' (11:11); and yet this is precisely what YHWH had already promised to David's line in Psalm 110, a new Davidic priesthood after that of Melchizedek, an order associated with Zion's mountain and the city of Jerusalem and that signifies the reign of righteousness (cf. Gen. 14:18–20). This new priesthood would be empowered by an indestructible life, for YHWH had sworn, 'You are a priest for ever [*lĕ'ôlām*]' (Ps. 110:4; Heb. 11:15–17). That indestructible life, as we will see, derives from the perfection into which the new high priest will himself have entered for ever.

The Son of God, who came as the son of David according to the flesh, descended for the purpose of establishing the new worship, the new and living entrance to God – a way that is opened to the reality of God's heavenly abode:

> Therefore, brothers, having boldness to enter the holiest place by the blood of Jesus, by the new and living way he opened for us through the veil, that is, his flesh, and having a high priest over the house of God, let us draw near with a true heart in full assurance of faith, having our hearts sprinkled clean from an evil conscience and our bodies washed with pure water. (Heb. 10:19–22)

As the high priest for God's people, the Son is able to lead others in this way, for he himself, as our forerunner, has already 'entered the most holy place once for all, having obtained eternal redemption' (Heb. 9:12). Indeed, after offering one sacrifice for sins for ever, he 'sat down at the right hand of God' (10:12). Having taken our humanity upon himself, the Son has brought that humanity to its divinely ordained end, to dwell with God in the inner sanctum of the house of God, beholding the face of God. He alone can now mediate our journey to the beatific vision: 'By one offering he has perfected for ever those who are being sanctified' (Heb. 10:14).

If we were to reduce to a single question the New Testament's development of the theology of Leviticus, it would be this: *How does the Son make possible our entrance into the heavenly abode of God?* This question involves a brief explanation, for the Old Testament's expectation for life with God gestures ultimately to the messianic kingdom of the eschaton, to life with God in the new Jerusalem of the new heavens and earth. Life with God in the eschaton, moreover, may be characterized as heaven on earth – in other words, as the end to the dichotomy between heaven and earth. In the Noah narrative we considered the probability that God's covenant had included the boundary delineation between God's abode in the heavens and humanity's abode on earth. The tabernacle, establishing the Levitical way of approaching God, therefore, was modelled after God's heavenly abode, with the holy of holies merely representing heaven. Generations later, during the dedication of the temple, Solomon had acknowledged the dichotomy of God's heavenly abode and the earthly temple 'which I have built', petitioning God that whenever his people or even foreigners pray 'toward this place' he would 'hear in heaven your dwelling place' (1 Kgs 11:30, 32, 34, 36, 39, 43, 45, 49). The eschaton, however, would bring an end to the dichotomy: the God of heaven would dwell among humanity in communion and fellowship on earth, once the earth itself had become heavenly. This reality is still the hope of God's people for the eschaton, a hope firmly anchored through the mediatorial work of the Son. *His accomplishment, however, has already ushered God's people into the reality of the eschaton, by opening the way of access to God's heavenly Presence now.* Until heaven descends to earth, he has opened the way for earth to ascend into heaven. In contrast to the former covenant's approach to God at an earthly mountain of this creation, therefore, God's people now enter the heavenly reality by faith:

For you have not come to the mountain that may be touched and that burned with fire, and to darkness and gloom and tempest . . . But you have come to Mount Zion and to the city of the living God, the heavenly Jerusalem, and to innumerable angels in festal gathering, to the assembly of the firstborn who are registered in heaven, to God the judge of all, to the spirits of the righteous made perfect, to Jesus the mediator of the new covenant, and to the blood of sprinkling that speaks better than that of Abel. (Heb. 12:18–24)

Comprehending this 'already but not yet' aspect of the eschaton, namely that we experience the eschaton of the new creation now through our taste of the heavenly reality, we may return to my original question: How does the Son make possible our entrance into the heavenly abode of God? The twofold answer, which will comprise the outline of this chapter, is that (1) *Christ's humanity must ascend* into the heavenly reality, and (2) *Christ's Spirit must descend* to earth, in order to unite us to him in that heavenly reality. Rephrased, the question is the same as the one I have pursued throughout this work, which springs up from the heart of Israel's cult: *Who shall ascend the mountain of YHWH?*

The ascent of Christ's humanity

To be sure, before Christ's humanity may ascend to God, the Son must first descend through the wonder of the incarnation, and then experience – and thereby open – the way of ascent through his life and crucifixion, burial, resurrection and ascension. 'No one has ascended but he who descended from heaven' (John 3:13). The subsequent movement of ascent through sacrifice will fulfil the cultic journey of worship – indeed, the entire first advent of the Son may be grasped as an, rather, *the*, offering to God.

Incarnation: the new dwelling of God

In the prologue of John's Gospel we read (1:14), 'The Logos became flesh and tabernacled [*eskēnōsen*] among us; and we beheld his glory, the glory as of the only Son [*monogenous*] from the Father, full of grace and truth.' Having taken our humanity upon himself, the Son became the new tabernacle, the Presence of God on earth veiled in flesh. He is in himself all that the temple signified: God's house and the way into that house. Because this reality cannot be grasped apart from understanding the Son's essential nature and relationship to the Father, the prologue is framed by that manifestation, opening with the Logos as the second person of the blessed Godhead eternally in relationship with God the Father, and then summarizing that relationship at the close (1:1, 18): 'In the beginning was the Logos, and the Logos was with God, and the Logos was God. . . . No one has ever seen God. The only Son, who is in the bosom of the Father, he has made him known.' Jesus says much the same in 6:46: 'Not that anyone has seen the Father, except he who is from God; he has seen the Father.' Just here it is critical to keep the Son's purpose in view:

he has come to draw humanity back into the Presence of God, to yield *the* revelation of God, bringing our fallen race to behold God. In the prologue we are given to know that this end for his and our humanity is nothing less than what he, as the eternal Son, has always enjoyed through the most intimate union with God the Father. The bosom (*kolpon*) of the Father he has come from is the place to which he will bring us. Repeatedly, Jesus' eventual ascent to the Father is linked to his prior descent from the Father (see 3:13; 16:26). More deeply, the Son's eternal role within the Godhead had already been that of mediator: as the life that was the light of humanity (v. 4), communicating the Father to Adam before his fall, facilitating the fellowship with the Father.[1]

In some respects the incarnation is itself the fulfilment of the temple, inasmuch as it means the union of humanity and God. Here we find the unveiling of the divine intent for humanity: nothing less than the fullest communion possible without collapsing the distinction of persons (even as the incarnation unites without obliterating the distinction between his two natures) – that is, a true fellowship indeed. The incarnation both springs from and impels toward an eternal love, creation from and to God. It is this dynamic of Christ's being – two natures, one person – that John seeks to convey later on in his first chapter, where Jesus declares to Nathaniel (1:51): 'Truly, truly, I say to you, hereafter you will see heaven opened, and the angels of God ascending and descending upon the Son of Man.' The precise repetition of Genesis 28:12 in 'the angels of God ascending and descending' leads the reader to Jacob's vision of a stairway whose summit reached heaven. As previously discussed in the chapter on Genesis, God was here vouchsafing by his grace the reality of what the tower of Babylon builders had sought through *technē* (craft): earthly access to God's heavenly abode.

What Jacob saw was the spiritual archetype of the temple – its inner reality and function as the connection between heaven and earth. He, therefore, referred to it as both the 'house of God' and 'the gate of heaven' (28:17).[2] It is this reality of what the Son has become through the incarnation that John sets forth – *in him* heaven and earth have intersected.[3] Nevertheless, as the future orientation of his remark bares out, it is Jesus' glorified body that will serve as the new temple, a point to which we will return. Through him, heaven, the abode of

---

[1] Cf. Canlis 2010: 55–88.
[2] See comments on this passage in ch. 2.
[3] Cf. also McKelvey 1969: 77.

God, will be opened. The original Jacob narrative contains a sixfold use of the word 'place' (*māqôm*). John's allusion, then, comprises another gesture that the place of the temple will soon give way to the person of the temple.[4]

The temple was, of course, more than a location, but included also the rituals of cleansing and atonement, the festival gatherings, and so on. In profound ways John's Gospel communicates how the Son's advent brought to fruition all that the temple stood for – not merely as a replacement for the temple, but rather, again, as the reality that, like new wine, bursts through the limitations of the Levitical wineskin. Through a theological angle akin to that of the author of Hebrews, John demonstrates the incompleteness of the Levitical system through a symbolic use of the number six, indicating that Israel had not yet entered into the seventh-day rest of God that is life with God.[5] The priesthood of the Son will bring to completion what the Levitical system, incomplete and bound to expire as it was, simply could not accomplish. In John 2:1–12, for example, we read of Jesus' first sign, turning water into wine for a marriage feast – the feast itself resonating with the end-days banquet of the Messiah, who is himself called the bridegroom (3:29). It is probably significant here that the water jars (*hydriai*) used for this miracle are described as 'of stone' (*lithinai*) – a common designation for the old covenant (cf. 2 Cor. 3:3, 7), that they were vessels used particularly for the 'Jewish rites of purification', and that they were six in number. Jesus' miracle served as a sign of the life and fulfilment he brings, the new wine of the messianic banquet. Moreover, this sign occurs on the seventh day.[6] His life and ministry will bring humanity through to its seventh-day end and, further, into the new creation of the new first (20:1, 19), or eighth (20:26), day.

After this first sign, Jesus ascends to Jerusalem during the Passover (John 2:13–22), where he makes a whip of cords and drives out the sellers from the temple, along with the sheep and oxen, pouring out their money and overturning their tables. When asked for a sign to

---

[4] Moreover, to behold Jesus as the new temple, one must be a part of the new Israel, that is, be 'without guile' (1:47) – following Nathaniel's example of being called out from under the fig tree (old Israel) and his confession of Christ as the Son of God (see Kerr 2002: 139–142). Note that both uses of 'you' in 1:51 are in the plural.

[5] Coloe 2001: 23.

[6] First day: Baptist's testimony about himself (1:19–28); second day: Baptist's testimony about Jesus (1:29–34); third day: Andrew and Simon Peter follow Jesus (1:35–42); fourth day: Philip and Nathanael (1:43–50); fifth and sixth day (none); seventh day: wedding at Cana (2:1–11) (Kerr 2002: 70).

demonstrate his authority for such a display, Jesus responds (v. 19), 'Destroy this temple, and in three days I will raise it up.' John then offers the following narrator's explanation (v. 21): 'But he was speaking of the temple of his body.' Here we have in explicit terms what John's Gospel has already been demonstrating implicitly. Two points are in order. First, this is the probable explanation for the accusation, dubbed 'false', levelled against Christ at his interrogation, as recorded by Mark (14:57–58): 'Then some rose up and bore false witness against him, saying, "We heard him say, 'I will destroy this temple made with hands, and within three days I will build another made without hands.'"' The accusation was false inasmuch as it was deliberately misconstrued as a malicious plot to attack the edifice at the heart of the Jews' life, and because, as John tells us, he was speaking of the temple of his body. Nevertheless, the temple of his body would bring the edifice into obsolescence and finally into judgment, so that the accusation cannot be read without a sense of irony. Mark's statement expresses, moreover, the significant expectation that the true temple of God's own abode would not be made by human hands (cf. Exod. 15:17). Secondly, the ultimate reference to Jesus' body as a temple must be understood as his resurrection body. Humanity can have no access to the heavenly abode of God whatsoever, through Jesus' body, apart from that body being his resurrection body. 'Therefore,' John writes, 'when he had risen from the dead, his disciples remembered that he had said this to them' (2:22). Uniquely, John's Gospel is narrated from the perspective of the ascension gift of the Spirit – it amounts to theological reflection upon the advent of the Son through the lens of the ascension. Using the categories by which we approached the book of Leviticus, we may describe, not unjustly, the result of the incarnation as Jesus' body becoming a *miškān*, a dwelling of God. He is, to be sure, a 'meeting place', as it were, *in himself*, through the union of his two natures, but not between the fallen race of humanity and God. Moreover, while it is also true that when encountering Jesus, human beings, whether Pharisees or publicans, had encountered God, nevertheless he had not yet become the means for them to enter the Presence of the Father, to be reconciled to him, nor to have union with the Godhead. It is his resurrection body that becomes the *'ohel mô'ēd*, the tent of meeting between humanity and God.

In John 4 Jesus encounters the Samaritan woman at Jacob's well, and this we are told took place around the sixth hour. The woman has had five husbands, along with a current man who is not her husband – six – but she now speaks with the bridegroom himself (John

3:29).[7] Jesus is, therefore, the seventh one, an idea buttressed by the context of the well, a common biblical setting for betrothal (see Gen. 24:11; 29:2, 9–11; Exod. 2:16–17). As this passage deals deeply with the outpouring of the Spirit, I will return to it below. For my purposes here, I underscore the woman's remark regarding the place of worship (v. 20): 'Our fathers worshipped on this mountain, but you [Jews] say that in Jerusalem is the place [*topos*] where one ought to worship.' Jesus' response manifests his mission (v. 21): 'Woman, believe me, the hour is coming when you will neither on this mountain nor in Jerusalem [earthly Mount Zion] worship the Father.' Once more place is substituted by the person of the Son, and this at the coming – that is, the seventh – hour. Nevertheless, when he negates the Jerusalem temple of the earthly Mount Zion as the place of worship, Jesus is not hereby announcing the utter end to approaching God at the mountain of God, for, as already noted, the new mountain will be unveiled: the Jerusalem of the heavenly Mount Zion (Heb. 12:22). After Jesus has revealed to the woman that he is the long-awaited Messiah, John then inserts a curious detail regarding her departure (4:28): 'the woman left her water jar [*hydrian*]'. With the water that he will give, Jesus has already slaked her thirst. As the only other use of this term in his Gospel, one wonders, too, whether John intends this obsolete vessel to be correlated with the six water jars of Levitical purification (see 2:6), as the seventh.

Turning now to John 14:1–6, we come in many ways to the heart of the Son's purpose. In the opening verses Jesus says:

> 'Let not your heart be troubled; you believe in God, believe also in me. In my Father's house are many rooms [*monai*]; if it were not so, I would have told you. I go to prepare a place for you. And if I go to prepare a place for you, I will come again and receive you to myself; that where I am you may be also. And where I go you know, and the way you know.'
>
> Thomas said to him, 'Lord, we do not know where you are going, and so how can we know the way?'
>
> Jesus said to him, 'I am the way, the truth, and the life. No one comes to the Father except through me.'

Jesus had previously mentioned that he would depart and that the disciples, as he had said to the Jews earlier (8:21–23), could not go with

[7] Cf. Coloe 2001: 97–99.

him (13:33). These grievous and startling words led to two questions from Peter: (1) 'Lord, where are you going?' and (2) 'Lord, why can I not follow you now?' (13:36–37), reiterated by Thomas with reference to the place of destination and to the way there (14:5). Jesus' response of consolation in 14:1–4, wherein he describes his journey to the Father, may be understood within the context of the gate liturgy, of entrance into the Father's house, the temple. McCaffrey,[8] in a superb treatment of this passage (and to which the present section is indebted), likewise writes that Jesus' journey may be interpreted as an entrance into the temple of the Father's house through his sacrificial death, a movement in line with the entrance of the high priest into the sanctuary to make atonement for sin. We have, therefore, the central mission of the Son aligned with the Levitical centre of the Pentateuch, the Day of Atonement ceremony. This movement will not only fulfil the cultic journey of expiation, consecration and communion with God, but *this ascent into the Father's house is the new exodus*. Indeed, the theological context for this discourse was 'the feast of Passover, when Jesus knew . . . that he should depart from this world to the Father' (13:1).

In his initial response Jesus had answered that his disciples could not follow him *now*, but would follow him *afterward* (13:36), a mystery unravelled by his explanation in 14:1–6. Jesus must first make the journey himself, as the incarnate Son, into the Father's house, taking his humanity with him. Then, having opened the way, he will return in order to take the disciples with him – *in him* – on the journey to the Father's house. Ultimately, then, this is why the Son has come: to bring God's people into the Father's house. The Father's house is the goal of Jesus' journey; yet it is also the place where he, as the eternal Son, the Logos, abides permanently – the bosom of the Father, therefore, becomes the goal of discipleship. Utilizing the table below,[9] let us explore this journey further.

	Goal = Father's House = *Terminus ad quem/a quo*		
	A	B	A'
Way Jesus	ascending movement ↑	descending movement ↓	ascending movement ↑
	I am going (*poreuomai*)	I am coming (*erchomai*)	I will take (*paralepsomai*)

[8] McCaffrey 1988: 129.
[9] Ibid. 172.

(A) The heavenly ascent of Jesus to the Father is the exaltation of humanity – his humanity, which he indeed shares with us. The Logos had descended in order to ascend as the incarnate Son, bearing a full humanity. Because the way of ascent is through his crucifixion and resurrection – the sacrifice is the journey as well as the means of ascent – John's Gospel can speak of the cross only in terms of exaltation, as the Son's being lifted up and glorified. Returning to the Father, to the place from which he came, was through the way of the cross. As such, *the cross is the means of ascent* – the means to the glory and perfection of humanity. This atonement, not only the death for sins but the conveying of his own blood and indestructible life into the heavenly abode of God, opens the way to the Father – opens the door to the Father's house. This is the 'new and living way which he consecrated for us, through the veil, that is, his flesh' (Heb. 10:20). This is how he prepares a place in his Father's house for his disciples, through his work of atonement. More than this, through the resurrection he himself – the new temple of his resurrection body – becomes the place prepared, a point to which we will return.

In the final sense of consummation, Jesus' return may be thought of as his second advent (B), when he descends bodily to usher his people into the house of the new heavens and earth, to dwell with the Father in glory for ever (A'). There is, however, a prior application that appears to be the true focus of Jesus' words: he will come back to the disciples through the outpouring of his Spirit (B), and, through the Spirit unite the disciples to himself so that where he is (in the bosom of the Father), there his disciples may be also (A'). Their journey is distinct from that of Jesus, but both ascents are directed to the same goal of the Father's house. Here we approach a depth of mystery too deep to fathom and a height of wonder beyond the intellect's ability to scale. The benediction of the Son's own humanity, through the incarnation, may, through his resurrection body, become the benediction of humanity itself – of his disciples – through the gift of the Spirit. Jesus says, I will come again and take you 'to myself' (*pros emauton*), indicating that union with the risen Jesus is both the goal of the journey and the way – they are one. This journey for the disciples is, consequently, ongoing in the sense of an ever-deepening movement into an ever-deepening union with the Son, in and through which he steadily reveals more and more of the Father. The Son, now incarnate and glorified, is in union with the Father through the Spirit – his humanity has entered into perfection, dwelling with the Father in the Father's house. As the Spirit unites us to the Son, the Son reveals to us more and more of the inner life of the Father. The Spirit brings us into the Son, and the Son unveils to us the Father. Because of the mutual indwelling of Father and Son, because as Jesus says, 'I am in the Father and the Father is in me' (14:11), when the Spirit brings us the Son, the Son brings us the Father. This mutual indwelling is given completion, encompassing humanity, with Jesus' promise in 14:23 'If anyone loves me, he will keep my word; and my Father will love him, and we will come to him and make our home [*monēn*] with him.' The many *monai* (rooms/homes) in the Father's house / the Son as the place prepared is matched by the singular *monē* (room/home) of the disciple as the place prepared for the Father and the Son. In other words, that there is room for all his children in the Father's house does not diminish the realization of personal fellowship with God. Humanity brought into the fellowship and communion, into the eternal and unbroken love, of the blessed Holy Trinity; here, finally, is the reality of the temple: the Son mediating the beatific vision, revealing the Father to us – not merely after a carnal manner, but rather by drawing us into the life of the Father through spiritual union with himself. As the means to our vision of the Father, as the means to our reconciliation and at-one-ment with the Father, as the place prepared within which we may abide with the Father – as the end and the means to that end, Jesus the ascended Son of God is the new temple. He is, as McCaffrey puts it,

> the mediator of an unbroken exchange between the Father's house and the disciples. . . . The disciples have access to the heavenly temple in the New Temple of the risen Jesus. In this New Temple, too, the goal of the heavenly temple and the way to it are one. . . . Thus the purpose of the earthly mission of Jesus to bridge the gap between God and man by his passion-resurrection is effective in the New Temple of the risen Jesus, where God and believers are one. . . . God becomes one with men in the temple of the flesh of Jesus (1:14) in order that men may become one with God in the New Temple of his glorified flesh (14:2–3). . . . It is the risen Jesus as the New Temple who spans in his risen body the distance which separates heaven and earth, and becomes the perfect mediator of a perpetual exchange between heaven and earth.[10]

In retrospect, we may say that all doctrinal roads lead to union with Christ: the temple theme, the Levitical cultus, its clean/unclean

[10] Ibid. 173, 196, 224, 252–253.

legislation all point to this most profound reality of union with the incarnate Logos, through which adoption into the household of the Godhead is realized.[11] Here is a high priest and mediator indeed, the inner dynamic of the temple itself; here is the stairway whose summit is in the heavens – in him the dichotomy of heaven and earth is reconciled. No one, Jesus says in 14:6, comes to the Father except 'through me' (*di' emou*), indicating that he is the means by which humanity may 'have access to the inner life of God, the manner also or the condition of their access'.[12] This relationship of mutual indwelling, spiritual in the purest sense, will be magnified at the consummation of history, when God's people are raised up in glory, with new-creation bodies no less spiritual than their souls.

We return now to the disciples' original confusion and concern: How can it be to their benefit that Jesus goes away? The answer to this question takes us to the paradigm shift that follows with the transition from the Levitical cultus of the old covenant to the living way of the new. A commonly made observation is that the goal for God's dwelling moves beyond his dwelling among us to his dwelling within us – this is certainly true and worthy of emphasis. Yet this truth may be perceived without appreciating the span of the Son's accomplishment. With the incarnate Son in their midst the disciples enjoyed the height of the old covenant – God's dwelling in the midst of his people, condescending to join their plight in the wilderness, as it were, in the old creation, full of death and pollution. Jesus' departure, therefore, would mean the absence of God's tabernacling Presence in their midst; this, *within the context of the Levitical system*, could signify only a detraction of fellowship with God and so was received as a disheartening word – for they did not have the new paradigm in their understanding. The Son had descended, however, not merely to bring God down to humanity's earthly situation, but – this is the new exodus – to lift humanity up into God's heavenly situation. So the disciples, in retrospect, were made sorrowful by the same naive ignorance and love that had once propelled David's desire to build a permanent house of stone for YHWH, and that, a thousand years later on the mountain of Jesus' transfiguration, had led Peter to blurt out, 'Master, it is good for us to be here; let us make three tabernacles: one for you, one for Moses and one for Elijah' (Luke 9:33). In John 14:17b–18 Jesus therefore goes on to tell the disciples, 'you know him

---

[11] On the doctrine of union with Christ, in relation to the temple theme, see Macaskill's monograph (2013).
[12] McCaffrey 1988: 217.

[the Spirit], for he dwells with you and will be in you. I will not leave you as orphans; I will come to you.' The Spirit dwells 'with' the disciples inasmuch as the Spirit is in Jesus, who is with the disciples; but, after Jesus' ascension, the Spirit will be 'in' them. Because the Spirit will unite them to Jesus, giving them Jesus within; however, the exchange is not the second person of the Godhead for the third. Rather, Jesus transitions from being with them to being in them – 'I will come to you' through the Spirit. Jesus gives them the Spirit; the Spirit gives them Jesus. He must go away, then, in order to give them more of himself, to have deeper union and fellowship with the disciples through the poured out Spirit. Yet the resurrection itself was required, finally, to shatter the disciples' old paradigm. The life of the new Israel is a post-resurrection life; more than this, it is nothing less than ascension life, life in heaven *with God*. How this idea fits within the scheme of cultic theology should not be missed. In my discussions on holiness in previous chapters I noted that, in practical terms and in relation to earthly objects, to be holy means to belong to God. Sacrificial animals, for example, were transferred to the ownership and realm of God. But this means being transferred from an earthly to a heavenly status, context and life. The programme for Israel's cleansing and sanctification, then, was nothing less than the gradual transference, and transformation, of Israel from the earthly to the heavenly realm, with God. It is this reality that Jesus accomplishes, first for himself, and then in and through him, for the people of God.

Crucifixion: the new Passover

On the eve of his crucifixion, as Matthew's Gospel records (26:36–46), Jesus was exceedingly sorrowful and deeply distressed, even to death. Falling on his face, he prayed, 'O my Father, if it is possible, let this cup pass from me; nevertheless, not as I will, but as you will' (v. 39). And again, a second and a third time, he prayed, 'your will be done'. This night of dark distress and profound struggle opens a window into the innermost dynamic and spiritual reality symbolized and solicited by the ascension offering. As the quintessential offering – indeed, the altar's namesake – the ascension offering represented utter consecration to God, total self-surrender. Such a life is the life that must ascend as a pleasing aroma to the heavenly abode of God. Jesus' tormented night of prayer in the garden of Gesthemane, therefore, is not only the counter to Adam's self-willed failure in Eden's garden, but it stands for Jesus' fulfilment of the Levitical cultus. Jesus' entire life was one of increasing sanctification and consecration; here in the final sacrifice of his own will, the focus of his consecration narrows resolutely upon the cross. On this night the forking paths lay before him: his own will and that of his Father. The point is vital for understanding the meaning of both the sacrificial system of Leviticus and the cross itself. The Levitical offerings were not merely about negation, the expiation of sins; rather, they were also about righteous obedience and sanctification, soliciting a life of pleasing submission to God – and it is the same with the cross. Jesus' whole life was that to which the ascension offering gestured, morning and evening; and the cross itself, being nothing less than his life writ large, was but the capstone upon that obedience. The cross, then, is the culmination of his utter consecration, that sacrifice which obtains its pleasing aroma not merely from the act itself but from *the life* of obedience and surrender that, through its flames, rises to God the Father. And he does indeed rise to the Father's heavenly abode, a movement not only in line with the Day of Atonement's entry into the holiest, but in line as well with the ascension offering. Jesus' life, death and resurrection ascent – which is to say, Jesus himself – are the historical embodiment of the ascension offering, the reality placarded before the Israelite in symbol form. We must understand the system of offerings, then, as related fundamentally to the human will. This is precisely the exposition given by the author of Hebrews in 10:1–10. After reminding his readers that it was not possible for the blood of bulls and goats to take away sins, he writes that, *therefore*, when Jesus came into the world he came to offer more than Levitical sacrifices. Rather, the Son says, 'Behold, I have come . . . to do your will, O God!' This fundamental difference the author of Hebrews explains as follows (10:9b–10): 'He [Jesus] takes away the first [the Levitical sacrifices] that he may establish the second [obedience to God's will]. By that will we have been sanctified through the offering of the body of Jesus Christ once and for all.' Jesus' life, death and resurrection ascent are now to Israel what all the Levitical cultus once was – and more, of course. Not merely substitution, but vicarious substitution, which, beyond the accomplishment of reconciliation, also solicits and empowers conformity – that all God's people would belong to God.

Jesus' fulfilment of the Levitical cultus as a whole is a significant point to be kept in mind inasmuch as we will be considering the cross primarily in terms of the Passover sacrifice alone. As we will see next, however, the veil of the temple's inner sanctum stood for the temple itself.[13] When the veil was rent, therefore, the whole cultus experienced the fissure caused by Jesus' crucifixion – a sign that he has 'taken away the first, that he may establish the second'. A sign, in other words, that he has fulfilled the whole Levitical cultus.

The rent veil

It is surely significant that the Synoptic Gospels – Matthew, Mark and Luke – each record the rending of the temple veil as a direct consequence of the crucifixion of Jesus Christ. Thereby, what he has endured and accomplished is associated with and brought to bear upon the temple, its significance and function. The Son's mission, once more, is to bring the new worship, the new way of access to God – moving Israel from the dramatic stage of the Levitical cultus, to its promised *telos* and reality in the cosmos. From the distinct perspective of Mark's Gospel we will examine this event briefly.

> 37 And Jesus cried out with a loud voice and breathed his last.
> 38 Then the veil of the temple was torn in two from top to bottom.
> 39 So when the centurion, who stood facing him, saw that he cried out like this and breathed his last, he said, 'Truly this man was the Son of God!' (Mark 15:37–39)

Here the rending of the temple veil is framed by two references to Jesus' death, woven together through resumptive repetition, with verse 39 repeating the substance of verse 37 and continuing on from that point. This literary technique, as it turns out, happens to be a trademark of Mark's Gospel, referred to as a 'Marcan sandwich', whereby he uses an interpolation in the midst of a story in order to demonstrate the story's theological significance. Mark 15:37–39 comprises, then, a Marcan sandwich in miniature, the main storyline being how Jesus' death leads to the centurion's confession, with the rending of the veil serving as the interpolation. How does the rent veil relate to the climactic confession that Jesus is the Son of God? As Chronis has insightfully demonstrated,[14] three major themes in Mark's Gospel culminate in and converge upon the death of Jesus. The first two are (1) Jesus' rejection in 15:37, and (2) his identity as Son of God in 15:39. Mark's particular portrait of Jesus, in relation to the first theme, is that of the man of sorrows, the one who came

---

[13] The weight of evidence favours a reference to the inner, not the outer, veil (cf. Gurtner 2006).
[14] Chronis 1982.

'to serve and to give his life as a ransom for many' (10:45). He repeatedly prophesies that he must suffer and be rejected by the temple authorities, and be condemned and killed (8:31–33; 9:31; 10:33–34); his 'own people' reject him (3:21; cf. 3:31–32), as does his 'own home town' of Nazareth (6:1–6); finally, even God must, as it were, turn his face from Jesus – and here is the culminating context for his loud cry and death in 15:37 – so that Jesus cries out in 15:34 the words of dereliction 'My God, my God, why have you forsaken me?'

Turning to the second theme, that of Jesus' identity, Mark opens his Gospel with the bold pronouncement that his is the Gospel of 'Jesus Christ, the Son of God'. While even – or, perhaps better, especially – unclean spirits acknowledge this identity (cf. 1:24; 5:7), the reader rather is taken on the journey with Jesus' disciples, invited to discover this truth through his words and works. When Jesus rebukes the wind and calms the sea, therefore, Mark allows the disciples' question to linger, wafting through the air, 'Who can this be that even the wind and sea obey him?' (4:41). Dramatically, Mark's narrative makes Jesus' self-disclosure *the reason* for his crucifixion (14:61–64). This theme, then, finds its culmination, too, in Jesus' death, as the centurion, presumably a Roman pagan, confesses Jesus to be 'the Son of God!' (15:39). Moreover, this confession is underscored as the centurion is the *only* human being in Mark's Gospel to confess Jesus as the Son of God (note e.g. the striking omission in 8:29). When chapter 15 is read directly from verse 37 to 39 (skipping over v. 38), the story already unfolds a profound theological statement: through his sacrificial suffering and death Jesus makes God known, leading the centurion to recognize his true identity as Son of God.

How, then, does the rent veil relate to the convergence of Jesus' suffering and the revelation that he is the Son of God? Mark inserts the rending of the veil so that a third theme, that of the temple, also converges upon Jesus' death.[15] Though in a manner altogether different from that of the fourth Gospel, Mark also portrays Jesus as the new temple – what he is and accomplishes demonstrates the obsolescence of the Levitical priesthood and its grand building. Jesus, for example, is the one who *makes* others clean, and his doing so serves as a testimony to the Levitical priests, whose role lay primarily in terms of diagnosing and declaring (cf. 1:40–45). Not only by his authority, a notable motif,

---

[15] All three themes are also evident in Mark 2:7 as the scribes accuse Jesus of blasphemy, asking, 'Who can forgive sins but God alone?' By this rejection of Jesus (theme one), they ironically identify him as God (theme two), through his ability to forgive sins, which replaces the temple's function (theme three).

but by his *being* – his life – Jesus is able to clean and draw into life, without the possibility of becoming unclean or polluted himself; he is all that temple rituals of cleansing signified. This point is made remarkably through the encounter with the Gadarene demoniac who, we are told, was indwelt by a legion of unclean spirits, and had made his dwelling among the tombs (5:1–20) – utterly defiled and defiling, this would be the last place to find a Levitical high priest. Jesus, however, as something of a walking temple cult, causes order and life, manifesting divine compassion. Who Jesus is, then, increasingly displaces the role and function of the Jerusalem temple. Moreover, for Mark, Jesus' visit to the temple (11:15–19) does not result in a cleansing but rather in its conclusive judgment,[16] a point underscored in a number of ways. First, in another Marcan sandwich, Jesus' visit to the temple interrupts the story of his cursing of the fig tree so that it withers from the roots. Juxtaposed with the temple judgment, the fig tree serves as a symbol for the Israel represented by the temple authorities, the vinedressers who yielded no fruit to the owner of the vineyard in the parable that immediately follows (12:1–12). Secondly, Jesus' rebuke in 11:17 is taken from two quotations, Isaiah 56:7, in relation to the temple's role for the sake of the nations, an idea that finds resolution with the centurion's confession, and Jeremiah 7:11, which condemns the temple as a den of thieves. With this latter reference a curious account by Mark may be explained. Jesus' first and somewhat ominous act upon entering Jerusalem was to visit the temple, where 'he looked around at all things' before returning to Bethany for the night (11:11), an incident not related by the other Gospels. In this manner Mark gives the impression that Jesus' judgment on the temple the next morning was an act of nightlong deliberation, as Scott has elucidated well,[17] and the reference to Jeremiah is even more revealing, as a fuller quotation of Jeremiah 7:11 demonstrates: '"Has this house, which is called by my name, become a den of thieves in your eyes? Behold, I, even I, have seen it!" utterance of YHWH.' The previous day's looking by Jesus, then, was part of the divine investigation before judgment, practised by YHWH elsewhere (cf. Gen. 6:5–7; 18:20–21). Within Jeremiah's context, what YHWH has seen makes the temple's destruction inevitable. Jesus' visit is one of judgment, foreshadowing the temple's ruin. Furthermore, quite unlike Luke's account, where after its cleansing Jesus reclaims the temple for his teaching ministry, in Mark's narrative Jesus never

---

[16] Cf. McKelvey 1969: 65–67; Chavez 2002.
[17] Scott 1952.

returns to the temple – and his departure is marked by a fateful prophecy:

> Then as he went out from the temple, one of his disciples said to him, 'Teacher, see what manner of stones and what buildings are here!' But Jesus answered and said to him, 'Do you see these great buildings? Not one stone will be left upon another, that shall not be thrown down.' (Mark 13:1–2)

Moving on to the interrogation of Jesus, we find that his relation to the temple is at the centre of the controversy, as false witnesses claim, 'We heard him say, "I will destroy this temple made with hands, and within three days I will build another made without hands"' (14:58). Even more significant and no less full of irony, the same accusation is levelled at him during his agony on the cross: 'And those who passed by blasphemed him, wagging their heads and saying, "Aha! You who are destroying [*katalyōn*] the temple and building [*oikodomōn*] it in three days, save yourself and come down from the cross!"' (Mark 15:29–30). As my translation brings out, the blasphemers' use of active participles for their derision underscores that, then and there, *as he is dying*, Jesus is about the work of destroying the old temple and rebuilding the new temple – of his body.[18] This temple theme thus culminates in the rending of the temple veil, from top to bottom, demonstrating that this event was an act of God. Jesus' ministry, which began with the rending (*schizomenous*) of the heavens and the Spirit's descent upon him (1:10), now ends with the rending (*eschisthē*) of the veil, the Levitical counterpart to the heavens (15:38).[19] The rent veil, standing for the whole temple cultus, indeed signifies the dissolution of the Levitical system, that the new way to God has been opened.[20] Returning once more to the question at hand, then, what does Mark's Gospel hope to accomplish by inserting the rent veil – the culmination of Jesus' displacement of the temple – between Jesus' death and the centurion's response to that death? The issue is pressing inasmuch as the centurion, who stood 'facing' Jesus, responded particularly to his view of Jesus' death – not to the

---

[18] Cf. Chavez 2002: 116.

[19] Motyer (1987) suggests that through this rending inclusio we have a Marcan version of Pentecost, Christ's death dispensing the Spirit.

[20] As such, the Jewish (temple) and Gentile (Roman centurion) establishments offer a double testimony to the efficacy of Jesus' death, making the Levitical cultus obsolete and manifesting God's light to the nations.

rent veil; rather, Mark has inserted the rent veil as commentary on the centurion's experience. Quite simply, the rent veil serves to help the reader interpret the death of Jesus according to the symbolism of the Levitical cultus. When his ignominious death is seen through the lens of the sacrificial system, the shame of his dereliction becomes the glory of his accomplishment and identity. In so doing, by associating the rent veil with the self-disclosure of Jesus, through his suffering and death, as Son of God, *Mark's literary strategy exhibits Jesus' death as serving to remove the veil that hides the face of God* – as he dies, God shows his face, and the centurion finds himself standing upon holy ground.[21] The rent veil, once more, serves to define the ignominy of the cross in terms of the sacrificial cultus, explaining Jesus' crucifixion as the atoning sacrifice that reconciles humanity to God. Here the culminating themes of Jesus' rejection unto death, the disclosure of his identity as the Son of God and his displacement of the Levitical cult all coalesce into a grand epiphany: in dying, Jesus' removes the veil from the face of God, and it is his own face, a revelation that is the undoing of Jerusalem's temple. The temple is the dwelling of God and, therefore, the place to meet with God; it holds the vision of God, as the place where one may behold his face, and it is the way to God – to this beatific vision – through the sacrificial cultus. The temple harmonizes the *glory* of perfection in beholding God and the *suffering* that is the way to that glory through sacrifice and the shedding of blood. This is what the temple is for, and Jesus' death fulfils these functions; his crucifixion opens the way to God and is itself the revelation of the face of God.

The feast of Passover

The New Testament interprets the crucifixion through the theological lens of the Passover, the first three Gospels doing so primarily in terms of Jesus' institution of the supper as the Passover meal of the new exodus on the eve of his death. Moreover, all four Gospels link Jesus' death with the sparing of a criminal in connection with the feast (Matt. 27:15–26; Mark 15:6–15; Luke 23:13–25; John 18:39–40). Not only does this event serve to portray the cross as a vicarious sacrifice of atonement, but it also unfolds the inner meaning of Passover. Significantly, all four Gospels record the criminal's name as integral to the exchange: Barabbas. Given that *bar Abbas* is Aramaic for 'son of the father', we are intended to associate him closely with Jesus –

---

[21] Chronis 1982: 110–111.

some early manuscript witnesses for Matthew 27:16 (see NU text) even read the man's name as 'Jesus bar Abbas'. Such a correlation manifests the redemption of Passover: Jesus is the Son, the first-born of the Father, who must be sacrificed in order for humanity, Adam and his posterity to be released. The New Testament delights in referring to Jesus Christ as the firstborn, and this title should be understood with reference to his role in redemption, as Passover theology:[22]

For, indeed, Christ our Passover was sacrificed for us. (1 Cor. 5:7)

[You were redeemed] with the precious blood of Christ, as of a lamb without blemish and without spot. (1 Peter 1:18–19)

And they sang a new song [to the Lamb], saying:

'You are worthy to take the scroll, and to open its seals;
For you were slain, and have redeemed us to God
   by your blood
out of every tribe and tongue and people and nation . . .'
(Rev. 5:9)

This latter passage in particular celebrates Jesus' crucifixion as the new Passover of the prophesied new exodus, the redemption that would release not only the Jews but also the Gentiles out of the misery of their long and dark exile (cf. Gen. 11:8–9).

Turning to John's Gospel, the Passover feast is mentioned on numerous occasions, as the theological context for Jesus' words and/ or acts (2:13, 23; 5:1; 6:4; 11:55; 13:1). Moreover, while the book of Revelation refers to Jesus as the slain lamb, John's Gospel introduces his ministry through a similar appellation voiced by John the Baptizer, identifying Jesus as the Passover redeemer: '"Behold! The lamb of God who takes away the sin of the world!" . . . And looking at Jesus as he walked, he said, "Behold the lamb of God!"' (John 1:29, 36).[23]

---

[22] See Holland 2004: 237–273.

[23] While there is some scholarly discussion as to whether or not John 1:29 refers to the Passover lamb in particular, yet alternative suggestions, such as the provision of a lamb awaited in Gen. 22, the lamb of the morning and evening daily service (Exod. 29:38–46), and even the suffering servant of Isa. 53, may be harmonized with the Passover lamb of Exod. 12 without controversy. Moreover, the typical reason for rejecting any reference to the Passover lamb, namely that this sacrifice did not involve atonement, is simply misguided.

The Gospel itself is framed by Jesus' identity as the Passover lamb, John 1:29 finding its counterpart in 19:31–37 and the detail that, since he was already dead, the soldiers did not need to break Jesus' legs. This took place, John remarks directly to the reader, in order to fulfil the Passover legislation, that 'not one of his bones will be broken' – in slaying, roasting, eating and burning the remains of the firstborn's substitutionary lamb, the animal's bones were not to be broken (Exod. 12:46; Num. 9:12; cf. Ps. 34:20). John is especially careful to set forth the timing of the crucifixion on the eve of Passover, precisely when the lambs would be slaughtered (19:14). The mention of hyssop in 19:29, which had been used to sprinkle the lambs' blood on the doorposts and lintels for the original Passover (Exod. 12:22), also serves to portray Jesus as the true Passover lamb. In the light of the fourth Gospel's Passover emphasis, scholars who find such an allusion in John 2:17 are probably correct,[24] where Psalm 69:9 is quoted, yet with a significant change: 'Zeal for your house will eat [*kataphagetai*] me.' Although both the Hebrew text and the LXX have 'has eaten' (*katephagen*) for this verse, John's quotation is future-oriented, pointing forward to the crucifixion. This statement within the context of the feast of Passover (2:13), and possibly forming an inclusio with it, may indeed have the sacrificial consuming of the Passover lamb in mind. More broadly, the Passover motif is reinforced by various allusions to the exodus in the fourth Gospel, allowing for John's narrative to be read as the new book of Exodus. Jesus' first sign of turning water into wine, for example, recalls Moses' opening sign of turning the Nile water into blood. In this new exodus, then, the former sign of death has been transformed into one of life. And there are also the 'I Am' sayings, which resonate with the burning bush revelation of YHWH, and are probably what Jesus refers to when he prays, 'I have manifested your name to those you have given me out of the world' (17:6, 11–12).[25] As with the exodus of old, the new exodus yields the knowledge of God; it reveals him – now as the Father – and chiefly through the Passover, which summarizes the redemption.

Resurrection and ascent: the new exodus

The exodus of Jesus is his passage from death to life, and therefore should not be restricted to the crucifixion, which is the Passover ordeal

[24] E.g. Kerr 2002: 85–86.
[25] Shirbroun 1985; Ball 1996; Kerr 2002: 323–335.

that generates the exodus. This point is brought out in a theologically rich manner by Luke's Gospel. When Jesus is transfigured, Moses and Elijah appear with him (9:28–36). While Moses and Elijah's significance upon the mountain has been a matter of debate, Luke makes his own intention plain. Moses, of course, had led the exodus out of Egypt; and Elijah was the promised forerunner of the new exodus (Mal. 4:5–6) – a role Luke's Gospel emphasizes (1:17, 76). These two men, furthermore, 'talked with Jesus', and Luke gives us the definite subject of their conversation: they 'spoke of his *exodon* he was about to accomplish at Jerusalem' (9:31). By this term, derived from *exodus*, Luke intends no mere euphemism for death, such as 'departure' or 'decease'. His aim, rather, becomes especially clear through Jesus' own lips when from the cross he tells the penitent criminal, 'Assuredly, I say to you, today you will be with me in paradise' (23:43). The Greek word *paradeisos* is used by the LXX in Genesis to designate the garden of Eden.[26] For Luke, who traces Jesus' genealogy back to 'Adam, the son of God' (3:38), the new exodus is nothing short of re-entry into the garden of Eden, the paradise of God. The cross, then, is the means of Jesus' ascent to paradise; the exodus pertains both to his crucifixion and ascent: 'Now it happened when the days had drawn near for his ascension, he set his face firmly to journey to Jerusalem' (Luke 9:51). That is the journey, after his exchange with Moses and Elijah, he determines to make. This exodus realizes the theological drama of the Day of Atonement entry into the holy of holies, further brought out in Acts 1:9 by Luke's account of the ascension: 'When he had said these things, as they were watching, he was lifted up, and a cloud took him up out of their sight.' That this cloud reference reflects priestly imagery, and particularly that of the Day of Atonement when the high priest would enter with the clouds of incense into God's Presence within the holy of holies, appears probable given Luke's previous depiction of the ascension, in Luke 24:50–51: 'He led them out as far as Bethany and, lifting up his hands, he blessed them. Now it happened that while he blessed them he was parted from them and was raised up into heaven.' The cultic ascent to God's heavenly Presence culminates in benediction, with the high priest lifting up his palms and pronouncing the Aaronic blessing. His Gospel ending as it had begun, in the temple, it may be the case that this benediction was meant by Luke as the resolution to Zecharias' emergence from the temple as a mute, unable to pronounce the blessing (1:22). Through the Passover

---

[26] Cf. Garret 1992: 15.

of the cross Jesus has made his exodus into the paradise of the heavenly Mount Zion; with the blood of atonement he has ascended through the veil of the heavens, entering into the holiest of God's house. In so doing, he has attained the benediction of his people.

Jesus Christ has thus fulfilled the cosmogonic pattern. He has gone through the waters of judgment and death, ascended to the heavenly mountain of God, for an indestructible life of glory before the face of the Father. *Who shall ascend the mountain of YHWH?* Jesus Christ, the Son of God.

The descent of Christ's Spirit

The eschatological outpouring of the Holy Spirit is the promised gift of the Father and the fruit of the Son's mediatorial work. Jesus ascended for the sake of the Spirit's descent; without the Spirit's descent, God's people cannot ascend. Apart from the outpoured Spirit, there is no new access to God the Father's heavenly abode – and, consequently, no new Israel. Just here it may be helpful to return to the words of Hosea 6:2:

> After two days he will revive us;
> On the third day he will raise us up,
> That we may live before his face.

The New Testament appears to solicit prophetic warrant for Christ's resurrection on the *third day* in particular. The apostle Paul, for example, says that Jesus 'arose again the third day according to the Scriptures' (1 Cor. 15:4), and Luke records Jesus' own words that 'thus it was written and therefore necessary for the Christ to suffer and to rise from the dead on the third day' (24:46; cf. 24:7, 21). The lack of third day prophecies in the Old Testament, therefore, has been a conundrum that has led to some scholarly consternation. Because Hosea 6:2, as the only explicit reference to third-day resurrection in the Old Testament, is itself considered vague, it is possible to avoid the problem altogether by understanding the 'according to the Scriptures' and 'thus it was written' statements of the New Testament as referring to the resurrection generally and not to the third day aspect in particular. Others, who sense the exegetical weight of the New Testament's emphasis on the third day, pursue a solution by resorting to Old Testament references that are more implicit or symbolic, such as Jonah's deliverance from the belly of the fish (Jon. 1:17). Be that as it may, the approach of Phythian-Adams is compelling,[27] that the New Testament's marked and methodical mention of 'the third day' is *precisely because* the authors, having the Hosea 6:2 prophecy in mind, are drawing their readers' attention to the one reference such a tacked-on phrase would evoke. Perhaps a first step toward understanding Jesus' third-day resurrection as a fulfilment of Hosea 6:2 would be to appreciate that he is himself the true and faithful Israel. In Matthew's Gospel, in particular, Jesus' wilderness testing, forty days and nights, is fashioned after Israel's forty years in the wilderness – yet, whereas Israel failed, Jesus is faithful, modelling the piety called for in Deuteronomy (Matt. 4:1–11). Moreover, Matthew quotes Hosea 11:1, a passage that appears to reference Israel originally, yet applies it directly to Jesus: when Joseph and Mary took the child and fled to Egypt, he tells us that this happened 'that it might be fulfilled which was spoken by the Lord through the prophet, saying, "Out of Egypt I called my son"' (Matt. 2:15). Along similar lines, then, one might suggest that the New Testament authors understood the prophecy of Hosea 6:2 to apply to Jesus as the true Israel, raised on the third day. It would, however, be a grave error to limit this passage merely to Jesus' own third-day resurrection in isolation. The theology of the New Testament is that Jesus' third-day resurrection was his experience of *the* resurrection of the dead, the eschatological event. In the study already referenced, Phythian-Adams notes well Paul's language in Romans 1:4, that Jesus was declared to be the Son of God by the resurrection *of the dead*, rather than 'from the dead'. This he rightly connects to Paul's teaching later in his epistle, regarding union with Christ: 'We were buried with him through baptism into death: that like as Christ was raised from the dead through the glory of the Father, so we also might walk in newness of life' (Rom. 6:4). Jesus' third-day resurrection, then, does not fulfil the prophecy of Hosea 6:2 *apart from* the Spirit's uniting Israel to Jesus (and his third-day resurrection), resurrecting God's people from the dead in and with him – this fulfils the third-day resurrection of Israel.[28] Through Jesus, for Israel – that is Paul's teaching. Jesus' resurrection was the resurrection of the corporate people of God, the new and *living* Israel.

> One of the first things they had learned as Christians was to think of our Lord's Resurrection . . . as an act of quickening power which

---

[27] Phythian-Adams 1942: 125–128.
[28] Holland (2004: 141–154) understands baptism in Rom. 6 to be a corporate event, as the new exodus of Jesus' Passover redemption.

procured the resurrection of all those who should 'seek him earnestly.' It was, in fact, not the bald reference to the 'two days' [or 'on the third day'] which linked this prophecy with its fulfillment but the profound mystery of a new and risen Israel to which it pointed. This was what God had promised, this was what He had done; but He had done it (*mirabile dictu!*) by Himself tasting death. And what voice could predict this great act more fittingly than that of the prophet [Hosea] who proclaimed most passionately the inexhaustible depths of Divine Love?[29]

We find this theology also in Ephesians, where, after describing the resurrection and ascension of Jesus (1:19–23), Paul immediately turns to the church's experience of the same: 'you he made alive, who were dead in trespasses and sin . . . God made us alive together with Christ . . . and raised us up together, and made us sit together in the heavenly places in Christ Jesus' (2:1–7). Here, then, is the resurrection of Israel prophesied by Ezekiel, for YHWH 'will put my Spirit within you, and you shall live' (37:14) – *the church is nothing less than the prophesied resurrection of Israel*, raised to live before the face of God.

The New Testament, then, does not stop with the ascension of Jesus; the fullness of its message and joy is the resurrection and ascension *of Israel* – with Jesus. That is to say, the new exodus from the depths of Sheol to the heights of the heavenly Mount Zion is no less a corporate redemption of Israel than the original exodus out of Egypt. The new exodus was promised to Israel and cannot, therefore, be restricted to the experience of Jesus alone. The church, Jew and Gentile who by faith have been united to Jesus through the Spirit, this church has experienced the resurrection, the new exodus out of bondage to sin and death, redeemed from exile in order to live before the face of God. The new exodus has created the new Israel.

In the sections below, therefore, we will consider the outpouring of the Spirit, essential to Israel's own experience of resurrection and ascension, as well as how this gift enables God's people to become his temple.

The outpouring of the Spirit

The role of the Spirit

To understand what the outpoured Spirit accomplishes, we must first grasp how the Spirit stands for the heavenly as well as the eschatological

---

[29] Phythian-Adams 1942: 128.

order, which are to a large extent one and the same reality.[30] The contrast between the Spirit and the flesh, for example, may be related to realms (heavenly vs. earthly), to time (the eschatological age vs. this present age) and also to creation (the new creation vs. the old creation that is passing away). When the Spirit is poured out, therefore, he ushers in the realities of heaven and the eschatological age. Put differently, heaven is now the foretaste of the eschaton (the new creation) until the eschaton arrives; the Spirit is the full reality, the dynamic and atmosphere (as it were), of the eschaton, which is presently a heavenly reality. The new heavens and earth of the eschaton will be the merging of heaven on earth, but, until that reality takes place, the eschaton is foretasted in the present heavenly reality. Because, furthermore, the eschaton is Israel's future, the hope of Israel's resurrection and renewal, the Spirit is the source of Israel's life. 'Until the Spirit is poured out upon us from on high' is Isaiah's plea (32:15).

Secondly, upon his resurrection and ascension into heaven, Jesus – as incarnate Son, bearing his humanity – enters the realm of the eschaton; for he has experienced the end-of-days resurrection from the dead and has been glorified and perfected.

Thirdly, he obtains the authority to dispense the Spirit of the eschaton into history – the life of the age to come within the age and creation that is passing away. Jesus is the one who pours out the Holy Spirit upon God's people. The Son dispenses the gift of the Spirit, the authority for doing so being a part of the incarnate Son's exaltation.

Fourthly, the result of this outpouring is union with the ascended Christ – that is the goal, and everything else follows from this bond. God's people are raised with Christ and, together with him – in him – form the household of God and the house, the living temple, of God. But also, the Spirit is the taste of – and down payment on – the eschaton, because in a manner of speaking he is the eschaton. The Spirit is the element or substratum, the circumambient atmosphere (as Vos has it) of the age to come. His outpouring, therefore, moves the future glory into present experience, his powers in the life of the church are 'the powers of the age to come' (Heb. 6:4–5). Here we have reached far enough to understand the illustration on p. 283 (beginning at the bottom with Jesus' death).

In summary, as God's firstborn Son, the last Adam and true Israel, *Jesus' earthly life reached the end of human history*, even to the

---

[30] My treatment of this topic will be found to be in basic accord with those of Vos (1912) and Gaffin (1989), to which I refer the reader.

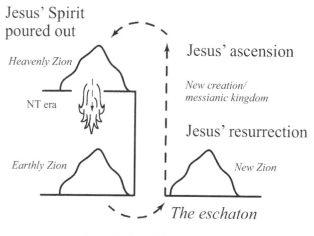

Jesus' Spirit poured out

Heavenly Zion

NT era

Jesus' ascension

New creation/ messianic kingdom

Jesus' resurrection

Earthly Zion

New Zion

The eschaton

Jesus' death/exodus

resurrection of the saints of God – their dying to the old creation and former age, and resurrecting as a new creation in the new Spirit age of glory, the eschaton (see John 11:23–25). To be sure, the new Zion exists now only as the heavenly Zion and not yet as the material reality of the new earth, so I intend by the illustration merely to communicate the *theological significance* of Jesus' resurrection, that he has indeed entered the glorious *state* of the eschaton. He then poured out his Spirit of glory, of new creation, of heavenly life, upon his people still within the bounds of history, and has, therefore, inaugurated the 'already but not yet' life of the new Israel. The Spirit who is poured out into this world is the Spirit as embossed both by Jesus' death to sin and to the old order, and by his resurrection glory, as the one who has entered the eschaton – the Spirit, therefore, is *his* Spirit. And the gift of the Spirit is, again, his gift – he is the dispenser. The work of glorification, of 'eschatonizing', however, is the role of the Spirit – he realizes the heavenly and eschaton states; he makes Jesus' resurrection body a new-creation reality. He is the Spirit of *the* resurrection of the dead. As a result of his outpouring, God's people experience the powers of the age to come now in history, have a heavenly citizenship presently on earth, and are new creatures abiding as foreigners and pilgrims within the old creation. Chiefly, through the outpoured Spirit, believers are united to the ascended Jesus Christ, born from above, and are enabled with all the church to make the heavenly ascent. The

Spirit's descent, through which Jesus returns to his disciples, is the church's ascent, this journey itself led by the Son into the Father's house. And so this heavenly reality is tasted and renewed liturgically, in the corporate Spirit-enabled approach of God's people, as they ascend with Jesus to the heavenly Mount Zion, Lord's Day by Lord's Day, through the new and living way – the veil of Jesus' flesh.

Through the Spirit, then, the new covenant, before its full consummation is enjoyed in the new earth of the eschaton, is nevertheless a heavenly reality now. *The church is a heavenly reality.* God's people are born of God, who resides in heaven (John 1:13), which means they are born from above (John 3:3), so that their citizenship by birth truly is heaven itself (Phil. 3:20).

Jesus, the baptizer

The Old Testament anticipates not only the advent of the Anointed One ('Messiah' from the Hebrew, 'Christ' from the Greek), who would be anointed by the Spirit (Isa. 11:1–2; 42:1), but also the anointing of God's people through the outpouring of the Spirit (Isa. 32:15; 44:3; 52:15; Ezek. 36:25–27; 39:29; Joel 2:28–29). In the New Testament era both expectations merge inasmuch as the Anointed One is announced to be the Anointer; that is, it is the Messiah who will pour out the eschatological gift of the Spirit. Indeed, having left his impress upon the Spirit, it may be said that the Messiah pours out *his* Spirit upon his people. Although John, the Elijah-like forerunner of the Messiah, is popularly dubbed 'the Baptist', yet he himself looked rather to the Messiah as the true baptizer: 'And he [John] preached, saying, "There comes one after me who is mightier than I, whose sandal strap I am not worthy to stoop down and loose. I indeed baptized you with water, but he will baptize you with the Holy Spirit"' (Mark 1:7–8). Matthew's Gospel records a similar saying: 'I indeed baptize you with water unto repentance, but he who is coming after me is mightier than I, whose sandals I am not worthy to carry. He will baptize you with the Holy Spirit and fire' (Matt. 3:11). Luke also provides this testimony from John: 'John answered, saying to all, "I indeed baptize you with water; but one mightier than I is coming, whose sandal strap I am not worthy to loose. He will baptize you with the Holy Spirit and fire"' (Luke 3:16). As the one consecrated to prepare the way of the Lord, to serve as the forerunner to the Messiah, it is surely significant that John's defining introduction of the coming one was in terms of this particular work of baptizing God's people with the Spirit. It is significant, further, that the Synoptic Gospels here introduce Jesus primarily according to this work, which he accomplishes only *after* his ascension. This emphasis upon Christ's act of pouring out the Spirit from heaven is, of course, a correction to the common understanding that considers Jesus' work merely from incarnation to crucifixion (and sometimes restricted to crucifixion alone). Reflecting on our consideration of John 14:2–3 above, with regard to the disciples' ascent to heaven through union with Jesus, one may define Jesus' work from incarnation to ascension as having the outpoured Spirit as its objective – this is what he suffered to accomplish. From a theological perspective, the reason is quite practical: without the Spirit's application of the redemption purchased by Christ there can be no salvation. It is true, moreover, that apart from Jesus' righteous obedience and atoning death, the Spirit, having no redemption to apply, could not be poured out from on high. In any case, my concern here is to emphasize that the outpouring of the Spirit is proclaimed by all four Gospels to be *the* work of Christ – a work, then, that required the incarnation, obedience, sacrifice, burial, resurrection and ascension of the Son to realize. As such, he is honoured as the giver, the enactor and dispenser of this gift – the Spirit's mighty work of restoration, in other words, is a subcategory of the Son's redemption, redounding to his own honour, even as he does all for the glory of the Father. To be sure, the Spirit is sent by both the Father and the Son, but this is nevertheless the special accomplishment of the ascended Christ who receives this authority, as the God-man, from the Father. Indeed, this same point forms the subject of Peter's proclamation on the Day of Pentecost: 'This Jesus God has raised up, of which we are all witnesses. Therefore being exalted to the right hand of God, and having received from the Father the promise of the Holy Spirit, he poured out this which you now see and hear' (Acts 2:32–33; see also 8:14–17; 10:44). How imperative the link is between Jesus' ascension and the outpouring of the Spirit may be demonstrated by Peter's singular statement in the verse that immediately follows (v. 34): 'For David did not ascend into the heavens . . .'

It is perhaps John's Gospel, given its focus on ascension theology, that most fully relates the pouring out of the Spirit as defining the person and work of the Son. In particular, John (1:32–33) notes the correlation between Jesus' being baptized with the Spirit from heaven and his role as baptizer with the Holy Spirit:

> John bore witness, saying, 'I saw the Spirit descending from heaven like a dove, and he remained upon him. I did not know him, but

he who sent me to baptize with water said to me, "Upon whom you see the Spirit descending, and remaining on him, this is he who baptizes with the Holy Spirit."'

While others had been baptized with water by John, yet it was only upon Jesus that the Spirit had descended and remained; the difference is significant, and related to his being the temple of God. I have already intimated that the Spirit could not have been poured out upon humanity until Christ's sin-conquering death and resurrection had supplied the redemption for the Spirit to apply to God's people. But this is also to say that the Spirit could not be poured out upon humanity because the Spirit of heaven does not abide the pollution of earth – that is, the Spirit would not fill the unclean 'tabernacle' of sinful humanity. Given the scriptural correlation between the Spirit and the Glory of God, when the Spirit descends from heaven upon the Son and remains on him, it can only be that the Spirit has identified the new Adam and Son of God as a clean and holy tabernacle fit for dwelling – the true temple of God. The Spirit's identification then becomes John's testimony of the same. Jesus' role as the dispenser of the Spirit is also linked with his character and function as the temple. To probe this point, we begin with Ezekiel's prophecy, wherein he describes a river flowing out of the new temple's inner sanctum, through the right side of the temple, south of the altar (47:1–12). As described, the river flows out and fructifies all within its compass:

> Along the bank of the river, on this side and that, will grow all sorts of trees used for food; their leaves will not wither, and their fruit will not fail. They will bear fruit every month, *because their water flows from the sanctuary*. Their fruit will be for food, and their leaves for medicine. (Ezek. 47:12)

Two points are relevant here. First, the incongruous portrayal of a river flowing from the holy of holies of the temple may be explained by recalling the correlation between the temple and the mountain of God – temples, again, are the architectural embodiments of the mountain of God, with the holy of holies corresponding to the summit. Thus understood, Ezekiel's depiction is not unlike the Eden mount, with a river flowing from the summit to water the earth (Gen. 2:10–14). The summit being the place of God's Presence, the river itself serves to symbolize his blessing: that all life on earth derives

286

from God as the source of life. Secondly, as elsewhere in Ezekiel (36:25–27), water symbolizes, more particularly, the cleansing and restorative work of the Spirit. The water that flows from the sanctuary describes, then, the pouring out of the life-giving Spirit. Returning to John's Gospel, Jesus' role as baptizer with the Spirit may now be seen to accord fully with his identity as temple.

Having identified Jesus in chapters 1 and 2 as the reality of the temple, who will pour out the living water, John 3 begins to address the dire need for the Spirit. The theology of John's Gospel revolves entirely around this point: Jesus will ascend in order to pour out the Spirit – he is the giver of the Spirit; and he is so *because the Spirit is the essence of life with God.* Luke, for example, depicts the seamless transition to the new covenant by beginning his Gospel with aged saints emblematic of the old covenant itself, Simeon and Anna, whose hope and yearnings finally give way to the young babe of the new covenant – with the birth of Jesus they are ready to die, having glimpsed the fulfilment of the divine promises in their final days of life (1:25–38).[31] The fourth Gospel, by contrast, stresses the method of interpretation – the hermeneutic – necessary for understanding this transition, particularly from the Levitical cultus with all of its legislation regarding purity, and so on, to the new reality and way of the Spirit. The outward cleansing with water, for example, had *always* symbolized the cleansing of the Spirit. The apostasy leading to the Assyrian and Babylonian exiles had demonstrated clearly the need for the cleansing and renewal of the Spirit – a reality proclaimed with one voice by the prophets. The temple, along with its rituals and symbolism, was meant to sustain, not satisfy, the longing for the reality. The Levitical cult was promissory and prophetic, given to foster a holy thirst for living water and an earnest expectation for the dawning of the day – thirst/water and darkness/light being two of the chief symbols in the fourth Gospel. Those who held to a false literalism unwarranted by the law of Moses, who rejected the reality for the sake of its symbol – indeed, who had monstrously fashioned the symbol into an idol as in Jeremiah's day – therefore, would be left with an obsolete structure, clinging to a carcass. The darkness, John writes, could not 'overcome' the light, fundamentally because it could not 'comprehend' (*katelaben*) it (1:4), the first of many double

---

[31] So Congar (1962: 120) writes, 'Simeon and Anna the prophetess, two old people, for the former Dispensation has grown old and is nearing the end of its life. . . . The whole of Israel's expectation is summed up in the persons of Simeon and Anna.'

entendres in his Gospel.[32] In John 3 the Pharisee Nicodemus comes to Jesus 'by night', and Jesus draws him immediately to reflect upon the need for the Spirit – for the spiritual reality: 'Truly, truly, I say to you, unless one is born from above, he cannot see the kingdom of God' (John 3:3). It is unfortunate here that many English versions of the Bible have chosen Nicodemus' misunderstanding of the double entendre by translating Jesus' teaching as merely 'born again'. This misunderstanding leads the ruler of the Jews to respond by asking, 'How can a man be born when he is old – is he to enter his mother's womb a second time and be born?' Ironically, the impossibility of the rebirth from a human perspective is nevertheless true; yet apart from understanding the particularity of Jesus' reference as the need for the *heavenly* birth – the birth 'from above' – the theology is easily missed. No fewer than three times Jesus' lips utter the phrase 'born of the Spirit' (3:5–6, 8), in addition to his twofold use of 'born from above' (3:3, 7), both phrases being linked with 'heaven' (3:12–13). John's Gospel has Israel's new heavenly citizenship in mind; as with Jesus himself, Nicodemus cannot ascend to heaven unless he has first descended from heaven – he must be born from above. But how can this be possible? The solution: he must be born of the Spirit, for the Spirit *is* heaven, its reality and atmosphere – he is the Spirit of the eschaton, of the new creation. He is the gift that Jesus, having descended to ascend, will give. Through the supernatural wonder of the heavenly birth, the new Israel may be, as Jesus was, in the world though not of it; as the Father sent Jesus (from heaven to earth), so Jesus sends his disciples (17:16, 18; 20:21); as the incarnate Son lives because of the Father through the Spirit, so the disciples will live because of the Son through the Spirit (6:57, 63).

The focus upon the work of the Spirit, as we find in John 4, remains unabated as Jesus persists in leading others to probe the logic and dire need for this gift. His encounter with the Samaritan woman begins with his own thirst as he says to her 'Give me a drink' when she comes to draw water, but soon thereafter turns upon the water he is able to give her:[33]

Jesus answered and said to her, 'If you knew the gift of God, and who it is who says to you, "Give me a drink," you would have asked

[32] See e.g. Wead 1970; Resseguie 2001: 51–58.
[33] This conversation, moreover, occurs at high noon (the sixth hour, 4:6), one of many contrasts between this account and the previous encounter with Nicodemus.

him, and *he would have given* you living water.'. . . Whoever drinks of this water [from Jacob's well] will thirst again. But whoever drinks of the water that *I will give him* will never thirst. But the water that *I will give him* will become in him a fountain of water springing up into eternal life.' (John 4:10, 13–14)

Note the threefold emphasis, italicized, on Jesus as the baptizer – the giver – of the Spirit. As with Nicodemus, however, her literalistic interpretation falls short of grasping the significance of Jesus' words. Give me this water, she says, wanting to bypass the continual chore of drawing water from the well (4:15). But Jesus has in mind the true entrance into God's Presence, the life with God that only the living water of the Spirit can supply:

The hour is coming and now is when the true worshippers will worship the Father in Spirit and truth, for the Father is seeking such to worship him. God is Spirit, and those who worship him must worship in Spirit and truth. (John 4:23–24)

Probably, the addition of 'and truth' forms a hendiadys with Spirit, and signifies *reality*: because God is Spirit, real worshippers will worship the Father in Spirit, that is, in reality. As Um remarks, the difference is not between external and internal religion, 'but rather *a new worship empowered by the reality of eschatological life found in the True Temple of God*'.[34] The narrative therefore brings together (1) the Spirit as the gift of God, (2) Jesus as the giver of this gift, and (3) the Spirit's role in the new worship, which is nothing less than real heavenly access to and fellowship with the Father. The dialogue, further, draws out a fundamental contrast between Jacob, the father of the twelve tribes, and Jesus, who has come to renew Israel through twelve apostles. In John 1:43–51 the implicit contrast was between Jacob who had recognized the house of God and Jesus who is the house of God – recognized by Nathaniel, an Israelite in whom there is no guile (quite unlike Jacob). In the present narrative the woman asks, 'Are you greater than our father Jacob, who gave us this well, and drank from it himself, as well as his sons and livestock?' (v. 12). Jacob had blessed Israel, in other words, by providing this physical water. How can Jesus promise perpetually satisfying water for his family: Is he greater than Jacob? Jesus, once more, as the reality of

[34] Um 2006: 173; emphasis original.

what the temple signified, will provide water that is living and gives eternal life, the Spirit.

In John 7:37–38 we read that Jesus stood and cried out, saying, 'If anyone thirsts, let him come to me and drink. He who believes in me, as the Scripture has said, out of his heart will flow rivers of living water.' Given the emphasis on Jesus as the giver of the Spirit, it may be the case that the 'his' here refers to Jesus rather than the believer: 'out of his [the Messiah's] heart will flow rivers of living water'. This reading accords well with the presumed background, for we are told that this statement took place on the great and last (*eschatē*) day of the feast, undoubtedly the feast of Tabernacles. The probable context for Jesus' words would then be the water-drawing ceremony, whereby the high priest would take a golden pitcher and draw water from the pool of Siloam; then, followed by a procession of priests, musicians and pilgrims, he would enter the temple through the Water Gate and approach the altar. He, along with the priestly host, would circle around the altar once each of the first six days of the feast and seven times on the last and seventh day, accompanied by the singing of the Hallel (Pss 113 – 118) by pilgrims. After three blasts from the shofar, he would ascend the steps of the altar and pour out the water as a libation into a silver basin while another priest poured out wine simultaneously into another, both basins having snouts so that the water and wine flowed down the altar. As with other festivals in general, the practice seems to have had both a seasonal significance, as a prayer for a fertile rainy season, and a spiritual significance, linked early on with Isaiah 12:3: 'Therefore with joy you will draw water out of the wells of salvation [*yĕšû'ā*; cf. *Sukkah* 48b]'. Moreover, within the prophetic corpus, Tabernacles is connected with the ingathering of the Gentiles, a new-covenant reality dependent upon the outpouring of the Spirit. Zechariah in particular depicts the nations ascending to Jerusalem to celebrate Tabernacles (14:16–21; cf. Isa. 2:1–4), this in connection with the Spirit's work: 'In that day it shall be that living waters will flow from Jerusalem' (14:8). Given the prophetic link between water and the Spirit, it is not surprising that 'the water-pouring at Tabernacles was interpreted eschatologically as the symbol of the outpouring of the Spirit of God in the messianic time',[35] understood as a prophetic act – a pleading not merely for rain from heaven, but for the promised gift of the Spirit. The connection is made by John's own gloss of Jesus' words: 'But this he spoke concerning the

---

[35] McKelvey 1969: 81.

Spirit, whom those believing in him would receive; for the Holy Spirit was not yet given because Jesus was not yet glorified' (John 7:39). Again the fourth Gospel speaks from and points to Jesus' state of ascension glory.

The role of the Spirit in John 14 has already been discussed and here I merely add that Jesus' entire farewell discourse is of a piece, unfolding the vital union the disciples will have with him through the Spirit (see e.g. 15:1–8; 16:5–15). His prayer gravitates to this centre:

> that they [who will believe] all may be one, as you, Father, are in me and I am in you; that they also may be one in us, that the world may believe that you sent me. And the glory which you gave me I have given them, that they may be one just as we are one: I in them and you in me; that they may be made perfect in one, and that the world may know that you have sent me, and have loved them as you have loved me. Father, I desire that they also whom you gave me may be with me where I am, that they may behold my glory which you have given me, for you loved me before the foundation of the world. (John 17:21–24)

Jesus' prayer is for the disciples to know that union with the Godhead that makes them one, even as the Father and Son are one – that is the glory he shares with them. Once more, as in John 14, Jesus intimates their joining him in his Father's house, their being 'with me where I am', that is, in the bosom of the Father, beholding the glory. Jesus concludes the prayer with his own role of declaring the Father, the revelation of the Father that will steadily yield the beatific vision: 'I have declared to them your name and will declare it, that the love with which you loved me may be in them, and I in them' (John 17:26). Union for revelation, revelation for deeper union, continually, all for the fellowship of love and communion of life with God – that is the dynamic John labours to unfold; that is the same joy he is burdened to explain elsewhere in his epistle: 'that you also may have fellowship with us, and truly our fellowship is with the Father and with his Son Jesus Christ – these things we write to you so that your joy may be full' (1 John 1:3b–4). Through Jesus, and his gift of the Spirit, humanity becomes God's household, participating in the Godhead, enjoying the *koinōnia* – the fellowship that is a communion of both love and friendship – of the Father, Son and Holy Spirit.

The gift of the Spirit continues thematically to the cross itself and Christ's declaration 'I thirst!' (19:28), a saying that recalls his earlier dialogues on the Spirit – his 'Give me a drink' to the Samaritan woman (4:7) and his crying out during the feast of Tabernacles, 'If anyone thirsts . . .' (7:37). Inasmuch as Jesus' death is the end of the Levitical cultus, 'I thirst' is a fitting cry, the final testimony to its own need for fulfilment. As the height and embodiment of the old covenant, of God's dwelling among his people, the temple of Jesus' body must be destroyed, though only to be raised again in three days, glorified, as the new temple of the new covenant – that, for John, is the continuity between the old and the new, as well as the vital distinction: the new covenant stands for the full consummation, the indestructible life of the resurrection in glory (even as it will be experienced ahead of the eschaton through the gift of the Spirit). The statement should not be severed, therefore, from his final gesture in verse 30: 'He said, "It is finished!" And bowing his head, he delivered the Spirit.' The Gospel that began with the phrase 'In the beginning' (*en archē*) now comes to a close with the declaration 'It is finished' (*tetelestai*). The sixth day of divine work and the incompleteness of the Levitical cultus will be brought into the seventh-day end, only to be born anew, from above, on the eighth day – the new creation. All translation requires interpretation, as is particularly evident in the last phrase of 19:30. The common English versions translate, 'he gave up his spirit', interpreting the phrase as a euphemism for death. This, however, would constitute an isolated instance of such a phrase, and simply lacks sensitivity to John's precise wording. The term *paredōkēn* does not refer to a loss or giving up, but rather to a passing on or delivering over, and *to pneuma* means not 'his spirit' but 'the spirit'. Given that, in the fourth Gospel, the cross is the first step in Jesus' exaltation, and that his exaltation is itself for the sake of pouring out the Spirit, John's precise description of Jesus' death is theologically weighted. The delivering of the Spirit was the goal of Jesus' mission, the heavenly key for unlocking all the promises he had made to the disciples, the persistent subject matter for so many of his dialogues, personal and public – John cannot help but offer a foreshadowing of the inevitable result of his sacrifice. That result is expressed more fully in a passage from John's Apocalypse, which echoes remarkably the fourth Gospel:

> He said to me, 'It is done! I am the Alpha and the Omega, the beginning [*archē*] and the end [*telos*]. To the thirsty, I will give from the spring of the water of life freely. . . . And let the one who thirsts come. Let whoever desires take the water of life freely.' (Rev. 21:6; 22:17)

And there is yet another anticipation from the cross of this abundant gift (19:34): 'But one of the soldiers pierced his side with a spear, and immediately blood and water came out.' This occurrence, which John is careful to underline by his testimony in the next verse, may recall the water-drawing ceremony of the feast of Tabernacles, where both water and wine were poured out. Some scholars have gone further, detecting here an allusion to Ezekiel's new temple, with the water flowing from the holy of holies and out of its side. McKelvey remarks:

> What is this but the river of life which Ezekiel said would flow from the new temple – the living water which if a man drink he will never thirst again (4:14; 7:38), and the blood which is drink indeed (6:55)? No sooner has Jesus been glorified (cf. 7:39) than the new life of the Spirit is made available for mankind.[36]

The whole narrative of his death, in fact, resonates with the words of Isaiah 44:3:

> For I will pour water on him who is thirsty . . .
> I will pour my Spirit on your descendants . . .

Finally, after his resurrection we read of yet another emblematic giving of the Holy Spirit, as Jesus breathes on his disciples and says, 'Receive the Holy Spirit' (20:22). From the beginning to the end of the fourth Gospel, then, Jesus is *the* baptizer, the one who will pour out the promised Spirit of God – the indispensable gift of the new covenant that he merits through his suffering and death, and is a chief aim of his exaltation.

As the one who pours out the Spirit from on high, Jesus inaugurates the new covenant of the new exodus – from the true mountain of God. Moses had ascended Mount Sinai, into the cloud of God's glory, in order to bring God's people the twin gifts of Sinai's summit: the torah and the tabernacling Presence of God. It is noteworthy that both gifts are regiven when Jesus ascends the heavenly Mount Zion – regiven yet transfigured by the manner with which they are conveyed, namely through the Spirit. Through the Spirit the torah is written upon the heart, brought within the people of God, instead of its merely being written on stone; through the Spirit the tabernacling

[36] Ibid. 83.

Presence of God is, similarly, brought within the people of God, instead of residing in a tent among them. In both cases there is a transfiguration of love, for love fulfils the law and is the new law (Rom. 13:8–10; John 13:34–35); and God's indwelling Presence is the love of God poured out in our hearts by the Holy Spirit (Rom. 5:5). The two are one in the Spirit, in the person who is also the principle of love shared between the Father and the Son, and now between the Son and the new Israel.

The new Israel as the new temple

The union with Christ that raises Israel from the dead and leads Israel through the new exodus to heaven itself is the same union with Christ that also transfigures Israel into the temple of the living God. And just as Jesus' exodus into heaven was for the sake of Israel's, so too his becoming the new temple through the resurrection is also for the sake of Israel's becoming the house of God. Jesus is, therefore, the son of David who God promised would build a temple for his name, a house of God that is also the household of God (2 Sam. 7:1–17). The author of Hebrews similarly describes Christ as both the builder of the house and as the Son who is over his own house (Heb. 3:1–6). Israel, resurrected on the third day, is also the temple he would rebuild in three days.

The house(hold) of God

Interwoven with the other themes we have considered, John's Gospel also develops the drama of Jesus' gathering to himself a household for God. Jesus is the 'Passover lamb and head of a household which he gathers to his Father through his death'.[37] John's Gospel began, of course, with this promise that those who received Jesus would become the 'children of God', having been 'born from above' – that is, of God (1:12–13; 3:3); God's intention being to 'gather together into one the children of God who were scattered abroad' (11:52). Returning to John 14 once more, Jesus' gathering of the disciples up to his Father's house is extremely relevant. First, Jesus as the firstborn prefaces this discourse by washing his disciples' feet on the eve of Passover, a profound gesture of hospitality on the threshold, as it were, of the Father's house. Secondly, the term used for the Father's house (*oikia*) in 14:2 is slightly different from that of the Father's house (from *oikos*) in 2:20. While *oikos* always refers to a building, *oikia* is

---

[37] Blanke 2007: vii.

broader and may refer to a household or family.[38] This idea coincides, thirdly, with Jesus' formal address of the disciples as 'little children' (*teknia*), the first and only such usage in the Gospel, as he begins his farewell discourse on the Father's house(hold) – they have become, at least by prolepsis, members of the Father's household, for the Son who abides in the house for ever is about to set them free (cf. 8:35–36). John's narrative, then, in a remarkable way demonstrates how Jesus' death yields the new household of God: at the foot of the cross he tells his own mother, 'Woman, behold your son!', referencing the disciple whom he loves; and to the disciple he says, 'Behold, your mother' (19:25–27). Finally, upon his resurrection, Jesus addresses 'my brothers' (*adelphous mou*) through Mary Magdalene in a manner that confirms this new divine household (20:17): 'say to them, "I am ascending to my Father and your Father, and to my God and your God."' In saying 'your Father', he acknowledges the disciples' heavenly birth, their being born of God; in saying 'my God', he acknowledges his own humanity, his being born of a woman. He ascends to his Father's house, to the bosom of the Father, and through him the disciples may with like justice say of that place prepared, 'my Father's house'.

The house of God

To understand how this household of God, born of God from above, also stands as the house of God, the new temple, we turn to the epistles.[39] In various places the apostle Paul unfolds his profound understanding of the nature of the church as the temple of God, asking in 1 Corinthians 3:16,[40] 'Do you not know that you are the temple of God, because the Spirit of God dwells within you?' The 'you' here (and elsewhere, as in 1 Cor. 6:19) being plural, having reference to the church rather than to the individual in isolation, his regular application is with regard to both the holiness and unity of the people of God: 'For the temple of God is holy, which temple you are' (1 Cor. 3:17). As an *architektōn*, a 'master builder', Paul lays the foundation of Christ (1 Cor. 3:10); and just as the Spirit had endowed artisans to build the tabernacle (Exod. 31:1–11), so now he endows his people to edify the temple (1 Cor. 12:4–11; 14:12; Eph. 4:7–16). In 2 Corinthians 6:16–18 he again states, 'For you are the temple of the

---

[38] McCaffrey 1988: 177–184.

[39] For the following passages, see the fine expositions of McKelvey (1969), Beale (2004) and Macaskill (2013).

[40] As my translation indicates, I take the *kai* as explicative.

living God,' anchoring that reality in the divine promises of Exodus 29:45 and Leviticus 26:12, promises he recognizes, by interpreting the force of the Greek preposition *en* to its fullest potential as 'within' instead of merely 'among', have only now come to fulfilment:[41]

> I will dwell *within* them, and walk among them.
> I will be their God, and they shall be my people.

The church is the temple in which God dwells, God's house. But more than this, in verse 18, the apostle offers an interpretative gloss to the Davidic covenant of 2 Samuel 7:14:

> I will be a Father to you,
> And you will be my sons and daughters.

The first change is from the original third masculine singular 'him' to the plural 'you' (in both cases), a significant change indeed and out of which Paul's second change springs: 'sons and daughters'. The original 'son' has become plural, and the phrase 'and daughters' has been added. This understanding can be explained only by the apostle's theology of union with Christ: the Spirit's outpouring enables all of God's people to be incorporated into the promise made to the Davidic Son – a household in and through the Son, which is also the house built by the Son. Paul brings out Christ's role of assimilation, through the Spirit's role of union, more clearly in his letter to the Ephesians:

> For through him we both have access in one Spirit to the Father. Now, therefore, you are no longer strangers and foreigners, but are fellow citizens with the saints and members of the household of God, having been built on the foundation of the apostles and prophets, Jesus Christ himself being the chief cornerstone, in whom the whole building, being joined together, grows into a holy temple in the Lord, in whom you also are being built together into a dwelling place for God in the Spirit. (Eph. 2:18–22)

In Christ, Jews and Gentiles are members of the household of God, and form together the house – the holy temple – of God, as each is united to Christ by faith and through the Spirit. While Jesus' glorified body may be called the new temple when considered in isolation, yet

---

[41] Cf. Phythian-Adams 1942: 173–174.

he is rather the chief cornerstone when considered together with all the redeemed, the one who integrates and builds God's people into the new and living temple of God, again through his outpoured Spirit. In a sense, all of Paul's theology flows into and out of his doctrine of the church – this is the new Israel, the new temple, filled with the Spirit of God. Christ is the centre, the builder and cornerstone; the Spirit is the means of union, as he applies the blood of Christ and unites believers, body and soul, to him; but the church, the living temple of God, is the result, the blossom and cluster of fruit whose increase is from God and whose liturgy of spiritual sacrifice is to the glory of God the Father.

Turning now to Peter's first epistle, itself structured by the temple theme,[42] we find a catena of 'stone' texts, including Isaiah 28:16, Psalm 118:22 and Isaiah 8:14, by which Peter sums up the gospel narrative of Jesus, along with the result for God's people:

Coming to Him as to a living stone, rejected indeed by men, but chosen by God and precious, you also, as living stones, are being built up a spiritual house, a holy priesthood, to offer up spiritual sacrifices acceptable to God through Jesus Christ. Therefore it is also contained in the Scripture:

'Behold, I lay in Zion
A chief cornerstone, elect, precious,
And he who believes on him will by no means
be put to shame.'

Therefore, to you who believe, he is precious; but to those who are disobedient,

'The stone which the builders rejected
Has become the chief cornerstone,
and
A stone of stumbling
And a rock of offence.'

They stumble, being disobedient to the word, to which they also were appointed. But you are a chosen generation, a royal priesthood, a holy nation, his own special people, that you may proclaim the praises of him who called you out of darkness into his

---

[42] See Mbuvi 2007.

marvellous light; who once were not a people but are now the people of God, who had not obtained mercy but now have obtained mercy. (1 Peter 2:4–10)

Jesus himself summed up his biography through the lens of Psalm 118: he was the rock the builders rejected, but that God chose to be the chief cornerstone for his temple (see Matt. 21:42; Mark 12:10–11; Luke 20:17; cf. Acts 4:11) – there is his rejection and death, his resurrection and exaltation, and, inasmuch as he is the cornerstone of God's temple (implying the rest of the building), there, too, is the outpouring of the Spirit and ingathering of believers. As people come to Jesus the living stone by faith, they themselves become living stones – resurrected, living – by union with him, and together form the dwelling of God through his Spirit. By use of appellations from Exodus 19:5–6 there can be no question that Peter understands the church, Jew and Gentile, to be the resurrected Israel proclaimed by the prophets, the new Israel of the new exodus who in the new covenant have become a royal priesthood and holy nation – even the sĕgullâ, the special possession, of God. Whereas the height of the old covenant was God's dwelling among his people, tabernacling finally as the incarnate Son, the wonder of the new covenant is a second sort of incarnation: God's dwelling within his people, the church gathered as a living temple of God. The height of the new covenant, its consummation, however, awaits with eager expectation the new creation.[43]

The new Jerusalem: Revelation 21 – 22

New covenant worship

Just at this point, having reflected upon the church as the temple of God, filled with the Spirit of God, it is necessary to return to the emphasis of John's Gospel and the book of Hebrews on the ascent of God's people through union with the ascended Jesus. The Spirit indeed fills the gathered people of God so that the church may be considered justly God's temple on earth. However, the mission of Christ was and is to bring them to himself in heaven, until the eschaton – this reality the church experiences by faith through the corporate ascent of worship, entering through the new and living way of Jesus' torn flesh and shed blood, ascending to the heavenly Mount Zion. The gift of the Spirit, once more, not only brings Christ to us, but,

---

[43] My theme of dwelling with God in the house of God, therefore, aligns well with the creation approach to biblical theology (see Beale 2004; 2011; Dumbrell 2001; 2009).

better, the Spirit raises us together to Christ in the heavenly places, that we may be where he is and behold his glory. The full resolution to this dynamic between God with his people on earth through the Holy Spirit, and his people with God in heaven through the same Spirit, awaits the consummation of the eschaton, the new heavens and earth, when the temple of God's people descends out of heaven from God, to dwell with him in the light of his glory.

The eschaton

> Now I saw a new heaven and a new earth, for the first heaven and the first earth had passed away. Also there was no more sea. (Rev. 21:1)

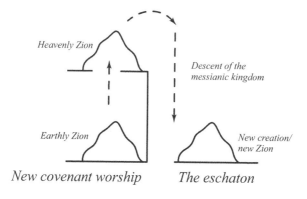

New covenant worship   *The eschaton*

With these words, and the transition they describe from the old creation to the new, one may perceive the full shift from the old covenant to the new. Here the cosmogonic pattern of redemptive history comes to an end, the final exodus: once God's people are brought to this mountain, singing the song of Moses and the Lamb (15:3), there is no more sea (cf. 20:13). The new Israel's heavenly birth is manifest in the descent of God's people out of heaven, born of God and described as a holy city, mountain and bride: 'Then I, John, saw the holy city, new Jerusalem, coming down out of heaven from God, prepared as a bride adorned for her husband' (Rev. 21:2). The worth of the Lamb's redemption is on display with this description, for Israel is 'of heaven'; that is, utterly fitting to dwell with God without any hindrance – spotless, blameless and holy, a companion suitable for God. Once more, this fellowship that is pure friendship with God, this union and communion, is the consummation of God's creation – the heart and deepest intent of his covenant:

And I heard a loud voice out of heaven saying,
'Behold, the tabernacle [*skēnē*] of God is with humanity!
He will dwell [*skēnōsei*] with them, and they shall be
  his peoples;
God himself will be with them and be their God.'
(Rev. 21:3; cf. Lev. 26:11–12; Ezek. 36:26–27)

The covenant formula's use here demonstrates that this reality of life
with God in the new earth is the substance of covenant theology,
unifying the covenants as their one definite *telos*. As the prophesied
new exodus encompasses the nations, the plural form of 'peoples' in
this declaration of the covenant formula is noteworthy.[44] YHWH
God was mindful of the nations he had scattered into exile from the
tower of Babylon; for this final declaration, he had created Adam,
delivered Noah, called out Abram, fashioned Israel and sent his Son.
Also significant, the Davidic covenant formula is applied to every
citizen of the new Jerusalem: 'I will be his God and he will be my son'
(21:7). The people of God, as the Lamb's bride and the new Jerusalem,
are again described as 'descending out of heaven from God, having
the glory of God' (21:9–11), and, given the four-square dimensions
of the new Jerusalem (21:16), are portrayed as the inner sanctum of
God's temple, the holy of holies. This reality fulfils the prophecy
of Zechariah, where he declares that 'holy to YHWH', the inscription
on the high priest's diadem, will be engraved even on the bells of
horses – even on every pot in Jerusalem (14:20–21). Since, moreover,
the holy of holies derives its status and nature from the intensely
manifested Presence of God, we are also to understand this as the
fulfilment of the final words of Ezekiel's prophecy, similarly describing the new Jerusalem: 'All the way around shall be eighteen thousand
cubits; and the name of the city from that day will be: YHWH
Shammah ['YHWH is there']' (Ezek. 48:35).

The gate liturgy
With every atom of the new Jerusalem possessing God's holiness
through the pervasive presence of the Spirit, we cannot be sur-
prised that entrance to this city, this sanctuary most holy, should be
conditional, bringing us once more to the (final) gate liturgy. There
is, in fact, a threefold emphasis upon the conditionality of entrance

---

44 Cf. Mathewson 2003: 51–54. Though there is some manuscript evidence for the
singular form, this reading, in terms of *lectio difficilior potior*, is to be preferred.

into this new creation and holy cosmos, as focused upon the new Jerusalem.

Revelation	Entrance	Exclusion
21:7–8	He who overcomes will inherit all things, and I will be his God and he will be my son.	But the cowardly, unbelieving, abominable, murderers, sexually immoral, sorcerers, idolaters and all liars will have their part in the lake which burns with fire and brimstone, which is the second death.
21:24–27	And the nations of those who are saved will walk in its light, and the kings of the earth bring their glory and honour into it. . . . And they shall bring the glory and honour of the nations into it.	But there will by no means enter it anything that defiles, or causes an abomination or a lie, but only those who are written in the Lamb's book of life.
22:14–15	Blessed are those who do his commandments, that they may have the right to the tree of life, and may enter through the gates into the city.	But outside are dogs and sorcerers and sexually immoral and murderers and idolaters, and whoever practises a lie.

Each of the three passages (21:7–8, 24–27; 22:14–15) draws a sharp contrast between those allowed within the city's gates and those who must for ever remain outside – every temple entrance liturgy thus far has gestured toward this final reality.[45] All things that defile are excluded, while all who enter are described in accordance with the blameless and just attributions given in Psalms 15 and 24. The question of Israel's liturgy may now be seen to enfold the drama of the ages – it is a deeply pressing, fate-determining, utterly relevant question for all humanity: Who shall ascend the mountain of YHWH? Just *who* will enter the new Jerusalem that is itself a holy of holies? Inasmuch as Jerusalem's gates remain open (a point to which we will return), it is evident that these three passages serve merely to punctuate the gate liturgy that has already taken place. In John's Apocalypse, *the* gate liturgy, the dread reality to which temple entrance and exclusion gestures, is the day of judgment. The excluded in 21:8, we are told, have their part 'in the lake which burns with fire and brimstone, which is the second death', the exile to which they have been sent upon the day of judgment: 'Then death and hades were cast into the lake of fire – this is the second death. And anyone not found written in the book of life was cast into the lake of fire' (Rev. 20:14–15). This is the final

---

[45] This statement includes excommunication from the New Testament church, which, moreover, the apostle Paul teaches within the context of the church as the temple of God (1 Cor. 5).

expulsion. In terms of the gate liturgy it is especially significant to weigh carefully the ultimate designation for the damned: 'anyone not found written in the book of life' – here is the only really germane distinction between those within the city's gates and those who remain in the eternal *outside*, which is the second death; here the distinction at the heart of the Levitical cultus, that between life and death, becomes absolute. The book of life is also mentioned as the determining condition in 21:27, though in this case it is called 'the Lamb's book of life', bringing us back to the Passover redemption of the lamb of God. All who enter the new Jerusalem are those who have been redeemed – ransomed and purified – by the blood of the Lamb, Jesus Christ. The shed blood and veil of flesh through which the church enters the heavenly places in corporate worship is one and the same shed blood and veil of flesh through which the church enters the new Jerusalem – liturgy is the silhouette of redemption. Through the Lamb's blood, God's people have their names written in the book of life, and so they enter the house of God. The twin paths of the identical goats of the Day of Atonement are here traversed in the ceremony's eternal consummation: the sinful and unclean, polluted and defiling, can by no means enter this holy city now; they go the way of the goat of damnation, 'cast into the lake of fire' (20:15). On the day of judgment they are sent into the full despair of dark and eternal exile, the final destination of Cain's footfall away from the face of God. And such is the fate for all humanity, if God had not chosen and endeavoured to author the book of life – '*But God!*'

> And you were dead in the trespasses and sins in which you once walked, following the course of this world, following the prince of the power of the air, the spirit now at work in the sons of disobedience – among whom we all once engaged in the lusts of our flesh, obeying the will of the flesh and the mind, and were by nature children of wrath, as with the rest of humanity.
>
> But God, being rich in mercy, because of his great love with which he loved us, even when we were dead in our trespasses, made us alive together with Christ – by grace you have been saved! – and raised us up with him and seated us with him in the heavenly places in Christ Jesus, so that in the coming ages he might show the immeasurable riches of his grace in kindness toward us in Christ Jesus. For by grace you have been saved through faith, and this is not your own doing – it is the gift of God, not of your works, so that no one may boast. (Eph. 2:1–9)

The people of God, once sinful and unclean, polluted and defiling, dead and awaiting the second death, yet now redeemed by the slain Firstborn, united to him by faith and through the Holy Spirit – which is to say, by the grace of God – they enter the holiest in, with and through the Son, to the eternal joys of the house of God where they will behold the face of God. The Day of Atonement is herewith fulfilled, the central ascent of Leviticus gives way to the clouds of glory. 'And I will dwell in the house of YHWH for ever' (Ps. 23:6).

> And the nations of those who are saved will walk in its light, and the kings of the earth bring their glory and honour into it. Its gates shall not be shut at all by day (there shall be no night there). And they shall bring the glory and the honour of the nations into it. (Rev. 21:24–26)

With the perpetually open gates of the new Jerusalem, the finality of the great white throne's gate liturgy has been signalled. By framing the open gates with references to the nations, streaming in with their glories and honours (cf. Isa. 2:1–4), the idea may be that the gates remain open *because* of the continual pilgrimage of the nations into God's Presence. The reference to no night also lends the idea of absolute safety and permanence, the destruction of all hostility – for, due to the usual dangers that attend the darkness of night, the ANE city would bolt its gates for the evening. The open gates, then, stand as the absolute counter gesture of closing them against enemies: with the end to all enmity by the blood of Jesus, the nations, one in him through the Spirit, are rather to be welcomed and constrained to enter the light of God's blessing. *This procession of the nations to the new Zion marks the profound reversal to the exile of the nations from the tower of Babylon.*

The new Eden

The last words of the expulsion from Eden's garden were with reference to the cherubim guarding 'the way to the tree of life' (Gen. 3:24), underscoring the barred life within the garden of Eden and the death awaiting those outside its gates. The cultic exodus of the high priest's entrance into the holy of holies, as we have considered, was a ritual re-entry of Eden. John's vision of the new earth in Revelation 21 and 22 presents us with the consummate reality of that ritual, the new exodus ascent of Zion, the eschaton's mountain of God, which is the new Eden:

> And he showed me a pure river of the water of life, clear as crystal flowing from the throne of God and of the Lamb; through the middle of its street, and on either side of the river, was the tree of life, which bore twelve fruits, each yielding its fruit every month. The leaves of the tree were for the healing of the nations. And there will be no more curse, but the throne of God and of the Lamb will be in it, and his servants will worship him. (Rev. 22:1–3)

The throne of God had been in the temple's holy of holies, the counterpart to the mountain of God's summit. Both images coalesce here as the river flows from the summit of the new Zion, the throne of God. Access to the tree of life, whose leaves will heal the nations, portrays the reversal not only of the expulsion out of Eden, but also, again, of its reassertion, the scattering of the nations from the tower of Babylon – the drama of Genesis 12 to Revelation 22 comprises the long journey of resolution to the primeval inclusio of exile (Gen. 1 – 11).

As the essence of that which the tabernacle and later temples were built to represent, recapture and re-enter, Eden was the *archetype* of the temple. Only as such is paradise called a temple – as its reality. And only as such is it said that the new Jerusalem includes no temple: 'But I saw no temple in it, for the Lord God Almighty and the Lamb are its temple. The city had no need of the sun or of the moon to shine in it, for the glory of God illuminated it. The Lamb is its light' (Rev. 21:22–23). In the new earth there is no temple in the sense that *God* through Jesus is humanity's temple; there is no temple in the sense that *humanity* is God's dwelling place; and there is no temple also because the *cosmos*, cleansed and consecrated, is finally the house of God, the context and stage for humanity's endless engagement with God. The end is life with God in Eden.

Conclusion

Leviticus, within the narrative context of the Pentateuch, unfolds how YHWH had opened a (Levitical) way for humanity to dwell in his Presence. That theme, I have endeavoured to demonstrate, is *the* drama and plot of the Bible, with the transition into the new covenant being most fully comprehended through the fundamentally new way of access opened through the mediation and priesthood of Jesus. Even the authority of his Davidic kingship is commissioned, in pouring out the Spirit and subduing his enemies, for the sake of his high priestly mediation, to usher God's people into the heavenly Presence of the Father – ultimately, within the new Jerusalem of the eschaton. The prologue to this work began with the lampstand beaming its light upon the twelve loaves of bread, within the holy place of God's wilderness tabernacle. This set up, we saw, symbolized the blessing of God upon the people of God, mediated by the priest of God – within the house of God. In a similar manner, the Aaronic blessing shone the light of God's face upon Israel, placing his name upon them. More particularly, given the Sabbath by Sabbath renewal of the bread of the Presence, the radiance within the holy place was a ritual theophany, presenting the Sabbath – as in eschatological – *end* for Israel: life with God in the house of God. John's Revelation yields the glimpse ahead: humanity dwelling within the fires of the glory of God, in the new Jerusalem whose lamp is the face of the Lamb. 'They will see his face, and his name will be on their foreheads. No night will be there. They need no lamp or light of the sun, for the Lord God shines for them. And they will reign for ever and ever' (Rev. 22:4–5). *This passage is the Sabbath.* In the words 'They will see his face, and his name will be on their foreheads,' the light of his countenance shining upon them and his name placed upon them, we glimpse the culmination of the Aaronic benediction, the life of blessing depicted by the twelve loaves renewed in the Sabbath light of the menorah – in the house of God. What sort of communion and joy will they experience who see his face, who dwell in the blessed light of his countenance, whose foreheads bear his own sacred name? The fellowship with the Godhead we taste in the present age, through our union with Christ, must only be increased to the fullest measure and degree possible in the eschaton, when all flesh itself will be spiritual and, as it were, *spiritized* – when we will know beyond our present understanding the joys of divine hospitality, know that by the Spirit we dwell in the Son and through the Son in the Father, and that by the Spirit the Father and Son indeed dwell within us and sup with us. Though categories for such intimacy with God who is Spirit are bound to falter and fail, Congar makes a noble attempt:

> Between God and ourselves there is, we may venture to say, reciprocal hospitality and indwelling, because there is between us both communication and communion (*koinōnia*). . . . If there is one obvious direction in the great story of God's Presence to his creatures as it has been made known to us by Revelation, if this story has one overall movement, it is surely this – it begins by

momentary contacts and visits, then passes through the stage of external mediations that draw God ever nearer to mankind, and finally reaches the state of perfectly stable and intimate communion. Whether it be through the temple, the sacrifice or the priesthood, God's plan moves towards a communion of such intimacy that duality between man and God, and therefore their external separation from one another, are both overcome in so far as this is possible without a meaningless confusion of beings or pantheism.[46]

Together united with the Godhead, there also are all the saints enjoying friendship with one another, bonded by the Spirit of love, seeing the image and likeness of God in each other's faces, radiant with the fires of his everlasting glory – the holy temple of God, the bride of Christ. That is life in the new Zion, the final mountain of God. That is what it means to bask in the Sabbath-day light of God's countenance. That is what it means to dwell in the divine Presence.

Who, then, shall ascend the mountain of YHWH? By the lovingkindness of the Father, the redemption of the Son and the outpouring of the Holy Spirit, a sure answer has been found: even the church of Jesus Christ.

> Yet she on earth hath union with God the Three in One,
> and mystic sweet communion with those whose rest is won.
> O happy ones and holy! Lord, give us grace that we
> like them, the meek and lowly, on high may dwell with thee.
> (Samuel J. Stone [1839–1900],
> 'The Church's One Foundation')

---

[46] Congar 1962: 230, 231–232.

Bibliography

Abba, R. (1977), 'The Origin and Significance of Hebrew Sacrifice', *BTB* 7.3: 123–138.

Abrahams, I. (2006), 'Tabernacle', in M. Berenbaum and F. Skolnik (eds.), *Encyclopaedia Judaica*, 2nd ed., Detroit: Keter, 19: 418–424.

Adams, D. L. (1996), 'Deus Praesens: The Present God in the Patriarchal Narratives', PhD diss., Cambridge: Cambridge University.

Adu-Gyamfi, Y. (2013), 'The Live Goat Ritual in Leviticus 16', *Scriptura* 112.1: 1–10.

Albright, W. F. (1920), 'The Babylonian Temple-Tower and the Altar of Burnt-Offering', *JBL* 39 (3.4): 137–142.

—— (1953), *Archaeology and the Religion of Israel*, Baltimore: Johns Hopkins University Press.

Alexander, T. D. (1995), 'The Passover Sacrifice', in R. T. Beckwith and M. J. Selman (eds.), *Sacrifice in the Bible*, Carlisle: Paternoster; Grand Rapids: Baker, 1–24.

—— (2009), *From Eden to the New Jerusalem: An Introduction to Biblical Theology*, Grand Rapids: Kregel.

Anderson, B. W. (1986), *Understanding the Old Testament*, Englewood Cliffs, N.J.: Prentice-Hall.

—— (1999), *Contours of Old Testament Theology*, Minneapolis: Fortress.

Anderson, G. A. (1989), 'Celibacy or Consummation in the Garden? Reflections on Early Jewish and Christian Interpretations of the Garden of Eden', *HTR* 82.2: 121–148.

—— (1991), 'The Praise of God as a Cultic Event', in G. A. Anderson and S. M. Olyan (eds.), *Priesthood and Cult in Ancient Israel*, JSOTSup 125, Sheffield: Sheffield Academic Press, 15–33.

—— (2001), 'Biblical Origins and the Problem of the Fall', *ProEccl* 10.1: 17–30.

—— (2009), 'Towards a Theology of the Tabernacle and Its Furniture', in R. Clements and D. R. Schwartz (eds.), *Text, Thought, and Practice in Qumran and Early Christianity: Proceedings of the Ninth International Symposium of the Orion Center for the Study* of the Dead Sea Scrolls and Associated Literature, Jointly Sponsored by the Hebrew University Center for the Study of Christianity, 11–13 January, 2004, STDJ 84, Leiden: Brill, 161–194.

———— (2011), 'Inauguration of the Tabernacle Service at Sinai', in S. Fine (ed.), The Temple of Jerusalem: From Moses to the Messiah: In Honor of Professor Louis H. Feldman, Leiden: Brill, 1–15.

———— (2015), 'Through Those Who Are Near to Me, I Will Show Myself Holy: Nadab and Abihu and Apophatic Theology', CBQ 77: 1–19.

Ashbel, D. (1965), 'The Goat Sent to Azazel', BM 11: 89–102.

Auld, G. (1996), 'Leviticus at the Heart of the Pentateuch?', in J. F. A. Sawyer (ed.), Reading Leviticus: A Conversation with Mary Douglas, Sheffield: Sheffield Academic Press, 40–51.

———— (2003), 'Leviticus: After Exodus and Before Numbers', in R. Rendtorff, R. A. Kugler and S. S. Bartlet (eds.), The Book of Leviticus: Composition and Reception, VTSup 93, Leiden: Brill, 41–54.

Averbeck, R. E. (1997a), 'Leviticus: Theology of', in NIDOTTE 4: 907–923.

———— (1997b), 'Clean and Unclean', in NIDOTTE 4: 477–486.

———— (2003), 'Tabernacle', in DOTP, 807–827.

Azevedo, J. (1999), 'At the Door of Paradise: A Contextual Interpretation of Gen. 4:7', BN 110: 45–59.

Balentine, S. E. (2002), Leviticus, Louisville: John Knox.

Ball, D. M. (1996), 'I Am' in John's Gospel: Literary Function, Background and Theological Implications, JSNTSup 124, Sheffield: Sheffield Academic Press.

Barre, M. L., and J. S. Kselman (1983), 'New Exodus, Covenant, and Restoration in Psalm 23', in C. L. Meyers and M. O'Connor (eds.), The Word of the Lord Shall Go Forth: Essays in Honor of David Noel Freedman in Celebration of His Sixtieth Birthday, Winona Lake: Eisenbrauns, 97–127.

Barrois, G. A. (1980), Jesus Christ and the Temple, Crestwood, N.Y.: St. Vladimir's Seminary Press.

Bartholomew, C. G. (2007), 'The Theology of Place in Genesis 1–3', in J. G. McConville and K. Möller (eds.), Reading the Law: Studies in Honor of Gordon J. Wenham, Edinburgh: T. & T. Clark, 173–195.

Batto, B. F. (1983), 'The Reed Sea: Requiescat in Pace', JBL 102.1: 27–35.

Baumgarten, J. M. (1966), 'The Counting of the Sabbath in Ancient Sources', VT 16.3: 277–286.

Beale, G. K. (2004), *The Temple and the Church's Mission: A Biblical Theology of the Dwelling Place of God*, Leicester: Apollos; Downers Grove: InterVarsity Press.

—— (2008), *The Erosion of Inerrancy in Evangelicalism: Responding to New Challenges to Biblical Authority*, Wheaton: Crossway.

—— (2011), *A New Testament Biblical Theology: The Unfolding of the Old Testament in the New*, Grand Rapids: Baker Academic.

Beauchamp, P. (1969), *Création et séparation: étude exégétique du chapitre premier de la Genèse*, Paris: Aubier-Montaigne.

Bender, A. (1903), 'Das Lied Exodus 15', *ZAW* 23: 1–48.

Bergen, R. D. (1990), 'The Role of Genesis 22:1–19 in the Abraham Cycle: A Computer-Assisted Textual Interpretation', *CTR* 4.2: 313–326.

Berman, J. (1995), *The Temple: Its Symbolism and Meaning Then and Now*, Northvale, N.J.: J. Aronson.

Bibb, B. D. (2001), 'Nadab and Abihu Attempt to Fill a Gap: Law and Narrative in Leviticus 10.1–7', *JSOT* 26.2: 83–99.

—— (2005), 'This Is the Thing That the Lord Commanded You to Do: Ritual Words and Narrative Worlds in the Book of Leviticus', PhD diss., Princeton: Princeton Theological Seminary.

—— (2008), *Ritual Words and Narrative Worlds in the Book of Leviticus*, London: T. & T. Clark.

Blanke, J. A. (2007), 'A Household to Be Gathered: The Anointing at Bethany and the Day of Jesus' Death in the Gospel According to John', PhD diss., St. Louis, Mo.: Concordia Seminary.

Blenkinsopp, J. (1976), 'The Structure of P', *CBQ* 38: 275–292.

—— (1992), *The Pentateuch: An Introduction to the First Five Books of the Bible*, New York: Doubleday.

Blocher, H. (1984), *In the Beginning: The Opening Chapters of Genesis*, Leicester: Inter-Varsity Press; Downers Grove: InterVarsity Press.

Bloch-Smith, E. (2002), 'Solomon's Temple: The Politics of Ritual Space', in B. M. Gittlen (ed.), *Sacred Time, Sacred Place: Archaeology and the Religion of Israel*, Winona Lake: Eisenbrauns, 83–94.

Blum, E. (1990), *Studien zur Komposition des Pentateuch*, Berlin: de Gruyter.

Bolger, E. W. (1993), 'The Compositional Role of the Eden Narrative in the Pentateuch', PhD diss., Deerfield: Trinity Evangelical Divinity School.

Bovell, C. R. (2004), 'Genesis 3:21: The History of Israel in a Nutshell?', *ExpTim* 115.11: 361–366.

Bromiley, G. W. (1949), 'The Significance of Death in Relation to the Atonement', *EvQ* 21: 122–132.

Brueggemann, W. (1976), 'Presence of God, Cultic', *IDBSup*, 680–683.

——— (1979), 'The Crisis and Promise of Presence in Israel', *HBT* 1: 47–86.

——— (1994), 'Exodus', in T. E. Fretheim, W. C. Kaiser and L. E. Keck (eds.), *Genesis to Leviticus*, NIB 2, Nashville: Abingdon, 25–32.

——— (2005), *Theology of the Old Testament: Testimony, Dispute, Advocacy*, Minneapolis: Fortress.

Büchler, A. (1967), *Studies in Sin and Atonement in the Rabbinic Literature of the First Century*, New York: Ktav.

Budd, P. J. (1989), 'Holiness and Cult', in R. E. Clements (ed.), *The World of Ancient Israel: Sociological, Anthropological, and Political Perspectives*, Cambridge: Cambridge University Press, 275–298.

Burden, J. (1987), 'A Stylistic Analysis of Exodus 15:1–21: Theory and Practice', in J. Burden, P. J. Botha and H. F. Van Rooy (eds.), *Exodus 1–15, Text and Context: Proceedings of the 29th Annual Congress of the Old Testament Society of South Africa (OTSSA)*, Pretoria: OTWSA/OTSSA, 34–72.

Burrows, E. (1935), 'Some Cosmological Patterns in Babylonian Religion', in S. H. Hooke (ed.), *The Labyrinth: Further Studies in the Relation Between Myth and Ritual in the Ancient World*, London: SPCK, 43–70.

Callender Jr., D. E. (2000), *Adam in Myth and History: Ancient Israelite Perspectives on the Primal Human*, HSS 48, Winona Lake: Eisenbrauns.

Canlis, J. (2010), *Calvin's Ladder: A Spiritual Theology of Ascent and Ascension*, Grand Rapids: Eerdmans.

Carmichael, C. M. (1976), 'On Separating Life and Death: An Explanation of Some Biblical Laws', *HTR* 69.1–2: 1–7.

——— (2000), 'The Origin of the Scapegoat Ritual', *VT* 50.2: 167–182.

Carpenter, E. E. (1997), 'Exodus 18: Its Structure, Style, Motifs and Function in the Book of Exodus', in E. E. Carpenter (ed.), *A Biblical Itinerary: In Search of Method, Form, and Content: Essays in Honor of George W. Coats*, JSOTSup 240, Sheffield: Sheffield Academic Press, 91–108.

Cassuto, U. (1961), *A Commentary on the Book of Genesis*, vol. 1: *From Adam to Noah*, tr. I. Abrahams, Jerusalem: Magnes.

—— (1967), *A Commentary on the Book of Exodus*, tr. I. Abrahams, Jerusalem: Magnes, Hebrew University.

Charlesworth, J. H. (ed.) (1985), 'Jubilees', in *Old Testament Pseudepigrapha*, tr. O. S. Wintermute, Garden City: Doubleday, 2: 35–142.

Chavez, E. G. (2002), *The Theological Significance of Jesus' Temple Action in Mark's Gospel*, Lewiston, N.Y.: Mellen.

Cheung, A. T. M. (1986), 'The Priest as the Redeemed Man: A Biblical-Theological Study of the Priesthood', *JETS* 29: 265–275.

Cheyne, T. K. (1895), 'The Date and Origin of the Ritual of the "Scapegoat"', *ZAW* 15.1: 153–156.

Childs, B. S. (1962), *Myth and Reality in the Old Testament*, London: SCM.

—— (2004), *The Book of Exodus: A Critical, Theological Commentary*, Louisville: Westminster.

Chirichigno, G. C. (1987), 'The Narrative Structure of Exod 19–24', *Bib* 68: 457–479.

Christensen, D. L. (1996), 'The Pentateuchal Principle Within the Canonical Process', *JETS* 39.4: 537–548.

Chronis, H. L. (1982), 'The Torn Veil: Cultus and Christology in Mark 15:37–39', *JBL* 101.1: 97–114.

Clark, W. M. (1971), 'The Flood and the Structure of the Pre-Patriarchal History', *ZAW* 83.2: 184–211.

Clifford, R. J. (1972), *The Cosmic Mountain in Canaan and in the Old Testament*, HSM 4, Cambridge, Mass.: Harvard University Press.

—— (1984), 'The Temple and the Holy Mountain', in T. G. Madsen (ed.), *The Temple in Antiquity: Ancient Records and Modern Perspectives*, Provo, Utah: Religious Studies Center, Brigham Young University, 107–124.

Clines, D. J. A. (1976), 'Theme in Genesis 1–11', *CBQ* 38: 483–507.

—— (1997), *The Theme of the Pentateuch*, 2nd ed., Sheffield: JSOT Press.

Coats, G. W. (1969), 'Song of the Sea', *CBQ* 31.1: 1–17.

Cohn, R. L. (1981), *The Shape of Sacred Space: Four Biblical Studies*, Chico, Calif.: Scholars Press.

Coloe, M. L. (2001), *God Dwells with Us: Temple Symbolism in the Fourth Gospel*, Collegeville, Minn.: Liturgical Press.

Congar, Y. (1962), *The Mystery of the Temple, or, the Manner of God's Presence to His Creatures from Genesis to the Apocalypse*, Westminster, Md.: Newman.

Cothey, A. (2005), 'Ethics and Holiness in the Theology of Leviticus', *JSOT* 30.2: 131–151.

Cross, F. M. (1973), 'The Song of the Sea and Canaanite Myth', in *Canaanite Myth and Hebrew Epic*, Cambridge, Mass.: Harvard University Press, 112–144.

Cross, F. M., and D. N. Freedman (1955), 'The Song of Miriam', *JNES* 14.4: 237–250.

Crüsemann, F. (1996), *Torah: Theology and Social History of Old Testament Law*, tr. A. W. Mahnke, Minneapolis: Fortress.

Currid, J. D. (1997), *Ancient Egypt and the Old Testament*, Grand Rapids: Baker.

Damrosch, D. (1987), 'Leviticus', in R. Alter and F. Kermode (eds.), *A Literary Guide to the Bible*, Cambridge, Mass.: Harvard University Press, 66–77.

Daniélou, J. (1960), *From Shadows to Reality: Studies in the Biblical Typology of the Fathers*, Westminster, Md.: Newman.

Davidson, R. M. (1988), 'Assurance in Judgment', *AR* 7: 18–20.

—— (2000a), 'The Eschatological Structure of the Old Testament', in J. Moskala (ed.), *Creation, Life, and Hope: Essays in Honor of Jacques B. Doukhan*, Berrien Springs: AUTS, 349–366.

—— (2000b), 'Cosmic Metanarrative for the Coming Millennium', *JATS* 11.1–2: 102–119.

Davies, D. (2009), 'An Interpretation of Sacrifice in Leviticus', *ZAW* 89.3: 387–399.

Davies, G. (1999), 'The Theology of the Exodus', in E. Ball (ed.), *In Search of Wisdom: Essays in Old Testament Interpretation in Honour of Ronald E. Clements*, JSOTSup 300, Sheffield: Sheffield Academic Press, 137–152.

Davies, J. A. (2004), *A Royal Priesthood: Literary and Intertextual Perspectives on an Image of Israel in Exodus 19.6*, London: T. & T. Clark International.

Dempster, S. G. (2004), *Dominion and Dynasty: A Biblical Theology of the Hebrew Bible*, Leicester: Apollos; Downers Grove: InterVarsity Press.

Di Vito, R. A. (1992), 'The Demarcation of Divine and Human Realms in Genesis 2–11', in R. J. Clifford and J. J. Collins (eds.), *Creation in Biblical Traditions*, CBQMS 24, Washington, D.C.: Catholic Biblical Association of America, 39–56.

Dorsey, D. A. (1999), *The Literary Structure of the Old Testament: A Commentary on Genesis–Malachi*, Grand Rapids: Baker.

Douglas, M. (1966), *Purity and Danger: An Analysis of Concepts of Pollution and Taboo*, London: Routledge & Kegan Paul.

—— (1972), 'Deciphering a Meal', *Daedalus* 101.1: 61–81.

——— (1993), 'The Forbidden Animals in Leviticus', *JSOT* 59: 3–23.

——— (1999a), *Leviticus as Literature*, Oxford: Oxford University Press.

——— (1999b), 'Justice as the Cornerstone: An Interpretation of Leviticus 18–20', *Int* 53.4: 341–350.

——— (2003), 'The Go-Away Goat', in R. Rendtorff, R. A. Kugler and S. S. Bartlet (eds.), *The Book of Leviticus: Composition and Reception*, Leiden: Brill, 121–141.

Doukhan, J. (1993), 'The Center of the Aqedah: A Study of the Literary Structure of Genesis 22:1–19', *AUSS* 31.1: 17–28.

Dozeman, T. B. (2009), *Commentary on Exodus*, ECC, Grand Rapids: Eerdmans.

Dumbrell, W. J. (2001), *The End of the Beginning: Revelation 21–22 and the Old Testament*, Eugene, Ore.: Wipf & Stock.

——— (2002), *The Faith of Israel: A Theological Survey of the Old Testament*, Grand Rapids: Baker Academic.

——— (2009), *Covenant and Creation: A Theology of Old Testament Covenants*, Eugene, Ore.: Wipf & Stock.

Eaton, J. H. (1976), *Kingship and the Psalms*, Naperville, Ill.: Allenson.

Eberhart, C. A. (2004), 'A Neglected Feature of Sacrifice in the Hebrew Bible: Remarks on the Burning Rite on the Altar', *HTR* 97.4: 485–493.

Edenburg, C. (2011), 'From Eden to Babylon: Reading Gen 2–4 as a Paradigmatic Narrative', in T. B. Dozeman, T. Romer and C. Schmid (eds.), *Pentateuch, Hexateuch, or Enneateuch? Identifying Literary Works in Genesis Through Kings*, Atlanta: Society of Biblical Literature, 155–168.

Eliade, M. (1987), *The Sacred and the Profane: The Nature of Religion*, San Diego: Harcourt.

Ellul, J. (1973), *The Meaning of the City*, Grand Rapids: Eerdmans.

Emmrich, M. (2001), 'The Temptation Narrative of Genesis 3:1–6: A Prelude to the Pentateuch and the History of Israel', *EvQ* 73.1: 3–20.

Enns, P. (2000), *Exodus*, NAC, Grand Rapids: Zondervan.

Eslinger, L. (1991), 'Freedom or Knowledge? Perspective and Purpose in the Exodus Narrative (Exodus 1–15)', *JSOT* 16.52: 43–60.

——— (1996), 'Knowing Yahweh: Exod 6:3 in the Context of Genesis 1–Exodus 15', in L. J. de Regt, J. de Waard and J. P. Fokkelman (eds.), *Literary Structure and Rhetorical Strategies in the Hebrew Bible*, Assen: Van Gorcum, 188–198.

Feder, Y. (2010), 'On Kuppuru, Kippēr and Etymological Sins That Cannot Be Wiped Away', *VT* 60.4: 535–545.

Feinberg, C. L. (1958), 'The Scapegoat of Leviticus Sixteen', *BSac* 115: 320–333.

Firmage, E. B. (1990), 'The Biblical Dietary Laws and the Concept of Holiness', in J. A. Emerton (ed.), *Studies in the Pentateuch*, VTSup 41, Leiden: Brill, 177–208.

———— (1999), 'Genesis 1 and the Priestly Agenda', *JSOT* 24.82: 97–114.

Fischer, G. (1996), 'Das Schilfmeerlied Exodus 15 in Seinem Kontext', *Bib* 77.1: 32–47.

Fishbane, M. A. (1975), 'The Sacred Center: The Symbolic Structure of the Bible', in M. A. Fishbane and P. R. Flohr (eds.), *Texts and Responses: Studies Presented to Nahum N. Glatzer on the Occasion of His Seventieth Birthday by His Students*, Leiden: Brill, 6–27.

———— (1998), *Biblical Text and Texture: A Literary Reading of Selected Texts*, Oxford: Oneworld.

Fletcher-Louis, C. H. T. (1997), 'The High Priest as Divine Mediator in the Hebrew Bible: Dan. 7:13 as a Test Case', in E. Lovering (ed.), *Society of Biblical Literature Seminar Papers*, Atlanta: Scholars Press, 161–193.

———— (2002), *All the Glory of Adam: Liturgical Anthropology in the Dead Sea Scrolls*, STDJ 42, Leiden: Brill.

———— (2004), 'God's Image, His Cosmic Temple and the High Priest: Towards an Historical and Theological Account of the Incarnation', in T. D. Alexander and S. J. Gathercole (eds.), *Heaven on Earth: The Temple in Biblical Theology*, Carlisle: Paternoster, 81–99.

———— (2006), 'Jesus as the High Priestly Messiah: Part 1', *JSHJ* 4.2: 155–175.

Fokkelman, J. P. (1989), '"On the Mount of the LORD There Is Vision": A Response to Francis Landy Concerning the Akedah', in J. C. Exum (ed.), *Signs and Wonders: Biblical Texts in Literary Focus*, Decatur, Ga.: Society of Biblical Literature, 41–56.

———— (2004), *Narrative Art in Genesis: Specimens of Stylistic and Structural Analysis*, Eugene, Ore.: Wipf & Stock.

Freedman, D. N. (1974), 'Strophe and Meter in Exodus 15', in H. Bream, R. Heim and C. Moore (eds.), *Light Unto My Path: Old Testament Studies in Honor of Jacob M. Myers*, Philadelphia: Temple University Press, 163–203.

———— (1980), 'The Twenty-Third Psalm', in *Pottery, Poetry, and Prophecy: Studies in Early Hebrew Poetry*, Winona Lake: Eisenbrauns, 275–302.

Fretheim, T. E. (1991a), *Exodus*, Louisville: John Knox.

———— (1991b), 'The Reclamation of Creation Redemption and Law in Exodus', *Int* 45.4: 354–365.

———— (1996), '"Because the Whole Earth Is Mine": Theme and Narrative in Exodus', *Int* 50.3: 229–239.

Frymer-Kensky, T. (1983), 'Pollution, Purification, and Purgation in Biblical Israel', in C. L. Meyers (ed.), *And the Word of the Lord Shall Go Forth*, Winona Lake: Eisenbrauns, 399–414.

———— (1993), *In the Wake of the Goddesses: Women, Culture and the Biblical Transformation of Pagan Myth*, New York: Ballantine.

Gaffin Jr., R. (1989), 'The Holy Spirit and Eschatology', *Keryx* 4.3: 14–29.

Gage, W. A. (2001), *The Gospel of Genesis: Studies in Protology and Eschatology*, Eugene, Ore.: Wipf & Stock.

Gane, R. (1992), '"Bread of the Presence" and Creator-in-Residence', *VT* 42.2: 179–203.

———— (2004), *Leviticus, Numbers*, NAC, Grand Rapids: Zondervan.

———— (2005), *Cult and Character: Purification Offerings, Day of Atonement, and Theodicy*, Winona Lake: Eisenbrauns.

———— (2010), 'The Unifying Logic of Israelite Purification Offerings Within Their Ancient Near Eastern Context', *JATS* 21.1: 85–98.

Garr, W. R. (2000), '"Image" and "Likeness" in the Inscription from Tell Fakhariyeh', *IEJ* 50: 227–234.

Garret, S. R. (1992), 'The Meaning of Jesus' Death in Luke', *WW* 12.1: 11–16.

Gayford, S. C. (1953), *Sacrifice and Priesthood: Jewish and Christian*, 2nd ed., London: Methuen.

Geller, S. A. (1992), 'Blood Cult: Toward a Literary Theology of the Priestly Work of the Pentateuch', *Proof* 12.2: 97–124.

Gennep, A. van. (1960), *The Rites of Passage*, tr. M. B. Vizedon and G. L. Caffee, Chicago: University of Chicago Press.

Gentry, P. J. (2007), 'The Atonement in Isaiah's Fourth Servant Song (Isaiah 52:13–53:12)', *SBJT* 11.2: 20–47.

Gese, H. (1981), 'The Atonement', in *Essays on Biblical Theology*, tr. K. Crim, Minneapolis: Augsburg, 93–116.

Gesenius, W. (1888), *A Hebrew and English Lexicon of the Old Testament: Including the Biblical Chaldee. From the Latin of William Gesenius . . .* , 25th ed., Boston: Houghton Mifflin.

Gispen, W. H. (1948), 'The Distinction Between Clean and Unclean', *OtSt* 5: 190–196.

Goldin, J. (1971), *Song at the Sea*, New Haven: Yale University Press.

Gordon, R. P. (2007), 'The Week That Made the World: Reflections on the First Pages of the Bible', in J. G. McConville and K. Möller (eds.), *Reading the Law: Studies in Honor of Gordon J. Wenham*, London: T. & T. Clark, 228–241.

Gorman, F. H. (1990), *The Ideology of Ritual Space, Time, and Status in the Priestly Theology*, JSOTSup 91, Sheffield: JSOT Press.

—— (1993), 'Priestly Rituals of Founding: Time, Space, and Status', in M. P. Graham, W. P. Brown and J. K. Kuan (eds.), *History and Interpretation: Essays in Honour of John H. Hayes*, Sheffield: JSOT Press, 47–64.

—— (1997), *Divine Presence and Community: A Commentary on the Book of Leviticus*, Grand Rapids: Eerdmans; Edinburgh: Handsel.

Grabbe, L. L. (1987), 'The Scapegoat Tradition: A Study in Early Jewish Interpretation', *JSJ* 18.2: 152–167.

Grant, J. A. (2004), *The King as Exemplar: The Function of Deuteronomy's Kingship Law in the Shaping of the Book of Psalms*, Leiden: Brill.

Gray, G. B. (1925), *Sacrifice in the Old Testament: Its Theory and Practice*, Oxford: Clarendon.

Greenstein, E. L. (2001), 'Presenting Genesis 1, Constructively and Deconstructively', *Proof* 21.1: 1–22.

Gros Louis, K. R. R. (1974), 'The Garden of Eden', in K. R. R. Gros Louis, J. S. Ackerman and T. S. Warshaw (eds.), *Literary Interpretations of Biblical Narratives*, The Bible in Literature Courses Series, Nashville: Abingdon, 1: 52–58.

Guillaume, P. (2004), 'Metamorphosis of a Ferocious Pharaoh', *Bib* 85: 232–236.

—— (2009), *Land and Calendar: The Priestly Document from Genesis 1 to Joshua 18*, New York: T. & T. Clark.

Gunkel, H. (1988), *An Introduction to the Psalms*, Macon, Ga.: Mercer University Press.

Gurtner, D. M. (2006), *The Torn Veil: Matthew's Exposition of the Death of Jesus*, SNTSMS 139, Cambridge: Cambridge University Press.

Hanson, K. C. (1993), 'Blood and Purity in Leviticus and Revelation', *JRC* 28: 215–230.

Haran, M. (1985), *Temples and Temple-Service in Ancient Israel: An Inquiry into Biblical Cult Phenomena and the Historical Setting of the Priestly School*, Winona Lake: Eisenbrauns.

Harper, E. A. (2011), 'Genesis 6:14–16: You Shall Make a Tebah', unpublished research paper.

Harris, J. M. (1996), 'From Inner-Biblical Interpretation to Early Rabbinic Exegesis', in M. Sæbø (ed.), *Hebrew Bible / Old Testament: The History of Its Interpretation*, Göttingen: Vandenhoeck & Ruprecht, 256–269.

Harris, R. L. (1961), 'Exegetical Notes: Meaning of Kipper', *JETS* 4.1: 3.

Hartley, J. E. (1992), *Leviticus*, WBC 4, Dallas: Word.

——— (2003a), 'Atonement, Day of', in *DOTP*, 54–61.

——— (2003b), 'Holy and Holiness, Clean and Unclean', in *DOTP*, 420–431.

Hauge, M. R. (2001), *The Descent from the Mountain: Narrative Patterns in Exodus 19–40*, Sheffield: Sheffield Academic Press.

Hauser, A. J. (1980), 'Linguistic and Thematic Links Between Genesis 4:1–16 and Genesis 2–3', *JETS* 23.4: 297–305.

——— (1982), 'Genesis 2–3: The Theme of Intimacy and Alienation', in D. J. A. Clines, D. M. Gunn and A. J. Hauser (eds.), *Art and Meaning: Rhetoric in Biblical Literature*, JSOTSup 19, Sheffield: Sheffield Academic Press, 20–36.

Hayes, C. (2006), 'Purity and Impurity, Ritual', in M. Berenbaum and F. Skolnik (eds.), *Encyclopaedia Judaica*, Detroit: Keter, 746–756.

Heijne, C. H. von (2010), *The Messenger of the Lord in Early Jewish Interpretations of Genesis*, Berlin: de Gruyter.

Helyer, L. R. (1983), 'The Separation of Abram and Lot: Its Significance in the Patriarchal Narratives', *JSOT* 8.26: 77–88.

Hendel, R. S. (1992), 'When the Sons of God Cavorted with the Daughters of Men', in H. Shanks (ed.), *Understanding the Dead Sea Scrolls: A Reader from the Biblical Archaeology Review*, New York: Random House, 167–177.

Hendrix, R. E. (1991), 'Miskan and 'Ohel Mo'ed: Etymology, Lexical Definitions, and Extra-Biblical Usage', *AUSS* 29.3: 213–224.

——— (1992a), 'The Use of Miskan and 'Ohel Mo'ed in Exodus 25–40', *AUSS* 30.1: 3–13.

——— (1992b), 'A Literary Structural Overview of Exod 25–40', *AUSS* 30.2: 123–138.

Hertz, J. H. (1988), *The Pentateuch and the Haftorahs*, London: Soncino.

Heschel, A. J. (2003), *The Sabbath: Its Meaning for Modern Man*, Boston: Shambhala.

Hicks, F. C. N. (1953), *The Fullness of Sacrifice: An Essay in Reconciliation*, 3d ed., London: SPCK.

Hieke, T., and T. Nicklas (eds.) (2012), *The Day of Atonement: Its Interpretations in Early Jewish and Christian Traditions*, Themes in Biblical Narrative: Jewish and Christian Tradition 15, Leiden: Brill.

Hilber, J. W. (1996), 'Theology of Worship in Exodus 24', *JETS* 39.2: 177–189.

Hoffmann, D. Z. (1906), *Das Buch Leviticus*, vol. 1, Berlin: M. Poppelauer.

———— (1971), *Sefer Vayikra*, tr. Z. H. Shefer and A. Leiberman, 2 vols., Jerusalem: Mossad Harav Kook.

Holland, T. (2004), *Contours of Pauline Theology*, Fearn: Mentor.

Holloway, S. W. (1991), 'What Ship Goes There? The Flood Narratives in the Gilgamesh Epic and Genesis Considered in Light of Ancient Near Eastern Temple Ideology', *ZAW* 103.3: 328–355.

Hui, T. K. (1990), 'The Purpose of Israel's Annual Feasts', *BSac* 147: 143–154.

Hutton, R. R. (1999), 'The Case of the Blasphemer Revisited (Lev. XXIV 10–23)', *VT* 49.4: 532–541.

Jacob, B. (2007), *The First Book of the Bible, Genesis*, ed. E. Jacob and W. Jacob, New York: KTAV.

Jacobs, L. (1975), 'Jewish Cosmology', in C. Blacker and M. Loewe (eds.), *Ancient Cosmologies*, London: Allen & Unwin, 66–84.

Janowski, B. (1995), 'Azazel', in *DDD*, 240–248.

———— (2008), 'Schöpferische Erinnerung: zum "Gedenken Gottes" in der biblischen Fluterzählung', in O. Dyma and A. Michel (eds.), *Sprachliche Tiefe – Theologische Weite*, BThSt 91, Neukirchen-Vluyn: Neukirchener Verlag, 17–47.

Janzen, J. G. (1997), *Exodus*, Louisville: Westminster John Knox.

Jenson, P. P. (1992), *Graded Holiness: A Key to the Priestly Conception of the World*, Sheffield: JSOT Press.

Jürgens, B. (2001), *Heiligkeit und Versöhnung: Levitikus 16 in seinem literarischen Kontext*, HBS 28, Freiburg: Herder.

Kaiser, W. C. (1994), 'The Book of Leviticus', in L. Keck (ed.), *The New Interpreter's Bible: Old Testament Survey*, Nashville: Abingdon, 985–1191.

Kalimi, I. (2012), 'The Day of Atonement in the Late Second Temple Period: Sadducees' High Priests, Pharisees' Norms, and Qumranites' Calendar(s)', in T. Hieke and T. Nicklas (eds.), *The Day of Atonement: Its Interpretations in Early Jewish and Christian Traditions*, TBN 15, Leiden: Brill, 75–96.

Kaminski, C. M. (2004), *From Noah to Israel: Realization of the Primaeval Blessing After the Flood*, London: T. & T. Clark International.

Kamionkowski, S. T. (2009), 'Leviticus 24, 10–23 in Light of H's Concept of Holiness', in S. Shectman and J. S. Baden (eds.), *The Strata of the Priestly Writings: Contemporary Debate and Future Directions*, Zürich: Theologischer Verlag Zürich, 73–86.

Kapelrud, A. S. (1965), 'The Role of the Cult in Old Israel', in J. P. Hyatt (ed.), *The Bible in Modern Scholarship: Papers Read at the 100th Meeting of the Society of Biblical Literature, December 28–30, 1964*, Nashville: Abingdon, 45–56.

Kaufmann, Y. (1947), *Toledot Ha-'Emuna Ha-Yiśra'elīt*, 2nd ed., vol. 1, Jerusalem: Mosād Bialik.

Kearney, P. J. (1977), 'Creation and Liturgy: The P Redaction of Ex 25–40', *ZAW* 89.3: 375–387.

Keel, O. (1997), *The Symbolism of the Biblical World: Ancient Near Eastern Iconography and the Book of Psalms*, Winona Lake: Eisenbrauns.

Kerr, A. R. (2002), *The Temple of Jesus' Body: The Temple Theme in the Gospel of John*, JSNTSup 220, London: Sheffield Academic Press.

Kiuchi, N. (1987), *The Purification Offering in the Priestly Literature: Its Meaning and Function*, JSOTSup 56, Sheffield: Sheffield Academic Press.

——— (2007), *Leviticus*, AOTC, Nottingham: Apollos; Downers Grove: InterVarsity Press.

Klawans, J. (2001), 'Pure Violence: Sacrifice and Defilement in Ancient Israel', *HTR* 94.2: 133–155.

——— (2009), *Purity, Sacrifice, and the Temple: Symbolism and Supersessionism in the Study of Ancient Judaism*, New York: Oxford University Press.

Klein, R. K. (1996), 'Back to the Future: The Tabernacle in the Book of Exodus', *Int* 50.3: 264–276.

Kleinig, J. W. (1992), 'What's the Use of Naming God?', *LTJ* 26: 27–34.

——— (2003), *Leviticus*, CC, St. Louis, Mo.: Concordia.

Kline, Moshe (2006), 'The Literary Structure of Leviticus', *Biblical Historian* 2.1: 11–28.

Klingbeil, G. A. (2007), *Bridging the Gap: Ritual and Ritual Texts in the Bible*, BBRSup 1, Winona Lake: Eisenbrauns.

Knierim, R. P. (1985), 'The Composition of the Pentateuch', *SBLSP* 24: 393–415.

——— (1995), *The Task of Old Testament Theology: Substance, Method, and Cases: Essays*, Grand Rapids: Eerdmans.

Knohl, I. (2007), *The Sanctuary of Silence: The Priestly Torah and the Holiness School*, Winona Lake: Eisenbrauns.

Knoppers, G. N. (1995), 'Prayer and Propaganda: Solomon's Dedication of the Temple and the Deuteronomist's Program', *CBQ* 57: 229–254.

Koorevaar, H. J. (2014), 'The Exile and Return Model: A Proposal for the Original Macrostructure of the Hebrew Canon', *JETS* 57.3: 501–512.

Kristensen, W. B. (1968), *The Meaning of Religion: Lectures in the Phenomenology of Religion*, The Hague: Martinus Nijhoff.

Kugler, R. A. (1997), 'Holiness, Purity, the Body, and Society: The Evidence for Theological Conflict in Leviticus', *JSOT* 22.76: 3–27.

Kurtz, J. H. (1998), *Offerings, Sacrifices and Worship in the Old Testament*, tr. J. Martin, Peabody: Hendrickson.

Lanfer, P. T. (2012), *Remembering Eden: The Reception History of Genesis 3: 22–24*, Oxford: Oxford University Press.

Lawlor, J. I. (2011), 'The "At-Sinai Narrative": Exodus 18–Numbers 10', *BBR* 21.1: 23–42.

Leach, E. (1985), 'The Logic of Sacrifice', in B. Lang (ed.), *Anthropological Approaches to the Old Testament*, IRT 8, Philadelphia: Fortress, 136–150.

Leder, A. C. (1999), 'Reading Exodus to Learn and Learning to Read Exodus', *CTJ* 34: 11–35.

——— (2010), *Waiting for the Land: The Story Line of the Pentateuch*, Phillipsburg: P. & R.

Leithart, P. J. (2014), 'Reenacted Exodus', *First Things* <http://www.firstthings.com/blogs/leithart/2014/03/reenacted-exodus>, accessed 31 Mar. 2015.

Levenson, J. D. (1976), *Theology of the Program of Restoration of Ezekiel 40–48*, Missoula, Mont.: Scholars Press.

——— (1984), 'The Temple and the World', *JR* 64.3: 275–298.

——— (1987), *Sinai & Zion: An Entry into the Jewish Bible*, New York: HarperSanFrancisco.

——— (1993), *The Death and Resurrection of the Beloved Son: The Transformation of Child Sacrifice in Judaism and Christianity*, New Haven: Yale University Press.

——— (1994), *Creation and the Persistence of Evil: The Jewish Drama of Divine Omnipotence*, Princeton: Princeton University Press.

Levine, B. A. (1965), 'The Descriptive Tabernacle Texts of the Pentateuch', *JAOS* 85.3: 307–318.

——— (2002), 'Ritual as Symbol: Modes of Sacrifice in Israelite Religion', in B. M. Gittlen (ed.), *Sacred Time, Sacred Place: Archaeology and the Religion of Israel*, Winona Lake: Eisenbrauns, 125–135.

Levine, N. (2006), 'Sarah/Sodom: Birth, Destruction, and Synchronic Transaction', *JSOT* 31.2: 131–146.

Levy, R. D. (1998), *The Symbolism of the Azazel Goat: A Dissertation Presented to the Graduate School of the Union Institute*, Bethesda, Md.: International Scholars.

Liss, H. (2008), 'Ritual Purity and the Construction of Identity', in T. Romer (ed.), *The Books of Leviticus and Numbers*, Leuven: Peeters, 329–354.

Lohfink, N. (1994), *Theology of the Pentateuch: Themes of the Priestly Narrative and Deuteronomy*, Minneapolis: Fortress.

Low, B. (2009), 'The Logic of Atonement in Israel's Cult', *Scripture and Interpretation* 3.1: 5–32.

Luciani, D. (2005), *Sainteté et pardon*, vol. 1: *Structure littéraire du Lévitique*, Leuven: Peeters.

Lundquist, J. M. (1983), 'What Is a Temple? A Preliminary Typology', in H. B. Huffmon, F. A. Spina and A. R. W. Green (eds.), *The Quest for the Kingdom of God: Studies in Honor of George E. Mendenhall*, Winona Lake: Eisenbrauns, 205–219.

——— (1984), 'The Common Temple Ideology of the Ancient Near East', in T. G. Madsen (ed.), *The Temple in Antiquity: Ancient Records and Modern Perspectives*, Provo, Utah: Brigham Young University, 53–76.

——— (2014), 'The Common Temple Ideology of the Ancient Near East', in L. M. Morales (ed.), *Cult and Cosmos: Tilting Toward a Temple-Centered Theology*, Leuven: Peeters, 49–67.

Lyonnet, S., and L. Sabourin (1970), *Sin, Redemption, and Sacrifice: A Biblical and Patristic Study*, Rome: Biblical Institute.

Macaskill, G. (2013), *Union with Christ in the New Testament*, Oxford: Oxford University Press.

McCaffrey, J. (1988), *The House with Many Rooms: The Temple Theme of Jn 14:2–3*, Rome: Pontifical Biblical Institute.

McCarthy, D. J. (1984), '"Creation" Motifs in Ancient Hebrew Poetry', in B. W. Anderson (ed.), *Creation in the Old Testament*, Philadelphia: Fortress, 74–89.

McEvenue, S. E. (1971), *The Narrative Style of the Priestly Writer*, AnBib 50, Rome: Biblical Institute.

McKelvey, R. J. (1969), *The New Temple: The Church in the New Testament*, London: Oxford University Press.

McNamara, M. (1992), *Targum Neofiti 1, Genesis*, Collegeville, Minn.: Liturgical.

Marcus, J. (2003), 'The Son of Man as the Son of Adam', *RB* 110: 38–61, 370–386.

Master, J. R. (2002), 'The Place of Chapter 24 in the Structure of the Book of Leviticus', *BSac* 159: 414–424.

Mathews, K. A. (1996), *Genesis 1–11:26*, vol. 1A, NAC 1A, Nashville: Broadman & Holman.

Mathewson, D. (2003), *A New Heaven and a New Earth: The Meaning and Function of the Old Testament in Revelation 21.1–22.5*, Sheffield: Sheffield Academic Press.

Mbuvi, A. M. (2007), *Temple, Exile and Identity in 1 Peter*, London: T. & T. Clark.

Meyer, E. E. (2013), 'From Cult to Community: The Two Halves of Leviticus', *VE* 34.2: 1–7.

Meyers, C. L. (1976), *The Tabernacle Menorah: A Synthetic Study of a Symbol from the Biblical Cult*, Missoula, Mont.: Scholars Press.

——— (2005), *Exodus*, NCBC, Cambridge: Cambridge University Press.

Middleton, J. R. (2005), *The Liberating Image: The Imago Dei in Genesis 1*, Grand Rapids: Brazos.

Midrash Rabbah: Genesis (1939), tr. H. Freedman and Maurice Simon, 10 vols., London: Soncino, 2: 625.

Milgrom, J. (1976a), 'Israel's Sanctuary: "The Priestly Picture of Dorian Gray"', *RB* 83: 390–399.

——— (1976b), 'Atonement, Day of', in *IDBSup*, 82–83.

——— (1990), *The JPS Torah Commentary Numbers = [ba-Midbar]: The Traditional Hebrew Text with the New JPS Translation*, Philadelphia: Jewish Publication Society.

——— (1991), *Leviticus 1–16: A New Translation with Introduction and Commentary*, AB, New York: Doubleday.

——— (2004), *Leviticus: A Book of Ritual and Ethics*, Minneapolis: Fortress.

——— (2008), *Leviticus 23–27: A New Translation with Introduction and Commentary*, New Haven: Yale University Press.

Miller, J. E. (1996), *The Western Paradise: Greek and Hebrew Traditions*, San Francisco: International Scholars.

Morales, L. M. (2012a), 'Crouching Demon, Hidden Lamb: Resurrecting an Exegetical Fossil in Genesis 4.7', *BT* 63.4: 185–191.

———— (2012b), *The Tabernacle Pre-Figured: Cosmic Mountain Ideology in Genesis and Exodus*, Biblical Tools and Studies 15, Leuven: Peeters.

———— (ed.) (2014), *Cult and Cosmos: Tilting Toward a Temple-Centered Theology*, Biblical Tools and Studies 18, Leuven: Peeters.

Morris, P. (1992), 'Exiled from Eden: Jewish Interpretations of Genesis', in P. Morris and D. Sawyer (eds.), *A Walk in the Garden: Biblical, Iconographical and Literary Images of Eden*, JSOTSup 136, Sheffield: Sheffield Academic Press, 117–166.

Motyer, S. (1987), 'The Rending of the Veil: A Markan Pentecost?', *NTS* 33.1: 155–157.

Muilenburg, J. (1996), 'A Liturgy of the Triumphs of Yahweh', in T. C. Vriezen (ed.), *Studia biblica et semitica: Theodoro Christiano Vriezen qui munere professoris theologiae per XXV annos functus est, ab amicis, collegis, discipulis dedicata*, Wageningen: H. Veenman, 233–251.

Nelson, R. D. (1993), *Raising up a Faithful Priest: Community and Priesthood in Biblical Theology*, Louisville: Westminster/John Knox.

Neusner, J. (1975), 'The Idea of Purity in Ancient Judaism', *JAAR* 43.1: 15–26.

Newing, E. G. (1981), 'A Rhetorical and Theological Analysis of the Hexateuch', *SEAJT* 22.2: 1–15.

———— (1985), 'The Rhetoric of Hope', *Colloq* 17: 1–15.

Niccacci, A. (1997), 'Workshop: Narrative Syntax of Exodus 19–24', in E. J. van Wolde (ed.), *Narrative Syntax and the Hebrew Bible: Papers of the Tilburg Conference 1996*, BIS 29, Leiden: Brill, 203–228.

Nihan, C. (2007), *From Priestly Torah to Pentateuch: A Study in the Composition of the Book of Leviticus*, Tübingen: Mohr Siebeck.

Ninow, F. (2001), *Indicators of Typology Within the Old Testament: The Exodus Motif*, Frankfurt am Main; New York: P. Lang.

Och, B. (1995), 'Creation and Redemption: Towards a Theology of Creation', *Judaism* 44.2: 226–243.

Oden, R. A. (1981), 'Divine Aspirations in Atrahasis and in Genesis 1—11', *ZAW* 93.2: 197–216.

Olson, D. T. (2005), *Deuteronomy and the Death of Moses: A Theological Reading*, Eugene, Ore.: Wipf & Stock.

Otto, E. (1994), *Theologische Ethik des Alten Testaments*, ThW 3.2, Stuttgart: W. Kohlhammer.

Palmer, B. M. (1980), *Theology of Prayer as Viewed in the Religion of Nature and in the System of Grace*, Harrisonburg: Sprinkle.

Parry, D. W. (1994), 'Garden of Eden: Prototype Sanctuary', in D. W. Parry (ed.), *Temples of the Ancient World: Ritual and Symbolism*, Provo, Utah: Deseret; Salt Lake City, Utah; Foundation for Ancient Research and Mormon Studies, 126–151.

Patterson, R. D. (2004), 'Victory at Sea: Prose and Poetry in Exodus 14–15', *BSac* 161.641: 42–54.

Philpot, J. M. (2013), 'Exodus 34:29–35 and Moses' Shining Face', *BBR* 23.1: 1–11.

Phythian-Adams, W. J. (1942), *The People and the Presence*, Oxford: Oxford University Press.

——— (1947), 'Shadow and Substance: The Meaning of Sacred History', *Int* 1.4: 419–435.

Pinker, A. (2007), 'A Goat to Go to Azazel', *JHS* 7: 2–25.

Plastaras, J. (1966), *The God of Exodus*, Milwaukee: Bruce.

Polak, F. (1996), 'Theophany and Mediator: The Unfolding of a Theme in the Book of Exodus', in M. Vervenne (ed.), *Studies in the Book of Exodus: Redaction, Reception, Interpretation*, Leuven: Leuven University Press, 113–147.

——— (1997), 'Water, Rock, and Wood: Structure and Thought Pattern in the Exodus Narrative', *JANES* 25: 19–42.

Postell, S. D. (2011), *Adam as Israel: Genesis 1–3 as the Introduction to the Torah and Tanakh*, Eugene, Ore.: Pickwick.

Poythress, V. S. (1995), *The Shadow of Christ in the Law of Moses*, repr., Phillipsburg: P. & R.

Propp, W. H. (1987), *Water in the Wilderness: A Biblical Motif and Its Mythological Background*, Atlanta, Ga.: Scholars Press.

——— (1999), *Exodus 1–18: A New Translation with Introduction and Commentary*, TAB, New York: Doubleday.

Rad, G. von (1962), *Old Testament Theology*, tr. D. M. G. Stalker, vol. 1, New York: Harper & Row.

——— (1972), *Genesis: A Commentary*, tr. J. H. Marks, Philadelphia: Westminster.

Radday, Y. (1972), 'Chiasm in Tora', *LB* 19: 21–23.

——— (1981), 'Chiasmus in Biblical Narrative', in J. W. Welch (ed.), *Chiasmus in Antiquity*, Provo, Utah: Research, 50–117.

Rainey, A. F. (1970), 'The Order of Sacrifices in Old Testament Ritual Texts', *Bib* 51.4: 485–498.

Rendsburg, G. (2008), 'The Two Screens: On Mary Douglas's Proposal for a Literary Structure to the Book of Leviticus', *JSQ* 15: 175–189.

Rendtorff, R. (1998), *The Covenant Formula: An Exegetical and Theological Investigation*, Edinburgh: Continuum.

———— (2003), 'Leviticus 16 als Mitte der Tora', *BibInt* 11.3–4: 252–258.

Resseguie, J. L. (2001), *The Strange Gospel: Narrative Design and Point of View in John*, Leiden: Brill.

Rickett, D. (2011), 'Rethinking the Place and Purpose of Genesis 13', *JSOT* 36.1: 31–53.

Rigby, P. (1980), 'A Structural Analysis of Israelite Sacrifice and Its Other Institutions', *EgT* 11: 299–351.

Robertson, O. P. (2004), *The Christ of the Prophets*, Phillipsburg: P. & R.

Rodriguez, A. M. (1986), 'Sanctuary Theology in Exodus', *AUSS* 24: 127–145.

———— (1996), 'Leviticus 16: Its Literary Structure', *AUSS* 34.2: 269–286.

Rooke, D. W. (2007), 'The Day of Atonement as a Ritual of Validation for the High Priest', in J. Day (ed.), *Temple and Worship in Ancient Israel*, New York: T. & T. Clark, 342–364.

———— (2015), 'The Blasphemer (Leviticus 24): Gender, Identity and Boundary Construction', in F. Landy, L. M. Trevaskis and B. D. Bibb (eds.), *Text, Time, and Temple: Literary, Historical and Ritual Studies in Leviticus*, HBM 64, Sheffield: Sheffield Phoenix, 153–169.

Rudman, D. (2005), 'A Note on the Azazel-Goat Ritual', *ZAW* 116.3: 396–401.

Rudolph, D. J. (2003), 'Festivals in Genesis 1:14', *TynB* 54.2: 23–40.

Russell, B. D. (2007), *The Song of the Sea: The Date of Composition and Influence of Exodus 15:1–21*, Frankfurt am Main: P. Lang.

Ruwe, A. (1999), *'Heiligkeitsgesetz' und 'Priesterschrift': Literatur-geschichtliche und rechtssystematische Untersuchungen zu Leviticus 17,1–26,2*, Tübingen: Mohr Siebeck.

———— (2003), 'The Structure of the Book of Leviticus in the Narrative Outline of the Priestly Sinai Story (Exod 19.1–Num 10.10)', in R. Rendtorff and R. A. Kukler (eds.), *The Book of Leviticus: Composition and Reception*, VTSup 93, Leiden: Brill, 55–78.

Sailhamer, J. H. (1992), *The Pentateuch as Narrative: A Biblical-Theological Commentary*, Grand Rapids: Zondervan.

Sanders, S. L. (2009), *The Invention of Hebrew*, Urbana: University of Illinois Press.

Sarna, N. M. (1989), *Genesis: The Traditional Hebrew Text with New JPS Translation*, JPSTC 1, Philadelphia: Jewish Publication Society.

—— (1991), *Exodus: The Traditional Hebrew Text with the New JPS Translation*, JPSTC 2, Philadelphia: Jewish Publication Society.

Schart, A. (1990), *Mose und Israel im Konflikt: Eine redaktions-geschichtlichte Studie zu den Wustenerzahlungen*, OBO 98, Freiburg, Switzerland: Göttingen: Vandenhoeck & Ruprecht.

Schmidt, W. H. (1983), *The Faith of the Old Testament: A History*, Philadelphia: Westminster.

Schwartz, B. (2001), 'The Literary and Ritual Unity of Leviticus 16', paper presented at the annual meeting of the Society of Biblical Literature, Denver, Colo.

—— (2003), 'Leviticus', in A. Berlin and M. Z. Brettler (eds.), *The Jewish Study Bible*, New York: Oxford University Press, 203–280.

Scott, E. F. (1952), *The Crisis in the Life of Jesus: The Cleansing of the Temple and Its Significance*, New York: Scribners.

Seidl, T. (1999), 'Levitikus 16 – "Schlussstein" des priesterlichen Systems der Sundenvergebung', in H.-J. Fabry and H.-W. Jüngling (eds.), *Levitikus als Buch*, Berlin: Philo, 219–248.

Sellin, E. (1936), *Theologie des Alten Testaments*, Leipzig: Quelle & Meyer.

Shea, W. (1986), 'Literary Form and Theological Function in Leviticus', in F. B. Holbrook (ed.), *The Seventy Weeks, Leviticus, and the Nature of Prophecy*, Washington, D.C.: BRI, 131–168.

Shirbroun, G. F. (1985), 'The Giving of the Name of God to Jesus in John 17:11,12', PhD diss., Princeton: Princeton Theological Seminary.

Ska, J.-L. (2006), *Introduction to Reading the Pentateuch*, Winona Lake: Eisenbrauns.

Sklar, J. (2005), *Sin, Impurity, Sacrifice, Atonement: The Priestly Conceptions*, Sheffield: Sheffield Phoenix.

—— (2008), 'Sin and Impurity: Atoned or Purified? Yes!', in B. J. Schwartz, D. P. Wright, J. Stackert and S. M. Naphtali (eds.), *Perspectives on Purity and Purification in the Bible*, New York: T. & T. Clark International, 18–31.

—— (2014), *Leviticus: An Introduction and Commentary*, TOTC 3, Nottingham: Inter-Varsity Press; Downers Grove: InterVarsity Press.

Smith, C. R. (1996), 'The Literary Structure of Leviticus', *JSOT* 21.70: 17–32.

Smith, M. (1997), *The Pilgrimage Pattern in Exodus*, Sheffield: Sheffield Academic Press.

—— (1999), 'Matters of Space and Time in Exodus and Numbers', in C. Seitz and K. Greene-McCreight (eds.), *Theological Exegesis: Essays in Conversation with Brevard S. Childs*, Grand Rapids: Eerdmans, 182–207.

—— (2010), *The Priestly Vision of Genesis 1*, Minneapolis: Fortress.

Sohn, S.-T. (1999), '"I Will Be Your God and You Will Be My People": The Origin and Background of the Covenant Formula', in B. A. Levine, R. Chazan, W. W. Hallo and L. H. Schiffman (eds.), *Ki Baruch Hu: Ancient Near Eastern, Biblical, and Judaic Studies in Honor of Baruch A. Levine*, Winona Lake: Eisenbrauns, 355–372.

Sommer, B. D. (2001), 'Conflicting Constructions of Divine Presence in the Priestly Tabernacle', *BibInt* 9.1: 41–63.

Souza, E. B. de (2005), *The Heavenly Sanctuary/Temple Motif in the Hebrew Bible*, Berrien Springs, Mich.: Adventist Theological Society.

Sprinkle, J. M. (1994), *The Book of the Covenant: A Literary Approach*, Sheffield: JSOT Press.

—— (2000), 'The Rationale of the Laws of Clean and Unclean in the Old Testament', *JETS* 43.4: 637–657.

Stadelmann, L. I. J. (1970), *The Hebrew Conception of the World*, Rome: Pontifical Biblical Institute.

Stager, L. E. (1999), 'Jerusalem and the Garden of Eden', *ErIsr* 26: 183–194.

Stökl Ben Ezra, D. (2003), *The Impact of Yom Kippur on Early Christianity: The Day of Atonement from Second Temple Judaism to the Fifth Century*, WUNT 163, Tübingen: Mohr Siebeck.

Talmon, S. (1978), 'Har; Gibh'ah', in *TDOT* 3: 427–447.

—— (2001), '"Exile" and "Restoration" in the Conceptual World of Ancient Judaism', in J. M. Scott (ed.), *Restoration: Old Testament, Jewish, and Christian Perspectives*, Boston: Brill, 107–146.

Tawil, H. (1980), 'Azazel the Prince of the Steppe: A Comparative Study', *ZAW* 92.1: 43–59.

Terrien, S. L. (1978), *The Elusive Presence: Toward a New Biblical Theology*, San Francisco: Harper & Row.

Trevaskis, L. M. (2009), 'The Purpose of Leviticus 24 Within Its Literary Context', *VT* 59.2: 295–312.

—— (2011), *Holiness, Ethics and Ritual in Leviticus*, Sheffield: Sheffield Phoenix.

Turnbull, M. R. (1926), *Studying the Book of Leviticus*, Richmond, Va.: Presbyterian Committee of Publication.

Turner, K. J. (2011), *The Death of Deaths in the Death of Israel: Deuteronomy's Theology of Exile*, Eugene, Ore.: Wipf & Stock.

Turner, L. A. (1993), 'The Rainbow as the Sign of the Covenant in Genesis IX 11–13', *VT* 43: 119–124.

Um, S. T. (2006), *The Theme of Temple Christology in John's Gospel*, LNTS 312, London: T. & T. Clark.

VanGemeren, W. A. (1981), 'The Sons of God in Genesis 6:1–4 (an Example of Evangelical Demythologization?)', *WTJ* 43: 320–348.

Vervenne, M. (2001), 'Genesis 1, 1–2, 4: The Compositional Texture of the Priestly Overture to the Pentateuch', in A. Wénin (ed.), *Studies in the Book of Genesis*, Leuven: Peeters, 35–79.

Vogels, W. (1975), 'Abraham et L'offrande de La Terre (Gn 13)', *SR/SR* 4.1: 51–57.

——— (1979), *God's Universal Covenant: A Biblical Study*, Ottowa: University of Ottawa Press.

——— (1997), 'The Cultic and Civil Calendars of the Fourth Day of Creation (Gen. 1:14b)', *SJOT* 11.2: 163–180.

Vos, G. (1912), 'The Eschatological Aspect of the Pauline Conception of the Spirit', in R. B. Gaffin Jr. (ed.), *Redemptive History and Biblical Interpretation: The Shorter Writings of Geerhardus Vos*, Phillipsburg: P. & R., 91–125.

——— (1975), *Biblical Theology: Old and New Testaments*, Edinburgh: Banner of Truth Trust.

Wagner, V. (2009), 'Zur Existenz des sogenannten "Heiligkeitsgesetzes"', *ZAW* 86.3: 307–316.

Walters, S. D. (1987), 'Wood, Sand and Stars: Structure and Theology in Gen. 22.1–19', *TJT* 3: 301–330.

Waltke, B. K., and C. Yu. (2007), *An Old Testament Theology: An Exegetical, Canonical, and Thematic Approach*, Grand Rapids: Zondervan.

Walton, J. H. (1995), 'The Mesopotamian Background of the Tower of Babel and Its Implications', *BBR* 5: 155–175.

——— (2001a), *Genesis: From Biblical Text . . . to Contemporary Life*, Grand Rapids: Zondervan.

——— (2001b), 'Equilibrium and the Sacred Compass: The Structure of Leviticus', *BBR* 11.2: 293–304.

Warning, W. (1999), *Literary Artistry in Leviticus*, Leiden: Brill.

Watts, J. W. (1995), 'Rhetorical Strategy in the Composition of the Pentateuch', *JSOT* 68: 3–22.

——— (1992), *Psalm and Story Inset Hymns in Hebrew Narrative*, Sheffield: JSOT Press.

Watts, J. D. W. (1957), 'The Song of the Sea: Ex. XV', *VT* 7.4: 371.

Wead, D. W. (1970), 'The Johannine Double Meaning', *RestQ* 13: 106–120.

Weimar, P. (2002), 'Struktur und Komposition der priesterschriftlichen Schöpfungserzählung (Gen 1,1–2,4a)', in M. Dietrich, O. Loretz, K. A. Metzler and H. Schaudig (eds.), *Ex Mesopotamia et Syria lux: Festschrift für Manfried Dietrich zu seinem 65. Geburtstag*, Münster: Ugarit-Verlag, 803–843.

Weinfeld, M. (1981), 'Sabbath, Temple, and the Enthronement of the Lord – the Problem of the Sitz im Leben of Genesis 1:1–2:3', in A. Caquot and M. Delcor (eds.), *Mélanges bibliques et orientaux en l'honneur de M. Henri Cazelles*, AOAT 212, Kevelaer: Butzon & Bercker; Neukirchen-Vluyn: Neukirchener Verlag, 501–512.

Wenham, G. J. (1979), *The Book of Leviticus*, NICOT, Eerdmans.

———— (1981a), 'The Theology of Unclean Food', *EvQ* 53.1: 6–15.

———— (1981b), 'Aaron's Rod (Numbers 17:16–28)', *ZAW* 93.2: 280–281.

———— (1983), 'Why Does Sexual Intercourse Defile (Leviticus 15:18)', *ZAW* 95.3: 432–434.

———— (1986), 'Sanctuary Symbolism in the Garden of Eden Story', in *Proceedings from the Ninth Congress of Jewish Studies, Division A: The Period of the Bible*, Jerusalem: World Union of Jewish Studies, 19–25.

———— (1987), *Genesis 1–15*, Waco: Word.

———— (1990), 'Original Sin in Genesis 1–11', *Chm* 104.4: 309–328.

———— (1995), 'The Theology of Old Testament Sacrifice', in R. T. Beckwith and M. J. Selman (eds.), *Sacrifice in the Bible*, Carlisle: Paternoster, 75–87.

———— (2003), *Exploring the Old Testament*, vol. 1: *A Guide to the Pentateuch*, Downers Grove: InterVarsity Press.

———— (2008), *Numbers: An Introduction and Commentary*, TOTC, repr., Leicester: Inter-Varsity Press; Downers Grove: InterVarsity Press.

———— (2012), 'Hearing the Pentateuch', in C. G. Bartholomew and D. J. H. Beldman (eds.), *Hearing the Old Testament: Listening for God's Address*, Grand Rapids: Eerdmans, 231–253.

Westermann, C. (1964), *The Genesis Accounts of Creation*, Philadelphia: Fortress.

———— (1981), *Praise and Lament in the Psalms*, Atlanta: Westminster John Knox.

———— (1984), *Genesis 1–11: A Commentary*, Minneapolis: Augsburg.

Whitekettle, R. (1996), 'Levitical Thought and the Female Reproductive Cycle: Wombs, Wellsprings, and the Primeval World', *VT* 46.3: 376–391.

Widengren, G. (1951), *The King and the Tree of Life in Ancient Near Eastern Religion (King and Saviour IV)*, Uppsala: Almquist & Wiksells.

——— (1984), 'Yahweh's Gathering of the Dispersed', in W. B. Barrick and J. R. Spencer (eds.), *In the Shelter of Elyon: Essays on Ancient Palestinian Life and Literature in Honor of G. W. Ahlström*, JSOTSup 31, Sheffield: Almond, 227–245.

Wilson, V. M. (1997), *Divine Symmetries: The Art of Biblical Rhetoric*, Lanham, Md.: University Press of America.

Wright, D. P. (1987), *The Disposal of Impurity: Elimination Rites in the Bible and in Hittite and Mesopotamian Literature*, Atlanta: Scholars Press.

——— (1992a), 'Unclean and Clean', *ABD*, 729–741.

——— (1992b), 'Azazel', *ABD*, 536–567.

——— (1996), 'Holiness, Sex, and Death in the Garden of Eden', *Bib* 77: 305–329.

Wyatt, N. (2001), *Space and Time in the Religious Life of the Near East*, Sheffield: Sheffield Academic Press.

Zenger, E. (1983), *Gottes Bogen in den Wolken: Untersuchungen zu Komposition und Theologie der priesterschriftlichen Urgeschichte*, SBS 112, Stuttgart: Katholisches Bibelwerk.

——— (1999), 'Das Buch Levitikus als Teiltext der Tora/des Pentateuch: Eine synchrone Lektüre mit kanonischer Perspektiv', in H.-J. Fabry and H.-W. Jüngling (eds.), *Levitikus als Buch*, Berlin: Philo, 47–83.

Zimmerli, W. (1982), *I Am Yahweh*, ed. W. Brueggemann, tr. D. W. Stott, Atlanta: John Knox.

Zlotowitz, M. (1977), *Bereishis*, vol. 1: *Bereishis, Noach*, Brooklyn: Mesorah.

Index of authors

Index of Scripture references

344

John (*cont.*)
1:32–33 *285–286*
1:35–42 *262*
1:36 *276*
1:43–50 *262*
1:43–51 *289*
1:47 *262*
1:51 *261, 262*
2 *287*
2:1–11 *262*
2:1–12 *262*
2:6 *264*
2:13 *276, 277*
2:13–22 *262*
2:17 *277*
2:19 *263*
2:20 *294*
2:21 *263*
2:22 *263*
2:23 *276*
3 *162, 287*
3:3 *284, 288, 294*
3:5–6 *288*
3:7 *288*
3:8 *288*
3:12–13 *288*
3:13 *260, 261*
3:29 *262, 264*
4 *263*
4:6 *288*
4:7 *292*
4:10 *289*
4:12 *289*
4:13–14 *289*
4:14 *293*
4:15 *289*
4:20 *264*
4:21 *264*
4:23–24 *289*
4:28 *264*
5:1 *276*
6:4 *276*
6:46 *260*

6:55 *293*
6:57 *288*
6:63 *288*
7:30 *292*
7:37 *292*
7:37–38 *290*
7:38 *293*
7:39 *291, 293*
8:21–23 *264*
8:35–36 *295*
11:23–25 *283*
11:52 *294*
11:55 *276*
13:1 *265, 276*
13:33 *265*
13:34–35 *294*
13:36 *265*
13:36–37 *265*
14 *291*
14:1–4 *265*
14:1–6 *264, 265*
14:2 *294*
14:2–3 *267, 285*
14:5 *265*
14:6 *268*
14:11 *267*
14:17–18 *268*
14:23 *267*
15:1–8 *291*
16:5–15 *291*
16:26 *261*
17:6 *277*
17:11–12 *277*
17:16 *288*
17:18 *288*
17:21–24 *291*
17:26 *291*
18:39–40 *275*
19:14 *277*
19:25–27 *295*
19:28 *291*
19:29 *277*
19:30 *292*
19:31–37 *277*

19:33–34 *182*
19:34 *293*
19:41 *182*
20:1 *262*
20:14–15 *182*
20:17 *295*
20:19 *262*
20:21 *288*
20:22 *293*
20:26 *262*

Acts
1:9 *278*
2:32–33 *285*
2:34 *285*
4:11 *298*
8:14–17 *285*
10 – 11 *163*
10:44 *285*

Romans
1:4 *280*
3:21–26 *30*
5:5 *294*
5:8–10 *30*
5:12–21 *182*
6 *280*
6:4 *280*
9:7–8 *72*
9:22–26 *251*
13:8–10 *294*

1 Corinthians
3:10 *295*
3:16 *295*
3:17 *295*
5 *301*
5:7 *276*
6:19 *295*
12:4–11 *295*
14:12 *295*
15:4 *279*
15:21–22 *182*
15:24–28 *235*

Titles in this series:

An index of Scripture references for all the volumes may be found at
http://www.thegospelcoalition.org/resources/nsbt

Finding the Textbook You Need

The IVP Academic Textbook Selector
is an online tool for instantly finding the IVP books
suitable for over 250 courses across 24 disciplines.

---

ivpacademic.com
